INSIGHT GUIDE

Greece

APA PUBLICATIONS

L

Part of the Langenscheidt Publishing Group

ABOUT THIS BOOK

Editorial

Project Editor
Melissa de Villiers
Editorial Director
Brian Bell

Distribution

UK & Ireland
GeoCenter International Ltd
The Viables Centre
Harrow Way
Basingstoke
Hants RG22 4BJ
Fax: (44) 1256-817988

United States
Langenscheidt Publishers, Inc.
46–35 54th Road
Maspeth, NY 11378
Fax: (718) 784-0640

Worldwide
APA Publications GmbH & Co.
Verlag KG (Singapore branch)
38 Joo Koon Road
Singapore 628990
Tel: (65) 865-1600
Fax: (65) 861-6438

Printing

Insight Print Services (Pte) Ltd
38 Joo Koon Road
Singapore 628990
Tel: (65) 865-1600
Fax: (65) 861-6438

© 2000 APA Publications GmbH & Co.
Verlag KG (Singapore branch)
All Rights Reserved
First Edition 1987
Fourth Edition 1998 (Updated 2000)

CONTACTING THE EDITORS
Although every effort is made to
provide accurate information in
this publication, we live in a
fast-changing world and would
appreciate it if readers would
call our attention to any errors or
outdated information that may
occur by writing to us at:
**Insight Guides, P.O. Box 7910,
London SE1 1WE, England.
Fax: (44 20) 7403-0290.**
e-mail:
insight@apaguide.demon.co.uk

This guidebook combines the
interests and enthusiasms of
two of the world's best known information providers: Insight Guides,
whose titles have set the standard
for visual travel guides since 1970,
and Discovery Channel, the world's
premier source of nonfiction television programming.

The editors of Insight Guides provide both practical advice and general understanding about a
destination's history, culture, institutions and people. Discovery
Channel and its Web site,
www.discovery.com, help
millions of viewers explore
their world from the com-
fort of their own home and also
encourage them to explore it
firsthand.

How to use this book

Insight Guide: Greece is structured
to convey an understanding of
Greece, its people and its culture,
as well as to guide readers through
its sights and everyday activities:

♦ To understand Greece, you
need to know something
about its past. The **Features** section covers
the history and culture
of the country.

♦ The main **Places** section ia a complete guide to

all the sights and areas worth visiting. Places of interest are coordinated by number with the maps.

◆ The **Travel Tips** listings section provides a handy point of reference for information on travel, hotels, restaurants, shops and more.

The contributors

The job of assembling this edition of *Insight Guide: Greece* fell to **Melissa de Villiers**, a London-based journalist and editor who has travelled widely in the country. Thoroughly revised and updated, this book builds on the original edition produced by **Karen Van Dyck**. Both editors sought out writers and photogra-

phers with the ideal combination of affection for, and detachment from, their subject that distinguishes the Insight Guide series.

John Chapple, a writer and editor who has lived in Greece since 1969, covered Athens, central Greece, the Ionian islands and the islands of the Saronic Gulf. He also revised the essays section. Fellow American **Marc Dubin**, a long-time resident of Sámos, not only contributed many photographs but explored northern Greece and the Peloponnese as well as the islands of the northeast Aegean and the Dodecanese.

Jeffrey Carson, who wrote the chapter on the Cyclades, has lived on Paros since 1970 and teaches art history at the Aegean Centre for the Arts. Crete was covered by tour leader and botanist **Lance Chilton**, who has written several walking guides to Greece as well as two botanical studies on Cretan flora.

Text retained from previous editions contains material from many experts on Greece, including **Jane Cowan, Katy Ricks, Mark Mazower, Charles Stewart, Haris Vlavianos, Peter Mackridge, Samantha Stenzel, Lucy Rushton, Fay Zika, Nelson Moe, Dimitri Gondicas, David Ricks, Julia Loomis, Stephanie Ferguson, Kay Cicellis, John Chioles, Stacy Rubis, Sean Damer, Nikos Kasdaglis** and **Aliki Gourdmichalis**.

Many of the photographs in this book are the vision of **Glyn Genin**. Others came from **Phil Wood**, a graduate of the London College of Printing with a passion for Greece; and **Terry Harris**, who runs the Just Greece picture library in London.

Jane Simmonds proofread the book, **Peter Gunn** indexed it, and **Sue Platt** edited Travel Tips.

Map Legend

▬ ▬ ▬	International Boundary
▬ ▬ ▬	Province
⊖	Border Crossing
▬•▬•▬	National Park/Reserve
▬ ▬ ▬	Ferry Route
Ⓜ	Metro
✈ ✈	Airport International / Regional
🚐	Bus Station
Ⓟ	Parking
❶	Tourist Information
✉	Post Office
† ✝	Church / Ruins
†	Monastery
☾	Mosque
✡	Synagogue
⌘	Castle / Ruins
∴	Archeological Site
∩	Cave
⌇	Statue / Monument
★	Place of Interest

The main places of interest in the Places section are coordinated by number with a full-colour map (e.g. ❶), and a symbol at the top of every right-hand page tells you where to find the map.

CONTENTS

Maps

A map of Greece is also on
the front inside cover, and a
map of the main ferry routes
is on the back inside cover.

Introduction

History

Features

The Acropolis towers above the market place of Athens on a white rocky platform

Places

Travel Tips

◆ **Full Travel Tips index**
  is on page 321

WELCOME TO GREECE

A heady mix of sun, sea and ancient sites bathed in brilliant Aegean light, Greece has enchanted travellers for centuries

Whether you arrive in Greece by boat, train or plane, your first impression as you stretch your legs and climb down the stairs is sure to be of the sun. Glimmering on the water, reflecting off metal and glass, casting shadows, the Mediterranean sun is omnipresent. Like the flash of a hidden camera, the brilliant light catches you unaware and transfixes you.

From the minute you set foot in Greece, you are a part of the Greek landscape – blue sky above, white sand below, the Parthenon, olive groves, a wine festival; whatever the scene, you are in the picture as well. There is a sense that, no matter how many holiday snapshots you may take, Greece will already have taken as many of you.

This country is not merely a holiday resort, ready to satisfy your every desire – it is a population of 10 million people working, eating, drinking, arguing and dancing, who will initiate you into the bustle of their everyday life, into the splendour of their mountains, their ancient temples and white pebbled shores and into the fellowship of their company. When an older woman offers you a sprig of basil, the traditional gesture of hospitality, she simultaneously introduces you into her world and enters yours.

This country is no escape from the everyday; it is an invitation to participate with all your senses – to dive in, smell it, hear it, feel it, taste it, consider it from another perspective, to roll the basil between your fingers, breathing in its fragrant greeting, and to exchange a smile with this generous woman who has invited you into her world. A Greek poet, Olga Broumas, remembered it this way in her collection *Beginning with O* (Yale University Press):

> *When the Greek sea*
> *was exceptionally calm*
> *the sun not so much a pinnacle*
> *as a perspiration of light, your brow and the sky*
> *meeting on the horizon, sometimes*
>
> *you'd dive*
> *from the float, the pier, the stone*
> *promontory, through water so startled*
> *it held the shape of your plunge...*

Just as Greece over the centuries has shaped Western civilisation, so it holds the shape of your plunge. Greece's history would be incomplete without you and all the other travellers who have come before you. Welcome to Greece. You are a part of the story that is about to be told. ❏

PRECEDING PAGES: Knossós fresco; island transport; windmills on Kárpathos; Cycladic architecture. **LEFT:** passengers descending the gangway of an Aegean ferry.

LA GRECIA
VNIVERSALE ANTICA
Paragonata con la Moderna da
Giacomo Cantelli da Vignola
Con le direttioni delle Carte Migliori e'è di più accre=
ditati Scrittori di Geografia   data in luce da Gio=
Giacomo Rossi in Roma alla Pace l'anno 1687...
con Priu. del S. Pont.

MARE DI SAPIENZA

Decisive Dates

MINOAN PERIOD: CIRCA 3000–1400 BC

3000 BC The Minoan civilisation arises on Crete; outposts are established and contact is made with the Egyptians.

2100–1500 BC Minoan culture – noted for its great cities and palaces, and sophisticated art – reaches its zenith.

Circa **1400 BC** The settlement at Akrotíri on Santoríni is annihilated by a volcanic eruption. Most other centres of Minoan power are destroyed by fire and abandoned.

THE BIRTH OF EUROPE

Greece – or to be more precise, Crete – was present at the birth of Europe. A myth, now thousands of years old, recounts how Zeus, the father of the gods, abducted a beautiful, shy princess from her palace in Phoenicia. He fell in love with her and gained her trust by posing as a white bull.

However, as soon as the princess sat on the bull's back she was carried away against her will to the shores of a distant continent, which from then on bore her name: Europa. The rest, as they say, is history...

MYCENAEAN AND DORIAN PERIOD: 1400–700 BC

1400 BC A Peloponnesian tribe, the Myceneans, rise to prominence, building grand fortifications to defend their citadels at Mycenae and Tiryns.

1200 BC The Dorian tribe conquer large areas of the Peloponnese.

776 BC The Dorians hold the first Olympic games, in honour of Zeus and Hera.

ARCHAIC PERIOD: 700–500 BC

700 BC onwards Dorian invasions create city-states, including Athens, Sparta, Thebes and Corinth, which compete for supremacy.

550 BC Sparta forms the Peloponnese League with neighbouring states. Rivalry with Athens increases.

500 BC The Greek city-states control large parts of the Mediterranean coast.

CLASSICAL PERIOD: 500–338 BC

490 BC The Persian king, Darius, attempts to invade and conquer Greece but is convincingly defeated by the Athenian army.

480 BC Xerxes, Darius's son, invades. The Spartan king, Leonidas, fails to hold back the Persian army at the Battle of Thermopylae. Athens is captured, but then in a surprise attack, Greek boats sink the Persian fleet off Salamína.

431–404 BC The Peloponnesian Wars, with Sparta and Athens the main protagonists. Athens capitulates; Sparta takes control of much of Greece.

338 BC Philip II of Macedonia defeats Athens and Thebes at the Battle of Chaeronea and unites all Greek cities except for Sparta.

HELLENISTIC AND ROMAN PERIOD: 338 BC–AD 395

336 BC Philip II assassinated. His son, Alexander the Great, develops Greece into an imperial power with Macedonia at the centre of government.

323 BC Alexander's huge empire is divided on his death amongst his successors, the Diadochi; the centres of political power consequently shift from Greece to the Middle East and Egypt.

320–275 BC The Diadochi war amongst themselves; Macedonia struggles to maintain its position. Rome emerges as a major power.

146 BC Rome annexes Greece as a province of the Roman Empire.

BYZANTINE PERIOD: AD 395–1453

395 The Roman empire is divided into East and West, with the Greeks dominant in the East.

1204 The Crusaders, assisted by the Venetians, attack and plunder Constantinople. The Franks and

Venetians divide Greek territory amongst themselves. Fortified harbours and fortresses are built in the Peloponnese and on Rhodes and Crete against the Turkish threat.
1453 The Byzantine Empire is defeated by the Ottomans.

OTTOMAN PERIOD: 1453–1821

1453 The sultan hands over the civil administration of Greece to the Greek Orthodox Church. Initially, life for the Greeks is tolerable.
1500s High per capita and land taxes prove to be a heavy burden for the Greek population.
1600s The burden of taxation now becomes unbearable and the Greek struggle for independence starts to take shape. The Church takes the side of the rebels.
1821 After a number of failed attempts, Archbishop Yermanós in the Peloponnese calls for an armed struggle against the Turks. Troops succeed in liberating Athens at the first attempt.

MODERN TIMES: FROM 1821

1820s The major European powers intervene in the Greek War of Independence. Their military assistance helps expel the Turks from southern and central Greece.
1832 Russia, France and Great Britian install Prince Otto of Bavaria as the new king of Greece.
1863 King George I succeeds the ousted Otto.
1909 The Liberal Party under Elesthérios Venizélos comes to power and governs until 1920.
1912 The Balkan Wars erupt. Greece wrests southern Macedonia, Epirus, Crete and the east Aegean islands from the Turks.
1917 Greece enters World War I after bitter wranglings between republicans and monarchists.
1922 Encouraged by the Allies, Greek troops attempt to annex Smyrna from Turkey but fail. King Constantine goes into exile; a parliamentary republic is established.
1923 The borders between Greece and Turkey are finally settled and in a traumatic population transfer, 1.1 million Orthodox Greeks leave Asia Minor and 380,000 Muslims leave Greece for Turkey.
1928–32 Venizélos is restored to power.
1933 The royalist Populist Party is voted in.
1935 The monarchy is restored.

PRECEDING PAGES: 17th-century map of Greece.
LEFT: ancient myth revived in a bust of Poseidon.
RIGHT: effigy of the great Liberal prime minister, Elefthérios Venizélos, a native of Crete.

1936–41 Military (and fascist) dictatorship under General Metaxás. When World War II is declared, Greece is initially neutral.
1940 Mussolini sends troops into Greece.
1941–44 Hitler's forces occupy Greece. Resistance groups base themselves in the mountains.
1944–49 The Germans retreat, and the Allies attempt to reintroduce civilian rule. Rebel forces defy the right-wing government the Allies install.
1950s The conservatives rule and an uneasy peace reigns. The Communist Party is outlawed.
1967 A group of army colonels under Yeórghios Papadhópoulos seize control of the country.
1974 The junta attempts to take over Cyprus but

fails and is forced to resign. The monarchy is abolished and Greece declares itself a republic.
1977 Andréas Papandhréou's socialist party, PASOK, makes large gains in the general elections.
1981–98 PASOK gains power and apart from a brief interruption (1989–93), Papandhréou remains the Prime Minister.
1993 A breakaway republic of the former Yugoslavia calling itself (to Greece's anger) Macedonia gains official recognition from the EC and UN as the Former Yugoslav Republic of Macedonia.
1995 Greece opens its borders with FYROM.
1996 Andréas Papandhréou dies; Kóstas Simítis succeeds him and wins re-election.
2000 Simítis narrowly wins a second term. ❏

CHANGE AND CONTINUITY

Overshadowed by the dazzling classical legacy, the origins of the
modern Greek state are richer and more complex than many suppose

In Greece the classical past overwhelms you. The visitor's first glimpse of Pláka, Athens' best-preserved old quarter, seems to dissolve the intervening centuries. In a country whose inhabitants proudly remind you of their ancient heritage, it is easy for the newcomer to assume that a simple thread of continuity runs from the ancient world to modern Athens.

But closer acquaintance throws up new historical and linguistic surprises: a crumbling 15th-century Pláka house offering a reminder of Ottoman Athens; communities to the south of the city where the old people, refugees from Asia Minor, still speak Turkish; and suburbs to the north where you can hear Albanian. Or further afield, the roadside shelters of a group of nomadic Sarakatsanái shepherds, a Roman Catholic church on a Cycladic island, or a Jewish cemetery in Ioánnina.

Migrations and invasions

The history of Greece is the story of endless movements of people: invasions, migrations, depopulation, resettlement. Sometimes the invasions were brief, as was the case with the Arab attacks from the sea in the 8th to 10th centuries. At other times they were gradual, bringing new settlers, such as the Dorian tribes three millennia ago, or more recently the Slavs, both entering Greece through Epirus and then moving down the west of the country into the Peloponnese (Pelopónnisos).

The other side of the coin was depopulation. In the face of invasion whole populations would leave their towns and villages. The Slav invasions wiped out urban life in southern Greece. Similarly, pirate raids led to the whole-sale evacuation of Aegina (Éghina) in AD 896 and the abandonment of Sámos late in the 15th century. Even later, in 1821, the inhabitants of Híos fled from Turkish savagery to Sýros.

Depopulation was often a major economic

headache: the strain of maintaining Alexander's empire weakened Macedonia for generations. Byzantine and Ottoman rulers both tried to improve matters by authorising mass transfers of settlers. At the same time, they welcomed new-comers. The Albanians were admitted to the Peloponnese in 1338 on condition they fought for the

local ruler and cultivated the land he gave them.

Albanian tribes were often ready to move; their livelihood involved shifting their sheep between mountain pastures in the summer and lowland grazing in winter. Such communities covered vast distances each year. Two other nomadic groups, the Vláchs and the Sarakatsanáoi, also moved into Greece in large numbers. The Vláchs in particular prospered during the 18th century, and produced a number of Greece's most famous poets and politicians.

In more recent times these large movements of population have continued. At the turn of the century there was a huge wave of emigration from the Peloponnese to the United States

LEFT: a kiosk-owner from Sýros proudly displays a picture of himself as a boy.
RIGHT: the picture in close-up.

caused by over-population and economic distress. And in 1923 a compulsory exchange agreed between Greece and Turkey led to the departure of 380,000 Muslims from Greece and the arrival of 1.1 million Orthodox Greeks from Asia Minor.

Continuities in daily life

In the long run, people change; the endless cycle of invasion and assimilation introduces new inhabitants with new customs. But over the same period of time, daily life may change very little, especially in the Mediterranean. Take security, for example, which until very

recently was a key issue of Greek social life.

The pirates who lurked in coves in the Máni in the 18th century – taking prisoners everywhere, as a French traveller reported, "selling the Christians to the Turks and the Turks to the Christians" – were merely following in the steps of their Homeric predecessors who had infested just the same area. When no naval power was strong enough to control their activities, the pirates operated on a large scale. The Genoese were obliged to move the inhabitants of Sámos *en masse* to Híos when pirate raids made a normal way of life impossible for them. And in the 8th century, Arab raiders from North Africa

BUILT FOR SECURITY

For most of recorded history, social life in Greece has been a precarious affair. Many towns and villages lie off the main road in foothills – a precaution against attack by wandering bands of highway robbers. Coastal settlements were often set on high ground at some distance from the shore, for better protection from frequent pirate raids. Local communities had to rely on their own devices as far as security was concerned – and while a pack of dogs may have been the cheapest burglar alarm, a good set of walls and an easily defensible location were more reliable.

left Páros such a wilderness that hunters used to sail over from Évvia (Euboea) after the deer and wild goats which had become plentiful on the island.

Highway robbery

Life on the mainland was no easier. Pirate bands were likely to raid villages inland, particularly in daylight when the menfolk of the village would be away working in the fields. For travellers by land, there was also the perennial problem of highway robbery.

As one 17th-century English traveller noted, "in order to insure the safety of Travellers, drummers are appointed in dangerous passages;

and in Macedonia, in a narrow passe, I saw an old Man beating a drum upon the ridge of a Hill; whereby we had noticed that the passage was clear and free from thieves." In those short periods when an effective central authority held sway, it generally had such limited resources that it could do little to enforce the law. At the end of the 19th century the Ottoman authorities refused to permit trains to run through Macedonia at night since they could not guard them against armed attack. The Germans faced a similar problem when they occupied Greece in World War II.

Though life was insecure, frightening and

from the moment that he picked up his weapon.

Such rules may have constituted the most reliable codes of justice, for statesmen and those in power often failed to keep their word. A traveller in Ottoman Greece was told, "in your petty Kingdoms and States men are tryed and convicted, but our great Empire cannot be so maintained, and if the Sultan should now send for my head, I must be content to lay it down patiently, not asking wherefore… in this country we must have… patience even to the losse of our heads and patience after that."

Rulers might come and go, but to the poor such patience remained a necessity. After all,

violent, it embraced rigidly observed codes of courtesy and honour. Today the blend is difficult to recapture, except in the Máni, and on Crete, where blood feuds still thrive. Vendettas, for example, which were common in most parts of Greece, were conducted according to strict rules which changed little over the centuries. In 18th-century Epirus, as in Homeric Greece, an intended victim of a blood feud was immune from attack while he was farming, but was considered fair game

LEFT: Ermoúpolis on the island of Sýros, built on a hill as protection against piracy.
ABOVE: the Dillesi gang, pre- and post-capture.

their very existence depended upon factors beyond their control. Even when their villages escaped the attention of bandits or the tax-man, a poor harvest raised the grim spectre of starvation. Certainly, the past has never offered them a "Golden Age".

The account that follows describes the changing fortunes of dynasties and kingdoms; however, the history of a country involves more than just a succession of names and dates. The essential backdrop is provided by the generations of nameless inhabitants whose lives involved those countless imperceptible changes which may escape our gaze, but which provide the real origins of modern Greece. ❑

ANCIENT GREECE

The rich civilisations which rose and fell in the Aegean have left
a precious inheritance still relevant today

The basis for the modern way of life in Greece was laid around 3000 BC, when settlers moved down from the northeast plains onto rockier land in the Peloponnese (Pelopónnisos) and the islands, and began to cultivate olives and vines, as well as the cereals they had originally grown. At about the same time a prosperous civilisation arose on Crete (Kríti), and spread its influence throughout the Aegean.

The Minoans, whose rituals have filtered down to us through the legend of Theseus and his labyrinthine struggle with the Minotaur, left proof of their architectural genius in the ruined palaces of Knossós and Festós. Adventurous sailors, they appear to have preferred commerce to agriculture. They established a number of outposts in the Peloponnese and made contact with the Egyptians.

By 1500 BC their civilisation had reached its zenith. Yet barely a century later, for reasons which remain unexplained, most centres of their power were destroyed by fire and abandoned. The settlement on Santoríni (Thíra), at Akrotíri, was annihilated by a volcanic eruption. But the causes of the wider disintegration of Minoan control remain a mystery. Only Knossós continued to be inhabited as Cretan dominance in the Aegean came to an end.

Its place was taken by Mycenae (Mykínes), the bleak citadel in the Peloponnese. We do not know whether the rulers of Mycenae exerted direct power over the remainder of the mainland. But in the *Iliad* Homer portrays their king, Agamemnon, as the most powerful figure in the Greek forces, and this suggests that Mycenae had achieved some sort of overall authority.

In its heyday the Mycenaean world contained men rich enough to commission massive stone tombs and delicate gold work. Rulers were served by a complex array of palace scribes and administrators who controlled the economic life of the state, exacting tribute, collecting taxes and allocating rations of scarce metals.

The Dark Ages

In the 13th century BC this civilisation, like the Cretan one before it, came to a violent end. Classical myth connects the decline of the

Mycenaean age with the arrival of Dorian tribes. In fact, there was no clear connection between the two events. Mycenaean power had broken down irreversibly by the time the Dorians entered Greece. These invaders, like later ones, entered Greece from the northwest, down over the Pindos mountains into the Peloponnese. Probably they were nomads, which would explain their willingness to travel and account for their lower level of culture.

They also brought their own form of Greek. In areas where they settled heavily we find West Greek dialects, whilst Attica, the Aegean islands and the Ionian colonies continued to use East Greek forms. The hostility, at a later date,

LEFT: sunrise at Cape Sounion on the Attica Peninsula, southwest of Athens.
RIGHT: figure of a goddess, found at Knossós.

between Athens and Sparta (Spárti) was based in part on this division between Ionian and Dorian peoples.

The Dorian invasion coincided with the onset of the Dark Ages. Historical evidence for the period between the 11th and 8th centuries BC is patchy, but it is clear that civilised life suffered. Trade dwindled and communities became isolated from one another. Building in stone seems to have been too great an effort for the small pastoral settlements that had replaced the centres of

A CULTURAL DECLINE

Although by the 13th century BC the Mycenaeans had adapted Minoan script into the first written Greek, the art of writing was all but forgotten during the Dark Ages.

Another, equally important Greek concept was borrowed from the Phoenicians; the notion of the *pólis* (city-state). In the Dark Ages small, isolated settlements were loosely grouped into large kingdoms. This system survived in both western and northern Greece into classical times when Thucydides described how "the Aetolian nation, although numerous and warlike, yet dwell in unwalled villages scattered far apart."

Elsewhere, however, a network of small independent states grew up. At first, these were

Mycenaean power. Homer's *Odyssey* is set in a simple society where even the rulers busy themselves with menial tasks; where wealth is measured in flocks and herds.

Writing revives

In the 8th century BC there were signs of revival: trade spread further afield. There were contacts with civilized peoples such as the Etruscans in the west, and the Phoenicians and Egyptians in the east. Artistic influence from the east was increasingly evident in metalwork and pottery. With the adoption of the Phoenician alphabet, writing revived amongst a much larger circle than before.

based around clusters of villages rather than one large urban centre. With the population explosion of the 8th century, however, large conurbations evolved and expanded as surplus population moved from the country to the town. Land became more intensively cultivated and highly priced. In the Dark Ages the slump in population had caused arable land to fall into disuse. Farmers turned from sowing cereals to stock-breeding; now the process was thrown into reverse. The available land could not support such a rapidly growing population. There is a clear parallel with the Peloponnese in the 19th century, and in both cases the outcome was the same: emigration on a massive scale.

Together with the division between the new pólis and the older éthnos (kingdom), there was now a further distinction. On the one hand, there were states, mostly in the Dorian-speaking parts of the country, with a serf population who were excluded from power, like Sparta, a major pólis, and Thessaly, an éthnos. On the other hand, there were states with a more broadly based citizen body, such as Athens.

From kings to aristocrats

In general the kings mentioned in Homer must have surrendered power towards the end of the Dark Ages to an aristocratic form of rule. But

had been reflected in the move from chariots to horseback fighting, so too the emphasis switched from cavalry to infantry; aristocracy lost ground to democratic pressure. Men would only fight in the new larger armies if the aristocrats granted them political rights.

Military power swung away from the traditional horse-breeding aristocracies of Chalkis, Eretria and Thessaly to new powers: Corinth (Kórinthos), Argos and, above all, Sparta, where the state was protected by a hoplite army whose core was a body of citizens who were trained as infantry soldiers from birth.

Often the demand for radical reform met with

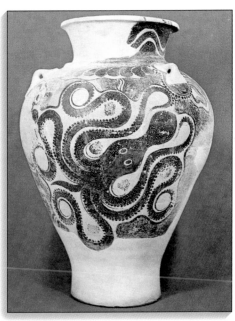

the aristocracy too became entrenched in power and increasingly resistant to change. As commoners settled on land and amassed wealth, pressure grew for constitutional reform. Aristotle seems to have been right in tying the demand for such reform to changes in military techniques. He noted that, "when states began to increase in size, and infantry forces acquired a greater degree of strength, more persons were admitted to the enjoyment of political rights." Just as the shift from monarchy to aristocracy

LEFT: dolphin fresco in the Palace at Knossós.
ABOVE: two early 6th-century vase designs; the one on the left depicts Theseus and the Minotaur.

resistance from the upper classes, but some individuals, more far-sighted, recognised the need for change. One such was Solon, elected in early 6th-century Athens to introduce sweeping constitutional changes. Realising that the city's strength would depend upon the organisation of the citizen body, he opened up the Assembly to the poorest citizens and in other ways loosened the grip of the aristocracy.

Inevitably these changes were attacked from both sides, as Solon himself complains in a number of his poems. But they did lay the foundations for the tremendous expansion of Athenian power throughout the next century.

Another symptom of these political tensions

was tyranny. To the ancient Greeks the word "tyrant" was not pejorative; it simply referred to a ruler who had usurped power instead of inheriting it. In the 6th century, tyrants seized power in a number of states. Usually they were dissident aristocrats, who gained the support of the lower classes with promises of radical change – promises which were often kept, as it was in the new ruler's interest to weaken the power of his peers. In the mid-7th century, for example, Kipselis of Corinth was supposed to have redistributed land belonging to his fellow aristocrats.

But it would be wrong to regard the tyrants as great innovators. They were symptoms of social

Thus it was the scale of its religious activities which provided some measure of the wealth of a community.

Greeks and outsiders

Now, alongside the rise of an artistic culture shared across state boundaries, a process of political unification began to grow. People in different cities started to become aware of a common Hellenic culture. The historian Herodotus was a keen promoter of the idea of one Greece, and asserted that the Greeks are "a single race because of common blood, common customs, common language and common reli-

change rather than causes of it. Conscious of their own vulnerability, they resorted to various propaganda expedients to stay in power. The most potent of these was the religious cult, and it is from the time of the tyrants that religion came directly to serve the purposes of the state.

Religion was not only important to the state as propaganda; it was also a major economic factor. While religious festivals and games earned revenues – enormous in some cases – for the city which staged them, temples, sacrifices and other rituals were very costly. Apart from wars, temple-building was probably the greatest drain on a community's resources.

gion". The increasing prominence of interstate religious games and festivals spread this view.

But the sharpest spur to unity was a threat from outside: the rise of the Persian empire. Cyrus, halfway through the 6th century, had conquered the Greek cities on the Asia Minor coast, and Persian aspirations were further encouraged by his son Darius (521–486 BC) who conquered Thrace, subdued Macedonia and, after quashing an Ionian revolt in Asia Minor, sent a massive expeditionary force southwards into Greece. Athens appealed for help from Sparta, the strongest Greek city, but succeeded in defeating the Persians at Marathon before the Spartan forces arrived.

This victory did more than save Attica; it also confirmed Athens as the standard-bearer for the Greek military effort against the Persians. This explains why a frieze displaying the warriors killed at Marathon (situated just over 23km/ 20 miles from Athens) was placed in a prominent and highly unusual position around the Parthenon in the 440s BC. Only then was Athens becoming a power to be reckoned with. The silver mines at Lávrion began producing enough ore to finance a major shipbuilding programme from early in the 5th century. For two generations after that, Aegina (Éghina) remained superior to Athens as a Saronic Gulf trading force.

banished than the Greek alliance broke up. There was intense suspicion, especially between Sparta and Athens. Thucydides described how, as soon as the Persians withdrew, the Athenians rebuilt their city walls for fear that the Spartans would try to stop them.

The development of a classical "cold war" became obvious as Athens extended its control over the Aegean with the help of the Confederation of Delos. Significantly, the Persian threat had receded long before peace was officially declared in 449 BC. Next, between 460 BC and 446 BC, Athens fought a series of wars with its neighbours in an effort to assert its supremacy.

Athens and Sparta

Ten years after Marathon, when Darius's son Xerxes organised a second attack on Greece, the city-states rallied around Sparta. For while Athens had the largest navy, the Spartans controlled the Peloponnesian League, with its considerable combined land forces. Both the crucial naval victory at Salamis in 480 BC and the military victory at Plataea the following year, were won under Spartan leadership.

But no sooner had the Persian menace been

LEFT: the ancient stadium at Delphi.
ABOVE: a vase painted in the red-figure style which became popular in the late 6th century BC.

THE RISE OF ATHENS

The Athenian Empire owed much to the Confederation of Delos, a naval alliance formed in 478 BC to liberate the East Greeks and continue the struggle against the Persians. It was also underlaid by much anti-Spartan sentiment. Sparta's own version of the alliance, the Peloponnesian League, consisted of land forces, requiring minimum financing. But the creation of a navy called for long-term planning and central coordination – a crucial difference. Athens' smaller allies found it increasingly difficult to equip their own ships, and turned instead to sending money for the Athenians. Thus Athens grew in strength as its allies became impoverished.

Naval rivals such as Aegina were singled out for attack.

In 430 BC war erupted again when Corinth appealed to the Peloponnesian League for help against Athenian attack. This, the Second Peloponnesian War, dragged on for years since neither side was able to deal the death-blow to the other. The Peace of Nikias in 421 BC gave both sides a breathing space, but lasted just six years. Only when the Spartans got financial support from the Persians and managed to inflict a final,

HOW TO BUILD EMPIRES

One reason the Greek city states failed as imperial powers, the Roman Emperor Claudius observed, was because they "treated their subjects as foreigners."

their subject territories. Nor could the military strength of Athens keep pace with its imperial commitments, which explains the permanent cycle of conquest and revolt. The Spartans had the additional headache of a large serf population, the helots, often prone to revolt in their own province.

The first half of the 4th century continued the pattern. On the one hand, there were long wars between cities; on the other, evidence of prolonged economic difficulties as Corinth fell into irreversible decline and Athens struggled to

catastrophic defeat on the Athenian navy was Athens forced to surrender.

Civic breakdown

Literature and art both flourished even during these incessant periods of fighting, but economic activity did not. In a world where each tiny *pólis* was determined to safeguard its independence at any cost, war was endemic. Such a world carried within it the seeds of its own destruction.

The paradox was that city-states with imperial pretensions chose not to take the steps that might have brought success. Unlike Rome, Greek city-states did not extend citizenship to

recapture its previous prominence. This it failed to do. Spartan power remained supreme until 371 BC when Thebes defeated the Spartan army at Leuctra.

The city-state system was gradually starting to fall apart. The old form of citizen army was superseded by a more professional force, which relied upon trained mercenaries. Aristotle noted that "when the Spartans were alone in their strenuous military discipline they were superior to everybody, but now they are beaten by everybody; the reason is that in former times they trained and others did not." Things had certainly changed.

The spread of mercenaries, in fact, reflects

the economic problems of the 4th century. Mercenary service, like emigration or piracy, was a demographic safety valve, and whereas in archaic Greece mercenaries had come from just a few backward areas, in the 4th century they were increasingly drawn from the major cities as well. This points to economic difficulties over an increasingly wide area.

As in earlier times, military changes linked up with political ones. The decline of the citizen armies coincided with a trend away from democracy in favour of more autocratic government. Power shifted from the city-states towards Thessaly, an *éthnos* state, and later still, towards Macedonia, which was another old-fashioned kingdom.

Both regions had the advantage over Attica in that they were fertile and not short of land. More rural than the city-states to their south, they managed to avoid the domestic political turmoil that periodically erupted in the latter. The military successes of the Thessalian tyrant, Jason of Pherae, in the early 4th century, indicated the confidence of these newcomers.

A little later Philip of Macedonia moved southwards, secured the vital Thermopylae (Thermopýles) Pass and, after gaining control of Thessaly, defeated an alliance of Thebes and Athens at Chaeronea in 338 BC. Banded together in the League of Corinth, the Greek city-states were compelled to recognise a new centre of power, Macedonia.

Alexander's Greece

In the *Republic*, Socrates asserts, "we shall speak of war when Greeks fight with barbarians, whom we may call their natural enemies. But Greeks are by nature friends of Greeks, and when they fight, it means that Hellas is afflicted by dissension which ought to be called civil strife."

This passage reflects three sentiments that were becoming widespread in the 4th century: first, that the Greeks were all of one race; second, that warfare between city-states was undesirable; third, that it was natural for the Greeks to fight their enemies in the east. It is ironic in this regard that a successful concerted effort against the Persians was made only under

the leadership of Macedonia, traditionally a border power in the Greek world.

The rapid growth of Alexander the Great's Asian empire drastically altered the boundaries of the Greek world. The city-states of mainland Greece no longer occupied centre stage. The mainland was drained of manpower as soldiers, settlers and administrators moved eastwards to consolidate Greek rule. At the same time, the intellectual and religious world of the Greeks was opened up to new influences.

The Greek-speaking world was not only expanding, it was also coming together: "common" Greek replaced local dialects in most

areas. In 3rd-century Macedonia, for example, local culture was "hellenised", and the native gods were replaced by Olympian deities.

For the first time coins became widely used in trade – something which had been impossible so long as each city had its own currency. Now the Attic drachma became acceptable in an area ranging from Athens to the Black Sea, from Cappadocia to Italy.

But there were limits to this process, for although the city-states gave up their political freedom, they clung to self-determination in other spheres. Local taxation and customs duties offer examples of this passion for independence. Likewise the calendar: in Athens

LEFT: Roman mosaic floor: a man from Kós welcomes the healer Asclepius, while Hippocrates looks on.
RIGHT: an "early owl" Attic drachma.

the year began in July, in Sparta in October, on the island of Delos, January.

Philosophers were debating ideas of communal loyalties which transcended the old civic boundaries. Perhaps this reflected the way in which these were being absorbed within larger units, such as the Hellenistic kingdoms, the Greek federal leagues and, eventually, the Roman Empire. Whatever the cause, the most influential philosophical school, Stoicism, emphasised the concept of universal brotherhood and talked of a world state ruled by one supreme power. In its moral fervour, Stoicism was very much a product of the Hellenistic age.

Roman expansion

Gradually but inexorably, the expansion of Macedonia curtailed the political autonomy of the city-states. In the 3rd century they formed federations, and tried to exploit disputes between the generals who had inherited Alexander's empire. The policy had only limited success, mainly because of the paltry military resources available to the Greek leagues.

Early in the 2nd century, disputes among the city-states brought about Roman intervention for the first time in Greek history. Within 20 years Rome had defeated first Macedonia, and then the Achaean League which had organised a desperate Greek resistance to Roman rule.

The Roman consul Memmius marked his victory by devastating Corinth, killing the entire male population, and selling its women and children into slavery. As a deterrent to further resistance this was brutal but effective. Conservative factions were confirmed in power in the cities and Greece became a Roman protectorate. In 27 BC, when the Roman Empire was proclaimed, the protectorate became the province of Achaea.

Greece – a Roman backwater?

By the 1st century AD, Greece was no longer the centre of the civilised world. Athens and Corinth could not rival Alexandria or Antioch, let alone Rome. The main routes to the east went overland through Macedonia, by sea to Egypt. But while Greece was certainly a commercial backwater, its decline was only relative: along the coast, cities flourished. The *pólis* remained much as it had been in Hellenistic times and the Roman authorities permitted a degree of political self-rule. Philhellene emperors like Hadrian even encouraged groups of cities to federate in an effort to encourage a panhellenic spirit.

But the *pólis* was no longer a political force. Hellenistic rulers had feared the Greek cities' power; the Roman, and later the Byzantine emperors feared their weakness and did what they could to keep them alive. After all, they were vital administrative cogs in the imperial machine. If they failed, the machine would not function.

Two centuries of relative tranquillity were shattered by the Gothic invasions in the 3rd century AD. The invasions were successfully repelled, but the shock led to a loss of confidence and economic deterioration. Civic building programmes continued on a much reduced scale. The wealthy classes became increasingly reluctant benefactors, and two centuries passed before imperial authorities and the church revived the demand for architectural skills.

By that time much had changed. Emperor Constantine had moved his capital from Rome to Constantinople. Christianity had been made the official religion of the empire. The transition from Rome to Byzantium had begun. ❏

LEFT: Roman head of Apollo, Benáki Museum, Athens.
RIGHT: coptic angel, reminiscent of St George the dragon-slayer.

BYZANTINE GREECE

The legendary wealth of Rome's eastern empire attracted many potential invaders, from the Franks and Venetians to the Ottomans

A revealing incident occurred in the Byzantine capital, Constantinople, in AD 968. Legates from the Holy Roman Empire in the west brought a letter for Nicephorus, the Byzantine Emperor, in which Nicephorus was simply styled "Emperor of the Greeks" while the Holy Roman Emperor, Otto, was termed

"august Emperor of the Romans." The Byzantine courtiers were scandalised. The audacity of it – to call the universal emperor of the Romans, the one and only Nicephorus, the great, the august, "emperor of the Greeks" and to style a poor barbaric creature "emperor of the Romans"!

Behind this reaction lies the curious fusion of cultures which made up the Byzantine tradition. From the Hellenistic world came the belief in the superiority of the Greek world, the summary dismissal of outsiders as barbarians. From Rome came a strong sense of loyalty to empire and emperor. And in the fervour which marked their belief in the moral superiority of *their* empire –

which they regarded not as the "Eastern Roman Empire" but as the only true empire – is the stamp of evangelical Christianity.

The inhabitants of this empire did not call themselves Greeks or Byzantines: they were Romans, "Roméï". But the mark of a *Romaiós* was that he spoke Greek and followed the rite of the Orthodox Church. Thus the three elements intermingled.

The end of antiquity

The real break with antiquity came late in the 6th century when Greece was first attacked and then settled by Slavic-speaking tribes from the north. The invasions marked the end of the classical tradition in Greece, destroying urban civilisation and with it Roman and Christian culture. But the empire fought back. Christian missionaries converted the pagan Slavs in the Peloponnese, and taught them Greek. The language survived but the old urban culture did not. The disappearance of the city-states is shown by the way in which the word *pólis* came to refer exclusively to Constantinople as though there were no other cities. A small urban elite studied and wrote in ancient Greek but had little impact on the mass of the population; their books were probably read by less than 300 people at any one time. Ancient monuments were left untouched because peasants thought that they were inhabited by demons.

The weaknesses of Byzantine rule

The Byzantine Empire lacked the resources to maintain tight control over its territories. It was beset on all sides by the Italian city-states, the Slav kingdoms to the north, the Persians and Turks in the east. The Greek provinces, being less vital than Anatolia, which supplied Constantinople with corn, were ceded more readily to other powers.

Byzantium's period of glory was short-lived, lasting from the mid-9th to mid-11th centuries. Its prosperity under a succession of Macedonian emperors ended in 1071 when a new enemy, Turkoman tribes of nomads from central Asia, cut its army to pieces at Manzikert in Anatolia. The threat from the west was soon felt, too. A possible Norman invasion was feared in the 12th century when the Norman Roger of Sicily invaded Greece, sacking both Thebes and Corinth.

But this was only a foretaste of still worse misfortune. In 1204 Constantinople itself was sacked by the Crusader forces en route to the Holy Land for the Fourth Crusade. The empire was fragmented. Successor states arose in Epirus, Nicaea and Trebizond. Greece itself

A FIERCE RESISTANCE

The Aegean islands held out longest against the Turks. Tínos resisted until 1715 – over 250 years after the mainland fell.

Southern Greece and the islands remained under the control of the Crusaders' successors until in the 14th century the Paleológoi re-established a Byzantine presence at Mystrás. This political confusion led to ethnically mixed populations.

Turkish mercenaries began to play a significant role. As the Byzantine Empire lacked the men to do its own fighting, Turkish forces were enlisted to act as a buffer against the Serbs and Bulgars. Their successes were alarming; even the occasional arranged marriage between

was divided into small kingdoms – the Duchy of Athens under the Burgundian de la Roche, islands to various Italian adventurers, crucial west coast ports retained by Venice.

Over the following 50 years Byzantium re-emerged as Nikean rulers, the Paleológoi, fought back into mainland Greece and recaptured Constantinople. But there was considerable confusion in western Greece, which briefly came under Serbian control, and in Thessaly, where the Vlachs established a separate principality.

LEFT: detail of Byzantine fresco: an old ascetic.
ABOVE: carved in stone at Mystrá: St George slaying the dragon.

Ottoman princesses and Greek princes failed to negate the threat they posed.

By 1400 the empire had shrunk to just Constantinople, Thessaloníki and the Peloponnese. In April 1453 Mehmet II besieged Constantinople and took it within two months. Eight years later, the rest of the mainland had succumbed, too.

The fall of "The City" reverberated throughout Europe: with it had fallen the last descendants of the Roman Empire itself. Although in the West this seemed the inevitable result of Byzantine decline, to the Greeks it was a much more traumatic moment. They had passed from freedom into slavery. ❑

OTTOMAN GREECE

Greek nationalism grew slowly as the Turkish empire declined – until,
in the 17th century, a bloody struggle for independence was launched

The Ottoman Turks who now controlled the Balkans were the latest in a stream of nomadic tribes who had moved westwards from central Asia. They were highly mobile, and their determination to pursue military conquests made up for their lack of numbers.

Religious tolerance was reflected in the

"millet" system of imperial government. The sultan in Constantinople recognised minority religions, and permitted each "millet", or religious community, a measure of self-government. The Greek Orthodox Church was granted special privileges and came to exert both religious and civil powers over Ottoman Greeks.

Under their new masters the Greeks lived in much the same way as they had done earlier. Their houses, like those of the Turks, tended to be miniature fortresses, built on two floors around a central courtyard. The restored merchant's house in Kastoriá gives a good idea of the effect. Most elements of contemporary Greek cuisine were common then – from the

resináto wine so distasteful to foreign travellers to the strong coffee which Ali Pasha, the "Lion of Ioánnina", found helpful in poisoning his rival, the Pasha of Vallona.

But autonomy did not rule out oppression. When, from the 17th century onwards, central authority weakened, local magnates were free to burden the peasantry with their own impositions. Many revolts in the Ottoman Balkans, notably that in 1805 which revived the state of Serbia, involved appeals to the sultan for help against corrupt local landowners or bishops.

Powerful enemies continually threatened the Ottoman grip on the country. The Venetians, and later the French, were thorns in the Ottoman flesh. Within the empire the wild Albanians, backbone of the Ottoman armies, often threatened to break loose. The resulting conflicts left Greece much weaker.

Thus in 1537 an Ottoman army carried off half the population of Corfu after an attack on the Venetian colony there, leaving the island with barely one-sixth of the numbers it had had in antiquity. The Peloponnese was also caught in a bloody tug-of-war between the same two rivals. It was ravaged by Albanian forces fighting for the Ottomans in 1715 and again in the 1770s. Further destruction came in the wake of the 1821 uprising. Greeks slaughtered Turks in Trípolis; Turks slaughtered the Greek inhabitants of Híos. Finally Egyptian troops, under Ibrahim Ali, laid waste most of the area.

Deadly foes

When, during the 17th century, the Ottoman empire ceased to expand, new problems appeared. In the hills and mountains, where the Ottoman grip had never been as firm as elsewhere, groups of brigands, known as *kléfts*, were formed. They were bandits, equally prone to plunder a Greek village as a Muslim estate, but in peasant folklore they came to symbolise the spirit of Greek resistance to the much hated Ottoman authorities.

Perhaps more important for the development of Greek nationalism was the growth of a

Greek merchant community. Commercial links with Europe introduced wealthy Greeks to European lifestyles, but they also encountered European cultural and political ideas. Late in the 18th century two ideas in particular, philhellenism and nationalism, found a fertile ground among young educated Greeks.

In 1814 three Greek merchants in Odessa formed a secret organisation called "The Friendly Society" (*Filikí Etaireía*) devoted to "the betterment of the nation", which rapidly acquired a network of sympathisers throughout the Ottoman lands. A number of vain attempts to secure themselves powerful backing were

belief that this was a national struggle was held with greatest conviction by the foreign philhellenes – Byron and others – who came to help the Greeks. These men were influential in getting Western public opinion behind the Greeks. Thus the major powers, initially unsympathetic to the Hellenic dream, came to put military and diplomatic pressure on the Turks to acknowledge Greek independence. The turning point came with the almost accidental destruction of the Ottoman fleet by an allied force at Navarino in 1827.

Count Ioánnis Kapodhístrias, a Greek diplomat formerly in the service of the Russian

finally rewarded when their members organised an uprising against Ottoman rule in 1821.

Yet the struggle for Greek independence, which lasted from 1821 to 1832, was not a straightforward affair. Fighting the Ottomans was a motley crew of *kléfts*, merchants, landowners and aristocratic families known as Phanariots – all as keen to further their own interests as to advance the cause of Greek nationalism. When they were not fighting the Turks they turned on each other. Ironically, the

Tsar, was elected president by a National Assembly in the same year. He encouraged Greek forces to push north of the Peloponnese and his efforts were rewarded when the 1829 Conference of London fixed the new state's northern boundary on the Árta-Vólos line. But numerous Greeks were dissatisfied with his administration and suspected him of aiming at one-man rule.

In 1831 he was shot by two chieftains of the Máni as he went into a church at Náfplio. While the major powers – Britain, France and Russia – tried to find a suitable candidate for the Greek throne, the country fell into a period of bloody anarchy and civil war. ❏

LEFT: 19th-century watercolour of Cretan costume.
ABOVE: a painting, *Dinner at a house in Chríssa*, taken from Dodwell's *Views of Greece*, 1801.

MODERN GREECE

*Despite plenty of setbacks for the new Greek state, today it is the voters
who choose the government in the birthplace of democracy*

The new state was desperately poor, overrun by armed bands of brigands, and beset by quarrelling among various political factions. In 1834 a rebellion in the Máni resulted in government troops being defeated and sent home without their equipment. There were few good harbours or roads. Athens remained a squalid,

provincial town. Internally, conditions were worse than they had been under Ottoman rule.

Bavarian absolutism was partly to blame. On Kapodhístrias's death the crown of the new kingdom was given to Otto, the son of Ludwig I of Bavaria, who arrived at Náfplio in 1833 on a British man-of-war. Since he was under age, a succession of regents ruled. Widespread calls for a constitution were ignored until, in 1843, a brief uprising in Athens forced Otto to dismiss his Bavarian advisers and accept the idea of constitutional rule and parliamentary government. Despite a poor economy, the 1844 and later the 1864 constitutions endowed the country with the trappings of a democratic state.

The "Great Idea"

The new kingdom contained less than one-third of the Greeks in the Near East. The prospect of "liberating" Ottoman Greeks, of creating a new Byzantium by recapturing Constantinople and avenging the humiliation of 1453 was known as the "Great Idea" and aroused enormous enthusiasm. This had roots embedded in the soil of a fervent nationalism. The Great Idea was rarely a realistic policy since the Greek army was never a match for the Ottomans; yet it survived repeated humiliations. After the defeats of 1897 and 1922 it continued to rear its head. King George I, who succeeded the ousted King Otto in 1863, was titled not only "King of Greece" but also "King of the Hellenes".

The most prominent populist of the late 19th century, Theodore Deliyiánnis, encouraged foolhardy expeditions to Thessaly and Crete. His more far-sighted rival, Harílaos Trikoúpis, realised that such a policy was unwise so long as Greece was dependent on foreign loans, which gave its creditors the whiphand over any foreign policy initiatives. Trikoúpis set out to reduce this dependency by boosting economic activity. Roads were improved, the Corinth Canal built. Piraeus expanded to become one of the Mediterranean's busiest ports.

But despite the appearance of a few textile and food factories, industrial activity remained minimal right up to World War I. Greece was a rural nation, a country of peasant smallholders. The lack of large estates may have ironed out social inequalities but it also meant most farmers remained miserably poor, too poor to adopt modern farming methods. The export of currants brought prosperity for a while, but a world slump in 1893 hit the entire economy. Greece became bankrupt and hunger drove many peasants to emigrate. By 1912 numerous villages lived on remittances sent from the United States by young exiles.

Such domestic problems only increased Greek enthusiasm for the Great Idea. Further territory had been acquired in 1881, without any fighting, as a by-product of the

Congress of Berlin. When troubles on Ottoman Crete in 1897 provoked a wave of sympathy on the mainland, Greek naval forces were sent to the island while the army marched northwards – only to be checked by Ottoman forces in a humiliating defeat.

On Crete and in Macedonia, Ottoman rule was crumbling. But the rise of the new Balkan nations – Serbia and Bulgaria – added a new complication to Greek ambitions.

Within Greece, political changes had often been forced through by military uprisings, something which happened again in 1909. Junior army officers staged a revolt against the political establishment and invited a new politician with a radical reputation, Elefthérios Venizélos, to come over from Crete and form a government. A consummate diplomat, Venizélos channelled the untapped energies of the Greek middle class into his own Liberal Party, which dominated politics for the next 25 years.

A decade of wars

When the Balkan Wars erupted in 1912, Greece was strong enough to wrest southern Macedonia from the Ottoman forces and then to defend its gains, in alliance with Serbia, from a hostile Bulgaria. The full gains from the fighting included – in addition to Macedonia – Epirus, Crete and the east Aegean islands. Greece's area and population were doubled at a stroke.

There was barely time to consider what burdens the new territories would impose before the country was embroiled in World War I. Venizélos and the new king, Constantine, quarrelled over whether to bring Greece into the war. The prime minister wanted Greece to give the Entente active support, while Constantine insisted on keeping the country neutral. The quarrel raised a number of vital issues: who had the final say over foreign policy – the king or parliament? The dispute reached the point of open civil war, ending only in 1917 with Constantine being forced to leave the country and Greece entering the war.

Venizélos had hoped that the Entente powers would reward Greece for its support with

PRECEDING PAGES: Zografou's *War of Independence.*
LEFT: Ioánnis Kapodhístrias, Greek President 1827–31.
RIGHT: a naive depiction of Elefthérios Venizélos.

> ### A RICH MIX
>
> The French term for fruit salad is a *macédoine* – a turn-of-the-20th century reference to Macedonia's rich and complex ethnic mix.

new territories. The annexation by Greece of Smyrna (Smyrni) with its rich hinterland and large Greek population had long been a basic tenet of the Great Idea. When the English, French, and Americans sanctioned the landing of Greek troops in Smyrna in May 1919, it began to look as though the dream might at last be realised.

It was not to be. In 1920 the pendulum of Greek political sentiment swung back, removing Venizélos from office and returning King Constantine from exile. Army morale was

damaged by changes in command according to royalist loyalty, but the revival of Turkish national fervour sparked by the Greek advance and the emerging Turkish leader, Mustafa Kemal, was even more dangerous to Greek interests. The Greek military forces advanced to 80 km (50 miles) from Ankara in June 1921, but were hampered by the European allies changing to a "neutralist" position and refusing to sell the Greeks arms. Kemal stopped the Greek advance and gradually forced the Greek army back behind long defensive lines ever closer to the coast. After a year-long stalemate, Kemal broke through the Greek lines in late August; the Greek army abandoned Smyrna a few days later. The Turkish army entered the city on 9 September 1922 and ran amok, burning both the Armenian and Greek quarters and killing an estimated 30,000 of the Christian inhabitants in the process.

The 1923 treaty, which finally ended the war between the two countries, fixed the boundaries which hold today (with the exception of the Dodecanese islands, held by the Italians until after World War II). In addition, a massive population transfer was agreed upon: 380,000 Muslim inhabitants of Greece moved to Turkey in exchange for 1.1 million Orthodox Greeks. But for a dwindling population in Istanbul, this

urban areas – often in squalid shantytowns outside the large cities – to search for jobs.

After the disaster of 1922, King Constantine was forced to leave Greece a second time, and a parliamentary republic was established. It lasted only 12 years, a succession of short-lived coalitions and minority governments, broken up by military dictatorships and abortive *coups d'état*. Governments regularly altered the electoral system to keep themselves in power. The only period of stability – Venizélos's years in power from 1928 to 1932 – was terminated by the shock of international economic depression. In 1933 the Liberals were succeeded by

10 SALONIQUE — Quartier Vardar, Groupe de Réfugiés - Vardar district, A groupe of Refugees

exchange ended a 2,500-year Greek presence in Asia Minor. The Greeks refer to these events as "the Asia Minor Disaster", and they remain a defining factor in the Greek perception of both themselves and the Turks.

The interwar years

Buffeted and impoverished by 10 years of war, the nation now faced the huge problem of absorbing these indigent newcomers into an already crowded country. The economy benefited from the cheap labour, and it was in the interwar period that Greece began to industrialise. But the refugees also increased social tensions. Over half a million of them settled in

the royalist Populist Party, whose timid leaders only half-heartedly supported the republic. Apart from the constitutional issue, little separated the parties.

Lacking popular support, parliamentary government remained vulnerable to military pressure. In 1935 this led to the king, now George II, Constantine's son, being restored. In 1936 the king dissolved parliament and offered the premiership to an extreme right-wing politician, Ioánnis Metaxás, a former senior army officer and a fervent royalist. Soon afterwards, Metaxás responded to a wave of strikes by declaring martial law. But the "First Peasant" (as Metaxás liked to be called) never managed to succeed in digging the solid foundations for his longed-for Third Hellenic Civilisation.

Renewed conflict

Metaxás had tried to steer a middle course in foreign policy between Britain and Germany. The latter's increasing dominance in the Balkans had to be set against Britain's naval strength in the Mediterranean. But Germany was not the only power with aggressive designs on the Balkans. In April 1939 Mussolini sent Italian troops into Albania and in 1940 he tried to emulate Hitler's record of conquest by crossing the Albanian border into Greece. Metaxás could no longer hope to keep Greece neutral. Receiving the Italian ambassador in his dressing-gown, he listened to a recital of trumped-up charges and responded to the fascist ultimatum with a curt "No!" Or so the story runs.

Fighting on their own in the mountains of Epirus, the Greek forces were remarkably successful and pushed the *Makaronádes* (Spaghetti Eaters) – as the Italians became known in later folk songs – back deep into Albania. But in the spring of 1941 Hitler sent German troops south to pacify the Balkans in preparation for his invasion of the Soviet Union. Victory was swift: their invasion of Greece began on 5 April; on 30 April they appointed General Tsolákoglou as a quisling prime minister.

Greece was occupied by German and Italian forces until late 1944. While their hold over the countryside was often tenuous, it was firm in the towns, which suffered most from the shortage of food, notably in the terrible winter of 1941–42. It was also from the towns that the Germans deported and exterminated Greece's old and varied Jewish communities. King George and his official government had left the country in 1941 and passed the war under British protection.

Yet in the hills, organised resistance began to emerge. The earliest and most important group was known as the National Liberation Front (EAM in Greek), organised by the Communist Party but commanding a broad base of support. Other groups, drawing on the *kléft* tradition of

---

LEFT: a group of refugees in Thessaloníki after the 1922–23 Asia Minor Disaster.

RIGHT: British troops liberate Athens in 1944.

mountain resistance, also formed, making occasional forays down into the plains, Inter-group clashes were common.

> **THE ANSWER IS NO**
>
> "Ochi" (No) Day, every 28 October, is a public holiday commemorating Mextaxás' famous rebuff to Mussolini's ambassador in 1940.

The dominance of EAM meant that when the British first began to establish contact with resistance groups in 1942, they found that military considerations collided with political ones. EAM, with over 1 million supporters, was well placed to pin down German troops. On the other hand, the British, suspecting that EAM intended to set up a communist state in Greece after the war, armed

other groups to act as a counterweight.

EAM, for its part, was concerned that Churchill wished to restore the monarchy without consulting the Greek people. In fact, Churchill had little sympathy for the guerrillas, whom he described as "miserable banditti".

In autumn 1944, the German forces retreated, to be replaced by British troops. In March 1947 the United States took it upon themselves to reintroduce civilian rule. But resistance forces mistrusted the Allies' intentions and refused to lay down their arms. The Allies, fearing the spectre of a communist rising, tried hard to find moderate politicians to whom they could hand over power. However, these politicians relied heavily on a right-wing militia to keep order. It was in such circumstances that the king returned to Greece in September 1946 after a bitterly disputed plebiscite. Inflation soared, the black market flourished and violence spread rapidly through the country as old wartime scores were settled.

Into the Cold War

Greece, sliding into open civil strife, had a key role to play in the rapidly evolving Cold War. Already dependent on Allied loans, the government adroitly exaggerated the threat posed by the communists in order to win fur-

Greece looks West

Democracy had weathered the civil war – but only just. In the following decade a certain stability seemed to have been achieved, with only two prime ministers – both conservatives – in power between 1952 and 1963. Yet this stability was precarious, relying as it did on a policy of discouraging all opposition to the regime.

Greece had joined NATO in 1951, and the pro-Western orientation of its foreign policy secured financial support from the United States. However, the relationship was not straightforward: when the Cyprus dispute flared

ther American support. In fact, it also had to abandon control of large parts of the countryside to the rebels.

Boosted by American aid, the government managed to defeat the rebel army in the mountains of northwest Greece in October 1949. But victory involved detaining suspected left-wing sympathisers and forcibly evacuating entire villages.

The violation of civil rights and the emergence of a powerful security service did not come to an end in 1950. Again, politics were polarised: the old prewar split between royalists and republicans gave way to one between Left and Right.

up in 1954 Greece refused to take part in NATO manoeuvres. This foreshadowed the problems later governments would have in defining Greece's role in Europe. Nonetheless, the Cyprus issue was resolved – for a time – when the island was created a republic in 1960.

A troublesome "miracle"

In the 1950s and 1960s, Greece, like Italy and Spain, experienced an "economic miracle" which transformed the country. Electric power became widespread and communications improved. Athens mushroomed outwards, a chaotic concrete sprawl, until it contained more than one-third of the country's entire population.

Old forms of political control which had operated best in the small rural communities began to erode. A new urban middle class arose which regarded the conservative political elite as rooted in the rhetoric of the Cold War and lacking a vision of Greece as a modern state.

The 1961 elections saw the resurgence of the political centre under the leadership of a former Liberal, Yeórghios Papandhréou. It was a bitter contest. When the results were announced in Karamanlís's favour,

A COMMON BOND

Greece's links with the West were greatly strengthened by its 1962 entry into the Common Market as an Associate Member.

power, an extended period of centrist rule now seemed possible, and the right-wingers in the military saw the new government as a threat.

When Papandhréou demanded a reshuffle of senior army officers he found his defence minister and the young king, Constantine II, opposed to him. The king tried clumsily to bring down the Centre Union Government, but when Papandhréou agreed with the main conservative opposition to hold elections in May 1967, Constantine was faced with the prospect of a further Centre Union victory.

Papandhréou alleged that they were fraudulent.

Public disquiet at possible links between the ruling party and extreme right-wing violence increased in May 1963 when a left-wing deputy, Yeórghios Lambrákis, was assassinated at a peace rally in Thessaloníki. Shortly afterwards Karamanlís resigned and in the elections that followed Papandhréou's Centre Union Party won power, the first centrist ruling party in Greece for over a decade. However, with conservative politicians prepared to surrender

LEFT: women fought with the Resistance during the Civil War.
ABOVE: Athens has mushroomed since World War II.

However, schemes hatched between the king and senior army officers for military intervention were dramatically pre-empted when a group of junior army officers, working according to a NATO contingency plan, executed a swift *coup d'état* early on the morning of 21 April 1967. Martial law was proclaimed; all political parties were dissolved. The Colonels were in power.

The Rule of the Colonels

The junta was motivated by a mixture of self-interest and hazy nationalism. This combination was certainly not new; on a number of occasions in the interwar period army officers had used the rhetoric of national salvation to head off a possible purge in which they feared they might lose their jobs. In their policies and attitudes, too, the Colonels drew on earlier traditions. They wanted the country to "radiate civilisation in all directions" by establishing a "Greece of the Christian Greeks" which would make it once again "a pole of ideological and spiritual attraction." This was the old dream: an escape from the modern world into a fantastic fusion of classical Athens and Byzantium.

The first signs of widespread discontent coincided with the economic downturn of 1973. The leaders of the protest were students, whose occupations of university buildings in March and November were brutally broken up. Increasingly the regime was proving incapable of dealing with the ordinary problems of general government. In the bloody aftermath of the November student sit-in at Athens Polytechnic, Colonel Papadhópoulos, the regime's figurehead, was replaced by a far more sinister figure, Dhimítrios Ioannídhes, who was previously the commander of the military police.

In the end, it was the Cyprus problem which toppled the junta. A foolhardy Greek nationalist coup, supported from Athens, against the Cypriot president, Archbishop Makários,

led the Turks to land troops in northern Cyprus. Ioannídhes ordered Greek forces to retaliate, but mobilisation had been so chaotic that local commanders refused to obey his orders. On 24 July 1974 the former premier, Karamanlís, made a triumphant return from exile in Paris to Athens to supervise the restoration of parliamentary democracy.

The transition to democracy proceeded remarkably smoothly considering the enormous problems which Karamanlís faced. Aware of his own vulnerability, he moved slowly in dismissing collaborators of the regime. At elections held in November 1974, Karamanlís's New Democracy (*Néa Dhimokratía* or ND)

A TOTALITARIAN APPROACH

With their peasant or lower-middle-class backgrounds, the Colonels symbolised a provincial reaction to the new world of urban consumers brought about by Greece's so-called economic "miracle" of the 1950s and '60s. They constantly stressed the need for a return to traditional morality and religion, and set about this with a fanatical attention to detail. Not only did they close the frontiers to bearded, long-haired or mini-skirted foreigners (or at least they did until the tourist trade was hit), they also prevented Greeks from reading "subversive" literature – Greco-Bulgarian dictionaries included. This grim period of Greek history was marked by torture and deportations.

party won an overwhelming victory, though many people seemed to have voted for Karamanlís simply as a guarantor of stability.

Karamanlís himself was well placed to make any necessary political reforms, since a referendum the month after the elections produced a decisive vote for the abolition of the monarchy, compromised by the king's actions before and during the junta. In its place Karamanlís created a presidency with sweeping powers. It was widely believed that in the event of a swing to the Left, Karamanlís would resign his parliamentary seat and become president.

A move to the Left

Signs of such a swing were evident after the 1977 elections in which Andhréas Papandhréou's Panhellenic Socialist Movement (PASOK) made large gains. The younger Papandhréou, Yeórghios's son, represented a new, postwar generation – at home with the "miracle" and its fruits. With his background as a professor of economics in the US, he was well placed to lead a party of technocrats. At this time he still had a reputation as a radical and he vehemently attacked Karamanlís's policies, taking a more belligerent stand over relations with Turkey, and threatening that a PASOK government would take Greece out of both NATO and the EEC, subject to a referendum. Support for PASOK grew, until in 1980 Karamanlís resigned as prime minister and was voted in as president by parliament.

After PASOK's victory in the October 1981 elections, based on a simple campaign slogan of *Allaghí* ("Change"), Papandhréou took office, forming Greece's first socialist government. His significance lies not in his socialism, which existed in name only, but in his remarkable success in articulating populist leftist views.

PASOK rhetoric carried the party until the elections of 1989, when accumulated financial and domestic scandals returned the New Democracy party to power. This proved to be only a short interruption, for PASOK won the next elections, in October 1993, returning Andhreas Papandhréou to power until illness forced him to leave office two years later. PASOK chose an uncharismatic pragamatist, Kóstas Simítis, as prime minister

whose task has been to oblige a population long accustomed to government largesse to accept economic reality. Particularly after Andhreas Papandhréou's death in June 1996, the government followed a tight economic policy to keep inflation down to allow Greece to meet the conditions for joining the European monetary union (EMU). This has not been easy, for many PASOK parliamentarians, not to mention labour unions, are unhappy with the apparent abandonment of their avowed socialist ideals, and the New Democracy party in its turn is not united.

In foreign affairs, Greece seems to have accepted that the country formed out of the for-

mer Yugoslav province of Macedonia will include the name Macedonia. Relations with Turkey, long beset by nationalist elements on both sides, have broken into a new dimension with warming relations initiated when both countries sent teams to help the other's earthquake victims in the summer and autumn of 1999.

Back on the domestic front, the 2000 election was the closest fought for many years, with Simítis just pulling ahead of Kóstas Karamanlís's ND, with 43.8 percent to 42.8 percent of the vote. The election was marked by a series of promises which the new government may well find hard to keep if it still wishes to keep the economy on track for EMU in 2001. ❑

LEFT: anti-dictatorship posters.
RIGHT: tourism has made a significant impact. Here, visitors soak up the sun on Crete's Váï beach.

A
JOURNEY
INTO
GREECE,
BY
George Wheler Esq;
In Company of
Dʳ SPON of LYONS.

𝕴𝖓 𝕾𝖎𝖝 𝕭𝖔𝖔𝖐𝖘.

CONTAINING

I. A Voyage from *Venice* to *Conſtantinople*.
II. An Account of *Conſtantinople* and the Adjacent Places.
III. A Voyage through the *Leſſer Aſia*.
IV. A Voyage from *Zant* through ſeveral Parts of *Greece*
    to *Athens*.
V. An Account of *Athens*.
VI. Several Journeys from *Athens*, into *Attica*, *Corinth*,
    Bœotia, &c.

With variety of Sculptures.

LONDON,
Printed for *William Cademan*, *Robert Kettlewell*, and *Awnſham Churchill*,
at the *Popes Head* in the *New-Exchange*, the *Hand* and *Scepter* in
Fleetſtreet, and the *Black Swan* near *Amen-Corner*.
MDCLXXXII.

THE EARLY TRAVELLERS

The first foreign visitors viewed Greece as supremely important,
both for their national culture and their own enlightenment

The ancient Greeks had a strong sense of identity. From the Homeric age until at least the disintegration of Alexander's empire, Greeks were conscious of themselves as a people distinct from all others. These others they called barbarians. "Barbarous" first meant only that: non-Greek. The word was probably imitative of unintelligible foreign speech. For it was in their common language and culture that the Greeks – however various and widely distributed – knew themselves to be Greek.

According to myth, the goddess Athena chose the land of Greece for her favourite people because of its ideal location between the frozen north and the torrid south. Later civilisations, particularly northern ones, have endorsed that myth. The Greeks, it was thought, were Nature's favourites.

Brilliant glimpses

We have learned a few epithets from Homer, and discovered that they were exact and telling: windy Troy, sandy Pýlos, Mycenae rich in gold. And in Pindar, Sophocles and Euripides there are brilliant glimpses of places within and around the limits of the Greek world: of Mount Tmolus and the golden Pactolus in the east, of Aetna in the west (where the Titans were confined), and of Kolonos, Thebes, Cithaeron and Delphi at the centre.

There were some extraordinary travellers among the heroes of Greek myth and legend: Odysseus, who took 10 years getting home from Troy; Herakles, whose labours took him north into the land of the Hyperboreans and west to the Garden of the Hesperides; Jason, who sailed to Colchis after the fleece.

The Greeks had a strongly mythical and religious sense of the places in their world; and this sense, or something like it in intensity, survived them and has inspired or coloured the

vision of travellers in their country ever since. It should excite the traveller to know that places of terrific mythical resonance really exist. They are not in a nebulous otherwhere but actually within it, substantial and real. Helicon (Hélikon), Parnassus (Parnassós), Olympus (Ólymbos) are real mountains and can be climbed – which

affects the imagination very curiously: it is exciting but also almost seems an offence. The Acheron still flows by the hilltop Nekromanteion of Persephone and Hades, just east of Párga. Párga was a fishing village and is now a holiday resort. It is not large, but there are many travel agencies, all offering the same thing: boat-trips to the entrance to Hades.

The ancients sited many of their myths very precisely indeed. Citizens of Athens, Corinth or Thebes constantly saw with their own eyes places their divinities and heroes had operated in. Travel was difficult, but people *did* travel; they went about their ordinary business in a country illuminated by myth. The everyday and

---

PRECEDING PAGES: St John the Theologian, Pátmos.
LEFT: title page of Wheler's pioneering travel book.
RIGHT: Odysseus, the archetypal traveller.

the mythical seem to coexist very easily in Greece. Judging from the leaden tablets unearthed at Dodona, they were often very ordinary men and women who made their way to the sanctuary and oracle there. The questions they put to Zeus through his priests who, as Homer says, slept "on the ground with unwashed feet," were often very mundane ones: "Will it be all right to buy the small lake by the sanctuary of Demeter?" "Is it good and possible to sail for Syracuse at a later date?" "Shall I be successful in my craft if I migrate?" The answers were given in the rustling of the leaves of the sacred oak.

The mythical and religious sense of place coexisted, from quite early on, with a concern for topographical accuracy. When travellers and critics called Homer a "truthful" poet, "a painter after Nature", they meant not just his depiction of human passions but also his eye (blind though it was) for the landscapes and topography of the real world.

Travellers were on equally firm ground when they took the historian Herodotus, the geographer Strabo and the tourist-cum-topographer Pausanias as their guides. The latter two are often referred to at great length in the early modern travel literature of Greece. Indeed, until

HOMER AS HISTORIAN

It was the 18th-century scholars and travellers who first made the important discovery that Homer had sited his epic stories precisely. When Lady Mary Wortley Montagu, wife of the English ambassador to Turkey, sailed through the Dardanelles it gave her great pleasure (or so she wrote to Pope) to check Homer's descriptions for herself and to find them exact. Others used the poet's works for their archaeological researches – most famously the German Heinrich Schliemann, who, inspired by the *Iliad* and *Odyssey*, uncovered numerous ancient sites at Troy, Mycenae and Tiryns in the 1870s and '80s. He was the most fanatical, credulous and fortunate of a long line.

the modern tradition itself became established, travellers in Greece seeking to locate places famous in antiquity *only* had ancient testimony to go on. Not only particular monuments – the Temple of Olympian Zeus in Athens, for example, or of Artemis at Ephesus – but even entire sanctuaries and cities of the very greatest importance (Delphi, Miletus, Sparta) had vanished if not from the face of the earth at least out of all local ken, and could only be located and identified by following ancient directions (converting *stádia* into miles, while allowing for changes in the landscape) and searching hopefully for telling inscriptions.

The ancients themselves, then, were the best

guides available to travellers when Greece began to be explored in modern times (Homer was thought to be accurate; Herodotus was good for honouring the myths and enhancing the glamour of places). The texts worked in a dual way: they located the sites and aroused what Dr Johnson called "local emotion". The knowledge the travellers gained was thus both factual and imaginative.

The rise of nostalgia

Serious exploration of Greece did not get under way until the late 17th century. Medieval Christian Europeans, though they took a great deal of

entirely figuratively: Jerusalem at the centre; the River of Death all around the circumference. If you look on that map for information about the classical lands, Greece itself has no general designation, unless the word ICAYA (Achaea) is meant as one.

Famous ranges and rivers are hopelessly misplaced, and there are some notable confusions: Athos appears as Atlas; Delphi as Dílos. Thássos and Pátmos have drifted north into the Black Sea. The Peloponnese is drawn as a rounded lump and labelled: INSULA. The Chersonese peninsula in Thrace has the shape which clever etymologists deduced for it from the

their learning from Plato and Aristotle, had no wish to visit Greece – unless as Crusaders or robber-knights to carve out feudal domains. Nor did these confidently Christian cultures have any impulse to map Greece (or, indeed, any remote country) accurately. During this period, geography was more figurative and symbolic than empirical.

The *Mappa Mundi* (of about 1290) in England's Hereford Cathedral illustrates this very well. The world is disposed there almost

name of its chief city, Cardia: a heart-shape.

Two-and-a-half centuries later, even among the learned, the degree of knowledge was scarcely higher. Martin Crusius, for example, a German scholar writing in the 1550s, asked a correspondent in Greece whether it was true that Athens no longer existed. The trade-routes passed the city and Piraeus by; ships rounding the Peloponnese crossed to Smyrna through the islands. On the first modern maps Athens occurred as *Stines* – which is what the Franks heard when the Greeks said *stin Athéna* (in Athens) – and by that misnomer all connection with the ancient city was effectively severed.

In Holland and Germany in the 16th and 17th

LEFT: the ruins at Delphi.
ABOVE: woodcut of Greece made in 1545; serious exploration did not begin until the late 17th century.

centuries scholars did write geographies of Greece, but bookish ones, entirely on the basis of classical texts. The author of one of them, Christoph Cellarius, was renowned for having taken only one short walk throughout the 14 years of his professorship in Halle. Such works prove the reverence that Renaissance learning had for Greece, and at the same time an almost medieval indifference to empirical knowledge.

Yet from the Renaissance onwards, nostalgia for Greece began to increase as the value of ancient Greek civilisation rose. Early modern travellers came to Greece from countries – England, France, Italy – whose cultures were

The shift that now took place is exemplified by the botanist Joseph Pitton de Tournefort who set off in 1700 to see for himself whether what the ancient geographers and botanists had written was true or false. It needed a cultural incentive to send travellers to Greece, and the Renaissance supplied that. But it also needed a shift in the way the world was apprehended, a radical shift towards belief in the value of empirical enquiry.

A lull in the wars between the Turks and Venetians, after the victory at Candia (Iráklio) in 1669, made trade and travel easier. Travel for pleasure or scientific purposes was greatly

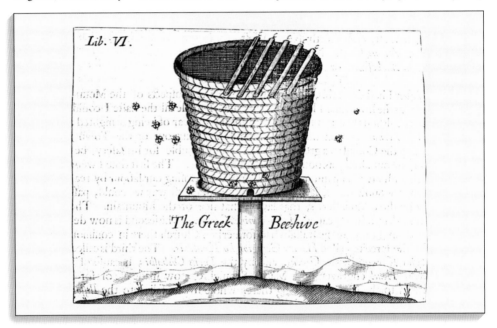

Lib. VI.

The Greek Beehive

deeply indebted to the classical world, and naturally, in varying degrees, they brought that influence with them and it affected their responses. It is worth noting that nostalgia for Greece, though not to the same degree, already existed in Roman and Alexandrian times. Both those ages were, in some respects, backward-looking to a civilisation which they thought superior to their own. European travellers of the 17th and 18th centuries found in Roman and Alexandrian sentiment towards ancient Greece a precedent and an authority for what they felt themselves. They would quote Cicero's lament for the decline of Athens at the appropriate moment in their own accounts.

facilitated when trade routes and commercial contacts were secure.

Opening up

Initially, much information about Greece and much assistance in the exploration of Greece was supplied not by tourists, but by people who happened to be there on other business. Such figures occur *passim* in the first published accounts, and travel writers were much indebted to them.

They were, for example, Capuchin priests who, as residents of Athens, accommodated the first European travellers in their own religious house, showed them around the still visible monuments and supplied them surreptitiously with maps. Merchants and consuls could be equally useful, Consul Giraud, for example, who served first French and then British interests in Athens for some 30 years, offered hospitality to travellers and showed them around the sights. He also engaged in scholarly researches, of which the French explorer, Jacques Spon, made grateful use.

Another powerful figure at this time was the French Ambassador in Constantinople, the extravagant Marquis de Nointel. He considered it part of his diplomatic duty to travel through Greece, his domain, with a large entourage and much ostentation, collecting and recording curiosities and antiquities as he went. A Flemish painter in his party did drawings of the Parthenon frieze which, though crude, are of great value still, since they were done before the bombardment of 1687 in which much was damaged. When Spon and his companion, Sir George Wheler, arrived in Greece in 1675 they were entertained by Nointel, who gave them protection as well as practical information.

Recording the visits

Spon and Wheler's explorations in Greece and their separate publications (Wheler's *A Journey into Greece* appeared in 1682) constituted the first coherent survey of the land in modern Europe. Spon especially wrote as a scholar and a Hellenist; Wheler followed him as well as he could. When he entered the church in 1685 he gave his souvenirs, the bits and pieces of marble he had brought back with him, to Oxford's new Ashmolean Museum, which already housed the Arundel collection. Spon, for his part, had copied thousands of inscriptions. The travellers recorded numerous instances of Greek neglect and Turkish maltreatment of ancient works – an architrave used in a cowshed here, a sculpted head used for target-practice there – and felt wholly justified in removing whatever they could.

These first journeys to Greece were, in some cases, extensions of the Grand Tour beyond Italy. Spon, who perhaps always intended to go, made up a party with Wheler and two other English gentlemen when they met in Rome.

Wheler had been travelling through France with his Oxford tutor to complete his education. He had money; Spon had a scholarship and enthusiasm. They were an interesting combination at the outset of the tradition. Both professed Protestantism (Spon went into exile for it after his return), but Wheler, although he was the younger of the two, was much more hidebound and hectoring.

Quite simply, he preferred Restoration England to Greece, even to Periclean Athens, as the imagination of a Hellenist might reconstruct it. He was not a very open-minded man. We may recognise his type even today: the per-

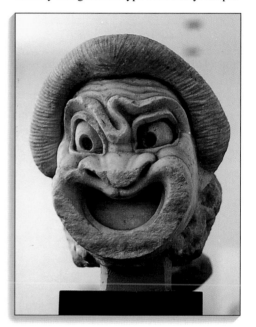

LEFT: 18th-century travellers took extensive notes, even detailing the local bee husbandry.
RIGHT: ancient gargoyle.

SOUVENIR RAIDERS

From the start, journeys to Greece were undertaken with the intention of bringing things back – information; copies of inscriptions; but also anything readily movable. The justification was simple: the Greeks were perceived by Western scholars and explorers as degenerate, and the Ottomans – their masters from the late 15th century onwards – as barbarians who would deface as a matter of religious duty whatever statuary they found. Thus it was the perceived duty of "civilised" travellers to "rescue" as many precious relics as possible. In modern times, debate on the real ownership of these sorts of treasures has been revived but, in many cases, not resolved.

son who travels to confirm his or her prejudices, and who is profoundly relieved to get home again unchanged.

Spon was the better traveller. True, he was disposed to feel in a certain way; but he was alive and awake on the spot to the places themselves. He was consequential in his passion for Greece. His travels, despite Wheler's assistance, impoverished him. When he went into exile he was penniless. Eventually, he died in a pauper's hospital.

That first enterprise was a private one, largely undertaken on Wheler's funds. Tournefort in 1700 and the Abbé Fourmont in 1728 were sent and financed by the French Crown. For serious exploration some such backing became increasingly necessary, and in France and England there were public bodies and a few wealthy private individuals who were willing to provide it. National pride was a factor, but also a sense of social and cultural responsibility, and of *noblesse oblige*. Tournefort, botanist to Louis XIV, was a man of the broadest learning and an excellent traveller, good humoured and resilient. He took in classical sites en route – not incidentally, but as part of a whole interest.

His book *Voyage du Levant* (1717) is the best of the early accounts. He gives the ancient and

Lib. III. Fig. IX.
Ruines att y end of y Gulfe of Samos a mile from y fea
caled by the Turkes
Iotan

present state of places, what they produce and pay in taxes, how they are administered, how the people live, where the best harbours are. He exerts himself, climbs a high hill to have a good vantage-point, enquires diligently of the priest and village elders who might be able to inform him. Later accounts constantly refer to Tournefort as an authority and as an important point of orientation.

The "Hellenic ideal"

By the 18th century travel literature had become an important and popular genre. Within it, accounts of Greece had a wide circulation, often went through several editions, and were very quickly translated. Furthermore, booksellers, knowing the market, engaged hack writers to plagiarise and excerpt from the best available accounts and to compose compendium volumes out of them. *The Travels of the late Charles Thompson Esq.*, for example, was put together in this way (in 1744), and was very well received.

When the London Society of Dilettanti sent its expedition to Greece in 1764 it was with a very specific, particularly Hellenist intention. Cultural demands had altered,

A LEAN TIME

The pioneering 18th-century traveller Tournefort's luck ran out on the island of Tínos, where "We were reduced to make pottage with Sea-Snails … a sorry fare."

doing so. In 1764, directed by Robert Wood, they sent a party to Greece and Asia Minor specifically to locate the ancient remains.

Chandler's account of the tour (in two volumes, 1775 and 1776), may be set alongside Tournefort's as the century's best. Its appeal is, however, rather different, just as the journey it describes was different. Chandler knew what he had to look for, and what it was his duty to report. Though his tone is throughout reasonable, unenthusiastic, and his prose style deliberately

and the society, founded in 1731 chiefly for convivial purposes, was by the middle of the century beginning seriously to respond to them. In 1751 it had taken up two energetic individuals, the architects James Stuart and Nicholas Revett, who had made their own way to Athens and were measuring and drawing the monuments there. The society financed the gradual publication of their work – as the *Antiquities of Athens* – and conclusively promoted the Greek style of architecture and furnishings by

LEFT: classical site – or pile of rubble?
ABOVE: engraving of a Turk and a Greek from Tournefort's *Voyage du Levant*, 1717.

plain, he was nevertheless writing in the service of a love and admiration of ancient Greece so assured in himself and in the society he represented as to need no special pleading.

With Chandler's expedition the archaeological exploration of Greece was put on a professional footing. He consolidated the tradition to date, and his publications, together with others under the auspices of the society, established a firm scholarly basis for serious-minded successors in the next century to build on.

Misconceptions

Notwithstanding the growth of this fine tradition, neither the Turks nor the Greeks had any understanding of what the travellers were about. If the travellers' interests were archaeological, they met with great incomprehension and mistrust. One energetic Turk, seeing a party inspecting the drums of a column, set to pulverising the marble with cannon balls in the belief that gold, at least, must be inside. Stuart and Revett, when they needed to erect ladders and scaffolding, met with objections from Turkish pashas who feared that the Westerners would be able to spy into their harems.

It was also frequently the case that places the travellers wished to explore were of military importance to the Turks. The Acropolis of

Athens was a Turkish citadel, the Parthenon was a store for powder and ammunition. It suffered accordingly when Morosini bombarded it. Drawing and measuring, which a traveller would naturally want to do, were extremely suspicious activities in Turkish eyes. Francis Vernon, examining the Theatre of Dionysos under the Acropolis, was fired on, and escaped only through the intervention of Consul Giraud. The Capuchin maps were drawn surreptitiously, which partly explains their inaccuracy, and circulated likewise.

In time the travellers produced their own maps. We know that Chandler in the Troad in 1764 had with him a map, done by a Frenchman, which Wood had with him in 1726. Their reliance on one another, and on the ancient authors, was very great. But how many books could they actually carry with them? Wood tells us that he and his companions took "a library, consisting chiefly of all the Greek historians and poets, some books of antiquities, and the best voyage writers." But they were perhaps unusually well-provided for, since James Dawkins, one of their party, was a very wealthy man. Spon and Wheler received the newly-published *Athènes ancienne et nouvelle* (by Guillet de Saint-Georges) just as they were sailing from Venice. They were able then to check its descriptions on the spot, and found them, in Vernon's phrase "wide from Truth".

A party would hire guides and interpreters and enquire locally, once they had established the area of their interest, whether any ruins were still apparent in it. The same employees would procure them food, and accommodation (often of a very wretched, flea-ridden kind). In many districts the travellers needed more than guides: they needed armed guards. Bocher, travelling alone, was murdered. James Stuart was two or three times set upon and robbed. The roads at the back of Smyrna were infested with bandits, and travellers there did well to join with caravans of merchants who had Janissaries riding with them.

These difficulties should be borne in mind when we evaluate the travellers' achievements. Chandler's party were deterred from climbing Parnassus by the menacing behaviour of some Albanian soldiery camped near them at the spring; they also kept well clear of Rhamnous because the local Turks there apparently "bore a very bad character".

HONOUR AMONG THIEVES

In early days, travelling in Greece was not for the faint-hearted. Yet the bands of thieves and brigands one risked encountering on the road often observed rigid codes. When one 19th-century aristocrat was ransomed by his friends, his captors turned out to be hospitality itself.

"Baron Stackelberg was then shaved by one of the gang, a ceremony which they never omit on these occasions, and handed back to his friends. They were all pressed to stay and partake of a roasted lamb and an entertainment about to be prepared … the robbers then wished them a good journey and expressed their hope of capturing them again at some future time …"

Other hardships

We should mention the sea's dangers, too. Spon and Wheler, crossing from Constantinople, were tossed to and fro for 37 days. Vernon was taken by pirates and stripped of all he possessed (he escaped with his life only to lose it a few months later in Persia, in a quarrel over a penknife). And had Chandler sailed home in the *Seahorse* as he intended, he and his party would very likely all have been drowned off Sicily when that ship went down.

Sir Giles Eastcourt, the fourth member of Spon's party, died on the road to Delphi near Náfpaktos. Wood's friend James Bouverie died at Magnesia on the Maeander. Plague was endemic still in many areas. It had a high season in the summer months. The Turks, with their fatalistic view of things, allowed it to carry them off in great numbers. The Franks were more circumspect and withdrew into isolation if they could. Chandler and his companions spent three months holed up in a village above Smyrna, the town itself being much too dangerous to enter.

A certain piety entered the tradition. Earlier fates were remembered and commemorated. Tournefort got the whole story of Vernon's death from the English Consul in Isfahan, and recounted it. Chandler searched for and found where Eastcourt and Vernon had scratched their names on the south wall of the Theseion (the names are still there and can still be read).

The journeys were often dangerous and – what with mosquitoes, heat, dirt and wolfish dogs – must almost always have been uncomfortable. Though some of the travellers were born adventurers, for others it was just an interlude, perhaps the only escapade of their lives, and they returned to Oxford common rooms and quiet country living with a few mementos and a fund of stories. They had many high moments to remember.

The "travel experience"

Discovery was the essence of early travel in Greece. For those travellers seeking to identify, after a lapse of nearly 2,000 years, a particular site famous in antiquity, the satisfaction when they were successful must have been very great

indeed. They weren't excavators; they didn't dig their way through to treasures like the Mask of Agamemnon or Helen's Gold: but, knowing their texts, they brought to such places as Marathon, Mystrás or Delphi considerable reverence and a willingness to be moved.

They were in a landscape such as they had not seen before. It was not only the botanists among them who were excited by the flowers and shrubs, by their vivid colours and rich scents. Again and again they saw scenes that painters in the 18th and 19th centuries loved to depict: ruins among olive trees, broken columns on a headland against the sun, animals grazing

in fields littered with marble. And their interest was not always antiquarian. Guys says rather pointedly of Spon that looking for ancient Greece he found only stones; Guys himself then, as a corrective, looked to the people and their present lives. True, he saw them through a veil of Homer and Theocritus, but perhaps our perceptions are always coloured. The first Western painters in Greece saw the landscape through a haze of Claude Lorraine. Our view may be harsher now and more historical, but the 18th-century images are still appealing. Indeed, at times, and in certain places, they are quite compelling.

Enormous changes – some, unfortunately,

LEFT: 19th-century drawing of a Kássos maiden.
RIGHT: detail of Skýriot embroidery, probably from the 17th century.

deeply damaging – have occurred as a result of travel in Greece. Large areas are going to perdition as rapidly as money will permit. Perhaps we will look even more to the past, in horror at what is being done in the present. Out of that past things have been brought to light – out of the earth, out of the sea, the like of which the early travellers never saw, though perhaps the poets of their day imagined them (the great bronzes in the National Museum, for example, the gold of Mycenae, the palaces on Crete).

Some sites have undergone marvellous resurrections. On Delos, at Delphi, Olympia and in Athens there is now infinitely more to be seen.

Chandler discovered Olympia, Spon and Wheler Delphi, but having identified those sites they saw very little. When we see the richness of Delos nowadays we can scarcely believe that by the early 18th century it was thought nothing there merited a visit.

We have more knowledge nowadays, the museums are richer, the sites more extensive. On the other hand, it may not be so easy in present-day Greece to get a sense of what early travel was like. Out of season, and out of the way, is best: at Dion, for example, under Olympus, or at Górtyn in the centre of Crete (where the road runs through what was the ancient

A GREAT BUT TROUBLESOME LEGACY

Thanks to the ancients "where'er we tread" in Greece is, as Byron put it, "haunted, holy ground". Shelley prefaced his poem *Hellas* (1821) with the dramatic proclamation: "We are all Greeks. Our laws, our literature, our religion, our arts have their roots in Greece. But for Greece… we might still have been savages and idolators."

Small wonder the modern Greeks have not had an easy time of it, being expected by Western Hellenists to live up to their glorious past. However, if travellers are prepared to leave their nostalgia and their rose-tinted spectacles at home, they will discover that the country has much more to offer than the ancient legacy.

Quite apart from the country's rich and diverse modern culture, the landscape and environment have their own delights. Indeed, Greece's special brand of seductiveness starts with something elemental – the earth and air itself. In *Europe without Baedeker* (1986), Edmund Wilson puts it like this: "Here is a paler, purer, soberer country [compared to Italy], which seems both wild and old and quite distinct from anything further west… there is a special apparent lightness of substance and absence of strong colour which characterizes Greece and sets it off from other countries. As you descend into the hot airport, you have a general grateful impression of simplification and gentle austerity."

city). And of course, when you least expect it, there are places where a few yards of old walling, or the remains of old irrigation channels, or ledges and niches in a goatherd's cave, will suddenly bring the whole experience upon you with a rush.

Crossing the boundaries

In Turkey, in old Ionia, there are some potent reminders. Ephesus, for example, ends in a marsh. There you may see fallen pillars, broken architraves and beautiful carvings sinking among the bulrushes. The Temple of Artemis, one of the Seven Wonders of the ancient world,

Ephesus for the castle walls, and even in the poorest houses, in some wretched slum, you may suddenly spot the glimmer of fractured marble. Your *pension* in Selçuk might well have a Corinthian capital as a seat in the shade by the door. The Roman aqueduct still steps through the town, and anyone so inclined can copy the inscriptions embedded topsy-turvy in its pillars. Such details are the stuff which fed the nostalgic imagination of the early travellers – and still feeds modern visitors today.

It is impossible not to feel empathy for those first explorers. Their interest was predominantly Hellenist. In what other spirit would they

lies (what little is left of it) on swampy wasteland, on a patch that serves as village green, football pitch, grazing ground and rubbish tip. The precinct falls away into a pond that looks malarial, and there blocks and drums of the temple, swarming with terrapins, emerge and sink according to the season. Selçuk was built out of the ruins of Ephesus. Dressed stones, portions of columns and many ornamented blocks bearing inscriptions were quarried from both the public buildings and the temples of

ABOVE: Edward Lear – in his lifetime as famous for his watercolours as his nonsense verse – painted this view of Thessaloníki.

have gone? True, others were in the country for quite different purposes – commercial, diplomatic, military – but they are not the ones who wrote accounts. The documentation of early travel in Greece is very much coloured by the travellers' perception of that land as supremely important, both for their own and for their national culture.

It is doubtful that any modern traveller can ever be quite rid of that sense. There is something compelling about the old images still. Myths are as necessary as they ever were, and some myths are more productive than others. We all know what the worst ones are: in Greece, still, we can glimpse some of the best.   ❑

THE GREEK WAY OF LIFE

The 20th century may not have had much impact in Greece until the 1960s,

but now traditional customs and attitudes are changing fast

Imagine that you are a guest in a Greek family house on a Sunday afternoon. You have just finished an immense and leisurely dinner and though your head floats with a pleasantly sleepy *retsína* high, the weight in your stomach keeps you earthbound. Buoyant dinner repartee subsides as appetites are sated, and someone lazily flicks on the television. A low clarinet wails plaintively, and as the picture focuses, you perceive a dozen human forms clasping hands and gravely circling a green hilltop: women shapeless in weighty layers of embroidered frocks with wide bronze belts and men in white skirts and tights and pom-poms on their shoes. "Epirots," your hostess remarks off-handedly. "How do you drink your coffee?"

Our Greek Folk Songs is broadcast every Sunday afternoon on one of the state-run television stations. With the traditional Sunday afternoon dancing now mostly a picturesque memory, the broadcast makes a peculiarly appropriate substitute, but the "Epirotness" which these symbols evoke is oddly tamed. In the 1990s, regional consciousness began to verge on a sentimental *folklorismós*. It often seemed a parlour game of regional trivia shorn of its divisive power: knowing that Kálymnians wrap *dolmádhes* in cabbage – not vine – leaves, that potatoes in the "village salad" signal a Cycladic chef, that the novelist Kazantzákis hailed from Crete and the popular singer Kazantzídhis, beloved of immigrants and workers, comes from Asia Minor.

But regionalism was in earlier days hardly a matter of songs and salads. Of neighbouring Italy in the early days of its nationhood, D'Azeglio remarked ruefully that "now that Italy had been created, it was necessary to invent the Italians." And was Greece so very different? The travel writer Patrick Leigh Fermor once described the Greek world as "an inexhaustible Pandora's box of eccentricities",

and doubtless an extreme topography has nurtured great variety in a relatively small land. Vlách-speaking shepherds in the Pindos mountains had little contact and little enough in common with the shipbuilders of Híos or the Jewish merchants of Ioánnina. Though not all communities were equally isolated by terrain they

tended to be introverted socially. *Xénos*, the "foreigner-stranger-guest", is in Greece an elastic designation, and brides marrying in from the next village forever remained "strangers" in their husbands' villages.

It was not just the land which came between them: but differences in language, culture, religion and class. At the same time, that Koutsovlách shepherd was typically polyglot, speaking his own Romance language with his kin, Greek with the cheese-merchants, a smattering of Albanian and Slavic with the villagers he encountered out with the sheep, and enough Turkish to outwit the odd Ottoman official. Under the tolerant Ottomans, a plethora of

---

PRECEDING PAGES: summer evening; Easter parade.
LEFT: young soldier on duty, Athens.
RIGHT: dolls in national costume are sold in kiosks.

religious and ethnic communities thrived: Greek-speaking Orthodox, Slavic-speaking Orthodox, Romaniot and Sephardic Jews, Turkish farmers, gypsies, Franco-Levantine Catholics in the Cyclades, Protestants converted by American missionaries in the Levant, Orthodox and Muslim Albanian shepherds, Dönme, Máamin, Sephardic Jews who converted to Islam in the late 17th century and more. From this multiplicity, the inhabitants of a newly invented, formally secular nation-state of Greece were charged with inventing *themselves* anew.

The cultural homogeneity which undeniably exists in Greece today is as much a goal and a

Even so, the monolithic vision of the official state, with its images of Pericles and Kolokotrónis, has always been quietly subverted from below. "The people" refuse to imagine themselves a lumpish mass, and remain stubbornly sure of essential differences amongst them. Stereotypes of ethnic groups coexist alongside other stereotypes of regions and topographies.

In a society fascinated with "appearances" the stereotype of a place becomes part of its reality, and to see the mountains, the plains and the islands as the Greeks do one must set out on a journey across their cultural terrain.

consequence as a precondition of this new nationalism. With one eye on the past and the other on the West, official policies of the Greek state have long worked to eradicate – or, at the very least, to trivialise – local variations in language, dialect and custom. Differences which seemed to threaten the integrity of the state – like the speaking of Slavic – have been systematically suppressed. More insidious, the traditional refusal of both the state and private investors to develop the provinces economically has inflamed a ruinous pattern of poverty, massive emigration to Athens and abroad, and a frequent sense of cultural inferiority in those who have remained behind in the backwaters.

In the mountains

"The picturesque is found any time the ground is uneven." If there is any truth to the wicked verdict of the French critic Roland Barthes, Greece is a paradise of the picturesque. From the scrubby hills of central Greece to the soaring peaks and wide wooded vales of the majestic Pindos mountains, the land seems in continuous undulation, and even from the plains – a relative term, so little do they recall the great flats of Nebraska or Hungary – the mountains seldom disappear from view. Romantics who seek the truth in the land often claim that the irregularity of its surfaces has most forcefully shaped "the Greek character".

The settlement of Greeks in mountainous areas has not been stable or continuous and, for many groups, is "traditional" only if we don't look back too far. Of course, some settlements are of a Byzantine or Frankish vintage. And certain tribal groups of transhumant shepherds – Sarakatsanáoi, Karagoúnides, Koutsovláchoi, Arvanítovlachoi – who herd their sheep and goats on mountainsides in summer and move them to the plains in winter, have probably always wandered widely across the Balkan territories. Of these, all except the Sarakatsanáoi built permanent villages where they and their livestock spent the winter. However, other sed-

Pirates did not venture very far inland, though, and in the first 100 years of Ottoman rule, when peasants enjoyed a level of justice and prosperity far above that of their counterparts in feudal serfdom throughout Europe, inaccessible mountain tops held fewer attractions. But as the centralised system – and the safeguards it had ensured – began to break down, Christian and Muslim peasants became increasingly vulnerable to exploitation from all sides: from their Turkish landlord anxious for profits from maize and wheat sold to the west, from local bands of brigands who periodically helped themselves to the peasants'

entary mountain villages found their *raison d'être* in conditions of Ottoman life.

In island and coastal regions, many towns were (and many still are) situated not at the port side but high on the crest of the mountain, even – indeed, preferably – hidden from view altogether. This town plan was a response to the threat of pirates. In the late 16th century when the Ottoman state began its long decline, the time-honoured random piracy of the Aegean became systematic.

LEFT: the traditional cuisine – here, grilled fish and Greek salad – is both simple and delicious.
ABOVE: Cretan shepherd.

A SONG OF THE MOUNTAINS

Throughout the centuries, the Greeks have used their landscape – rugged mountains, rolling plains – as a metaphor to describe the different natures of the people living there, a device this old Cretan folk song (composed by hill-dwellers, one presumes) cunningly exploits:

> *"Fie on the young men down on the plains*
> *Who taste the good things in life,*
> *The choicest foods,*
> *And are base to look at, like creeping lizards.*
> *Joy to the young men up in the hills*
> *Who eat the snow and the dew-fresh air*
> *And are fine to look at, like the orange-tree."*

crops and livestock, to unruly Janissaries – the sultan's professional army, recruited from local communities – extorting tributes for their "protection". By the 17th century, vast stretches of countryside began emptying as peasants fled to the cities and upwards to the mountains.

Mountain settlements multiplied, interspersed among already established villages whose inhabitants made a living (sometimes a handsome living) not only by farming and shepherding, but as itinerant stone-masons and charcoal-burners, as wandering merchants and muleteers and mountain guides to Turks and

The "traditional" village

Every Easter, Athens spits out its millions towards numberless villages, only to swallow them up again two weeks later, laden with baskets of olive oil, cheese, homemade bread. Every Athenian, every Thessalonikan speaks reverently of "his or her" village, usually, of course, a mountain village. The mountain village is never merely real but partakes of the archetype, the village poor in all but rocks. Ah, but so beautiful…

The mountain village typically comprises a cluster of houses, often with adjoining walls, circling a central church and a square. This

travellers, and as artisans and immigrant labourers to richer regions of the empire. Still required to pay the annual tax to the sultan, newly settled peasants terraced the rocky mountain sides, wresting a meagre living from their flocks and gardens, and from small fruit orchards.

Still vulnerable to extortion by brigand and Ottoman official alike, the community drew inward, socially and physically. And so developed the particular ethic and organisation of village life which has come to be regarded – not only by foreigners, but by Greeks, as well – as something which is quintessentially Greek.

physical arrangement reveals a moral geography, for the boundary between the "civilised" human space and an unsanctified wilderness teeming with human and supernatural dangers is marked by a ring of tiny churches and shrines. United by Orthodoxy and a common way of life, villagers were nonetheless divided into separate households. The family, not the individual, was – and still is – the central unit of Greek society, enormously interdependent economically, socially and emotionally, and whatever the harmony or tumult within its four walls, to the outside the "house" stood, and stands, united. The unconditional loyalty to the family and the demand that each member must help further its collective interests made friendships outside the house inevitably fragile. Tenuously bound by ties of religion and patriotism, these families competed for scarce resources: land, water, pasturage, and for that most ephemeral and valued substance, honour.

Anthropologists who have studied small villages have conventionally identified "honour" and "shame" as key moral values in Greece. According to this code, a family could rarely be considered honourable if its women were seen to be immodest. Since Orthodox teachings

AN ISOLATED LIFE

More than 32 percent of the Greek population still lives in communities of fewer than 2,000 people.

nity to the next, and depends on whether one is rich or poor, male or female.

Today, to be *filótimos*, to "love honour", can mean something as vague as acting as a "good" person should, though this presupposes no small knowledge of what the community considers good. It differs from the Protestant idea of "conscience" in one crucial way: one must be *seen* to act honourably, for it is a judgement which only others – almost begrudgingly – bestow. In such conditions, reputation becomes an all-important attribute.

and native thought both agreed that woman was by nature sensual and seductive, social chaos was avoided by strictly segregating unrelated men and women, and defining various tasks as "male" or "female". This was relaxed only during feast days and weddings.

Today, of course, the image of meek womenfolk in household purdah and domineering but protective men is both outdated and overly simplistic. Moreover, what acting "honourably" actually means varies from one Greek community to the next, and depends on whether one is

LEFT: stringing tomatoes at Pyrghí on Híos. The women work …
ABOVE: … while the men play backgammon.

The myth of the mountain man

The mythology of the mountains is emphatically masculine. Greeks are inclined to see in the mountain man an embodiment of alpine virtue. In his "craggy" face they discern a "harsh" pride, a "rugged" individualism, a moral "purity" as pristine as the mountain springs. For the ferocious clans of the Máni and Crete which always kept the Turks at bay, and the Souliot women who danced into the abyss rather than submit to the finally victorious Turks, they reserve their highest praise. In the figure of the *kléft* they celebrate a more pugnacious heroism. Scholars protest that the *kléft* ("thief") was, in fact, seldom more than a self-serving outlaw, preying on landlord and peasant alike, building a local empire in the time-honoured Balkan style, coercing the weak and awarding the spoils to his own minions. But in the national mythology, the *kléfts* became symbols of resistance to the "hated Turkish oppressor". If the myth glorifies a selfless *kléftic* patriotism, the Greeks do not fail to relish the cunning which turned patriotism to personal advantage.

On the slopes of Crete's Mount Ida shepherds steal each other's sheep to prove their honour and daring, and insist that their way of life upholds a Greek ideal degraded by morally slack, soft-palmed Athenian bureaucrats. And in the 1940s, during the German occupation, resistance fighters lived like *kléftic* heroes, in wandering bands, and attacked from the mountains. The great rebel leaders, the *kapetáni*, absorbed that heroic aura and held control of a newly democratised, mountainous "Free Greece" long after the Germans were ousted.

To many, the *kapetáni* resuscitated a dream of a Greece liberated from foreign domination – not by Turks this time, but by Germans and British and Americans. The image still lives on, and the dream won't quite die.

There is, however, an underside to the myth

A WAY OF LIFE ON THE WANE

Modern life in the rural villages of Greece is still a hard one. Since the 1960s, an enduring paucity of opportunity in such communities has spurred a mass exodus to the main cities; as a result, many settlements are hardly more than "old people's homes" these days, with too few children to support a school.

Locals lament the fact that the only weddings are those of the children of urban migrants returning for a "traditional" celebration in their parents' beloved village, and where the gypsy musicians may well complain that celebrations have become "cold". At the funerals – far outnumbering weddings – old women mourn not only their dead kin but the empty houses of these isolated places which have been – as they put it – "forgotten by God".

Mountain settlements – and particularly those scattered on the lower slopes – at least have the option of combining small-scale shepherding and livestock-raising with the growing of high-quality tobacco and cereals, and of cultivating orchards: peaches, apples, pears, cherries, walnuts and chestnuts all thrive in the cooler climate.

If a village is particularly beautiful and not too hard to find, then it might be fortunate enough to attract tourists, and then sweaters, weavings and souvenir hand-carved shepherds' crooks may bring in much-needed income.

of mountain man. The word *vláhos* – both the ethnic label of many of Greece's transhumant shepherds, and the simple occupational term for "shepherd" – holds a hint of scorn. It is the Greek equivalent of the term "hill-billy" and draws on the same imagery. Moreover, *vláhos* sounds almost like *vlákas*, "idiot", and though Greek ears keenly distinguish *chi* from *káppa*, the phonic resemblance is gleefully savoured. Vlachs – the lot of them – are the butt of countless jokes, which portray them as brawny but dull and silent.

This underside reveals less about ethnic slurs than about a vaguely guilty disdain for a whole way of life. As people have gradually abandoned the mountains for Athens and Chicago and Vancouver, they have learned to reject that life, even to see that once "heroic" shepherd as uncouth, unlettered, even slightly ridiculous.

On the plains

The plains – the *kámbi*, as Greeks call them – hold no hallowed place in the national mythology. Marshy and malarial, muggy in summer and muddy in winter, they have seldom inspired the poets, who find few metaphors in their flatness. So, absent among the rocks and mountains and sea and sun of tourist board posters, we are almost surprised that plains exist here. Redeemed at times by the curiosities of human architecture (the abundance of windmills on Crete's Lassíthi Plain) or by the surprise of mountains (Mount Parnassós rising from the Boeotian plains) the *kámbi* arouse our respectful interest, not our passions.

Yet the plains – flat, rolling, and if we stretch the term, sloping patches of plateau – have been among the most coveted of spaces in Greece. The major way of making a living here has always been farming. Despite the richness of much of this land, most farmers have remained poor, especially in relation to their European counterparts. This is less a consequence of peasant fatalism, familism* and superstition, than of a complex combination of factors, including historical patterns of land ownership, Greek state policies, patterns of economic interdependence between Greece and the West, and various commercial priorities and practices

over which the farmer, unfortunately, has had absolutely no control.

A chronic problem of Greek agriculture has always been too many farmers for the land to support. Small plots and inefficient farming methods made life on the land quite marginal, yet few alternatives outside of emigration to America existed until the early 20th century.

Historical conditions have also quite literally shaped agricultural lands. Large farmsteads are rare; rather, farmers have traditionally clustered their houses in a village and walked out daily (and today, ride out on donkeys or tractors) to scattered fields. Inheritance practices,

though varying somewhat among localities, have generally ensured that a father's fields, and those his wife had brought as part of her dowry, would be divided equally among all his children, with daughters given their portion – or its equivalent in livestock, a house, or cash – as a dowry at marriage. Since fields varied in fertility, protection from wind and access to water, it has not been uncommon for even small parcels to be subdivided, and then re-subdivided, with each generation.

The system is not as mad as we might think. It is surprising to learn, accustomed as we are to thinking that only massive fields and monocropping make sense, that a handful of tiny

---

LEFT: today's youth, torn between tradition and modernity.
RIGHT: tradition on parade.

plots, growing varied produce, may provide the farmer with real stability in areas where rain is unpredictable and soil fertility marginal. "A little bit of everything" can be better than a big crop that fails.

Yet the land's progressive fragmentation has sometimes reached ludicrous proportions. Tales abound of single trees – an olive or walnut tree, say – in which 15 households of second and third cousins own shares. Such a tree often goes unharvested: trying to gather all 15 representatives (some of whom have moved to Athens,

THE GODDESS OF CORN

In ancient times, farmers used to worship Demeter, Zeus's sister, who is the goddess of corn, the harvest and agriculture.

were – and are – vulnerable to all manner of disaster: drought and pestilence, crop failures, sudden, radical fluctuations in the price of agricultural produce internationally and locally, and the whims of changing governments. Indebtedness – to the grocer, as to the state-controlled Agricultural Bank (established in 1929) which they approach for loans – has been the rule. Farmers, once dependent on the wealthy estate-owning landlords, have become dependent on the state.

Indeed, one of the basic themes in farming

others to Australia) to harvest together is a logistical nightmare.

The large agricultural estate – whether an Ottoman legacy or a more recent conglomeration – can be found, too. From Náfplio's citrus groves to Naoússa's peach orchards and Thessaly's fields of cotton, estate owners search for extra hands at harvest time. Along with impoverished tourists and local day-labourers, it is the gypsies (and, increasingly, Albanian immigrants) who figure importantly in this migrant labour force. Though wages are often low, this type of seasonal work – following the harvest – is a way of preserving independence.

Like peasants everywhere, Greek farmers

life is the confrontation between the farmer and the state bureaucracy. Traditionally, the only place more crowded than the land was the civil service. When the state apparatus was being developed after 1830, politicians and lawyers with "pull" handed out endless minor clerkships to constituents fleeing rural poverty. (By 1880, Greece had seven times as many civil servants per 10,000 as Britain.)

Thus was created a bloated bureaucracy of barely literate peasants, mostly from the then-politically dominant Peloponnese. Even today, if you talk to plains farmers from the north (and since most such farmland is in Thessaly, Thrace and Macedonia their attitudes reveal a double antagonism: north versus south, farmer versus functionary), they are scornful of southerners who – until recently – seemed to occupy with all the self-importance they could muster the bulk of the clean and comfortable civil posts: as doctors, teachers, lawyers, policemen. Northerners are fond of saying that the poor but powerful southerners are parasitical on the north's wealth. "The civil service is a big cow," they explain, "and we Macedonians, we are the grass she eats and eats. When she is finished, the politicians milk her dry, and then she is so happy, she drops a great load of dung on us!"

To farmers, the impersonal bureaucracy was

Understandably daunted by this state of affairs, farmers turned to those they considered to have the clout (*méson*) to intervene at higher levels and push through their modest requests. The local politician, the ambitious lawyer, the doctor with connections, all helped the less powerful, obliging them to return the favour (their votes or their custom) afterwards. Born of such conditions, patronage became endemic.

Providing individualistic solutions to systemic problems (and also carefully obstructing the requests of the "uncooperative"), patronage thwarted collective action among farmers, at the same time as it ensured that they remained

just as arbitrary as any Ottoman official and infinitely less responsive. Its hierarchical character has meant that petty clerks refused to process even the most routine applications without the immediate superior's approval; while he, in turn, checked with *his* superior, and as requests climbed, so did the piles of paper. Moreover, unless the farmer had some moral claim on him – as a relative, godparent or co-villager – the bored civil servant would offer him only the most perfunctory assistance.

LEFT: a delighted farmer during the harvest season.
ABOVE: farm-workers stop for a break and a welcome mid-morning snack.

politically and socially docile. Yet resentment to the system grew as well, and it was in no small part PASOK's pledge to make war on *rousféti*, "string-pulling", that landed its election victory in 1981.

The changing face of the plains

On a drive through the towns and farming villages of the plains, one is struck by the amount of new house construction and farm machinery. Postwar economic aid helped rebuild the countryside. But the noticeable bourgeoisification of the wealthier farming villages has also depended on the surplus of farmers emigrating to Germany and Australia in the 1950s and 1960s, or to the oil rigs of Saudi Arabia in the 1970s. The village prospered from the money sent back to their families; at the same time, relatives and neighbours could rent or sharecrop the fields left behind.

It is one of modernisation's contradictions that mechanised farming has frequently marginalised women, whose farming skills and labour are rendered obsolete. While women have not left the land completely, many find themselves imprisoned in a domesticity their mothers never knew. They remember the drudgery of farming in the pre-tractor era with little fondness, yet the often heard remark that

income and most social security benefits. Other women work in shops or small enterprises.

It is partly in response to the village's limited work opportunities that parents want an urban bridegroom for their daughter, and a professional job for their son. In towns, women with no special skills may find jobs in light industry cutting or stitching in garment workshops, or stuffing sliced pears into cans. In a gesture which promotes – not just anticipates – this move, the "dowry" flat is now likely to be bought or built in Athens or Thessaloníki, or in one of the larger plains towns, like Sérres, Kateríni, Trípolis.

such a housewife "just sits" reminds them of their economic dependency on their husbands. It also betokens a loss of status and power, for men are sceptical when "the little housewives" (nikokyroúles) start talking feminisimós. "It's men who are oppressed," they protest. "We work so you can eat."

High inflation and rising material aspirations mean that most families want the woman to bring in wages, but opportunities in farming villages are limited. A woman might earn a little extra by contracting with large garment companies to do piecework at her own sewing machine, a practice which alleviates the problem of finding childcare but denies her a secure

Some farming villages look more affluent, and some farmers are no doubt wealthier than before. Yet farming life is still perceived as dirty, exhausting and unpredictable, and the horizons of village life limited by few jobs and a dearth of entertainment and cultural life. The farmers' children tend to marry out, and the migratory current still flows towards the cities.

It remains to be seen whether decentralisation schemes – bringing small hospitals, daycare centres, adult education and greater administrative autonomy to the countryside – combined with the increasingly unlivable conditions of overcrowded, polluted Athens, can turn the stream.

On the islands

When the foreigners began to descend on the islands, first in dribbles and then in droves, it was perhaps their worship of the sea which first amazed the island inhabitants. But tourists, who appear in the summertime, are to the sea only fair-weather friends, lured by its tranquil visage, azure and benign. They lie dreamily on the sands, courting the sun for a colour eschewed not so many years ago by the island aristocrats as the mark of a common labourer, in a state of public undress unimaginable to the sartorially puritanical natives.

> **A LAND OF ISLANDS**
>
> Greece has over 1,400 islands, some 160 of which are currently served by a variety of passenger ferries, catamarans and hydrofoils.

If the tourist regards the island as a temporary escape and the sea as soothing and benevolent, the perspective of those who live, and who have lived for generations, on the islands, is rather different. In the early days of tourism, islanders seldom knew how to swim, and children who ventured too far into the waters were regularly snatched by shrieking mothers who had no reason to romanticise the sea. To them, the sea was no less treacherous for its beauty. "There are three things to fear in the world," goes an old proverb, "fire, woman, and the sea." Death by the sea is both a memory and an expectation to those who live, winter as in summer, at its edge. They know the winter squalls, the convulsions of rain and wind that erupt without warning and toss fishing caïques (*kaíkia*) like so many toy boats in a bathtub. The sea gives life with its fish and its sponges, but also takes it back.

Geologically, the 1,425 isles in Greek territorial waters are born of the meeting of sea and mountain, for the isles are merely the crests of now submerged mountain ranges. About one-tenth of these are inhabited, some by only a few monks and goats. It is tempting to stretch the comparison, for the individuality of each island in its architecture, costume and dialect is striking, and would seem to suggest an isolation reminiscent of the high mountain villages. Yet this individuality is not a simple matter of remoteness. On the contrary, there has always been frequent, intense contact among clusters of islands, and within each island group – the central Cyclades, the eastern Dodecanese, the northerly Sporades and the Ionian islands of the western coast – songs are traded, wives are sometimes sought, house styles remain familiar. Rather, embedded in the houses and faces and words of each island is its own particular history of labour and of foreign domination.

The pre-modern economy of sea-piracy and plunder, ship-building, sponge-diving and trade made the islands until this century among the richest and most coveted territories in the Mediterranean world. The Ottomans held a much more tenu-

ous and intermittent grip on the islands than on the mainland. European principalities, from the Hospitaler Knights of St John to the Venetians, the Genoese, the French and the British, sought through political control and trading privileges to exploit the strategic position and trade of particular islands.

Although the object of the European principalities was to extract wealth which passed as merchandise through the islands, some wealth stayed on the islands, concentrated in the hands of an indigenous elite. This local elite owned land or ships and shipyards on islands spread from Hydra (Ídhra) to Híos, and often co-operated with the Europeans on mutually prof-

LEFT: a staple diet on the islands: octopus being cleaned...
RIGHT: ...and neatly hung out to dry.

itable terms. At the beginning of the 20th century, many islands had a clear class hierarchy.

On islands blessed with good soil and adequate water resources, some inhabitants lived then, as today, as farmers, and farmed very much as their compatriots did on the mainland. Grapes, melons, figs, tomatoes, oranges and lemons thrive in the arid summer heat, and beans and onions can be coaxed to grow as well. On luxuriant Corfu (Kérkyra), tenant farmers laboured on the estates of local aristocrats, while in the pre-independence Cyclades, the rocky hills were shared between the islanders and a powerful monastery.

out their money and moved – to Athens, to Tarpon Springs, Florida, to Argentina. On the skeleton of this affluence a new prosperity is being built. For it is the stark and lovely grandeur of these abandoned houses and harbours which tourist agencies translate as "picturesque" and which draws the concrete-weary foreigners.

The myth of the island woman

In the mythology of the land, the mountain man finds his apogee in the island woman. Mainland Greeks contrast their own heroic traditions of the "masculine" mountains with the "femi-

In many ways, the distinctiveness of each island is a legacy which is not always easily understood. The island economies of the present, for all except those blessed with fertile land and plenty of water, depend largely on the remittances of island migrants (and their pensions when they return home to retire) and on the development of tourism. The elegant mansions which rise along the hill encircling the Sými harbour bear mute witness to the incredible wealth of the sea traders and shipbuilders, and the renowned sponge-divers, but they are empty now, mausoleums, mute testimonies to a way of life which collapsed when upstaged by a steamship economy. The wealthy pulled

AN ABSORBING STORY

From pre-classical times right up until the 1930s, Sými and Kálymnos were the centre of a thriving sponge-fishing trade in the Dodecanese. Local sponge-divers pushed themselves relentlessly in quest of wages and prestige, daily risking death in the form of "the bends" in the deep waters. Fewer men dive for sponges now, however; for one thing, World War II destroyed much local sea trade, scattering many of the islands' inhabitants, and the industry never really recovered. For another, almost all the Aegean's sponge-beds were devastated by disease. Sadly, most of the sponges sold in local souvenir shops these days come from Florida.

ninity" of the islanders. Island dances are soft and undulating, like the sea, and very quick, they insist, while theirs are upright, rigid and proud, like warriors dancing on mountain peaks. (They forget the low, quick, sweeping *zonarádhiko* of the Thracian hills.)

The music, too, is "sweet." In this, they have given a sexual nuance to what is probably more accurately the difference between a smooth urban sound and a raucous, village style. Never mind that the ubiquitous synthesiser has infiltrated the *nisiótika* of popular cassettes – it hasn't destroyed the lightness of that most popular and familiar genre of island music, a

Island songs, with an almost courtly and Venetian chivalry, celebrate love, courtship, beauty: from the Cretan verse-romance *Erotókritos* whose verses still tunefully resound throughout the Aegean, to the improvised teasing couplets, the *pismatiká*, of the Cyclades and Dodecanese islands.

The "femininity" which mainlanders attribute to the islands is no doubt intertwined with their suspicion that women actually run things there. And indeed, the seasonal exodus of men as they followed the ships, the fish, the sponges or the factory job in Mannheim or Melbourne, has given many an island a strikingly female

music developed in a network of wealthy Aegean port cities, including the vibrant Greek-dominated Asia Minor cities of Smyrna and Constantinople. This style uses an ensemble of stringed instruments: a dolorous, hauntingly human-voiced violin; a *santoúri* – hammer dulcimer of the Middle East – whose resonating strings create a waterfall of sound; and the long-necked and deep-throated voice of the Turkish *ud* (in Greek, the *úti*), or its smaller substitute, the strummed *laúto*. (The reedy island bagpipe, the *tsambúna*, goes unmentioned.)

character. If tourism has enabled many men to return, the "feminine" quality is still perceptible in the way women dominate neighbourhood spaces. "A man is a visitor in his own house," Greeks say, and islanders with even more reason, as men are shooed out of the house every morning so women can get on with their chores. Mainlanders slyly insinuate that island women not only dominate their men, but cuckold them. After all, they speculate, how do they manage while their husbands are away for months and years at sea? Tales of bored housewives and exhausted island-bound lovers proliferate even on the islands, although their veracity remains, of course, quite unverifiable.

LEFT: transporting fish between the islands.
ABOVE: evidence of an angry sea, Ionian islands.

Yet on some islands, the family of an unmarried girl guards her reputation against slander ("Better your eye come out than your name," the proverb warns) with a vehemence rarely found now on the mainland. On Kálymnos, co-education in secondary schools was long resisted; it is only a few years since teenagers first began to attend classes together, and some parents are sceptical that the camaraderie of these mixed student *parées* (*see page 96*) can really be innocent.

Consequently, an explicit moral and religious

WINTER ISLAND-HOPPING

If you plan to travel between November and March, remember ferry services drop to a minimum, and schedules are often unreliable.

used to move in with their mothers-in-law, here the mother still gives her house to her oldest daughter when she marries, moving herself (and her husband) to smaller quarters: a tiny flat in the basement, a shed on the edge of the property, a rented room nearby. Second and third daughters, who once could expect little in the way of dowry, now almost always get a house as well.

Today, now married, that island daughter probably shares a room or two of this house with strangers. Like innumerable island houses,

conservatism accommodates a tradition of feisty women with most peculiar results: the same community which, pleading local "custom", petitions the bishop to negotiate a Kálymnian exemption from Greek law, giving them permission to marry daughters off at 14 before they lose their hallowed chastity, amiably tolerates the 25-year extra-marital liaison of a lusty yet commendably fastidious housewife.

This last word translates badly. *Nikokyrá* (house-mistress), though an entirely ordinary title, holds no slur, and all the more so in the Aegean, for on many of these islands the houses belong to women. If mainland brides

hers features a scrawled sign: "ROOMS. CHAMBRES. RAUME" and, summer after summer, countless blonde and sleek foreigners skip down her stairs on the way to the beach and struggle back up after a bout in the disco. They may pass in the hallway, but in many ways their worlds remain separate. She sells postcards in the family tourist shop, while her husband works in the construction crew of a new hotel development. She watches an American soap on TV as she crochets another doily for her daughter's trousseau. She worries about her son becoming a *kamáki* and about her daughter passing her university examinations. "Tourism is good. It brings money," she hears everyone say – and she says it, too, but sometimes she wonders.

In the city

Viewed from the heights of Pendhéli, which flanks the city to the east, Athens resembles – as the novelist John Fowles put it – a mass of dice scattered across the Attica plain. Block after block of more or less identical six-storey cement "multiple dwellings" (as they are known in Greek) do not make it the most beautiful urban centre in Europe. Moreover, the rapidity with which the city was thrown up effectively postponed questions of urban planning, zoning, and

Beneath the dominant cement of Athens lies a palpably human heart. Nowhere better than here does the ancient formulation "Man is the measure of all things" ring true. More than just a heart, Athens has soul and some districts, such as Athinás Street around the meat market or Pláka on a hot night, are downright funky.

What makes Athens attractive are its temperamental inhabitants. Clicking their worry-beads, making funny gestures with their hands, by turns provocatively rude or unexpectedly friendly, arguing and laughing… it is enlivening to walk among these people. Athenians do not hesitate to show their feel-

the siting of local parks to a later date. With over 4 million people living in the greater Athens area (over a third of the population), Athens is today a concrete matter of fact.

Planners and politicians are making the city more attractive by protecting those few houses still standing which possess any architectural merit and by converting some side-streets into pedestrian walkways. A good many political points are nonetheless scored for trying to make Athens, a more livable city, notably the recently opened Athens metro, a blessing.

LEFT: street musicians celebrate newly-weds.
ABOVE: a tourist portrait-painter confers immortality.

ings and it often seems that emotional states constitute a more powerful communicative device than words.

After a few days, visitors who expected to remain casual observers find themselves expressing long-forgotten feelings, exercising new facial muscles and vocal chords, unexpectedly at ease and unselfconscious. Aristotle described these as the effects of watching good drama and labelled them "catharsis". In modern Athens catharsis is always on offer, only there is no strict demarcation between audience and actors and the drama never ends.

It should be kept in mind that Athens, as a sprawling urban metropolis, is a very recent, and unforeseen development. The city was suddenly transformed – increased by one quarter practically overnight – in 1923 with the influx of Greek refugees from Asia Minor. These newcomers were exceedingly poor, in many cases arriving from Turkey with just the clothes on their backs. At first they were settled in makeshift barracks around the city in areas such as Néa Ionía or Néa Smyrni, names which recall their land of origin. Thus the trend of urban expansion was founded, and other characteristics such as inner-city poverty, the dark underworld of petty criminals (*mánges*), which found its expression in the sounds and

smog also mixes with atmospheric humidity to form an abrasive acid which has been dissolving stone monuments that have stood for millennia in the city. In recent years a restricted area has been drawn around the city centre in order to alleviate the problems of traffic and smog. On alternate days private cars with even and odd licence plate numbers are allowed to circulate within this exclusion zone. This is a great boon to taxi drivers but inevitably there aren't enough cabs to cope with the rush-hour demands. Be prepared to accept a jitney-like arrangement where other people may share stretches of the journey with you.

texts of *rembétika*, came to form part of the capital's image.

Athens has mushroomed in the past 60 years, a period which saw the city's population soar from 453,000 to more than 4 million. That's an 883 percent increase over a stretch of time when the population of the country as a whole rose only by 93 percent. Clearly, there has also been a significant movement from the countryside into the city. All roads lead to Athens.

The sheer density of people makes for monumental traffic jams twice a day and four times when there is late shopping. Cars are a prime cause of smog (the so-called *néfos*) which chokes the city during windless periods. This

SAGANAKI

Look out for this tasty traditional snack in Athenian *ouzerí*. Usually, one large slice of cheese is fried in a *saganaki* dish and then served individually at table.

    4 finger-thick slices of hard cheese (**Kasseri**
      or **Kashkaval** is best)
    2 tablespoons olive oil
    4 eggs
    Salt and pepper for seasoning.

Fry the cheese in hot oil in a heavy frying pan, large enough to hold the 4 slices. When the cheese begins to bubble, break an egg over each slice and cook until the white has set. Serve immediately.

Urban attraction

While the disadvantages of the metropolis are all too apparent to the casual observer, the benefits which Athenians enjoy are less obvious. There are more doctors, medical specialists, and hospital beds here than in any other region of Greece. Educational opportunities are also superior. There are more schools, teachers and university places per capita in Athens than elsewhere. And when the studying is finished, there are jobs. Furthermore, Athenians are often more highly paid than workers in other parts of the country.

Greece as a whole may be underdeveloped industrially, but 50 percent of the nation's industries (employing 10 or more people) are located in or around the capital; everything from chocolate factories and breweries to the massive dockyards and refineries sited along the coast at such locations as Pérama, Skaramangá and Elefsína. The drive from Athens to Corinth is virtually a tour through Greece's industrial heartland.

Those who hold a high-school diploma are eligible for a number of prestigious civil service positions which mean anything from working for the electricity company to serving as a government adviser. Such positions are desirable because salaries are inflation-indexed and hiked every year; best of all, they are secure for life and include a pension scheme. The permanence and security are highly prized in a society which is emerging from a primarily agrarian mode of existence (up until 1960 more than 50 percent of the population were living on the land).

The joys of office life

Whereas in former times it was hoped that a son would work his father's fields and flocks, such a proposition is now scoffed at by young men in villages. Supreme admiration is no longer accorded the rugged, autarchic shepherd able to provide his family with goats' milk, cheese, meat and other basic needs. The image of the educated civil servant or professional has usurped earlier ideals, office workers do not dirty their hands or sully their clothes.

Education is thus consummately valued as it facilitates upward social mobility. In this striving for knowledge and in the fascination for

LEFT: ice-cream and *loukoumádhes* – hot puffs of batter soaked in honeyed syrup – on sale in Athens.
RIGHT: Athenian cafés play an important social role.

foreign goods and ideas – for which the Greeks have a word, *xenomanía* (*see page 123*) – one may discern many symptoms of the so-called "developing country" syndrome. People are engaged in the effort to secure white-collar employment which they associate with an image of modernity and sophistication. Yet Greece has neither the industrial base nor the GNP to support such aspirations at present. In relation to the GNP there are twice as many students pursuing higher education in Greece as in the United States. Given that most businesses originate in family enterprises, no real demand has arisen for managers at the executive level. Thus

many of those who complete courses of higher education end up in positions which under utilise their talents.

Some go to work as teachers in the private tutorial schools (*frontistíria*) which one sees all around Athens. These institutions help students to cram for the state university entrance exams. Many talented students go abroad to study and, aware of how limited their opportunities for research or employment would be back in Greece, they remain abroad. Who can blame them when, by some estimates, there are more lawyers in Athens than in all of France?

In the view of villagers, the move from the country to Athens is one which is likely to secure employment, relative financial prosperity, and prestige, though in which order it is not exactly clear. In any case it is not easy to move back to the village except for holidays or retirement because this would mean re-adapting to village life, which pales after a stretch of time in the city. Athens is the centre of Greek political, commercial and cultural life. More than 17 major newspapers are printed every day in the capital, accounting for 90 percent of national circulation. Most Greek television also emanates from Athens, a fact apparent in the advertisement of products designed for the city dweller or in the promotions for Athenian stores, not to mention

for the first time. This is also the place where most Europeans will form a first impression of Greek culture.

It is said that, approached from the east, Athens is the first European city, and approached from the west, it is the first Asian city. This, albeit simplistic, interpretation of the city's place in the Mediterranean may be put to use in making sense of the cityscape as well as the people living, working and interacting within it.

On the Western pole, ideologically speaking, is Sýndagma Square bounded by the offices of international airlines, deluxe hotels and the

the weather reports, which concentrate on the capital. Living in this city, one feels oneself to be connected to the navel of the Hellenic world. It is very difficult to cut the cord.

East meets West

Athens is the primary point of entry into Greece. Around 2 million tourists, over half of all those arriving by air in Greece, land at Athens' Hellenikon Airport each year (to be replaced at some point by the ongoing project at Spata). In this respect Athens is the main interface between Greece and the rest of the world.

Here, villagers from outlying rural areas will probably encounter international culture

House of Parliament. Sýndagma bears a smart Western look; Gucci, St Laurent and Chanel vie for custom in this zone where English is the *lingua franca*. Rural Greeks may well feel awed when they stray into this area, or feel slightly uncomfortable, for there is nothing here to which they may readily relate. Indeed, it hardly seems Greek at all.

Less than a mile away is the opposite pole, Omónia Square. Here one may savour a Greek coffee in some of the largest coffee houses (*kafeneía*) in the country. (Two worth trying are the "Alexander the Great" or the "Neon".) Women are served but one cannot help noticing that they form a distinct minority.

Omónia is filled with hawkers who peddle anything from wristwatches to rice pudding. At night, men appear wheeling large copper samovars with a warm drink called *salépi*, a delicious and creamy concoction made from finely ground orchid roots which is said to be the perfect antidote for an oncoming cold. Here, it is the tourist's turn to feel foreign.

Omónia and Sýndagma are representative of two extremes of Athenian (one could even say Greek) identity. These two styles, the traditional

A CURIOUS VIEW

What colour is the Acropolis? The novelist Evelyn Waugh thought it most resembled "the milder parts of a Stilton cheese into which port has been poured."

The more "progressive" Greek, the Hellene, would probably take a course so as to pass through Sýndagma and then proceed down Stadíou Street past the numerous cinemas showing subtitled foreign films, department stores and neat shopping arcades.

At one point there is the National Historical Museum with a statue of Kolokotrónis, the hero of the Greek War of Independence, standing before it. For the Hellene, carrying their ideologies of the Enlightenment, Greek traditionalism is a strange sign

and the modern, are to some degree apparent in every individual in what amounts to a cultural bipolarity. As a hypothetical illustration, if a *Romaiós* (that is, a Greek of traditional leanings) needs to go from Plaka to Omónia, he would possibly choose a route past Athens' cathedral, the Mitrópolis, then proceeding through a district of smaller shops selling cloth, household and religious objects; that is, if he had decided against dropping down to Athinás Street, which is itself practically a full-scale bazaar.

LEFT: tourists are fair game in Athens' flea market.
ABOVE: lunch-time in the city.

of backwardness and an embarrassing indication of Asian influences. To them it belongs in museums.

In the different routes which they might choose, the imaginary Hellene and *Romaiós* confirm two very separate experiences of the capital – and life in general. This overlapping of histories and geographies is partially what makes Athens so attractive to the visitor. The city's appropriation by western travellers as the cradle of European civilization, at odds with its geography and recent history, makes it at once familiar and foreign. But, above all, Athens is a vibrant, modern city, and the visitor should revel in that as much as its glorious past. ❑

MIXING PIETY WITH PLEASURE

Greek religious festivals – and there are many – celebrate saints' days and other events in the religious calendar with devotion and high spirits

Greek island life is punctuated throughout the year by saints' days and religious festivals or *panighýria*. As there are around 300 saints in the Orthodox calendar, there is an excuse for a party most days of the year.

Easter is the most important festival (often preceded by a pre-Lenten carnival known as "Clean Monday"). It's a great time to visit, with traditional services marking the Resurrection everywhere from humble chapels to mighty monasteries. Colourful, noisy and potentially dangerous – in Kálymnos they throw dynamite to ensure Christ has truly risen – it's like Firework Night and Christmas rolled into one.

During Holy Week, or *Megáli Evdhomádha*, churches are festooned in black. On Maundy Thursday monks on Pátmos re-enact the washing of Christ's feet at the Last Supper. On Good Friday the *Epitáfios*, or bier of Christ, is decorated by the women and paraded through the streets (*see above*) as they sing hymns.

On Easter Saturday the churches are decked in white. On the stroke of midnight everything is plunged in darkness as the priest lights the first candle from the holy flame to represent the light of the world, and intones: "*Hristós anésti* [Christ has risen]". This the the signal for all the congregation to light their candles. Fireworks explode, rockets soar, dynamite sometimes shatters windows. Families then break the Lenten fast with Easter soup made from the lamb's viscera and then play conkers with red-dyed eggs.

On Easter Sunday there's great rejoicing as a lamb or kid is barbecued outdoors over charcoal with the usual music and dancing. There are often parties on Easter Monday and in some islands an effigy of Judas is filled with fireworks and burned.

▽ **AFTER MIDNIGHT**
In the early hours of Easter Sunday, crowds head home in candlelit processions. Families mark the sign of the cross over their door with their candle to bring good luck.

▷ **SCARLET SHELLS**
Hard-boiled eggs, dyed red to symbolise the blood of Christ, are cracked in a game like conkers on Easter Day.

◁ **EASTER TWISTS**
A sweet, twisted bread called *houlourakia* is made for Easter in various shapes, often with a red egg in the centre.

◁ MONDAY MAYHEM

"Clean Monday" is the end of the pre-Lenten carnival, with exuberant celebrations on some islands, including kite-flying and flour fights.

▽ STEPS TO SALVATION

Devout women crawl in penance to the church of the Panaghía Evangelístria on Tínos at the feast of the Assumption in August.

◁ MOUNTAINTOP MASS

Saints' days are celebrated by *panighýria* (festivals) at hundreds of small chapels throughout the islands. Here Cycladic islanders honour Aghía Marína, the protector of crops, on 17 July.

△ ALL DRESSED UP

In Ólymbos, the remote mountain village on Kárpathos, the eldest daughter or *kanakará* wears her traditional costume and dowry of gold coins for major festivals.

◁ EASTER PARADE

Priest and villagers join in traditional chants in an Easter procession on Páros.

CELEBRATING ALL YEAR ROUND

Greeks mix piety and pleasure with gusto for all their festivals from the most important to the smallest fair. The biggest religious festival after Easter, the Assumption of the Virgin (*Panaghía*) on 15 August, draws Greeks home from all over the world.

Following the long liturgy on the night of the 14th, the icon of the Madonna is paraded and kissed. Then there's a communal feast – and the party can go on for days. The celebrations are spectacular in Kárpathos, with dazzling costumes, special dances and traditional songs.

Every month there are festivals on the islands for everything from sponges to snakes, and national holidays like *Óhi* or "No Day" (28 October), with patriotic parades to mark the Greeks' emphatic reply to Mussolini's surrender ultimatum.

Celebrations begin the night before feast days and everyone in the community takes part from babies to grannies. Patron saints are honoured with services followed by barbecues, music and dance. The picture above shows the feast of Ághios Dimítris on Síkinos in October, which is conveniently when the first wine is ready to drink.

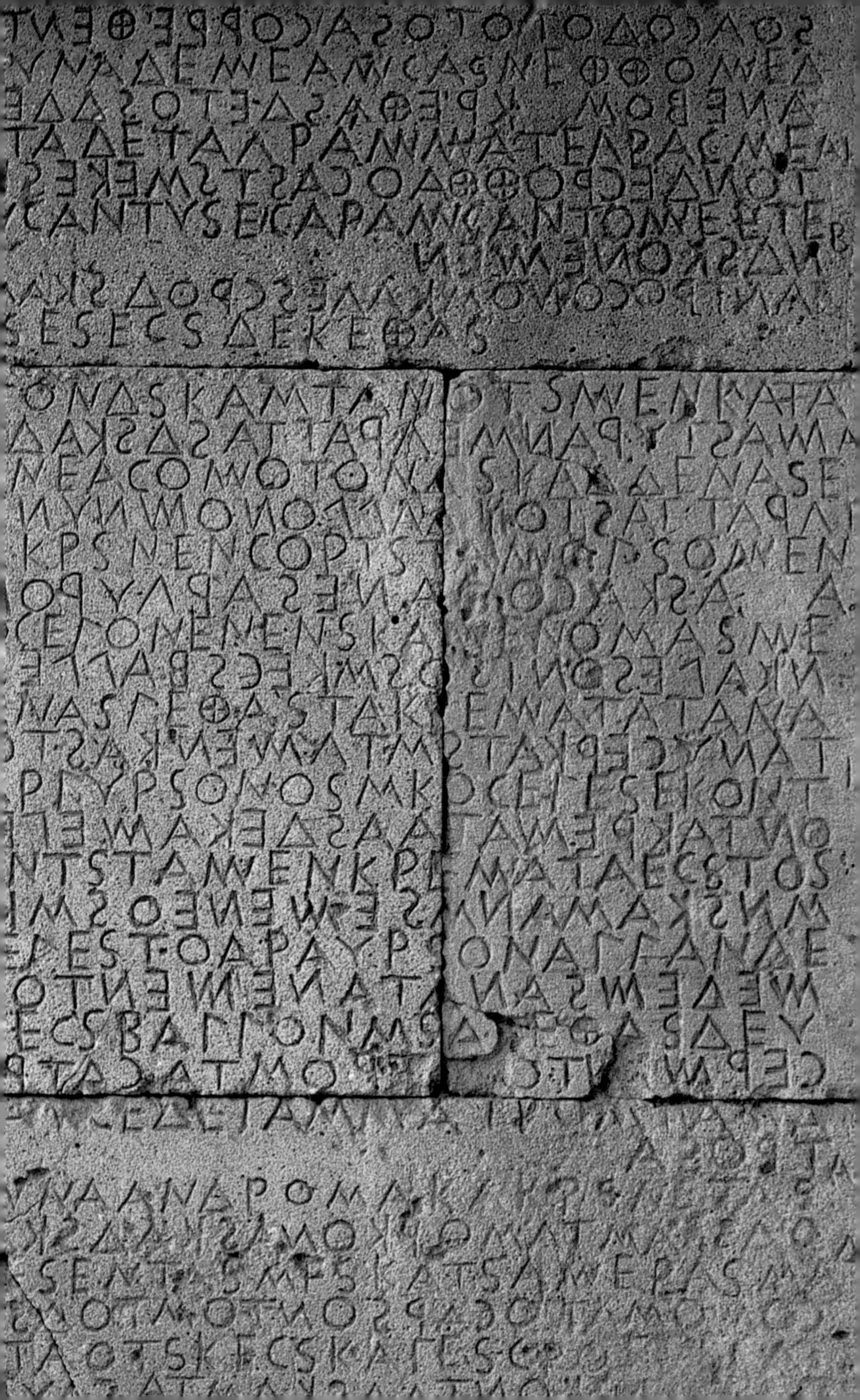

CULTURAL ABCS

An alphabet's worth of indigenous phenomena to guide
visitors through the maze of contemporary Greek culture

Newcomers to Greece are often baffled by the Greek alphabet. Even if they have trouble understanding other European languages they can at least read road signs and figure out which is the Ladies and the Gents. In Greece, however, even international catch words like EXPRESS have a bizarre appearance. Perhaps as much as anything else it is the strange alphabet that makes foreigners throw up their hands and utter the ancient words of despair: "It's all Greek to me!"

The cultural ABCs that follow won't help anyone overcome their fear of this odd-looking alphabet, but it may provide a key to another set of symbols that are equally strange. Greece is full of untranslatable concepts. What follows is an alphabet's worth of these indigenous phenomena. From E for Evil Eye to K for *Kamáki* to Z for Zorba, these entries introduce the newcomer to aspects of contemporary Greek culture which are not immediately obvious. Here readers will find out why no one bothers about birthdays (*see Namedays, page 108*), why kiosks dot every corner (*see Períptera, page 112*), why old women dress in black (*see Women, page 119*), and why Greeks are at odds over tourism (*see Xenomanía, page 123*).

Of course, this kaleidoscope of incongruous items is only one of many possible collections. The various writers who have contributed to this alphabet are not set on fixing Greece's cultural topography: on the contrary, each – whether linguist, anthropologist or journalist – is interested in tapping the shifting assumptions that go into making myths and shaping cultural identity. Sometimes humorous, sometimes serious, these entries map out another Greece, as important as the one already represented by geographical region in the following section. As a dictionary or as a set of social commentaries, use these pages as you please. ❑

LEFT: the law code of Górtyn on Crete must be read one line from left to right, the next line from right to left, and so on, "as a field is ploughed."

ACRONYMS

Even classicists who can bumble their way through scrupulously formal Greek would have a difficult time deciphering the strings of acronyms which seem to crop up so regularly now in modern Greek journalism. Always used for political parties (KKE, PASOK, ND, DIKKI, EPEN), acronyms now also stand in for everything from social services (IKA, EES, ANAT, IKY, DEH) to soccer clubs (PAOK, AEK).

Acronyms are the fast food of modern Greek discourse. Just as Americans have begun to wonder what "McDonald's" really

means, so Greeks are beginning to wonder what the acronyms are all about. Why have public announcements and newspaper articles started to resemble their ancient stone predecessors, with their long lines of unpunctuated capitals?

Acronyms, like junk food, have an uncanny ability to camouflage what they contain. One forgets what an acronym really stands for, until suddenly it acquires an association all its own. The former prime minister Andhréas Papandhréou took advantage of this slippage when he decided to use the same acronym for the Greek police force as the left-wing resistance fighters had used during Greece's civil war. ELAS now

stands for both; the acronym a subtle way of legitimising a moment of left-wing history.

But even though it might take a lifetime to decipher the politics of acronyms, it doesn't take long to learn those that are most frequently used. You would be hard-pressed to phone overseas if you didn't know that the public phones in every Greek town or city were housed in a building called OTE (pronounced "oté"). You might save yourself quite a bit of time if you knew that the Greek tourist organisation is called EOT (pronounced "eót"), and embarrassment if you knew that the great hordes shouting PAOK (pronounced "paök") in the streets of Thessaloníki on Sunday were not political activists but soccer fans.

BYZANTINE MUSIC

An interview with Markos Dragoumis, of the University of Athens' music department

Q: *In most parts of Greece on Sundays and Namedays [see Namedays, page 107] radios are turned on full blast and towns resound with the nasal half-tone and less than half-tone dips of the Athens' Mitrópolis' cantors. Why does this chanting sound "Eastern" to the ears of a Westerner?*

A: Traditional modern Greek music has many oriental features: not only tones and semitones, but other smaller and larger intervals, oriental chromatic scales, a nasal quality in the voice and characteristic motifs decorated with grace-notes – all particularly common in the East.

How did Byzantium give birth to two such different church musics as the Roman Catholic and the Greek Orthodox?

Plenty of scholars doubt whether these two kinds of music were really so different 1,000 years ago. For example, Igor Reznikoff says: "At the end of the 19th century, French Benedictines wanted to revive the Gregorian chant and created melodies based upon notes with identical time-value, often indeed beautiful, but which have no connection with the genuine ancient chant as we know it from manuscript sources on the one hand and from the tradition of model music on the other."

What does Orthodoxy have to say about music? Has it always been an integral part of the Greek church service? Has there ever been any instrumental accompaniment?

Music has been used in the Christian Church since Apostolic times, and is regarded by the Orthodox Church as an integral part of the liturgy, to be preserved by each generation as a holy relic and to be performed contritely, humbly and with due decorum. Ancient ecclesiastical tradition, which is still maintained, holds that musical instruments are alien to the spirit of Orthodox worship, because their sounds are associated with worldly festivity. That is why Orthodox church music remains purely vocal.

pupil still has to overcome a very considerable obstacle before he can be considered a good *psáltis* or cantor. He must learn to chant in the appropriate style, and in this no written music can help him, only his teacher.

If visitors want to hear chanting at its best, where should they go?

There are churches with good cantors and choirs in every Greek city and many large towns. In Athens, visitors should look out for Lykoúrgos Angelópoulos and his choir, who used to perform in Aghía Iríni, prior to that church's long restoration.

The history of Western music seems closely connected with the evolution of church music. How has this music survived? Are cantors trained or are they just expected to pick it up from their elders?

Up to AD 950, religious music of the Byzantines, and of the Greeks in general, was handed down by oral transmission. But once a special system of notation had been worked out, the music could be transmitted with the help of manuscripts and, since 1820, books. But the

LEFT: acronyms abound during election time.
ABOVE: traditional music still finds a wide audience throughout the country.

A CONTROVERSIAL BLEND

An interesting experiment in Greek contemporary music during the 1970s and early 1980s was an attempt to marry Byzantine chants with folk music. The best-known proponent of the style is the arranger and instrument-maker Hristodhoulos Halaris. He first hit the musical headlines in 1976 with his version of the romantic Cretan epic poem, *Erotókritos*, featuring Nikos Xilouris and Tania Tsanaklidhou as vocalists. Subsequently, Halaris has concentrated exclusively on Byzantine chants – including a reworking of I Melodhi tou Pathous, the hymns of Constantinople composer, Petros Peloponnisios, which caused much controversy amongst traditionalists.

Coffee

"Would you like a cup of coffee?" It's the classic come-on from Sýndagma to Sámos, for the homely brew of ground coffee-beans has long been the drink of erotic encounters.

Among Greeks themselves, offering coffee to a stranger is a gesture of hospitality and an excuse for light conversation. A chance invitation for coffee with an acquaintance and his or her *paréa* (circle of intimates) isn't easily refused. And why not? After all, it's the

---

A Change of Name

Known as "Turkish coffee" (*toúrkiko kafés*) until the 1974 war in Cyprus, the Greeks' favourite brew is now called *ellinikó kafés*.

In name, as in quality, it's much closer to the Arab original, *qáhwah*, than the West's watery brew. Ground into a fine powder and boiled with water and varying amounts of sugar, *kafés* is served in tiny cups. You can order it sweet (*glykó*), very sweet (*polý glykó*), medium (*métrio*) and unsweetened (*skéto*) – and if those few teaspoonfuls don't satisfy your caffeine addiction, double (*dipló*). Connoisseurs know that what distinguishes the exquisite cup from the - mediocre is a thick topping of froth (*kaïmáki*).

perfect drink for "exploratory" sociability, for jokes and mild flirtation, and many a romance has begun with shy glances over the coffee cups.

Its place in more mundane social intercourse is just as prevalent. Greek men drink it in the ubiquitous *kafenía*, housewives drink it at home with their neighbours. Working people drink it, too, but you won't find a coffee machine at their workplace. They "order out" from the local *kafenío*, and on city streets, ducking in and out of office buildings, you can often see the white-aproned waiter carrying an ingenious deep-dished tray crowded with coffee cups, the entire dish suspended, lantern-like, from three metal supports.

Even the dregs have their uses. For example, if you leave a trace of liquid so that the dregs can be swished around the cup, you can turn it over and let the wet residue run down the sides of the cup into the saucer. This leaves swirling patterns, and many a Greek woman will be able to decipher the symbols to "predict" your future.

Most men wouldn't be caught dead "saying the cup" and, since the Church frowns on it, many women hesitate to admit to it. But in their houses, women trade cups and interpretations "for a laugh". Curiously enough, wedding rings and tall, dark, handsome men often seem to populate the cup.

DELECTABLES

"And I, hungry once more, gaze at the sweet biscuits." This yearning, expressed more than 2,000 years ago by a female character in one of Sophocles' lost plays, is still experienced in today's Greece, where sweets supply an important national need.

The *zaharoplastío* (sweet-shop) is a mouth-watering sight, with mounds of crescent- and cone-shaped biscuits decorated with chocolate, almonds, sesame, apricots or coconut; with its giant baking-tins (*tapsiá*) crammed with diamond wedges of *baklavás* glossy with syrup and bulging with nuts; with its extravagant European-style *pástes* too.

But the *zaharoplastío* is more than a shop. You can often sit for some time, as in a café, eating a *kataïfi* (finely shredded pastry stuffed with almonds and soaked in honey) or a *profiterol* (not the light French *choux* pastry but sponge softened with syrup and liqueur, covered with chocolate custard and cream), always served with a glass of iced water.

In the northern cities – where the abundance of almonds and fruit and the large population from Asia Minor have fostered a sweet tooth among the inhabitants – sweet-shops are plentiful and often very smart. The city-dweller will eat a *baklavás* – or the even sweeter zeppelin-shaped *touloúmba* – in the early evening, after a siesta and before dinner.

At home deliciously fragrant sweet rusks, *koulourákia*, are dipped into tea or coffee at any time. On entering a home you are likely to be offered – refuse at your peril – a piece of preserved fruit in syrup, a *glykó tou koutalioú* (off the spoon), a cross between jam and crystallised fruit. All sorts of fruit and vegetables are preserved in this way; especially delicious are the green walnuts and little damsons of Thássos. The more adventurous will sample a jar of baby aubergines or marrows such as cram the stalls in Thessaloníki's street market.

The very humblest variety of the "spoon" family is the "submarine", a spoonful of vanilla (a vanilla-flavoured mastic cream) served in a glass of iced water, which then makes a delicately perfumed drink.

LEFT: coffee, the sociable drink.
RIGHT: vendor selling doughnuts on the beach at Mália.

Greek confectionery has a greater range than some disappointed visitors – used to the ubiquitous stale *baklavás* or the oily, foil-packaged *halvás* – might suppose. The very best *baklavás* is to be found on Thássos, made, unusually, with walnuts, and heavily spiced. Two delicious variants of this oriental pastry are *galaktoboúreko*, or milk pie (*fílo* pastry filled with a thick custard flavoured with orange flower and cinnamon) and *ravaní*, a Madeira-type sponge soused with a cognac and orange syrup. Be sure to try them when visiting Aegina (Éghina).

Halvás comes in many types. Smyrnan *halvás*, now hard to find in shops, is made in

huge flat circles and is of a coarse, grainy texture and rich amber colour. Pharsalian *halvás*, to be found in Thessaly, is more gelatinous, closer to Turkish Delight (be sure to call it *loukoúmi*). Both are excellent when sprinkled with lemon and cinnamon. *Halvás* should be bought in the street market, sliced from huge loaves, spotted with pistachios and almonds or marbled with chocolate. Even more sybaritic is *karidhóplastos*, a rich "pâté" made from chocolate and walnuts. When surrounded by the proliferation of unknown delicacies, don't be overwhelmed. Ask for a bag of *amigdalotá* – almond macaroons of numerous shapes and flavours – and you can't go wrong.

EVIL EYE

Greeks seldom call it the "evil eye" – just "the eye" (*to máti*). Perhaps the malevolence of "the eye" goes without saying. Belief in the existence of "the eye" is not confined to those from remote or provincial places. The jet set, the middle class as well as the proletariat, and not a few university-educated, swear that it exists. They insist that even doctors acknowledge its reality, just as the Church accepts the existence of demonic possession. Undoubtedly, the experience of "being eyed" is widespread, however much one might quarrel with its diagnosis.

much, for that invites jealousy and bad will. Out of this paradox – the need to be better, the need to be the same – comes "the eye". It is a consequence of envy, but it is envy expressed surreptitiously, even unconsciously. This qualification is important. A Greek will rarely give "the eye" to someone intentionally. What we'd call "sorcery" – saying special words or doing special actions in order to make something happen to someone – falls into a rather different category, that of "magic" (*máyia*). "The eye", by contrast, is cast by accident.

The kind of person who casts "the eye" on you or yours is probably a neighbour or an

Concepts of the "evil eye" abound. Whether these different concepts are about the same thing is hotly contested by scholars of this region. But the debate itself underscores just how much the "evil eye" is a social affliction rather than anything particularly metaphysical.

Probably, the "evil eye" is about envy. It tends to appear in communities relatively undifferentiated by social class or wealth – "egalitarian" in a sense, but where resources are scarce and competition keen. In such places, the increments of "superiority" of one family over another are tiny, yet all-important.

Prestige or honour, variously, requires one to "stand out" from one's neighbours – but not too

acquaintance, someone with whom relations are – if not warm – at least cordial. It can happen inadvertently when something is praised, or even silently admired.

The living beings and inanimate objects which are most vulnerable to "the eye" are those of unusual beauty, rarity or value. Tiny babies, appealing toddlers, pretty girls and twins are all at risk. This is why people take precautions by pretending to spit delicately (*"Phtoo! Phtoo! Phtoo!"*) near an infant. Livestock can be afflicted as well. When automobiles "die" for no apparent reason, people blame it on "the eye", and in certain parts of Macedonia you can find one tractor after another with an apotropaic string of blue beads hanging from its front bumper.

On a parched islet in the Dodecanese, the water supply for one household is stored in whitewashed barrels on its rooftop; on each barrel has been painted, with unabashed simplicity, a large blue eyeball.

Certain people are said to be prone to casting the eye. Often, such an individual (sometimes called a *grousoúzis*) is quarrelsome, odd, or marginal in some way to the community. Wearing blue – blue beads or the little blue pupil encased in plastic – repels that danger. Many adults place one of these blue plastic eyes next to the cross they wear on a chain around their neck. And until recently all children had some sort of charm – a cross, an eye, an image of the Virgin and Child – pinned to their underclothes.

There is no way to know precisely who has cast "the eye". First, the effects are noticed, and only afterwards is a culprit surmised. All concerned pool their memories to reconstruct the recent past, straining to identify possible suspects with possible motivations. This response of suspicion reinforces belief in "the eye". It also reinforces its precipitating conditions: those of superficial cordiality and subterranean mistrust among unrelated families. Oddly enough, then, identifying the culprit is usually irrelevant to the cure's effectiveness.

Symptoms of affliction are fairly well defined: in humans, they include sudden dizziness, headaches, a "weight" on the head or a tightening in the chest, a feeling of paralysis. Significantly, the head and chest are the sites of "breath" and "spirit". Animals show their affliction by bizarre behaviour or suddenly falling sick, while vehicles break down. When it happens, people know who to go to. It's often an old woman who is trusted and respected and who "knows about these things".

The cure has many variations, but this one is typical: the curer takes a glass of water and makes the sign of the cross over it three times. Then she repeats three times silently to herself a special, secret set of holy words, usually a short passage from the Bible, and simultaneously drops from her finger three droplets of olive oil into the glass. If the oil remains in glob-

ules, the person is not afflicted with "the eye". If it dissolves, this is both the proof and its cure. The curer may yawn and her eyes may fill with tears, while the afflicted person may feel a dramatic "lifting". The water is then dabbed on the forehead, belly, and on two points on the chest – that is, at the points of the crucifix.

Often, it works. Why it works isn't clear, but the moral is that illness isn't about germs alone. It's also about social relations – which could be called taking the holistic approach. If that fact has eluded the Western medical establishment, Greeks know it all too well.

CELEBRATING THE EPIPHANY

"E" also stands for the Epiphany, one of Greece's most colourful religious festivals. The 12 days of Christmas are a time when wicked spirits called *kalikántzari* are supposed to roam the earth, and 6 January – the Epiphany – is when they are banished back to the underworld by special Church rites. The most important of these is the blessing of baptismal fonts and all outdoor bodies of water. If you're visiting on this day, you'll see entire communities turn out to follow their priest down to the seashore or river-front, where – as the ciimax of the ceremony – he will cast a crucifix into the water. Local youths then compete for the honour of retrieving it.

LEFT: "the eye" painted on the prow of a fishing-boat.
RIGHT: you'll see strings of blue beads like these hanging on car bumpers to ward off bad luck.

FRIENDS

The French, with their word *compagnie*, come closest to the Greek notion of *paréa*. For *paréa* combines both senses of the French word: companionship, and the group of friends itself. "Do you have *paréa*?" means "Do you have company?" In Greece, without *paréa*, things aren't worth doing. Living alone, going off by yourself for a vacation, taking a lone stroll, these are not signs of independence but of desperation. This is a society whose language has no word for privacy. The closest translation is *monaxiá* (isolation), connoting deprivation,

loneliness and loss. Who would choose such a state? Young women on their own are especially suspect: surely they're "looking" for something. Before mass tourism, big-hearted Greeks felt obliged to "adopt" lone tourists wandering their countryside, to "protect" the woman and befriend the fellow. Even today, "Do you have *paréa*?" is less a question than an offer: "I'll come along."

The "naturalness" of *paréa* for Greeks is fostered in their family experience. Traditional peasant houses had one main room for cooking, eating, working and sleeping, and even in new village houses and Athenian apartments, everything seems to happen in the living room-kitchen. With television droning in the background, the teenage girl pores over her school books while her father passionately argues politics with his brother-in-law, her brother shouts into the phone and her mother clangs pots and scolds the grandchildren.

People often say that the primary unit of Greek society is the family, not the individual, and this is manifested in a different sense of personal boundaries. Greek families are not a place for "respecting the other person's space". They are interactive – indeed, interfering. How else can they show they care? Greeks advise, criticise, make sacrifices for and demand them from those they consider "their own". No *laissez-faire* here. If American individualism is about the lone cowboy, the Greek version is about the leader of the pack. "Twelve Greeks," they remark wryly, "13 captains."

Paréa partakes of both fixity and flux. "My *paréa*" can mean a fairly fixed group. For young Greeks, it's usually school friends. For those still childless, or far from home at university, the *paréa* becomes an alternative family which can last for years. Its members are always together, and think and talk about each other obsessively. They create a shared history. For their parents, especially if they've lived most of their lives in one place, the *paréa* combines long-time friends with relatives and new in-laws with their spouses, people with common interests and common responsibilities.

For the young and unattached, the *paréa* can be all-consuming activity. Its members meet for coffee before lunch, coffee after, a brandy at 4pm, and a meal in a *tavérna* at 10pm. Their political convictions won't diverge much (only kinship sometimes bridges political quarrels),

DRINKING AS A FINE ART

Greeks drink only with food, and never alone – for the point is not to get drunk. Drinking is first and foremost a means of "opening up", to enter a pleasant, sociable state known as *kéfi*. There are actually fewer alcoholics here than anywhere else in Europe.

As you might imagine, then, they regard with distaste tourists who drink to stupefaction – and especially women. Greeks may grudgingly respect a woman who can hold her liquor, but they are unforgiving when she can't. The double standard operates here with a vengeance, and in more puritanical locales, women will ostentatiously spike their retsína with soda water.

yet over these cups of coffee, they debate the fine points of their differences incessantly. They also joke and tell stories, and in their fragmented state of twos and threes, take up their other favourite subject: relationships. Friendships, family relationships, the continuing saga of lovers – all are minutely examined and emotional intimacies are thus forged. Friends measure their closeness by the pain they've shared.

Like a family, such a *paréa* sometimes has a kind of incest taboo. Jokey flirtations are part of the *paréa*'s spice but, for serious affairs, members of the opposite sex are so familiar that they seem more like siblings. Except per-

In the *tavérna*, the *paréa* members submit these creaturely needs to a grander, collective ideal. Endless plates of food come to rest not at each individual's place, but haphazardly on the table. Each wields his fork to spear a morsel, then rests it. Meals like this can last for hours. That is the point. The table must be brimming – stinginess Greeks find contemptible, but greediness in *paréa* is almost as bad. So, for all their exhortations to others to "Eat!" they can be surprisingly reluctant themselves.

As they've eaten collectively, so do they pay. Once, men always paid for women, splitting the bill among themselves. Things are more in

haps at marriage, people don't leave the *paréa* to form a "couple".

The *paréa* nurtures vehement loyalties, especially in the face of outsiders' criticisms. But such relentless intimacy can also be suffocating. *Paréa* life can verge on melodrama: imagined slights take on huge proportions. Sooner or later, there's a fight, or a cooling, and the membership changes.

For *paréa* life has its own etiquette. "Being together" is its object, not eating or drinking.

LEFT: for young Greeks, *paréa* means school friends. **ABOVE:** in the *tavérna*, there's always room at the table for friends who happen to come by.

flux these days. Men will pay for wives and girlfriends, but in university *parées* everyone is equally poor, regardless of sex, so all contribute. Guests, especially if they are foreigners, are a stickier matter.

Greeks are proud of their reputation for hospitality. And they would never let a foreigner pay his – and especially her – way without a fight. But they are sensitive about being taken advantage of. The best policy is always to plonk your money down with the rest – indeed, to show your willingness to pay with as much drama and determination as you can muster – and if (as may well be the case) you find yourself overruled, to accept graciously.

GRAFFITI

In Procopius's day, Constantinople was brought to a standstill as fans of rival chariot teams, the Reds, Blues and Greens, rampaged through the streets. Nowadays the chariot-racing is gone, but its place in Greek life is filled by politics.

Come election time, Athens' streets are jammed solid with thousands of banners, flags and posters as supporters flood into Sýndagma Square for the big rallies. Walls, bridges and the bare sides of apartment blocks become mottled configurations of slogans. Squads from the political parties' youth groups will head out at night

to whitewash opponents' slogans and paint up their own. Outside the towns, it's the same story.

Graffiti are essential to political success in Greece and they impose requirements of their own. Above all, colour. The choice is limited: white is out since it won't show up against whitewash; yellow likewise. Black has long been monopolised by the anarchists. The right-wing, whether ultra-nationalists or the centrist New Democracy has bagged blue, which conveniently echoes the national flag. The communists, now two parties, of course use red.

One key to the success of the socialist party, PASOK, it's said, was its appropriation of the colour green: highly visible, suggesting close ties with the natural world, which helped to offset the party's radical reputation in the eyes of conservative farmers.

PASOK's rise to power took place under the painted rays of a bright green sun, a symbol which lacked the disturbing effects one might have expected. Defying the laws of nature seemed only to underline the party's potency.

This idea of a political rebirth, the dawning of a new era, was helped by the charisma of Andhréas Papandhréou himself, but we may have come to the end of a long line of charismatic leaders in Greece. Andhreas Papandhreou was succeeded as prime minister by the decidedly uncharasmatic Kostas Simitis, who seems almost embarrassed to be in the public eye. He is, however, exceedingly effective, accomplishing much with a minimum of rhetoric. Yeorghios Papandhreou, Andhreas's oldest son (grandson of his namesake) is the gentle minister of foreign affairs who is improving Greece's relations with all her neighbours, most notably Turkey.

A SUCCESSFUL SLOGAN

Just one word won the 1981 election for Andhréas Papandhréou: *allaghí* – which means "change". This simple formula had already worked wonders for Papandhréou's socialist PASOK party four years earlier against a feeble array of alternatives such as New Democracy's "It Found Chaos: It Created a State" – which might, arguably, have been true but certainly fell completely flat, failing even to rhyme properly.

Then there was the centre party's motto, *allaghí me sigouriá* ("change with security"), which was nothing more than a laughable imitation of PASOK and a virtual admission of defeat.

HOSPITALITY

Almost every guide to Greece opens its entry on "hospitality" with the story of Zeus, the disguised stranger-guest. And who are we to break tradition? In its ancient form – and still so, today – the word usually translated as "hospitality" was a bit of an oxymoron. *Filoxenía* is a compound word, combining *fílo*, "to love", and *xénos*, a word meaning – oddly – both "stranger" and "guest".

Zeus liked to travel incognito, the better to seduce lovely mortals. So, opportunistically perhaps, he decreed *filoxenía* not just an exalted virtue, but also an obligation. The *xénos*, he said, should be treated in a princely fashion, because – who knows? – that stranger might really be a god in disguise, even Zeus himself.

Despite the onslaught of mass tourism, hospitality remains a virtue. Indeed, it is the very quality Greeks believe most distinguishes them from other peoples. They're positively competitive about it: every house insists its own hospitality is more genuine than the neighbour's, and "our" village is somehow always more hospitable than the village further down the road.

In some ways, the truth is in the declamation. But certain places achieve a national reputation.

The guest, receiving, becomes obliged to the host. Once you know this, the common power-struggle over food makes sense. The guest is obliged, ultimately, to receive but is at the same time ashamed to seem too eager. Proverbially, the guest was supposed to refuse an offer of food or drink twice, and only – after much coaxing – to relent the third time. It's quite a delicate game, and can be disastrous for the unsuspecting traveller, for the Greek host thinks your refusals are just politeness and that by saying "no", you really mean "yes". There aren't any magic solutions. You can try to argue "diabetes" or "bad teeth" if you can't bear the sight of another dish

Cretans – never a folk for middling gestures – are thought to be as extreme in hospitality as they are in temper. Predictably, the label becomes self-fulfilling. Other locales (Híos? The Máni?) fare less well in the eyes of their compatriots – but this being an issue of local patriotism, well, it's all rather subjective, isn't it?

Hospitality creates a relationship, but it is not of equals. The host brings the guest into his own domain; then increases his prestige by giving.

LEFT: Thessaloníki PASOK rally.
ABOVE: although tourism has become big business in Greece, hospitality remains a virtue here.

of jellied fruit, but be prepared to accept something so as not to insult your hosts.

If you are invited for coffee, your hostess will retire to the kitchen to set a tray with a tiny cup of coffee, a saucer of biscuits and a glass of water. Take the coffee first: raise it up slightly, and say *Stin yghiá sas!* ("To your health!"). When you've finished, raise the glass slightly, toasting your hostess, and drink the water. When you leave, you can say *Sas efharistó!* ("I thank you") or even better, *Hárika polý*. The latter is something you say when you've just been introduced ("I'm very pleased [to have met you]") but here, it can also mean "I've enjoyed myself." Hospitality, after all, is about both.

IDENTITY: MACEDONIA

The Greeks took several years to come to terms with the creation of a new state calling itself "Macedonia", but now many Greek firms are rushing North and making major investments. The issue stirred intense national feelings, and it is worth understanding why.

Modern Greeks still revere the memory of the ancient Macedonian kingdom which reached its zenith under Philip II and his son Alexander the Great. But this empire was shortlived, its core territory succumbing to Romans, Slavs, Byzantines and finally the

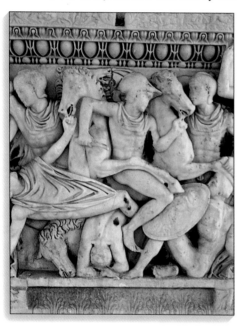

Ottomans. By the 19th century, "Macedonia" retained only its geographical sense: an area bounded by the Néstos river on the east, the Pindos to the west, the Aegean (and Mount Olympus) on the south, and various barrier hills nearly 200 km (125 miles) inland to the north.

It supported the most heterogenous population in Europe: Muslim Turks and Albanians; Orthodox Greeks, Bulgarians, Serbs and unaffiliated Slavophones; Gypsies and Jews. No one group predominated, and the Orthodox Greeks were often a distinct minority. With the rise of virulent nationalisms, and the steady weakening of the Ottoman Empire after 1870, armed bands – Bulgarian *comitadjidhes*, Serbian *chetniks* and

Greek *makedhonomáhes* – formed in preparation for a struggle to seize this rich territory. Briefly allied during the First Balkan War which saw the "Young Turks'" regime driven from most of Europe in 1912, an Orthodox coalition of Serbia, Bulgaria and Greece fragmented as the Greek Army liberated Thessaloníki 12 hours before the entry of the Bulgarians – who contested Greek supremacy, and were soundly beaten by a coalition of the Greeks, the Serbs and the Romanians in the Second Balkan War of 1913. But they returned to occupy most of eastern Macedonia during each world war, and only since 1950 has Bulgaria renounced all claims on Macedonia (and on Thrace).

Meanwhile, Greece consolidated its grip: population exchanges after each war replaced potentially troublesome Slav-identifying minorities with patriotic Greek refugees, and government-imposed Greek language and Orthodox primacy diluted Macedonia's multi-ethnic character. The Metaxás dictatorship forcibly renamed villages with Slavic tags; surnames like Dhimitrov became Dhimitropoulos; and if Bulgarian or "Macedonian" was your first, at-home language, there it stayed, on pain of stiff fines for public use.

During the 1940s, the communist resistance briefly supported "self-determination for Macedonia", widely interpreted as dismemberment of northwestern Greece and union with a hypothetical Macedonian state. This only made life harder for those Greek Slavophones still living on the northern frontier, between the Áxios river and Albania. More postwar repression ensued, prompting massive emigration to Canada, Yugoslavia and Australia; yet there remain approximately 40,000 "Macedonian" speakers in northern Greece, despite steadfast official refusal to recognize them as a minority.

When Yugoslavia disintegrated in 1991, its southerly "Macedonian" republic declared independence and the issue reared its head once more. The infant state took the "Star of Verghína" of the ancient Macedonian kings for its flag, printed banknotes showing the White Tower of "Solun" (Thessaloníki in Slavic), and promulgated a constitution allegedly referring to "unredeemed Aegean territories" containing "Slav minorities".

Greece's reaction, faced with the threatened reversal of all its hard-won gains of 1912–20, was predictably apoplectic. Million-strong demonstrations filled Greek streets, chanting the poster-slogans; a crippling commercial embargo was slapped on the new country's south frontier, lifted only in 1995; the Greek government resisted local fire-eater's demands for military action; and Greek diplomats lobbied other governments not to recognize any state calling itself "Macedonia". Finally, an EU and UN compromise, pleasing no-one, welcomed the "Former Yugoslav Republic of Macedonia" (FYROM) – a name which endures

PENNY LANE

Alexander the Great of Macedonia is depicted on the "heads" side of the 100-drachma coin – bearing an uncanny resemblance, so it is often said, to Sir Paul McCartney.

arly position), and on who are the true descendants of Alexander.

Of recent analyses, one of the most interesting is Greek anthropologist Anastasia Karakasidou's well-researched *Fields of Wheat, Hills of Blood* (University of Chicago Press, 1997), which describes the social changes in a small agricultural town outside Thessaloníki as the process of Hellenisation absorbed different ethnic groups into the largely homogeneous culture of the modern Greek state.

to date – to the community of nations. But the Greek press often refers disparagingly to the territory as *Ta Skopia* (after the "Macedonian" capital); "Macedonia", except thus in inverted commas, is still very much a no-no.

The polemic has – as you might expect – also invaded academic debate. Modern political legitimacy, it is argued, hinges on the identity of those ancient Macedonians: "proto-Slavs" (the Slav view), "pure Hellenes" (the Greek view) or Hellenised "barbarians" (the neutral schol-

---

LEFT: ancient success in Macedonia depicted in a frieze in the Archaeological Museum, Athens.
ABOVE: a grim moment in April 1967.

JUNTA

At 2am on 21 April 1967, the people of Greece discovered that the army, in a swift, well-planned coup, had overthrown the government and in its place established a military regime. Using a NATO contingency plan developed for use in the event of a communist invasion from Greece's northern neighbours, and code-named "Prométheus", the conspirators justified their putsch on the grounds that they "were saving Greece from the precipice of communism".

Later that morning martial law was proclaimed. Various articles in the constitution guaranteeing human rights were suspended, military courts were established in Athens and Thessaloníki, political parties were dissolved and the right to strike abolished. Newspapers were submitted to strict censorship, and all gatherings, indoors or outdoors, were forbidden. Many thousands of people with a record of left-wing political views or activity were arrested and sent into exile in bleak camps on remote islands. A large number of parliamentary leaders were taken into custody.

The new government ran true to form. Like other military dictatorships, its measures were alternately savage and ludicrous. Its leaders, the Colonels, were fanatical, if unintelligent,

anti-communist salvationists who saw politics as a simple and fierce contest between good and evil. Like the pre-war dictator General Metaxás, they emphasised the need to discipline and reform the Greek character, condemning long hair on men and mini-skirts on women and ordering both to go to church.

Even foreign tourists were subjected to some of these regulations, though the government was anxious not to frighten them away altogether. But like other "moralists", they did not escape making themselves ridiculous. For example, through the official propaganda machine, they tried to humiliate the Nobel Prize-winning poet George Seféris for handing out a memorable statement of

protest against the dictatorship; they deprived the film star Melína Merkoúri of her citizenship for criticising them; they banned the songs of Míkis Theodhorákis, a leading composer, because he had been a communist, and they censored the tragedies and comedies of the classical theatre.

After the coup, little was heard of the communist threat which was supposed to justify it and the seizure of the papers of the left-wing party failed to produce any evidence in support. The coup was a simple seizure of power by a handful of military bigots. The regime resorted to torture and brutality as a deliberate instrument of policy to maintain its grip on power.

The American government, under Richard Nixon, viewed these developments with no more than embarrassment and after a brief period of indecision gave the regime its accolade in the shape of arms supplies. Greece as a *place d'armes* for NATO seemed more important than Greece as a conforming member of the society of free and democratic nations which NATO was proclaimed to be.

The first blow in the downfall of the junta was initiated by students. In November 1973 a large number of them occupied the Athens Polytechnic and university buildings in Thessaloníki and Pátra. When it became clear that they were attracting widespread sympathy, and when the Athens Polytechnic students began broadcasting appeals on a clandestine radio band for a worker-student alliance to overthrow the dictatorship, the regime sent in troops and tanks to crush them. The eviction of the students from the Polytechnic was carried out with extreme brutality, and at least 40 students and other sympathisers were killed. This ruthless demonstration of force turned the stomachs of most Greeks. From then on, the days of the dictatorship were numbered.

The regime collapsed eight months later, in July 1974, under the weight of its bungling in Cyprus; this led to a confrontation with Turkey and a military call-up for which the Colonels had prepared with a farcical incompetence reminiscent of the equally empty militarism of an earlier Mediterranean dictator, Mussolini. The conservative leader Karamanlís, who had been living in exile in Paris, returned to Greece in the early hours of 24 July to oversee the dismantling of the dictatorship and the return to democratic rule. The brutal dictatorship ended as abruptly as it had begun.

KAMÁKI

Kamáki literally means a fishing trident, or harpoon, but the word also refers to picking up or "hunting" foreign female tourists, and to the "hunter" himself (the sexual metaphor is obvious). It is a practice which has grown alongside the Greek tourist industry over the past 30 years, and while it rarely descends to physical harrassment, is one which can become intensely irritating to any female traveller in Greece.

> **NIMBYS**
>
> The *kamáki's* two-faced nature means he will not risk the social approbrium that would come from targeting Greek women.

but also ignores the fact that contemporary Greek society now affords women much more sexual freedom. Any idea that *kamáki* is a sophisticated "game" of seduction, as its exponents like to imagine, is at once dispelled by its most common manifestation, a kind of "cheeping" noise is more appealing to a budgie than an independent woman. The best way to deal with young and deluded Greek males is to ignore them, and to try and remember, difficult as it may be, that losing your temper will only make things worse.

In the 1960s, most young Greek women were extremely restricted in their movements, and were kept closely tied to the family. There was therefore little prospect for romance, sex, or even an evening out with a girl for the would-be young man-about-town. The men saw the arrival of, in their eyes at least, sexually liberated women tourists as an opportunity not to be missed.

Whatever the social situation of its origins, *kamáki* is not only insulting to foreign tourists,

LEFT: posters for the Communist Party – the Colonels' greatest threat – stuck to a decorative wall.
ABOVE: *kamáki* in action.

LANGUAGE

Imagine a language which has two sets of unrelated words for basic concepts, such as "nose", "cheek", "shoe", "house", "moon", "red" and "white". Suppose, also, that, together with its own distinct grammar, one set is used in everyday life, while the other is obligatory in official parlance, in education, and newspapers.

That language is Modern Greek, or at least it was up until 1974. For the first 150 years after Greece gained its independence from the Ottoman Empire in 1821, there were two versions of Greek, used in different situations, which overlapped in pronunciation and in many areas of vocabulary and grammar, but differed radically in others. This is not unique to Greece. The Arabs, for instance, also use different versions of Arabic in different circumstances.

The Greeks have traditionally revered the language of ancient Greek literature and the New Testament – almost as much as the Arabs have valued the language of the Koran. For centuries they have felt that their writings should depart as little as possible from the language of their illustrious ancestors and of their holy book.

Some acquaintance with the history of Greek language is essential for an understanding of Greek culture as a whole over the past 200

years, since the controversies over the language sum up the conflicting attitudes of the modern Greeks to their ancient compatriots. It has never been doubted in Greece that its present-day inhabitants are the direct descendants of the ancient Greeks, who laid the foundations of European civilisation.

This assumption presented the Greeks who were preparing the way for independence in the 1820s with the problem of what national ideology to adopt in order both to unite the nation and to present a national image to the outside world. Within Greece itself – and among adherents to the Greek Orthodox faith in general – a bewildering variety of languages was spoken

and the Greek language itself was split into various dialects, some mutually incomprehensible. Nevertheless, Greek was the most commonly used and Greek (albeit the Greek of more than one and a half millennia before) was the language of the Church. So Greek intellectuals of the early 19th century agreed that the best way to cement national unity and, incidentally, to secure assistance from the West in their national liberation struggle was to promote their links with ancient Greece, to which Europeans and Americans had a romantic attachment. Their case was supported by the close connection between the ancient and modern Greek languages.

From here on, however, there was profound disagreement. Some intellectuals believed that the modern language was barbaric (thanks to centuries of Turkish rule) and that the only way for the Greeks to prosper was a return to the pristine beauties of ancient Greece. This would ensure the rebirth of ancient Greek culture, their belief being that anyone who learned to speak like Plato would also begin to think like Plato.

A related problem was that of what the modern Greeks should call themselves. From the early Christian era until the beginning of the 19th century almost all Greeks had called themselves "Romans" and their spoken language "Romaic", since they were conscious of belonging to the traditions of the Byzantine Empire, which was historically the continuation of the Roman Empire. They tended to reserve the words "Hellene" and "Hellenic" (Greek) for the pagan ancient Greeks and their language.

By insisting on calling themselves and their compatriots "Hellenes", some intellectuals were able to envisage the resurrection of the Ancient Greek language along with its name. But whereas everyone knows the difference between the Italians and the Romans, "Greek" is used to refer to the people and language of both ancient and modern Greece. Others, realising the impracticality of persuading the Greeks to renounce their mother tongue, looked at the example of the French, who had reached cultural eminence after abandoning Latin and cultivating their own language. These intellectuals argued that only through the use of the spoken language could the Greeks become sufficiently educated and enlightened to drag their country out of its economic and cultural morass. They wanted to follow the example of the ancient Greeks, who had used their mother tongue to reach the heights of civilisation.

Among those who opposed the imposition of a fully resurrected Ancient Greek was Adamántios Korais (1748–1833), a former merchant and physician living in Paris who became the leader of the intellectual movement preparing for Greece's independence. But although he constantly attacked the archaists, he was equally scathing about those who insisted on using the modern language as spoken by the common people. He proposed a "cleansed" ver-

> **ADULTS ONLY**
>
> Ancient Greek used to be a compulsory high-school subject, but these days it isn't usually studied before the age of 16.

promise language, which was neither fully ancient nor fully modern (and had never been spoken by anyone), was adopted by the fathers of the nation as the basis of the official language, later known as *katharévousa* (literally "the purifying language").

It is difficult for non-Greeks to imagine the almost magic power invested in the ancient written word in Greece. Throughout the 19th century Greek intellectuals, frustrated and disillusioned by the problems facing the Greek state, seemed convinced that every aspect of

sion of Modern Greek, one which conformed to the rules of Ancient Greek grammar.

This language would have the advantage of being not too far removed either from any of the modern Greek dialects (thus avoiding giving an unfair advantage to the speakers of any one dialect) or from Ancient Greek. It would display both the underlying unity among the modern speakers of Greek and the profound identity (despite superficial differences) between the ancient and the modern Greeks. Korais's com-

LEFT: an engrossing read, Híos.
ABOVE: a little word in your ear…

modern Greece represented an inferior and tarnished version of some glorious ancient counterpart. The ancient language was looked upon, quite irrationally, as an instrument of absolute perfection; and – precisely because it was no longer spoken, but only written – it appeared to be timeless and eternal, exempt from the change and decay that affect all living bodies (including, of course, spoken language, which is constantly in a state of flux).

It is notoriously difficult to create a standardised language. Look at the differences between the varieties of English spoken within any one English-speaking country, let alone in different English-speaking countries. The

Greek intellectual leaders created an added difficulty of trying to forge a standard that would contain material from two separate, albeit related, languages (ancient and modern Greek), each of which had never been standardised in itself but was split into widely diverging dialects.

So any user of *katharévousa* had to walk an unsteady tightrope and avoid falling into either incomprehensibility or vulgarity. Those without laborious training in such verbal acrobatics (the vast majority of the Greek population) could choose to ignore the official language altogether and thus exclude themselves from direct access to the law and the state appara-

tus. Alternatively, they could parrot-learn set formulas which would enable them to muddle through it.

While the academics were busy deriding the popular language, the poets were writing in it and exhorting people to abandon their prejudices against it. By the end of the 19th century almost all creative writers were using the "demotic" (spoken) language, so that *katharévousa* became solely the language of official parlance and no longer that of cultural life.

Nevertheless the struggle continued: people were killed in riots involving adherents of the two opposing linguistic variants in 1901 and again in 1903, and the article of the

Greek Constitution specifying *katharévousa* as the official language (inserted in 1911, in response to this violent polarisation) was not abolished until after the fall of the Colonels in 1974.

During the 20th century the language controversy often tended to be identified with political divisions; *katharévousa* being promoted by the Right and demotic by the Left. It was partly because *katharévousa* had become tainted by its identification with the Colonels' regime that the more liberal (though still conservative) Karamanlís government was able to begin replacing *katharévousa* by demotic in all areas of public life.

But the Greeks haven't stopped arguing about their language; indeed, it is still a frequent topic of discussion among both intellectuals and non-intellectuals alike. Beginning in 1981 Papandhréou's socialist government continued the process of dismantling *katharévousa*; the more laid-back style of its speeches and pronouncements has offended many unused to a casual use of language for official purposes. The government's abolition of many of the actually functionless diacritics used in writing Greek for 2,000 years (but not in the classical period), which caused so much misery and embarrassment both to school-children and adults, has been widely criticised.

Nevertheless, one positive consequence of the language controversy is a fondness shared by all Greeks – whether peasants, poets, neither, or both – for playing with the varieties of their language. Language isn't simply a means of expression, but an arena in which they can practise their creativity, display their wits, and generally have fun.

MOVIES

On sultry summer nights in Greece, most of the evening entertainment occurs outdoors, and movies are no exception. Very few indoor cinemas are air-conditioned. Some are equipped with a rare innovation: the convertible roof remains closed during the screenings before sundown, then movable panels creak apart to expose the audience to cool breezes and an occasional starry sky.

The rest of the indoor cinemas move to empty gravel-covered lots, alleys or rooftops where people are usually seated on folding deck chairs. Here, the atmosphere is appropriately relaxed. Whole families attend, and snack bars serve sandwiches, beer, soft drinks, crackers, chocolate and popcorn. A few establishments even operate as cinematic *ouzerís*, where one can sit at little tables and nibble on *mezédhes* (hors d'oeuvres) while sipping an *oúzo*. Drive-in movie theatres haven't been able to hold their own against video, and the very few remaining mostly show pornographic films.

SCREEN TEST

The union of outdoor cinema owners report that a tourist survey named their cinemas as Athens' No.2 attraction after the Acropolis.

Since many theatres are located in the centre of the city, the volume is decreased during the late showing out of consideration for the neighbours. One has a choice of viewing a rather dim picture with adequate sound at the first screening, which starts before dark, or a clearly defined image with a faint soundtrack during the late showings. Fortunately for foreign viewers, Greeks – in contrast to the French or Italians – prefer subtitles to dubbing, so only original language versions are shown.

In any case, open-air cinemas are a relaxing, quaint form of entertainment. No new releases are shown during the summer. But there is always a feast of films to choose from, including re-releases of the previous season and week-long festivals of older classics, plus the inevitable slapstick comedies.

Traditionally, domestic fare topped the popularity list but this has been reversed in recent years when foreign action adventures and romances have sold the most tickets. The heavy European influence in Greek cinema made many of the quality films too "arty" and slow-moving for general audiences who have grown used to a diet of fast-paced imports, or the crudely made buffoonery of Greek comedies. Here, as elsewhere throughout the world, it is Hollywood's blockbusters that dominate.

Greeks occasionally wander into an outdoor movie theatre in the middle of the film and talk throughout it. Yet, lest one should think there is no serious audience, a few art-houses in central Athens do a solid business by booking up earnest European imports as well as a smattering of avant-garde American independents. Meanwhile, the after-midnight movie trend has re-emerged in a few central cinemas, which show "B" grade thrillers, science fiction and horror flicks to die-hard fans.

Only a few Greek low-budget farcical comedies and a handful of quality films sold more than 100,000 tickets in recent seasons. The gulf between commercial movies and artistic ones has been great. However, the most popular domestic films of recent years have managed to combine "Greekness" with well-developed scripts that have international appeal.

NAMEDAYS

"What's in a name?" asked Romeo. He should have asked a Greek! For here, all sorts of stories piggyback onto names, if you know how to read them. Place of origin, for instance: *Theodhorákis* is clearly Cretan, for names ending with *ákis* (meaning "little") bear the slyly ironic tag of this ferocious people. Any *Yánnoglou* is sure to have ties to "The City" (Constantinople), and the common suffix *poulos* (meaning "bird", or "child of") to the Peloponnese, as in the case of the leader of the 1967 Colonel's junta, Papadhópoulos, which means "son of the priest".

LEFT: in Greece, body language is just as important a part of the communication process as the words.
RIGHT: open-air cinemas are a Greek institution.

Before the revision of Family Law (*see box*), it was rare for a woman – unless she were rich or Melína Merkoúri – to even contemplate keeping her father's surname. In the possessive case, female surnames (single and married) are telling: Mrs Papadhópoulos really reads "Papadhópoulos's Mrs". In mainland Greece, a woman traditionally lost even her first name at marriage, and was known by the feminised form of her husband's: Yiórgos's wife became "Yiórgina". The symbolism persists. At weddings, the bride's girlfriends will jokingly write their names on the sole of her shoe, for she whose name is rubbed out first will, according to tradition, also marry first.

A Greek baby is not fully a person until it is baptised and given a name. Baptism – a ritual more solemn than marriage, for it initiates the child into the Orthodox community – is celebrated between 40 days and a year after birth, and until then, the child is called simply "Baby".

Greeks are amazed at how Westerners name their children, guided by little more than fashion and personal whim. They themselves follow strict rules: the first boy is named after the father's father, and the first girl after the father's mother (in mainland Greece) or the mother's mother (in most of the Aegean islands). Naming the son after the father, as Americans do, is thought extremely unlucky, even vaguely incestuous: a premature usurping of the father's name. But between grandparents and grandchildren, the inheritance is not fraught. The grandmother greets with delight the baptism of a child with her name. While it ritually acknowledges her individual mortality, it nonetheless assures family continuity: "The name will still be heard."

Property, too, may be linked to names. On many islands, first-born Kalliópe inherits the house from her mother, Marína, who inherited it from her mother, Kalliópe, and so on in an infinite alternation of Kalliópes and Marínas. Likewise, the boy "with the name" will inherit his grandfather's fields, and he (and his wife) will be obliged to mourn for him when he dies.

Certain events can distort this ideal pattern. A man with many nephews bearing his father's name will yield to his father-in-law's desire for a namesake, or a woman trying to conceive may visit the miraculous icon of a particular saint and entreat its help by promising to give the child its name. These do not alter the Greeks' sense that names connect one to a long line of ancestors, perpetually reproducing itself.

If you are Greek, your name links you not only to your own blood ancestors but to the entire Greek (or more accurately, Orthodox) community. Most Greek names refer to a saint or some holy quality, hence, "Sofía", the sacred wisdom. Birthday parties are for kids; the adult Greek has instead a "nameday", the day when the saint for whom he or she was named was "born into" the life hereafter, usually through a rather unpleasant martyrdom. This day is now celebrated by the Orthodox faithful. It's an ingenious system; everybody knows your nameday, sparing you the embarrassment of dropping hints to your friends when you want somebody to celebrate with. But there are a few new twists.

The one who celebrates "treats" the guests. The guest may bring sweets or flowers or a bottle of whisky, but the host provides the feast. On St Dhimítrios's Day, everyone with a friend or relative named Dhimítris or Dhímitra must "remember" him or her (and people often know many Dhímitrises and Dhímitras) by phoning or stopping by, and at the houses of all these Dhímitrises and Dhímitras, the evening is a jolly chaos of doorbells buzzing, phones ringing and a constant flow of guests slightly green with the evening's fifth peppermint liqueur, proffering formal good wishes, and absently munching roasted chickpeas.

Mortal namedays blend the formal and the festive, but for the saint it's a more lavish affair. Every community has a saint (and sometimes several) who specially protects it, and on that patron saint's feast-day, the Orthodox community celebrates with a *paniyíri*. The word derives from ancient Greek, referring to a public assembly: all (pan) those gathered in the marketplace (*agora*). Today's *paniyíri* also involves the entire community.

MAIDEN NAMES

Since 1983, Greek women have been obliged by law to keep their maiden names for life as far as legal matters are concerned.

"Poúli" ("Birdie"). Women hardly ever get *paratsoúklia*, however, except by way of men. The man who has worked for 20 years in America and returned home to marry is dubbed "Amerikános", and his wife, "Amerikána", even though she has never left Macedonia.

Badges of individual peculiarity are thus passed on to sons and grandsons, until (with the real surname erased from memory) the shaggy, secret *paratsoúkli* slips quietly into the bland respectability of an official surname.

The saints are honoured with prayer and processions, followed by a great deal of feasting and dancing into the small hours.

Baptismal names are public and fixed, but *paratsoúklia* celebrate the idiosyncrasies of individual lives. Nicknames of a sort, *paratsoúklia* are an insiders' code; strangers and tax collectors aren't supposed to know them. They generally commemorate quirks of body and character: Manólis's brawny virility wryly recalled in the feminised "Manóla", Yiórgos's philanderings in

LEFT: a gift of flowers to celebrate a saint's feast-day – and all those named for the saint, too.
ABOVE: both birthdays and namedays are marked.

ORAL TRADITION

Poetry matters in Greece, and this is due, in part, to the fact that for centuries it was sung, not read. Poetry has always been a kind of performance in Greece, a social event. Even today, contemporary poets can fill soccer stadiums with keen fans.

Yet until the late 19th century Greek poetry had little in common with the written traditions of Western European cultures. This may be because oral poetry was a much more successful way of preserving Greek national identity during the centuries of foreign rule: writing could be censored, but no despot could confiscate songs.

Even in this century, oral transmission has been relied on as a means of thwarting censorship. Yánnis Rítsos (1909–94), one of Greece's best-known poets, was sent to prison along with many other suspected communists during the civil war. There he continued to write his poems. He would bury them in bottles to keep them from the guards, but the only way he could get them to his readers was with the help of freed prisoners who learned his poems by heart and smuggled them out.

Paradoxically enough, the fall of Constantinople (or "The City", as Greeks commonly call it) marked not only the end of Byzantium

but also the beginning of modern Greek poetry. It is at this point that versions of folk songs still sung today were first recorded or referred to in literary texts. The stock formula "I come from The City", although obviously referring to the fact of the fall, is also found in modern folk songs, and the well-loved 16th-century Cretan romance *Erotókritos* incorporated many verses from folk songs, verses that are still familiar to most Greeks.

Since oral transmission is an inherently creative process, phrases in such songs are not expected to resemble their antecedents word for word; the old phrases serve merely as a structure on which to base new variations.

While not all critics believe in a continuous poetic tradition dating back to Homer, most agree that a certain continuity can reliably be traced from the 15th century.

Until the War of Independence in 1821 and the founding of the Greek state, song and poetry were inseparably linked, whether composed on paper or passed down orally from generation to generation. In fact writing and singing were often equated. But with the emancipation from the Turks, national identity was no longer a clandestine matter. Oral transmission, formerly the *only* transmission possible, now was seen as unreliable. Writing – more fixed and more permanent – became the preferred means for spreading nationalist ideology. The folk song was a stepping stone for poets but not an adequate means of expression in itself. It wasn't reliable enough.

One of the first proponents of a National Greek Literature was the poet Dhionýsios Solomós (1798–1857; *pictured left*), who came from the Ionian islands. In a letter to a friend he expressed his interest in *kléftic* folk songs but also stressed that the poet's task was different: "*Kléftic* poetry is fine and interesting as an ingenuous manifestation by the *Kléfts* of their lives, thoughts and feelings. It does not have the same interest on our lips; the nation requires from us the treasure of our individual intelligence clothed in national forms."

Solomós may have brilliantly reworked the oral tradition's ingenuousness, but it would be too simple to suggest that Greek poetry in the 19th and 20th centuries was all lyricism and nationalism. Over in Alexandria, Greece's greatest modern poet, Constantine Caváfy (1863–1933), did something totally different. His poetry emphasised the importance of writing over song, and seemed to suggest that the human intimacy associated with the oral tradition was no longer possible. His historical framework was neither classical Greece nor the emancipation from the Turks but rather the slow decay of the pre-Christian and Christian eras. He invoked the pathos of deterioration; repeatedly, poetry was the only possible solace.

Written language had the power to construct something material out of what was being lost. Writing for Caváfy was not just a more durable substitute for singing, but a radically different means of expression. The poem took the place of what was missing. It could even fill the geographical space left by the destruction of a once-mighty city.

The two great 19th-century nationalist poets Solomós and Palamás, were followed by Angelos Sikelianós (884–1951). But in Sikelianós's poetry "being Greek" has become less of the collective project it was in Palamás's poetry and more a matter of personal identity. The Delphic priestess with her wild, windswept words is the inspiration for the incantatory verse of this modern poet, who was also a resident of Delphi.

> ## A POEM FOR SINGING
>
> The *Hymn to Freedom* composed by the Nationalist poet, Dhionýsios Solomós, has become the Greek national anthem.

Greece to the modernism of T. S. Eliot with its reliance on myth; Elytis, for his part, imported that other extreme of modernism, French surrealism.

Perhaps it is telling that their poetry gained popularity by the oldest trick in the book, oral transmission, this time through the ingenious scores of the composer Míkis Theodhorákis. As it was with the folk song, the bard in Seféris's and Elytis's poetry speaks for the community. Their poetry is meant to be read in the context of this longer oral tradition.

Very much a part of the established canon and probably best known of all modern Greek poets are the Nobel prize winners George Seféris (1900–71) and Odysséus Elytis (1911–96). Although their poetry is not devoid of questions about the nature of writing, both these poets of the 1930s generation draw heavily on the oral tradition. But rather than comprising a Greek avant-garde, they were just extremely adept at incorporating the techniques of other European genres. Seféris introduced

Oral tradition as a means of passing on culture and ideology is not restricted to oral texts, but also plays a large part in the transmission of traditional musics. Greek traditional musicians have a large vocabulary describing the ways and means of presenting and elaborating melodies. These include the concept of a *skeletós*, "skeleton", or framework around which the musicians may simultaneously improvise, and the variations themselves, described both as *stolídhes* ("ornaments"), and using words derived from *dáktylos* ("finger"), referring to the physical correspondence between the melodic patterns and the movements made by the musicians' fingers.

LEFT: Dhionýsios Solomós, national poet and the Ionian islands' most famous son.

ABOVE: poetry has always been a performance here.

PERÍPTERA

Although they may appear limited by their diminutive structures, kiosks are really multi-purpose powerhouses. Besides filling the obvious, ubiquitous function of newsagent-cum-sweetshop, they can also double as mini-amusement parks (complete with children's rides), sporting goods stores (some even sell sleeping bags), ironmongers and locksmiths. For customers with problems, the proprietor may dispense psychiatric or medical

FAMILY FORTUNES

Although it has only a quarter of the population of Great Britain, Greece has nearly the same number of retail shops – mostly family-run.

advice – whether asked for or not.

Running a kiosk is like conducting an orchestra – one eye on the telephone meter, one hand giving change and one ear tuned to the voice of a friend who has stopped around the back for a chat. How do kiosk owners cope?

The view from inside a kiosk, or *períptero* as it is called in Greek, is tight, complex and most resembles the cockpit of a DC-9. In the centre sits the proprietor, jammed into two square feet of space yet firmly in control of the till, responding to the images as they appear on the screen – that small opening to the front where customers pronounce their orders. It is not unusual for a *peripterás* to work shifts of 12

hours in conditions which vary from furnace-like in summer to chill and damp in winter (when most cramp their already tiny space with electric fires or some form of heating). Yet they remain a generally good-humoured lot, eager to oblige the lost foreigner, or to recommend a good local *tavérna*.

The kiosks were originally gifts from the government to wounded veterans of the Balkan Wars and World War I. Many will remark on the similarity between the architecture of kiosks and that of military guardposts such as those used by the honour guard in front of the Parliament Building on Sýndagma Square. In a symbolic way the *períptera* are also rather like guard houses where old soldiers prolong their duty, emerging from the military into the commercial sector, watching over and attempting to serve the community.

In Greece people want to run their own business and 3,000-plus *períptera* in Athens alone obviously make this a possibility. Kiosks are almost all family-run; one cannot help noticing the children or grandchildren of the proprietors stopping by for a sweet on the way home from school, or in summer the whole family sitting around a seafront *períptera* eating watermelon, which customers may be asked to share.

This has a lot to do with the charm of the kiosks, a charm which is part of Greek commerce in general – everything is personal. If a kiosk owner finds that you know a few words of Greek, it may take a bit longer to conclude your purchase. He (or she) will want to know where you are from.

The swollen number of retail shops in Greece is partly the reflection of a society which subdivides itself sharply into kindred groups, each of which seeks to own a shop, a *magazí*. The idea of working for a stranger is odious; in fact, the word for "employee" in Greek literally means "someone beneath another".

Consequently, instead of expanding, businesses have tended to remain relatively small in size while new businesses are opened to accommodate an expanding market. Thus the profusion of kiosks throughout Greece is more than just a peculiarity or a coincidence; it is an essential part of a whole economic mentality – the *períptero* mentality – the basis of which may be summed up in the slogan, "One family, one business".

QUEUEING

Americans call it "standing in line". Born of American straight dealing, it falls positively flat next to the elegant British verb, "to queue", from the Latin *cauda*, for "tail". American "lines" exude a democratic egalitarianism; British "queues" demonstrate fair play mixed with social distance. But both reveal a belief in rationality and order.

The Greek version is something else altogether. Can you really call it a "queue"? Waiting at a bus stop in Akademías in central Athens, you can just make out a semblance of

guaranteed seat number, passengers trip all over one another to board the plane. A different body language is no doubt part of the explanation. Greeks are comfortable with their bodies, and they touch each other constantly – in handshakes and kisses of greeting, in the loving pinch to a baby, in the slap on the arm to a comrade – in ways the colder northerners touch only their intimates. So you must interpret no hostility in the face of that old lady whose sharp finger jabs into your back and propels you forward on to the bus.

This impersonality has a logic, though. It's the inverse of the much-vaunted "personalism" of the Greeks, but not its opposite. Greeks don't

linearity among the bodies, if only because the metal rails installed for this purpose nudge them into orderliness. Once the bus appears, however, the pretence collapses and a chaos of anxiously pressing bodies pushes relentlessly through the doorway.

Some Athenians say it's just life in a city bursting its seams – too many passengers squeezing into too few buses. That's indisputable. But you see the same anxious crowding on airport runways where, clutching a boarding pass with a

imagine they live in a rational universe where all things come to those who wait. For Greeks, the universe is arbitrary and unpredictable – and that goes for God, the Turks and the Greek bureaucracy. Life is a struggle. You've got to push forward or you're lost.

For centuries, the little guys have survived through personal ties to the landowner, the grocer, the banker, and by making friends with more powerful men who had means (*méson*) enough to help, or in turn even more powerful friends. Perhaps these chains of influence linking the peasant farmer to the highest ranks in the centres of power are the nearest thing you get to an indigenous queue.

LEFT: although they appear diminutive, pavement kiosks have a multitude of uses.
ABOVE: the Greek queueing system is highly informal.

REMBÉTIKA

An interview with Markos Dragoumis, of the University of Athens' music department

Q: *What is* rembétika? *The old* rembétika *composer Rovertákis said:* "Rembétika *songs were written for people who sing* rembétika *by people who sing* rembétika. *The* rembétis *is a man who had sorrow and threw it out." But what political/historical environment originally brought about* rembétika? *How is its early history linked to the 1922 Asia Minor disaster?*

A: The *rembétika* is the most original kind

FORBIDDEN FRUIT

In the 1920s and '30s, the place to hear *rembétika* was in the *tekédhes* – the dens where workers and wide boys gathered to drink coffee and smoke hashish in small *narghilés* (water-pipes). It was identified as the sound of the urban dispossessed, and the musicians suffered ongoing persecution from the authorities. After the Metaxás dictatorship came to power in 1936, police crackdowns saw many placed behind bars, while possession of a *bouzoúki* became a criminal offence. Under the Colonels, *rembétika* verses were banned – which, ironically enough, merely aided the music's rediscovery by a new generation of rebellious youth.

---

of song to have appeared in Greece over the past 100 years. While a few examples of the type were already known throughout Greece as early as 1930, *rembétika* went on to become more and more popular over the following 15 years – although the style failed to secure any sort of a following among the well-to-do classes. It only received recognition from the "respectable" critics in the 1950s.

Unfortunately, however, we do not know when or where or amongst whom the songs originated. Was it in 1850, in 1880, or in 1910? In Smyrna, on Sýros, or in Piraeus? The destruction of Smyrna in 1922 and the 1923 exchange of populations meant that over a million Asia Minor Greeks poured into the country, many of whom were forced to settle in shantytowns around Athens. Their presence certainly increased the production of *rembétika* songs and speeded up the processes that led to the development of the style's singular quality.

Do you think that in contrast to the rural folk song – often a communal expression of a common sorrow or joy – these urban folk songs are an expression of a more alienated individual?

The words of the *rembétika* certainly express more specialised and individualised feelings than do the demotic or rural folk songs. They also differ to some extent from the demotic songs in their vocabulary and metrical structure, borrowing new elements from the lyrics of the light songs popular in the period between the wars, but using the phraseology in a different way, transforming it from the sugary and insipid into something serious and often tragic.

When and why did rembétika *come back into fashion? What made it possible for a larger audience to appreciate this music?*

Rembétika never completely lost its public. It is simply that in the 1960s this public changed; by now, the music was no longer particularly fashionable in the working-class districts of the towns, where most people had succumbed to the craze for light popular songs and "smooth" *rembétika*. Instead, it found a new following among the students and intellectuals.

These intellectuals initiated the rest of the middle class into the world of *rembétika*, which it had despised. Thus *rembétika* finally addressed itself to everyone, because it brought back a nostalgic and picturesque past, poverty-stricken perhaps, but in a way more carefree and certainly more genuine than the alienated present.

Do you think there's any use in comparing rembétika *with the American blues?*

Not only are the conditions that gave birth respectively to the *rembétika* and the blues completely different, but the vast geographical distance which separates Greece from the United States rules out any mutual influence. So the occasional similarities one meets in the verses are entirely accidental.

What was the role of the rembétissa, *the woman*

become a powerful symbol of the independent woman in Greek society.

Could you tell us something about two of the most important rembétika *instruments, the* bouzoúki *and the* baglamá?

These are very ancient instruments, used by the Assyrians, the Egyptians and the ancient Greeks. In fact, the Greeks never ceased to use them, but from time to time they simply modified them and changed their names. Thus the ancient *pandoúra* or *pandoúris*, the Byzantine *thamboúra* and the post-Byzantine *tamboúras* do not correspond exactly to the modern

who traditionally sang with and inspired the rembétis?

Woman – as mother, daughter, lover – is the central figure in the verses of the *rembétika.* But the title of *rembétissa* is appropriate only to the woman who follows the shiftless life of the *rembétis.* Very importantly, though, she follows him because she has a good voice and wants to *be* someone. She in her turn inspires the men who surround her. Through this process she is able to liberate herself – which is why she has

LEFT: the music is traditional, the electronic amplifiers more recent.
ABOVE: on the hunt for a handmade *bouzoúki.*

bouzoúki, but they certainly belong to the same family. The word "*bouzoúki*" came into Greece from the Lebanon – it is not known when, but it can be found in various demotic songs.

SHADOW PUPPETS

Shadow puppet theatre first emerged in Java, China and India, spreading from there to Turkey and then Greece. Karaghiózis, the Greek version's barefoot, ragged protagonist, takes his name from his prominent black pupils or "*karagöz*" ("black eye" in Turkish).

A short, balding hunchback with a long arm which he uses to club others over the head,

Karaghiózis is comical rather than pathetic. He survives by his cunning, impersonating prominent local personalities as the need arises. These ruses provide only temporary solutions to his problems, and he is often caught, beaten and thrown in jail. Although he frequently moans *"Ach manoúla mou, ti épatha?"* ("Oh Mum, what's befallen me?"), he always reappears undaunted in the next episode.

Figures are designed by the player, and made of painted leather and synthetic materials. Flat, simple silhouettes, they are manipulated by horizontal rods, hinged to facilitate movement. The action takes place behind a semi-transpar-

array of intonations to suit all roles of both sexes. He is judged by his mastery of mimicry of regional dialects and speech defects such as stuttering. Energy and skill are needed to coordinate the actions of the figures with the speech. Besides all this, the player often recites poetry, sings, and plays an instrument such as the guitar for the musical themes often associated with particular characters. Classic plots are adapted to satirise local personalities and events.

Before World War II, Mollas, a famous puppet-master, commented: "A monster has come to us from America." He was referring to the cinema, whose technical sophistication was

ent white screen, back-lit, which makes the figures shine through like stained glass.

Legends about Karaghiós's origins identify him as a Turkish blacksmith who lived during Sultan Orhan's reign (1326–59). While working on a mosque in Bursa, he and his friend, the mason Hadjiavat, had such humorous exchanges that all construction ceased as their fellow workers listened. The enraged sultan had them hanged but was later remorseful; to console him, one of his subjects manipulated likenesses of the two dead men on a screen, and Karaghiózis theatre was born.

Although the Karaghiózis player has assistants, he is still a one-man wonder with a vast

to enrapture the general audience previously devoted to shadow theatre performances. With the emergence of television in Greece in 1969, the shadow plays which were once the entertainment highlight of many a neighbourhood, seemed old-fashioned and naïve.

Fewer than 10 older Karaghiózis players now perform in Greece, with no young apprentices being recruited. Just one summer theatre and a weekly television programme are regularly devoted to shadow theatre. Yet this folk art has not lost its appeal, for Karaghiózis is the embodiment of the innate spirit of the Greek nation. He survives all adversity and starts every new adventure with renewed optimism and energy.

THEODHORÁKIS

Markos Dragoumis discusses the influence of the celebrated Greek composer Míkis Theodhorákis, who is best-known abroad for his sound-track for *Zorba the Greek*.

Q: *What was happening in music during the 1967–74 military junta?*

A: Certain songs which, in the ordinary way, would have circulated freely, went underground, while there was an increase in songs with hinted messages against the dictators; in fact, a kind of resistance activity went on through the medium of song.

Theodhorákis and the ballad-writers of the Néo Kýma *(New Wave) had enough success in the 1960s to ensure that Greek popular music remained largely unchallenged by disco and other Anglo-American imports. Why do you think this happened?*

The 1960s were a time of political unrest and saw the suppression of democratic institutions. Since the words "Greece" and "democracy" are inseparably linked, a tyrannical regime must always be foreign to Greece. In times of slavery all peoples go back to their roots, from which they derive the strength to survive as peoples. Nevertheless, this does not mean that the Greeks turned their backs on music from abroad during this period.

Could you describe some of the differences between the calculated compositions of Theodhorákis, Hadzidhákis and other modern Greek composers who have studied abroad, and rembétika and folk music, which is part of a tradition of spontaneity?

In certain of their songs (especially those written for the cinema), Theodhorákis and Hadzidhákis faithfully follow the spirit of *rembétika*. But in their genuinely important songs they express themselves more personally, and in these one seldom finds striking similarities with *rembétika*, even when these songs have a *bouzoúki* accompaniment.

LEFT: who needs satellite television when the shadow puppeteer's in town?

RIGHT: musical traditions are learned early on.

The public, of course, has its preferences, but it is not uncommon for admirers of modern Greek "composer" songs to like *rembétika* too.

> **A SHIFT TO THE RIGHT**
>
> Composer Mikis Theodhorákis was imprisoned between 1967–70 as a communist dissident. In 1989, however, he was elected an MP for the right-wing ND party.

Even if Greek popular music is not anything like classical, rock, disco or punk, could you still say that it is influenced by the West rather than the East? What is especially noteworthy in the music of Theodhorákis and Hadjidákis – as in quite a number of their successors – is how well they blend the frequently contradictory Western

and Eastern (that is, the Greco-Byzantine) compositional processes. Which sources influence them most? In this matter, surely each composer must choose his own path.

What is the extent of the collaboration that goes on between Greece's contemporary composers and poets?

I don't think we can really talk about "collaboration" between composers and poets. The composers usually open anthologies of poetry and simply set to music those poems which they like, as they like; in fact, they often choose to set the work of poets who are no longer alive, such as Solomós, Kálvos, Sikelianós and Kavadías.

UNFINISHED BUILDINGS

There are many jokes about Greek bureaucracy and endless red tape. It's a well-known fact that in the Greek civil service there are five people to every one job. This may diminish unemployment, but it has its side-effects: it often takes five times longer to do anything, whether it's going through customs, paying road tax, changing money or registering for school.

For many outsiders it is unfathomable that such simple tasks could take so long. But you have only to take into consideration such practices as *hartósima* (the tax stamps) to realise

that efficiency is not one of the main objectives. By law you are required to affix these tax stamps to most official documents, but state offices rarely have a stock. So in the middle of filing an application you must run down to the nearest kiosk to buy some. Then, after climbing four flights of stairs or surviving the ancient elevator crammed with people and coffee-trays, you arrive only to find that the coffee you so charitably balanced on your shoulder in the elevator on the way up was meant for the very civil servant who had been serving you and would therefore hold you up another half an hour.

After his coffee break you find out that you will also need three copies of one page and a passport-sized photograph of yourself taken by a particular photographer on the other side of town... and so the story goes.

One of the main symptoms of this bureaucracy, or *grafiokratía* as the Greeks call it, is the multitude of unfinished buildings that dot the Greek cityscape. If paying road tax takes a day, just think how long a building project could take. It is not unusual for families who have raised the considerable funds needed to get a licence to build from the state to then rush to throw up the frame before the zoning laws change – again.

Cultural expectations shift as well. Twenty years ago, most parents felt obliged to build their daughters houses as part of their dowry, even if it was beyond their means. Now, though a young woman may receive an education as a dowry instead, many of these building projects persist, gaining a floor, a wall, a fence or even an extension every year, as money allows.

VENDETTA

Unlike brigandage, once common throughout Greece, the vendetta tradition was found in only a few regions, where large families, a passionate sensitivity to personal honour and a love for fighting formed an unholy trinity. Epirus was one such feud-ridden region, but the heartland of the Greek vendetta was the Máni. William Leake, visiting the Máni village of Vathiá in 1805, decided not to spend the night there after learning that a feud had been raging for the past 40 years, "in which time they reckon that about a hundred men have been killed".

Some observers, debunking the vendetta "myth", claimed that reports of casualties had been much exaggerated and that there was more shooting than bloodshed. But the 18th-century casebooks of Dr Papadhákis, a Mániot surgeon with a flourishing practice, present a different picture of heads crushed by rocks, bullet-ridden limbs, stiletto and sword wounds being commonplace.

Today, however, the turbulent Máni described by the doctor has subsided into a desolate silence. The main road constructed after the war transformed the old ways. Now the last signs of the vendetta visible to the traveller are the gaunt stone towers in every village – like "bundles of petrified asparagus", as Patrick Leigh Fermor put it – from which rival clans of only a century ago attempted to exterminate one another.

WOMEN

In the traditional view, a woman without a house is as incomplete as a house without a woman. To a modern woman, a house may seem a paltry kingdom to inherit, especially if it is one box in a concrete block. But the link between the woman and the house has been a constant in Greece. Those wealthy merchants' houses of the 18th and 19th centuries which can still be seen in towns such as Kastoriá and Siátista were decorated inside with a painted profusion

VOTES FOR WOMEN

Greek women had to wait until 1956 before their right to vote was universally achieved.

riage chances and the balance of male and female children in families has been critical for economic success or failure. Sons have sacrificed their inheritance to dispose of their sisters, women have been driven to the brink of suicide as their market value plummets in a family crisis.

Attempts are now being made to limit the power of these expectations, and the dowry is technically illegal. In northerly areas the normal pattern is the reverse: it is the man's family which expects to provide a house, or house room, for each new couple. Tradition-

of flowers, fruit and friezes of wide rolling countryside. They were gilded cages for the women whose lives were spent within them.

A woman's relationship to her house, to its physical fabric, affects her whole life. In many areas of Greece (broadly speaking, the south and the islands) there has traditionally been the expectation that the family of a woman who is about to be married will provide a house as well as some furniture and other goods or property. The dowry has strongly affected women's mar-

ally, families extended as the sons married and brought their wives to the parental house where they were subject to the often tyrannical rule of the *petherá* (mother-in-law) who had no doubt suffered at the hands of her own *petherá* when she was the new bride. As families began to expect more comfort and privacy and, it is said, became less willing to have patience with each other, it became normal for only the latest married son to remain at home. Now new houses or flats are routinely made available for the new couple. But in these cases it is still most likely that the mother-in-law will keep a supervisory eye on the household management and child-rearing practices of her son's wife.

LEFT: Máni clansmen built towers like these to defend themselves during fierce local feuds.
ABOVE: the role of women is changing fast.

Once a woman is established in her own house, she can exhibit her worth through the objects in it. As a visitor to a Greek house, you may be shown into the *salóni*, and the shutters may be thrown open in your honour so that every item in the room sucks up light like a sponge. The furniture gleams with a limpid varnish, the mirror-backed cabinet is filled with phalanxes of glasses of every category. There are glinting ornaments in every direction and, above, a formation of globes or crystal drops which defies both gravity and any creep-

> **MADE IN HEAVEN**
>
> Until 1982, adultery was a punishable offence in Greece, with cases regularly brought to court.

ing invasion of darkness at the room's edges.

The challenge to the housewife is clear; every speck of dust which is allowed to settle will be reflected back as two. But all is under her control. Her banner is raised victoriously on every side. Every item of furniture is dressed overall with a festive array of fabrics embroidered, crocheted, tasselled and trimmed. What's more, they are crisply ironed and draped just so, pressed so the corners hang precisely at the midpoint of the table edges, or pushed into ripples by heavy vases.

The visitor who is left alone for a little longer, while the *kyría* goes to make coffee in her back kitchen, may begin to dwell upon the stitches,

the accumulated moments of women's hours and days – subtly toned flowers in blues and reds and gold, with silky green leaves, intricately counted patterns of crosses, and patient repetitions in the millions of brightly coloured tugged loops of a crocheted curtain.

Greek women's handiwork is no mere pastime. It is bound closely to the traditional sense of woman's role and destiny. A young girl learns to sew so that she will be marriageable. These skills symbolise, obscurely, all that she must be. The bride must show that she has the wherewithal to "dress" the house, all the ornamental and comfortable fabrics which will line the nest of marriage. The usually impressive accumulation of both fabrics and furnishings is brought to the new house with some ceremony – in the past on the backs of a string of well-laden mules, now more often in a truck which creeps through village or neighbourhood with the horn sounding and shouts of merriment issuing from the back.

Housework is, of course, a kind of display and in Greece the performance is almost always virtuoso. Many tasks are appropriately done in public view – hanging the washing, beating rugs, airing bedclothes, taking food to the bakeries to be cooked and shopping. A woman's work is manifested to the world.

A powerful tradition

It would be difficult to exaggerate the importance given to marriage in Greece. The feeling that there is no more appropriate mode of living for an adult of either sex is prevalent, and it is widely assumed that monks and nuns who explicitly reject it must have been disappointed in love. The fact that marriage is essential for a complete life is symbolised by the ritual in which a young adult who dies unmarried must be dressed in wedding clothes and, in a poignant ceremony, is "married" in the coffin with a single wedding crown.

The pressure for women to marry is intense. They are given less time to do so than men; an unmarried woman in her late twenties is a matter for concern to her relatives whereas a man can retain his "freedom" (unmarried people are always called "free") until 40 or so. Although child-bearing is their fulfilment, Greek mothers often talk of the suffering involved in having children. They don't just mean the pains of childbirth, either. They expect to suffer anxiety on the child's behalf from its first breath right until it is safely married. They share this suffering with the *Panaghía*, the Virgin Mary, who is the model of womanhood explicitly offered by Greek Orthodoxy, and whose sufferings on behalf of her son are remembered during the course of the Church's year. Women are "Eves", caught in the trammels of human sexuality and only redeem themselves by bearing a child, as the Virgin Mary did.

Quite simply, motherhood means nurture. The mother gives substance to her child while she is pregnant and the process does not stop

pastítsio and *píta*, for example – take hours to prepare and involve a number of different processes. A *hortópita* even requires that the cook should wander the fields in search of the right kinds of greens.

Although the ideal of motherhood is nurturing, ideally a mother should train her family to fast – that is, to control the types of food they eat at certain times in order to achieve religious purity. Fasting is regarded quite flexibly these days in many households, with the consequence that women often casually enquire what other families are eating – so that their standards are neither higher nor lower than the average. Strict

there. Mothers tend to feed their children with great anxiety (a reason sometimes given for preferring bottle-feeding is that "at least you can see what it has eaten"). Unfortunately many a Greek child is aware of this and exploits the mother's sensitivity on this matter.

The degree of a mother's love for her family can be represented by the effort she puts into preparing food. If she produces boiled macaroni day after day she will be aware that she is skimping. The favourite dishes – *dolmádhes*,

LEFT: widowed women still habitually dress in black.
ABOVE: life is hard in the rural areas, where women may lack the benefit of modern conveniences.

fasting means abstention from meat, all animal products and oil. Special dishes are made with oil and vegetables as a kind of intermediary level of restraint.

There are women, mostly old, whose faces light up as they say, during a fast period, "Not a drop of oil have I eaten, not a drop…", who take their gift of abstention to the Vespers every evening and appear to enjoy a peaceful detachment from physical needs. These women may be viewed with suspicion by the less devout and the irreligious, lest they start to use their piety as a ground for judging others. For families there is a balance of opposing values to be maintained, for to make children fast more than is generally thought to be necessary is a denial of motherly love.

Changed values

Today both old and new values coexist – the importance of being a wife and mother with the importance of being able to earn a good income. What has remained important has been the need for a woman to know that she has value. Where a woman's dowry has been external to herself she has been able to feel, once she is married, a certain solidity and security in relation to her husband. Where her value has been symbolised by the trivia of household fur-

nishing she has still had a means of display and self-presentation. Now more substantial, though less visible, qualities are being appreciated: education, competence, the quality of being a *drastíria*, a "woman of action". But these new values do not necessarily mean freedom, and certain visible indicators of a woman's character – the way she dances, what she drinks, whether she smokes – are still given weight. Most of all, a woman is still expected to be linked to a family.

This is the most shocking thing about foreign women in Greece. Women travelling in Greece are often a little unnerved by the separation of men's and women's worlds. Add to this the obvious attentions from men which foreign women attract in areas accustomed to tourism and the female traveller is left wondering how she is viewed by locals.

Because Greek fathers and brothers have traditionally been the guardians of female sexuality (the assumption being that individuals of either sex are not all that good at saying "no" on their own account), women who evidently have freedom of movement and economic independence are thought likely to be unconstrained in other ways. In this, they resemble men. Foreign women are often given small chances to be "pseudo-men", offered cigarettes or strong drink (offers which women from small villages would take as a joke or an insult, but which Greek city women take in their stride) and even a seat in a *kafenío*. Acceptance of "privileges" such as these makes overt the foreign woman's peculiar position.

Women are likely to respond to the visiting anomaly with a barrage of questions: *"Mamá, babá, zoúneh?"* ("Mum, Dad, are they alive?"); *"Adélfia?"* ("Brothers and sisters?"); and, pointing to the ring finger of the right hand, *"Andras?"* ("Don't you have a husband?"). These are not routine polite enquiries but attempts to clarify what is, for them, the most important thing about a person – the link with their family responsibilities.

How visitors are viewed

The traveller can, of course, conduct herself as she wishes. She can allow herself to be placed in the sexually free category or she can emphasise that she's a nice family girl. But, powerful as these stereotypes are, there is no need for them to be pushed into either. There is such a strong sense of "how we do things" that there is a corresponding streak of open-mindedness in most Greeks, who are ready to accept that in your country you obviously do things differently.

This acceptance of other values is having to be exercised more and more within the Greek family, between generations. The family's sphere of interests was once visibly contained within its own four walls and its fields. Now it is inter-penetrated by the world, by television, by education, by its members' movements throughout Greece and further afield. But it represents, still, the front line of contact with the real moral issues of human weakness, human needs and mortality. This is where women are effectively at work.

XENOMANÍA

As a small country, Greece has always had to contend with the *xénos*, the foreigner. Whether as invader or visitor, the *xénos* has had a big impact on the Greek conception of self. A *xénos* isn't simply a non-Greek, he or she might be a Greek from another town. In the past when a woman married a man from over the mountain she married a *xénos*. The songs sung at her wedding were often laments wishing her well in the "after-life". But whereas 50 years ago it was

THE RISE OF TOURISM

Greece has over 10 million annual visitors, who bring over $2.5 billion a year in tourist revenue.

can earn three times their salary by renting out spare rooms to foreigners may not reflect too much about architectural aesthetics or the possible influx of unsavoury modern mores – the sex, drugs and rock'n'roll variety – when they decide they are going to add some more guest rooms to the family house.

Another interesting thing about Greek tourism is the way it attends to foreigners' material needs but still obstinately refuses to accommodate their different pace of life. A trendy hotel on Hydra (Ídhra), for example, may serve all

xenophobia (*xenofovía*) which predominated, today its flip side, *xenomanía*, is by far the more prevalent.

Tourism has been on the rise since the early 1960s. By the end of the 1980s, it was bringing in almost as much money as all other industries combined – from olive oil to scuba masks to large-scale machinery. But *xenomanía* is not without its problems; in many ways Greece was not prepared for such a development. For example, a baker and his wife on Amorgós who

the right cocktails in its bar but the owner will refuse to get up before 10am to fix breakfast. According to him, no one who is anyone gets up that early. He hasn't thought that a trendy young German may not have the same sleeping habits as a trendy young Greek.

The speed with which Greece has become a holiday success story has meant that until recently it was more equipped for backpackers than the clientele of luxury liners. But this, too, is changing as the Greeks realise that they need to attract the latter in order to profit from tourism. Tourists can now expect more varied services – and also, perhaps, a less manic reception; neither *xenofovía* nor *xenomanía*, but *xenofilia*.

LEFT: being a *drastíria* – a woman of action – is a quality now accepted by society.
ABOVE: tourism brings mixed benefits.

YOGHURT

Rich, thick and creamy (the best still available in small clay pots rather than the more convenient plastic containers) in its commercial form, or tart and slippery in the *spitikó* (home-made) version, Greek yoghurt is a much more substantial food than the watery stuff you find elsewhere. Indeed, the American habit of "drinking" a yoghurt for lunch is completely unfathomable to a Greek.

Yoghurt is neither a beverage nor a meal. It has its own peculiar culinary function. Like parentheses, it separates the meal from the rest of daily activities. It cleans the palate, and helps

digestion. Meals often start with a plate of *tsatzíki* (a delicious thick spread of yoghurt, cucumber and garlic) or finish with a bowlful smothered in the region's honey and walnuts.

Once upon a time tourists would take back pockets full of pebbles and shells as mementos of their trip. These days, they can forego the fuss – a quick trip to the supermarket now provides all the ingredients for real Greek *tsatzíki*. And although British commercial brands of yoghurt barely resemble their tangy, crusty *spitikó* counterpart, a good imagination can still conjure up the smell of thyme and oregano and the distant bells of sheep and goats scampering across a mountainside.

ZORBA

Nobody has done more for the image of the earthy, passionate, impulsive Hellenic hedonist than Hollywood's ethnic chameleon, Anthony Quinn. Níkos Kazantzákis may have invented Zorba but only Quinn could have danced that lusty rogue of a peasant into the hearts of millions. Kudos must go, too, to director Elia Kazan, who captured in stark black-and-white the austerity (of the social mores no less than the mountains and architecture) of a highland village on Crete.

Though most foreigners know him as "Zorba the Greek", the novel is titled *The Life and Adventures of Aléxis Zorbás* – Kazantzákis would have found "the Greek" superfluous. In fact, Zorba was a real person – George Zorbas, a Macedonian labourer and adventurer with whom the author embarked upon an unsuccessful lignite-mining scheme in the Máni.

He may have been mortal once, but Zorba has acquired mythic qualities. He's a modern stereotype, perhaps, but with a distinguished lineage. European elites long regarded peasants as "noble savages" close to home, and romantic literature and travellers' accounts abound with rustic peasants dancing their troubles away. In Greece, there's a special twist; the peasants' "wild" dances and "discordant" music get likened to ancient Dionysian revels.

Yet however trivialised they have become, Zorba and his predecessors represent quite sober explorations of a very old philosophical problem in Greece: the power of passion and the limits of reason. This has also been a core issue of Orthodoxy, whose rational, worldly power has always coexisted with the most mystical of theologies. This otherworldly faith flourished in the sensuous landscape (from rugged hills to orange groves) of Kazantzákis's beloved Crete.

Kazantzákis was preoccupied with spiritual questions all his life. Though he eventually left the Orthodox Church, there is no doubt that his own personal conflicts over sex as well as his literary themes come from some early religious experiences. His novel about Zorba explores the problem of body and soul which obsessed him.

In the story, "the Boss" – who many say was really Kazantzákis himself – is an intellectual trapped in a world of words, struggling to escape from "pen-pushing". He keeps himself from sin by repressing all feelings of desire for forbidden things – indeed, for all sensual engagement. Yet he is totally unable to act.

The Boss's paralysis finds its antithesis in Zorba, who confronts his desires – for food, for wine, for the charms of women – naturally, even defiantly. Kazantzákis may be forgiven his hint of romanticism, for the rude peasant here is not just noble but wise. It's the scholar who needs to be taught by Zorba, the unlettered labourer who "knows himself".

Zorba as a celluloid, rather than a literary, figure, is somehow apt, for words are not his *forte*. Despite his pearls of earthy wisdom

ic self-assertion before a sceptical public, about the pleasures and tensions of sociability, about passion and control.

If foreigners barely understand what dancing, feasting, even smashing plates, mean to Greeks, we nonetheless find the exuberance we see there irresistible. For in Zorba and the rest we are able to discern a spontaneity and collective *bonhomie* which has somehow got lost in the sterile anonymity of our own more industrialised societies. This is why Greeks and foreigners alike keep Zorba alive, because Zorba is "good to think with" – not just about Greeks, but about ourselves. ❏

(laced with Quinn's exclamations in superbly accented Greek) Zorba knows the limits of words. When something profound happens – like the death of his daughter – Zorba must dance! Be it ecstasy or sorrow, he seems to say, the body is better at translating the ineffable.

Zorba, Mélina, Dionysios, the dancing Greek reincarnated under tourism in various distorted guises to sell everything from package holidays to tape cassettes, still expresses something about what it means to be Greek: about dramat-

---

LEFT: the name *Zorba* has become a modern Greek stereotype, selling everything from T-shirts to menus.
ABOVE: plaque marking author Níkos Kazantzákis.

A NON-CONFORMIST LIFE

Thanks to his unorthodox views and writings, Níkos Kazantzákis was to court controversy not only throughout his life – but even after his death in 1957. When his book *The Last Temptation of Christ* was first published, the Orthodox Church sought to prosecute him. When it was made into a film in 1958, Athenian priests marched on the cinemas and projection screens were slashed in anger. Today, admirers can make for the Kazantzákis Museum in the village of Mirtiá, 24 km/15 miles due south of Iráklio, where well-arranged displays illustrate what can be regarded as an extraordinary literary and political life.

PLACES

*A detailed guide to the entire country, with principal sites
cross-referenced by number to the maps*

As Henry Miller wrote in *The Colossus of Maroussi*, "marvellous things happen to one in Greece – marvellous *good* things which can happen to one nowhere else on earth. Somehow, almost as if He were nodding, Greece still remains under the protection of the Creator. Men may go about their puny, ineffectual bedevilment, even in Greece, but God's magic is still at work and, no matter what the race of men may do or try to do, Greece is still a sacred precinct – and my belief is it will remain so until the end of time."

It is easy to fall in love with Greece – its beauty is self-evident. Travellers return time after time, for the mirror-smooth Aegean Sea shimmering in the still of the morning, for the *kafenía* with their rickety tables offering some shade from the blistering afternoon heat, and for the silvery olive groves where the cicadas drone at evening time. It is a land for connoisseurs and explorers, with an ancient inheritance that remains relevant to this day. The Acropolis in Athens, the oracle sites at Delphi and the ruins of Olympia are places of unique importance in western culture.

In this section, our expert writers will take you on 12 individual journeys, each author to the part of Greece he or she knows best. Starting with the capital, Athens and then heading up to the northeastern corner of the country near Turkey and Bulgaria, we'll travel in a zigzag fashion down to Crete; en route, you'll find the history, geography and local culture of each area covered in detail. All the sites of special interest are numbered on specially drawn maps to help you find your way around.

The sections have been loosely designed as two-week itineraries, but of course the longer you stay, the better. Perhaps, like Lord Byron, you will one day be able to declare: "It is the only place I ever was contented in." ❑

PRECEDING PAGES: fishing-boats moored off Kálymnos; a dramatic setting for little Kastráki town in Thessaly; ancient olive-grove, Crete.
LEFT: sun, sea . . . and the radiant Aegean light.

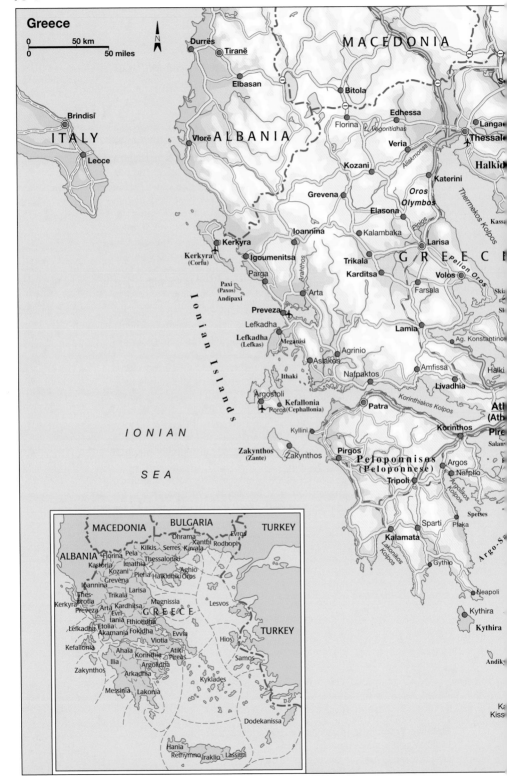

Greece

0 — 50 km
0 — 50 miles

N

Durrës
Tiranë

MACEDONIA

Elbasan

Bitola

S

Brindisi

Edhessa

Florina   L. Vegoritidhas

Langa

ITALY

Vlorë **ALBANIA**

Veria

Thessal

Lecce

Kozani   Aliakmonas

Halki

Katerini

Grevena

Oros
Olympos

Thermekos Kolpos

Elasona

Pinios   Kassa

Ioannina   **Kalambaka**

Larisa

Kerkyra

Igoumenitsa

Aranthos

Trikala

GREEC

Pelion Oros

Kerkyra
(Corfu)

Parga

Karditsa

Volos

Paxi
(Paxos)
Andipaxi

Arta

Farsala   Ski

Sl

Preveza

Lefkadha

Lamia

Lefkadha
(Lefkas)   Meganisi

Ag. Konstantino

Agrinio

Aslakos

Ithaki

Nafpaktos

Amfissa

Halki

Livadhia

Argostoli

Kefallonia
Poros (Cephallonia)

Patra

Korinthiakos Kolpos

At
(Ath

Korinthos

Pire

I O N I A N

Kyllini

Salan

Zakynthos
(Zante)   Zakynthos

Pirgos

Peloponnisos
(Peloponnese)

Argos

Nafplio

S E A

Tripoli

Argolikos Kolpos

Spetses

Sparti   Plaka

Kalamata

Argos-S

Lakonikos Kolpos

Gythio

MACEDONIA   BULGARIA   TURKEY

Dhrama   Evros
Xanthi   Rodhopi
Kilkis Serres Kavala

ALBANIA Florina Pela
Kastoria Imathia Thessaloniki
Kozani Pieria Aghio
Grevena   Halkidhiki Oros
Ioannina
Thes-   Larisa   Trikala
protia Kardhitsa   Magnissia   Lesvos
Kerkyra Arta Evri
Preveza   tania Fthiotidha
Lefkadha Etolia   **GREECE**
Akarnania Fokidha   Evvia
Viotia   Hios
Kefallonia
Ahaïa   Atiki
Ilia   Korinthia Pireas   Samos
Argolidha
Zakynthos   Arkadhia
Kyklades
Messinia Lakonia

TURKEY

Kythira

Kythira

Andik

Dodekanissa

Hania
Rethymno Iraklio Lassithi

Ka
Kiss

Neapoli

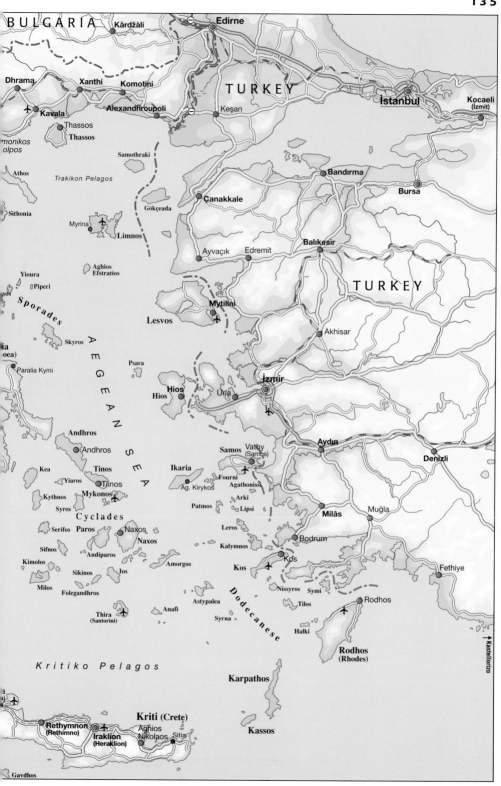

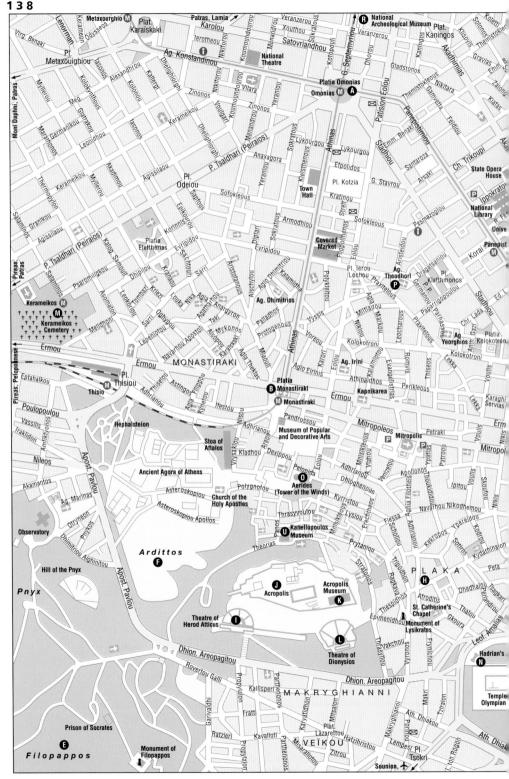

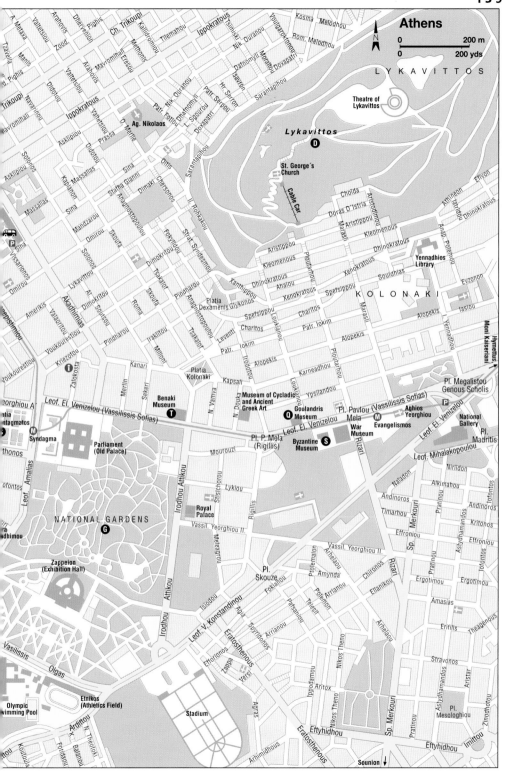

ATHENS

Both East and West converge in this vibrant metropolis, lively and brimming over, just like its inhabitants – and home, too, to some of the country's most important historical sites

Map, pages 138–9

If there is one quality which Athens should be credited with unreservedly, it is elasticity. It might be compared to an indestructible old sweater which has shrunk and stretched repeatedly through the centuries, changing its shape as circumstances required.

Athens is barely mentioned in Homer. It emerged as a growing power in the 6th century BC. Then came the Periclean high noon, when Athens became a great centre of art and literature, commerce and industry. With Macedonian expansion came the first shrinkage, though Athens remained a prestigious intellectual centre with particular emphasis on philosophy and oratory.

In the Hellenistic age, Athens was overshadowed by the great monarchies founded by Alexander's successors – but not obliterated. The rulers of Egypt, Syria, Pergamum courted the old city with gifts of buildings and works of art. Yet it was already beginning to rest on its laurels, to turn into a museum-city, a "cultural commodity" rather than an active, living organism. Besieged and sacked by Sulla in 86 BC, restored and pampered under two philathenian Roman emperors, Augustus and Hadrian, sacked again by the Herulians in AD 267 and Alaric the Goth in AD 395, Athens entered the Byzantine era shorn of all its glory – a small provincial town, a mere backwater. The edict of the Byzantine emperor Justinian forbidding the study of philosophy there (AD 529) dealt the death-blow to the ancient city.

PRECEDING PAGES: the Acropolis. **LEFT:** aerial manoeuvres. **BELOW:** this 17th-century icon is in the Byzantine Museum.

A sudden elevation

Under Latin rule (1204–1456), invaded, occupied and fought over by the French, Catalans, Florentines and Venetians, Athens shrank even further. It was only after the Ottoman conquest in the 15th century that it began to expand again, but still falling far short of its ancient limits. There were more setbacks, including a devastating Venetian incursion in 1687. Athens finally rose from its ruins after the War of Independence, an "exhausted city", as Christopher Wordsworth noted in 1832, and was suddenly raised, unprepared, to the status of capital of the new Greek state.

Athens is thus a city that has grown haphazardly, and too fast. It never had a chance to mellow into venerable old age. Old and new have not blended too well; you can still sense the small prewar city pushing through the huge sprawl of today's modern capital, like the proverbial thin man struggling to get out of every fat man. Occasionally, you come across what must have been a country villa, ensconced between tall office buildings, its owner still fighting against the tide, its windows hermetically closed against dust, pollution, the roar of the traffic

Traffic in Athens can be unbelievable, particularly when there is some protest demonstration going on

small chain of stone or wooden "worry-beads" – is good for relieving tension.

and traffic is forced off the main streets. The new metro, however, has worked wonders. From the day it opened, huge numbers of Athenians have been using it, making journeys of just a few minutes through the heart of the city that once took well over an hour by car. Suddenly, central Athens has become accessible.

But branching off from the frenzied central arteries are the minor veins of the city, relatively free from congestion. Most apartment blocks have balconies and verandas, and there you can see the Athenians in summer emerging from their afternoon siesta in underpants and nighties, reading the paper, watching the neighbours, watering their plants, eating their evening meal.

The hot weather makes life in the open air a necessity; this in turn means gregariousness – it is no accident that there is no Greek word for "privacy" – though nowadays the pale-blue flicker of television draws more and more people indoors. Yet even television sometimes turns into an excuse for the Athenian's unique brand of social exhibitionism: there are improvised World Cup parties and election-night parties, collective viewing while eating, drinking and playing cards.

Taxis, too, are something of a communal institution. They are cheap in Athens and therefore in great demand. If you're lucky enough to get one, you soon find you have to share it with others. But what began as a necessity has evolved into one more occasion for social exchange, whether heated argument or comfortable chatting. Are the Athenians then such sociable and fun-loving creatures? Not really; they are simply easily bored and immensely restless. Byron called the Greeks "an intriguing cunning unquiet generation".

There is a constant struggle to catch up with the West while still clinging to the old traditional ways. Tavernas, competing with pizza and fast-food shops, try to keep up a semblance of *couleur locale* (which is fast turning into *couleur*

BELOW: angelic dreams in the National Gardens.

internationale: you find better *taramosaláta* in London supermarkets than in Athens). Arranged marriages are still going strong, but the matchmaker is now competing with a computer service. Doughnuts and *koulourákia*, popcorn and *passatémbo*; a priest, majestic in flowing black robes, licking an ice-cream cone or riding a motorbike – unthinkable ten or 15 years ago. Coexistence – but the edges are still jagged.

Map, pages 138–9

City streets

The city's heart lies within an almost equilateral triangle defined by **Platí Omónias ◊** in the north, **Monastiráki ◊** in the south, and **Platía Sýntagmatos ◊** to the southeast. Except for three small cross streets, no cars are permitted in this area, which means it has taken on a new lease of life. **Ermou**, once a traffic-clogged mess, is now a long pedestrian walkway with reinvigorated shops, enlivened by pavement buskers and push-carts. Many buildings have been refurbished, while improved lighting makes this an attractive area to wander in the evening in search of the perfect taverna.

The entire area is a huge sprawl of shops, more upmarket towards Platí Sýntagmatos. Monastiráki brings to mind the market described in a 2nd-century BC comedy by Euboulo: "Everything will be for sale together in the same place at Athens, figs, summoners, bunches of grapes, turnips, pears, apples, witnesses, roses, medlars, honeycombs, chickpeas, lawsuits, beestings-puddings, myrtleberries, allotment machines, irises, lambs, waterclocks, laws, indictments."

Beestings-puddings and allotment machines sound mysterious enough, but the weird assortment of objects to be found in the market today is just as intriguing. Kitsch-collectors will find much to interest them; Greek kitsch is perhaps the

ABOVE: traditional sandals for sale, Monastiráki.
BELOW: the Theatre of Herod Atticus.

most orgiastically hideous in the world. Mass-produced trinkets for the tourist trade abound, too. Indeed, even the shops around the **Mitrópolis**, specialising in ecclesiastical articles, have turned touristy; perhaps the manufacturers have caught on to the fact that tourists often find bronze candle-stands just the thing for a garden-party; a priest's heavily embroidered robes could be turned into a stunning evening dress in no time at all, while pectoral crosses outshine the flashiest *faux bijoux*.

But move away from the robust vulgarity of **Pandróssou Street** to the narrow side streets off the **Flea Market**, and you step back into time into an almost pre-industrial era. This is the district of traditional crafts (crafts minus "arts"), wholesale shops selling refreshingly non-decorative, down-to-earth stuff like screws, chains of varying thickness, nails, boxes and crates, brushes and brooms, mousetraps and herbs (the mountains of Greece are a botanist's paradise), shops selling resin in big amber-coloured chunks alongside incense and bright blue chunks of sulphate of copper used for plants (and catching octopus) – truly a serendipitous accumulation.

As are the goods in the old covered market, a 19th-century gem roughly halfway between Monastiráki and Omónia squares on the north side of **Athinás Street** (you can also enter far more dramatically from the passageway at 80 Eólou Street). This is the city's main meat and fish market, crowded with shoppers milling between open stands displaying fish, seafood and any variety of poultry and meat you can imagine, all being loudly praised by vendors. Fruit and vegetables are available in the far less successful open area directly across Athinás Street to the south, but the milling scene there is just as vibrant.

ABOVE: vase for sale, Pláka district. **BELOW:** classical kitsch abounds.

Head for the hills

There's a peaceful busyness in these narrow streets. Yet only a few steps beyond, you are back in the great melting-pot, the high-rise buildings, the fumes, the heat. The saving grace of Athens is that there are easy – and visible – ways out. Just when you're feeling buried alive in the asphalt jungle, you see at the end of a street a fragment of mountain, a slice of open country, trees – peaceful breathing outlets.

Athens is full of bumps, some big enough to deserve the name of hills, others mere excrescences. Eight of them have been counted (one up on Rome!) but there may be more. There's **Mount Lycabettus** (Lykavittós) **D**, of course (you can't miss it); the equally conspicuous rock of the **Acropolis**, flanked by the **Pnyx** on one side, and the hill of **Philopappus** (Filopáppos) **E** on the other, where Athenians fly kites on the first day of Lent; the hill of **Ardittós F**, next to the marble horseshoe **stadium**, built by Herod Atticus in AD 143 and totally reconstructed in 1896 (the first modern Olympic Games were held there); the hill of the **Nymphs**, capped by the grey dome of the **Observatory**; the barren, windblown **Tourkovoúnia**; and the hill of **Lófos Stréfi**, the poor man's Lycabettus (it's far less touristy, and the efforts of landscape-gardeners appear more strenuous here than on the other hills).

Along with the small hidden cafés there is more

than a measure of coolness on some of these hills. For a real escape, however, you have to go further afield, up one of the three mountains that encircle Athens. **Mount Hymettus** (Ymettó), 5 km (3 miles) east of Athens, beloved of honey-bees, glowing violet at sunset, is perhaps the most beautiful. Driving up the winding road past the monastery of **Kaisarianí** you reach a tranquil vantage-point from which to contemplate the whole of Attica. The city is panoramically visible, yet totally, eerily inaudible. On **Mount Párnitha** (Parnés), just over an hour northwest, you can walk in a dark wilderness of fir trees, play roulette at the casino, ski in winter. **Mount Pendéli**, to the north, is crowded, lively, pop-ular, with all the ensuing disadvantages: the air is thick with *souvláki*-smoke and the screams of overactive children.

But if you're not much of a climber, you can escape to the **National Gardens** (open sunrise to sunset; free), within a stone's throw of the Byzantine, Benáki and War museums. Walk down **Herod Atticus Street**, watch – if you must – the changing of the *Évzone* Guard (whom Hemingway referred to as "those big tall babies in ballet skirts"), then turn right, into the park. Suddenly there is thick shade, tangled bowers, romantic arbours, and relative quiet.

Do not expect anything as lush or generous as the green expanses, lakes and cascades of other European parks. Here are only modest fish-ponds, thin but constant trickles of water running along secret leafy troughs; ducks, and a large population of cats, fed (and neutered) by Athens's few committed animal-lovers. Cicadas whirr away, peacocks cry, mournful for all their spotted blue-green glory. Here you can observe the Athenians at rest; lovers meet, old men medi-tate, mothers brood, businessmen hastily wolf sandwiches and weary hitch-hikers sleep on wisteria-shaded benches.

Map, pages 138–9

TIP

Take the funicular up Mount Lycabettus (Lykavittós) for a spectacular view – it starts from Ploutárhou Street, near Platía Kolonáki, and runs every 20 minutes in summer, 8am–10pm.

BELOW: *Évzone* Guard in traditional ceremonial dress.

There is also a solitary, unexpected stretch of green lawn on **Vasilissis Sofías Avenue**; beautifully designed, it serves as the setting for the giant bronze statue of the eminent statesman Venizélos (1864–1936), who seems on the point of plunging into the traffic, and then thinking better of it. If you climb over the green slope to the back of the site, you come upon the **Park of Freedom**. It is not a park, by any stretch of the imagination; as for the word freedom, it has here a propitiatory (perhaps expiatory) function; during the military dictatorship (1967–74) this was the HQ of the dreaded military police, where dissidents were detained and tortured.

Today, there is a pleasant café, a lecture-hall, a tiny open-air theatre. The torture-chambers have been turned into a museum, posing again that difficult moral problem: what does one do with places like this? Cover them up, preserve them, embellish them? Remember or forget? Remembrance may breed hatred, oblivion begets apathy. Here the effort seems to have been to preserve and transform at the same time; to commemorate the horror while creating around it an atmosphere in which the ghosts may be laid to rest.

Not particularly green but certainly an oasis is **Pláka** , the old quarter clustering at the foot of the Acropolis. Now refurbished and restored to its former condition (or rather to a fairly good reproduction of it), the garish nightclubs and discos have been closed down, motor-vehicles prohibited (for the most part), houses repainted and streets tidied up. It has become a delightful, sheltered place to meander in; you might almost imagine yourself in a village, miles from the urban monster below. It is full of small beauties, too: look out for the Byzantine churches, the Tower of the Winds, the Old University, the fragmented ancient arches and walls.

Night moves

Most nocturnal activities (restaurants, cafés, theatres, cinemas) take place in the open air. Yet do not mistake the open-air cinemas for drive-ins; they have rows of seats like ordinary cinemas, and the only customers on wheels are the midnight babies brought there in their pushchairs by their harassed mothers and silenced with ice-cream. As for theatres, apart from the **Herod Atticus Theatre** ❶ there is a large one on Mount Lycabettus (used mostly for concerts of modern music) along with several abandoned quarries which have been converted into theatres, all providing starkly dramatic settings for their – generally high-quality – productions.

The night is long in Athens; Athenians fiercely resist sleep, or make up for lost night-sleep with a long afternoon siesta (caution: *never* telephone an Athenian between 2pm and 6pm). Cafés and bars stay open until the small hours; bars and pubs here are unlike those of other European capitals; they are larger, they have tables, provide music (usually loud) and serve food (usually expensive) as well as drinks.

Three o'clock in the morning, and the traffic still won't give up; groups linger on street-corners, good-nights take forever. The main streets are never entirely deserted; perhaps this is one of the reasons why Athens is a safe city to walk in at night, except for

Map,
pages
138–9

he occasional bag-snatcher, for real violence is rare. The "unquiet generation" inally goes to bed; verandas and balconies go dark, cats prowl, climbing jasmine smells stronger – and all the conflicting elements in the patchwork city eem momentarily resolved in the brief summer night.

Seeing the sites

Seen from the right angle driving up the **Ierá Odós** (the Sacred Way) or looking up at its rocky bulk from high in Pláka, the **Acropolis ❶** still has a presence that makes the grimy concrete of modern Athens fade into insignificance. Climb up in early morning in summer or early afternoon in winter, when the crowds are thinnest, and a strip of blue sea edged with grey hills marks the horizon. On a wet or windy day, walking across its uneven limestone surface feels like being on a ship's deck in a gale (open summer: Mon–Fri 8am–6.30pm; Sat–Sun 8.30am–2.30pm; winter: daily 8.30am–2.30pm; entrance fee.

The Acropolis nowadays looks like a stonemason's workshop, much as it must have done in the 440s BC when the **Parthenon** was under construction as the crowning glory of Pericles' giant public works programme. Some of his contemporaries thought it extravagant: Pericles was accused of dressing his city up like a harlot. In fact, the Parthenon celebrates Athena as a virgin goddess and the city's protector. Her statue, 12 metres (39 ft) tall and constructed of ivory and gold plate to Phidias's design, once gleamed in its dim interior; in late antiquity it was taken to Constantinople, where it disappeared.

Conservators have lifted down hundreds of blocks of marble masonry from the Parthenon to replace the rusting iron clamps inserted in the 1920s with non-corrosive titanium (rust made the clamps expand, cracking the stone, while acid

ABOVE: exhibit in the Acropolis Museum.
BELOW: a peaceful corner, Pláka.

Towering above Athens on its white, rocky platform, the Acropolis has a history mirroring that of the city.

rain turned carved marble surfaces into soft plaster). The restorers also succeeded in identifying and collecting about 1,600 chunks of Parthenon marble scattered over the hilltop, many blown off in the 1687 explosion caused by a Venetian mortar igniting Ottoman munitions stored inside the temple. When they are replaced, about 15 percent more building will be on view. New blocks cut from near the ancient quarries on Mount Pendéli (14 km/9 miles north of Athens), which supplied the 5th-century BC constructors, will fill the gaps.

The **Erechtheion**, an elegant architecturally complex repository of ancient cults going back to the Bronze Age, is already restored. The Caryatids now supporting a porch over the tomb of King Kekrops, a mythical founder of the ancient Athenian royal family, are modern copies. The surviving originals were removed to the Acropolis Museum to prevent further damage from the *néfos*, the ochre blanket of atmospheric pollution often hanging over Athens.

Completed in 395 BC, a generation later than the Parthenon, the Erechtheion also housed an early wooden statue of Athena, along with the legendary olive tree that she conjured out of the rock to defeat Poseidon the sea god in their contest for sovereignty over Attica. In Ottoman times, the building was used by the city's Turkish military commander as a billet for his harem.

The **Propylaia**, the battered official entrance to the Acropolis built by Mnesikles in the 430s BC, was cleverly designed with imposing outside columns to awe people coming up the hill. Parts of its coffered stone ceiling, once painted and gilded, are still visible as you walk through. And roped off on what was once the citadel's southern bastion is the small, square temple of **Athena Nike** finished in 421 BC. It supposedly stands on one of the spots – the other is at Cape Sounion – where Theseus's father, King Aegeus, threw himself to his death on

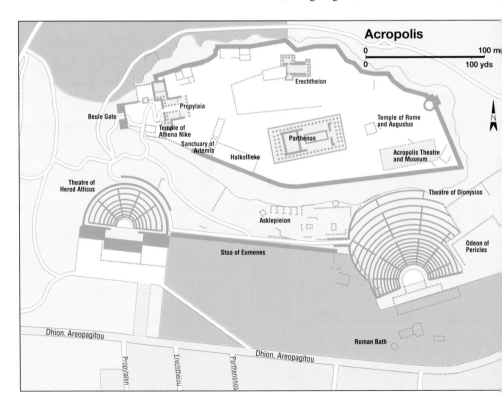

seeing a black-sailed ship approaching the harbour. Theseus had promised to hoist a white sail for the return voyage if he succeeded in killing the Minotaur on Crete, but carelessly forgot.

The sculptures that Lord Elgin left behind are in the **Acropolis Museum** Ⓚ. The four surviving Caryatids that are in Greece (one was taken by the Ottomans and lost, another is in the British Museum in London) stare out from a nitrogen filled case, scarred but still impressively female. The coquettish *koraï* reveal a pre-classical ideal: if you look closely, you can still make out the traces of make-up and earrings, and the patterns of their crinkled, close-fitting dresses (open summer: Mon–Fri 8.30am–6.30pm; Sat–Sun 8.30am–2.30pm; winter: daily 8.30am–2.30pm; entrance fee included in Acropolis entrance fee).

The Acropolis was mainly used for religious purposes. Situated north of the Acropolis, the ancient Greek **Agora** was for all public purposes; commercial, religious, political, civic, educational, theatrical, athletic. Today it looks like a cluttered field of ruins. If archeologists had their way, the whole of Pláka would have been levelled. The reconstructed **Stoa of Attalos**, a 2nd-century BC shopping mall, contains a wonderful, small architectural museum (open Tues–Sun 8.30am–3pm; entrance fee included in ancient Greek agora site fee). The **Hephaisteion**, the Doric temple opposite, will help you appreciate that the Parthenon is truly a masterpiece (entrance on Adhrianou Street or below the Areopagus; open Tues–Sun 8.30am–3pm; entrance fee).

Across from the Agora, on the far side of the Piraeus metro line, one corner of the **Painted Stoa** has been exposed in Adhrianoú Street. This building gave its name to Stoicism, the stiff-upper-lip brand of philosophy that Zeno the Cypriot taught there in the 3rd century BC.

Map, pages 138–9

In his 1811 poem "The Curse of Minerva", Byron angrily wishes vengeance beyond the grave on Lord Elgin, on Minerva's (or Athena's) behalf, for removing sculptures from the Parthenon's frieze.

BELOW: the Erechtheion was completed in 395 BC, a generation after the Parthenon.

A GAME OF MARBLES

Britain calls them the Elgin Marbles, but to the Greeks they are the Parthenon Marbles. They are a 76m² (500ft²) stretch of sculpted figures – mostly from the frieze – carved under the direction of the master-sculptor and architect Phidias himself. By 1799, when Lord Elgin was appointed British ambassador to Turkish-occupied Greece, the Parthenon was in a sorry state, having been damaged by a powder-keg explosion in 1687 (the Ottomans used it as a munitions depot), and by a series of plunderers. In 1801 Elgin negotiated a permit from the sultan to remove "some blocks of stone with inscriptions and figures", shipped the marbles back to Britain, and in 1816 sold them to the British Museum, where they remain today.

A new museum is now being planned for the slopes of the Acropolis, where all the sculptures may be housed together, in controlled conditions which will prevent pollution damage. The marbles are an integral part of one of the most beautiful buildings that still survives from antiquity, say the Greeks, and can be better appreciated in the city that made them. The British, on the other hand, claim that they have acquired nine points of the law by careful possession, and that to return the marbles would set a disastrous precedent. The debate continues.

ABOVE: statue housed in the Great Mitrópolis church.
BELOW: an Athenian pleasure: eating outdoors in Pláka.

On the south side of the Acropolis lies the **Theatre of Dionysios** ⬤. The marble seating tiers that survive date from around 320 BC and later, but scholars are generally agreed that plays by the likes of Aeschylus, Sophocles, Euripides and Aristophanes were first staged here at religious festivals during the 5th century BC. A state subsidy for theatre-goers meant that every Athenian citizen could take time off to attend (entrances on Leofóros Dhionissíou Areopayítou and above the Herod Atticus theatre; open daily 8.30am–2.30pm; entrance fee).

Past Monastiráki, the **Kerameikós Cemetery** ⬤ in the potters' district of the city, was a burial place for prominent ancient Athenians. An extraordinary variety of sculptured monuments – tall stone urns, a prancing bull, winged sphinxes and melancholy scenes of farewell – overlooked the paved Sacred Way leading to the Dipylon Gate from Eleusis, where the mysteries were held. The site museum's collection of grave goods is a magnificent guide to Greek vase-painting: from a squat geometric urn with a rusting iron sword twisted around its neck to the white *lekythoi* of classical Athens and self-consciously sophisticated Hellenistic pottery (open Tues–Sun 8.30am–3pm; entrance fee).

Hadrian's Arch

A few Roman monuments recall a time when Athens was a city to be revered, but stripped of its movable artworks. The 2nd-century **Emperor Hadrian**, a fervent admirer of classical Greece, erected an ornate **arch** ⬤ marking the spot where the classical city ended and the provincial Roman university town began. Little of this Roman city can be seen beneath the green of the **Záppeio Park** and the archeological area behind the towering columns of the **Temple of Olympian Zeus**, but recent excavations in the corner of the Záppeio indicate that many

Roman buildings were in this area, stretching at least to the stadium built by Herod Atticus. Work on the Temple of Olympian Zeus had been abandoned in around 520 BC when funds ran out, but Hadrian finished the construction and dedicated the temple to himself (open Tues–Sun 8am–2.30pm; entrance fee).

Later in the century, Herod Atticus, a wealthy Greek landowner who served in the Roman senate, built the steeply raked theatre on the south slope of the Acropolis (now used for Athens Festival performances) as a memorial to his wife. And a 1st-century BC Syrian was responsible for the picturesque **Tower of the Winds** , in the Aomanagora, a well-preserved marble octagon overlooking the scanty remains of the Roman Agora. It is decorated with eight relief figures, each depicting a different breeze, and once contained a water-clock (open Tues–Sun 8.30am– 2.45pm; entrance fee).

Byzantine Athens is scantily represented: a dozen or so churches, many dating from the 11th century, can be tracked down in Pláka and others huddle below street level in the shadow of the city's tall, modern buildings. One of the handsomest is **Ághii Theodhóri** **P**, just off Platía Klafthmónos. It was built in the 11th century on the site of an earlier church in characteristic cruciform shape with a tiled dome. The masonry is picked out with slabs of brick and decorated with a terracotta frieze of animals and plants. The church of **Sotíra Lykodhímou** on Filellínon Street dates from the same time but was bought by the Tsar of Russia in 1845 and redecorated inside. It now serves the city's small Russian Orthodox community; the singing is renowned.

On Athens's eastern and western limits there lie two famous monasteries: Kaisarianí and Daphní. **Kaisarianí** on Mount Hymettus, surrounded by high stone walls, is named after a spring which fed an aqueduct constructed on

Map, pages 138–9

TIP

Opening hours for sites and museums throughout the country are subject to change without notice. To be sure of getting in, visit between 9am and noon.

BELOW: two's company on top of the National Archeological Museum.

Hadrian's orders. Its waters, once sacred to Aphrodite, the goddess of love, are still credited with healing powers (and encouraging child-bearing). The monastery church goes back to AD 1000 but the frescoed figures who gaze out of a blue-black ground date from the 17th century. The monks' wealth came from olive groves, beehives, vineyards and various medicines made from mountain herbs (open Tues–Sun 8.30am–3pm; entrance fee).

Daphní, a curious architectural combination of Gothic and Byzantine, decorated inside with magnificent 11th-century mosaics, occupies the site of an ancient sanctuary of Apollo. A fierce-looking Christ Pandokrátor, set in gold and surrounded by Old Testament prophets, stares down from the vault of the dome. The present building dates from 1080 and the Gothic porch was added in the 13th century when Daphní belonged to Cistercian monks from Burgundy and was used as the burial place of the Frankish Dukes of Athens (open Tues–Sun 8.30am–2.45pm; entrance fee).

Museum notes

Going back to 3000 BC, the **Goulandrís Museum of Cycladic Art Q** displays a unique collection of slim, stylised Cycladic idols in white marble, beautifully mounted. These figures were scorned by 19th-century art critics as hopelessly primitive, but their smooth, simple lines attracted both Picasso and Modigliani. Mostly female and pregnant, the figures derive from robbed graves scattered throughout the Cyclades islands; to this day, scholars are still uncertain of their true purpose (open Mon, Wed–Fri 10am–4pm, Sat 10am–3pm; entrance fee).

Crammed with badly labelled treasures from every period of antiquity, the **National Archeological Museum R** should be visited early in the morning

ABOVE: not only ancient designs…
BELOW: the modern city has mushroomed outwards since World War II.

before the guided tours turn the echoing marble halls into a deafening Babel. (Open Mon 10.30am–5pm, Tues–Sun 8.30am–7.45pm; entrance fee; *see also pages 154–5*.)

Map, pages 138–9

The bronzes in the **Piraeus Archeological Museum** are more workmanlike, but still fascinating. The graceful, archaic Apollo, pulled from the sea in 1959, was made in 520 BC and is the earliest life-sized bronze statue. Two other bronze statues, of Athena and Artemis and both dating to the 5th century BC, were found at about the same time in Piraeus (Pireás) when new sewers were being dug (open Tues–Sun 8.30am–3pm; entrance fee).

The **Byzantine Museum ⑨**, a mock-Florentine mansion built by an eccentric 19th-century duchess, contains a brilliant array of icons and church relics from the 13th to the 18th centuries. The **Benáki Museum ❼** houses a wonderfully eclectic collection of treasures from all periods of Greek history – including jewellery, costumes and two icons attributed to El Greco in the days when he was a young Cretan painter called Dhomeniko Theotokópoulos (the museum has been closed for some time, undergoing extensive rearrangements, and is due to reopen sometime in 2000).

The **Kanellópoulos Museum ⑪**, a 19th-century mansion in Pláka, is a smaller treasure-trove of objects from many periods of Greek art, acquired by an erudite, obsessive collector. Also in Pláka is the excellent **Museum of Popular Instruments–Research Centre for Ethnomusicology** (open Tues, Thurs–Sun 10am–2pm; Wed noon–6pm; closed Mon), based around the collection of Fivos Anoyanakis. The **City of Athens Museum**, an accumulation of 19th-century furnishings, pictures and fittings in a house once occupied by the teenage King Otto, evokes upper-class life in newly independent Greece (for both, open Tues–Sun 8.30am–3pm; entrance fee).

ABOVE: relief in the National Archeological Museum.
BELOW: the Lysikratous monument.

Outside Athens, a 69-km (43-mile) drive to **Cape Sounion** on the windy tip of the Attica peninsula takes you to the Doric Temple of Poseidon. Completed in 440 BC, its slender, salt-white columns are still a landmark for ships headed toward Piraeus. Lord Byron carved his name on a column on the north side. The marble came from nearby Agríleza (open daily; 10am–sunset; entrance fee).

Following an impressive classical fortification wall down the hillside, you reach the remains of ancient shipsheds in the bay below: the Athenians once organised warship races off Sounion and it later became a pirates' lair.

More out of the way is the **Sanctuary of Artemis** at **Brauron** (now called Vravróna) on the east coast of Attica, 35 km (22 miles) from Athens through the wine-growing Mesógheio district. A 5th-century BC colonnade visited by owls at twilight is flanked by a 16th-century Byzantine chapel, built on the site of an altar to Artemis.

In classical times, well-born girl children aged five to ten ("little bears") performed a ritual dance at a festival honouring Artemis as the goddess of childbirth. Their statues – plump, with solemn expressions, and dressed like miniature adults – are now in the site museum (both the site and the museum open Tues–Sun 8.30am–3pm; entrance fee). ❑

A NATIONAL TREASURE TROVE

The National Archeological Museum in Athens is a storehouse of the wonderful art and artifacts that adorned ancient Greece

A walk through the rooms of the National Archeological Museum provides a survey of Greek art available nowhere else in the world. Some people are intimidated by the apparent size of the collection but in fact you can breeze through in under an hour and be content with an overview, or spend days in more detailed study.

The simplest way to visit the museum is to head directly into Room 4 (directly in front of the main entrance), containing material from the Mycenaean period (1600–1100 BC). Room 5, to the left of the Mycenaean room, has prehistoric finds, and Room 6, to the right, has finds from the Cycladic Period, most of them dating between 3000 and 2000 BC.

After visiting these rooms, if you return towards the entrance and enter Room 7, to the right as you face the museum's main entrance, you may begin a visit of the rooms encircling the Mycenaean Room and containing examples of ancient Greek sculpture from the Archaic Period (700 BC– 480 BC) through the Classical (480 BC–338 BC) and Hellenistic (338 BC– 146 BC) periods to the Roman Period (146 BC–AD 330).

The museum's second floor has a vast array of ancient Greek pottery from 900 BC to 300 BC and, far more rewarding, the room with the extraordinary Minoan frescoes from the island of Thera.

The picture at the top of this column is of the bronze Horse and Jockey of Artemesium (2nd century BC).

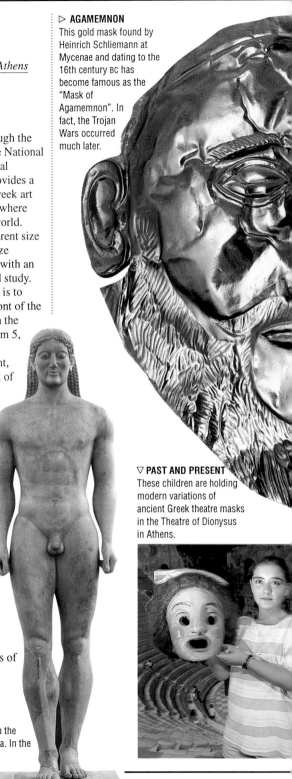

▷ **AGAMEMNON**
This gold mask found by Heinrich Schliemann at Mycenae and dating to the 16th century BC has become famous as the "Mask of Agamemnon". In fact, the Trojan Wars occurred much later.

▽ **PAST AND PRESENT**
These children are holding modern variations of ancient Greek theatre masks in the Theatre of Dionysus in Athens.

▷ **HUNK OF STONE**
This *kouros* (statue of a young man) was found in the Sanctuary of Poseidon at Sounion, the tip of Attica. In the Archaic style, it was carved in the 7th century BC.

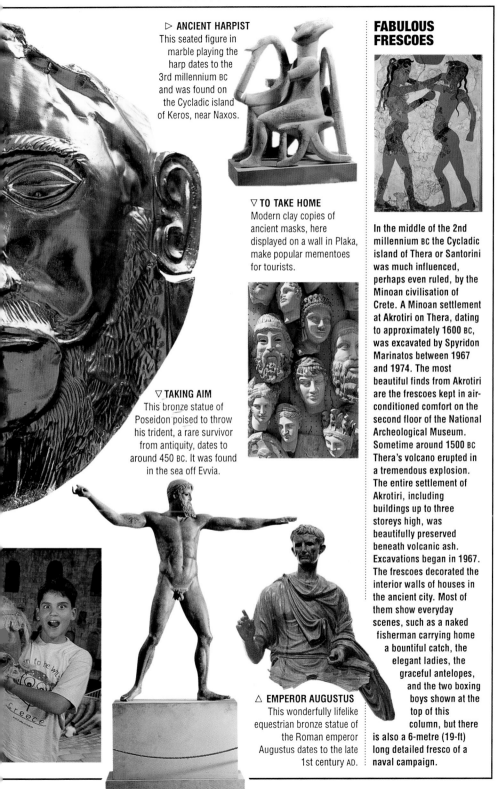

▷ **ANCIENT HARPIST**
This seated figure in marble playing the harp dates to the 3rd millennium BC and was found on the Cycladic island of Keros, near Naxos.

FABULOUS FRESCOES

▽ **TO TAKE HOME**
Modern clay copies of ancient masks, here displayed on a wall in Plaka, make popular mementoes for tourists.

▽ **TAKING AIM**
This bronze statue of Poseidon poised to throw his trident, a rare survivor from antiquity, dates to around 450 BC. It was found in the sea off Evvia.

△ **EMPEROR AUGUSTUS**
This wonderfully lifelike equestrian bronze statue of the Roman emperor Augustus dates to the late 1st century AD.

In the middle of the 2nd millennium BC the Cycladic island of Thera or Santorini was much influenced, perhaps even ruled, by the Minoan civilisation of Crete. A Minoan settlement at Akrotiri on Thera, dating to approximately 1600 BC, was excavated by Spyridon Marinatos between 1967 and 1974. The most beautiful finds from Akrotiri are the frescoes kept in air-conditioned comfort on the second floor of the National Archeological Museum. Sometime around 1500 BC Thera's volcano erupted in a tremendous explosion. The entire settlement of Akrotiri, including buildings up to three storeys high, was beautifully preserved beneath volcanic ash. Excavations began in 1967. The frescoes decorated the interior walls of houses in the ancient city. Most of them show everyday scenes, such as a naked fisherman carrying home a bountiful catch, the elegant ladies, the graceful antelopes, and the two boxing boys shown at the top of this column, but there is also a 6-metre (19-ft) long detailed fresco of a naval campaign.

THE NORTHEAST

*Along with a landscape of fertile plains and forbidding mountains,
you'll find the major holiday playground of Halkidhikí here,
as well as Greece's "second city", Thessaloníki*

Map,
pages
158–9

Standing about halfway between the Adriatic to the west and the Évros river to the east, Thessaloníki is Greece's second city, and "capital" (since 1923) of Macedonia and Thrace. Scarcely 100 km (60 miles) north, the frontiers of FYROM (the Former Yugoslav Republic of Macedonia), Bulgaria and Greece meet – a boundary settled only after World War I.

The Northeast does not possess the magnificent archaeological sites and stunning ruined temples of central and southern Greece. Its latitude spells a short summer season, a consequent dearth of cheap flights from abroad, and sparse, often overpriced accommodation (except on the Halkidikí peninsula). However, its proximity to other Balkan states and relatively recent acquisition by Greece give it greater ethnic variety, including lively music and cuisine. Ancient sites fall into two categories: either too sparse to astound, or palimpsests where layers of civilisation can be read, one after another. One of the best examples of the latter is Thessaloníki itself.

Thessaloníki

To a visitor approaching by sea, contemporary **Thessaloníki** presents the uniform façade of modern apartment blocks characteristic of so many Mediterranean seaside cities. At the beginning of this century, the same view was marked by minarets rising elegantly from a tile-roofed town picturesquely climbing between medieval ramparts to an upper quarter, with vast cemeteries outside the walls. When more than half the town was destroyed by the Great Fire of August 1917, British and French architects (who were accompanying Allied expeditionary forces at the time) were promptly commissioned to produce a new town plan. Surviving Art Deco buildings enhance the wide, sea-facing boulevards they designed, although their advice to ban high-rises was disregarded.

But the fire spared much, including the old hillside quarter of **Kástra**. Roman ruins, Byzantine churches, Ottoman public and domestic buildings and displaced Jewish tombstones lie encircled by Roman and Byzantine walls, or scattered alongside asphalt boulevards and pedestrian lanes. And after years of neglect, this great architectural heritage has finally been signposted and selectively renovated, a happy result of Thessaloníki's 1997 stint as European Cultural Capital.

Thessaloníki was founded in 316–315 BC by the Macedonian king Kassander, who named it after his wife, but it rose into prominence under the Romans, boosted by their **Via Egnatia** "trunk road" which stretched from the Adriatic coast to the Hellespont (Dardanelles). Saint Paul visited twice, and wrote two Epistles to the Thessalonians; Christianity (and the

LEFT: interior of Ághios Dhimítrios, Thessaloníki.
BELOW: the Rotunda of Ághios Yeórghios in Thessaloníki.

city) got further boosts from the Byzantine emperors, especially Theodosius (who issued his edict here, banning paganism) and Justinian, who began new churches to supplement those adapted from Roman structures. Despite Slavic and Saracen raids, frequent earthquakes, fires, adjacent malarial swamps and a spotty water supply, resilient Thessaloníki prospered. Even in temporary decline it made a rich prize for the Ottomans in 1430.

After 1500, large numbers of Sephardic Jewish refugees from Iberia settled here, giving Salonica – as they called it – its most distinctive trait for the next four centuries. On the eve of the Balkan Wars they accounted for just over half the population of 140,000, making it the largest Jewish city of that era. In 1943, 70,000 remained to be deported to the Nazi death-camps, leaving less than a thousand today. In the wake of the year as European City of Culture, their contribution to the city is being belatedly recognised with a memorial and a small museum.

Following the three wars leading up to 1923, the city came to epitomise a Greek refugee town: in absolute numbers Athens may have had more, but by proportion of population, Thessaloníki is the most purely Anatolian city in the land, with its blatantly Turkish surnames (Dereli, Mumtzis, etc) and spicy cuisine rarely seen elsewhere in Greece. Its own self-deprecating nicknames have long been *I Protévousa tón Prosfighón* (The Refugee Capital), after the ring of 1920s settlements, all prefixed "Néa", across eastern Macedonia, and *Ftohomána* (Mother of the Poor).

But 21st-century Thessaloníki is not all changing demographics. After years in Athens' shadow, it is finally coming into its own. The International Fair held every October in permanent grounds by the university already makes it an

Thessaloníki has the dubious distinction of being the first town in Greece to introduce satellite television – unavailable in Greece until the late 1980s.

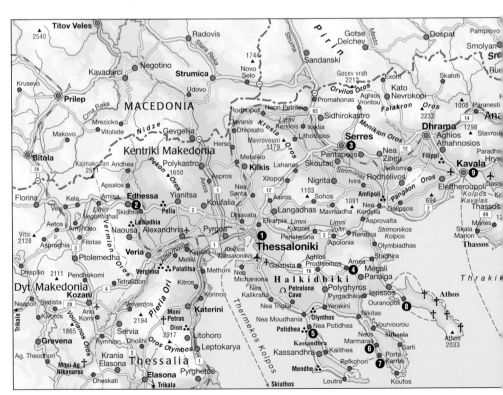

important Balkan trade centre, and the port is the natural gateway to the upper Balkans. Even before its year as European cultural capital, Thessaloníki was confidently on the move, with innovative restaurants and clubs occupying historic buildings, its native musicians (such as Savvopoulos and Níkos Papázoglou) frequently at the forefront of Greek song. They say you can always tell a Thessalonian in the rest of the mainland; with a spring in their step, they seem a head taller than the characteristically hunched-over, downtrodden Athenians.

A city tour

Begin at the **Archeological Museum Ⓐ**, which displays Macedonian, Hellenistic and Roman finds from the entire region, including the notable **Síndos** collections. Sumptuous jewellery and household effects in gold, silver and bronze vie for your attention (open Mon 12.30–7pm; Tues–Sun 8.30am–7pm; winter: Mon 10.30am–5pm, Tues–Sun 8.30am–3pm; entrance fee). The magnificent **Verghína** treasures, of what are thought to be the royal tombs of the Macedonian king, Philip II, and his relatives, are now housed at a specially designed museum at the site itself.

Roman Thessaloníki is mostly subterranean. The most extensive excavations, off pedestrianized **Dhimitríou Goúnari** and adjacent **Platía Navarínou**, are those of the palace of Christian-hating Emperor Galerius Caesar, he who martyred the city's patron saint Demetrius in AD 305. Above ground survives **Galerius**'s triumphal **Arch Ⓑ**, erected over the Via Egnatia in AD 297 to celebrate a victory over the Persians. Just northwest, the **Rotunda of Ághios Yeórghios Ⓒ** – perhaps originally intended as Galerius's mausoleum – is one of the few remaining examples of circular Roman architecture, enduring largely

Map, page 160

A gold casket found at Verghína. Its lid bears the star which was the emblem of Philip II's Macedonian dynasty.

BELOW: exhibit in Thessaloníki's Archeological Museum.

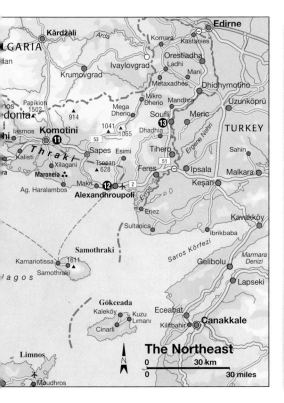

The Northeast

0   30 km
0   30 miles

During Ottoman rule, most Byzantine churches were converted into mosques, and their interiors coated in whitewash. This fresco, from Thessaloníki's Ághios Dhimítrios, was one that survived.

through conversion into a church, then a mosque. Glorious wall mosaics – seldom viewable since a 1978 quake prompted the Rotunda's closure – partially survive, high up inside; the truncated minaret is the city's last surviving one.

Byzantine Thessaloníki

A baker's dozen of Byzantine churches survive in Thessaloníki, more than in any other Greek town. The earliest examples are clear adaptations of the colonnaded Roman basilica, in turn descended from Greek temples, with the outermost columns replaced by walls. Highlighted here are the best (and the ones most likely to be open) among them.

Both 5th-century **Ahiropítos ⓓ** (open 8am–1pm; Sun till 5pm) and the heavily restored, coeval **Ághios Dhimítrios ⓔ** (open Mon 1.30–7.30pm; Tues–Sun 8am–7.30pm) are three-aisled basilicas. In Ahiropítos, hunt for fine mosaic patches under the arches, between ornate columns. Ághios Dhimítrios was founded shortly after the saint's demise, on the site of his martyrdom – the crypt is, thought to be the Roman baths where he was imprisoned. It is the largest church in Greece, almost entirely rebuilt after the 1917 fire which spared only the apse and the colonnades. Six small mosaics of the 5th to 7th century, many featuring the saint, survive mostly above the columns standing on either side of the altar.

Tiny, 5th- or 6th-century **Ósios Dhavíd ⓕ**, all that's left of the **Látomos Monastery**, is tucked away in the Kástra district (open Mon–Sat 8am–noon, 5–6pm; Sun 8–10.30am, by caretaker whim otherwise). The west end of this church has vanished, but visit for the sake of an outstanding early mosaic in the apse, only revealed in 1921 when Ottoman whitewash was removed. It depicts

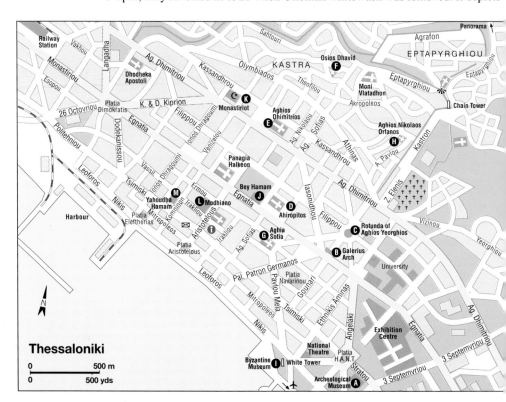

Thessaloniki

0   500 m
0   500 yds

Map, page 160

the vision of the Prophet Ezekiel of Christ Emmanuel, shown as a beardless youth seated on the arc of heaven, surrounded by the symbols of the Evangelists. Together, the mosaics of Ósios Dhavíd and Ághios Dhimítrios rank as the best pre-Iconoclastic sacred art in Greece, and predate the more famous work at Ravenna in Italy.

Back down in the flatlands near the waterfront, 8th-century **Aghía Sofía** (Holy Wisdom) **G** was built in conscious imitation of its namesake in Constantinople. This is one of the earliest successful experiments with domes; the 10-m (33-ft) wide one here has a vivid Ascension, with the Apostles watching Christ borne heavenward by angels, rather than the *Pandokrátor* (Christ Enthroned) that became the rule later. In the apse, unhappily obscured by scaffolding and the *ikonostásis*, you can detect traces of an earlier, Iconoclastic mosaic of the Cross behind the Virgin Enthroned. It was one of a pair, and the other figural cross survives in the adjacent vault.

Another batch of churches, all well uphill from the Via Egnatia, date from the 13th and 14th centuries – examples of a cultural "golden age" at odds with the Byzantine Empire's political decline and the numerous disasters visited on Thessaloníki from the 10th through to the 12th century. More modest financial resources meant that frescoes, rather than mosaics, were the preferred ornamentation in these churches, most of them attached to now-extinct monasteries. By far the best of these is **Ághios Nikólaos Orfanós H**, at the northeast edge of Kástra (open Tues–Sun 9am–2.30pm; warden at Irodhotou 17). Among the better-preserved and more unusual frescoes are Christ mounting the Cross and Pilate sitting in Judgment, the very image of a Byzantine scribe; in the Washing of the Feet, it seems the talented painter inserted an image of himself on horseback, wearing a turban.

Thessaloníki's de facto **Byzantine Museum I** is a collection of Byzantine secular and sacred art – top-notch icons, pottery, jewellery, coins – housed in the **Lefkós Pýrgos** (White Tower) by the waterfront. The tower itself, effectively the city's logo, was originally built during the brief Venetian occupation as an addition to the Roman-Byzantine walls. The Ottomans used it as a prison; that, and the massacre of unruly Janissaries here in 1826, earned it the epithet "Bloody Tower". The Greeks whitewashed it post-1912 – thus the new alias – and then removed the pigment in 1985. A spiral staircase with tiny windows connects the exhibit galleries, emerging at a lovely (and decently priced) cafe and finally the crenellated roof terrace, affording fine views over the seafront and up to Kástra (Tues–Sun 8am–2.30pm; entrance fee).

The vanished curtain wall leading inland from here linked the White Tower with the **Chain Tower**, the northeastern corner of the fortifications; beyond lay Eptapyrghíou, the inner citadel (Yedikule in Turkish), the site of a notorious prison from Ottoman times until 1989. The steep alleys of Kástra itself lie a 20-minute walk from the seafront. Since the late 1980s this neighbourhood of dilapidated half-timbered houses has been transformed from poor, despised and "Turkish" to renovated and trendy, with scattered taverns and cafes.

BELOW: the White Tower, Thessaloníki.

Ottoman and Jewish Thessaloníki

Thessaloníki was taken by the Ottomans in 1430, just 23 years before the fall of Constantinople. The new overlords converted most churches into mosques during the first century of their rule, tacking on minarets and whitewashing over mosaics and frescoes. As a result, there are few purpose-built Ottoman mosques, though there are other interesting civic buildings. Worthy 15th-century specimens include the graceful Ishak Pasha or **Alatza Imaret Mosque** at the base of Kástra – around the corner from the **Yeni Hamam**, or bath-house, engagingly restored as a bistro, concert hall and summer outdoor cinema – and the dilapidated **Hamza Bey Mosque** on the Via Egnatia, last used as the Alcazar cinema. Perhaps it may soon get the same treatment as the nearby **Bezesténi**, a refurbished six-domed covered market now tenanted by luxury shops. The nearby **Bey Hamam** ❶ has intact stalactite vaulting over the entrance.

Two more contemporary "Turkish" monuments may appeal to specialists. At the rear of the Turkish consulate stands the wooden house where Mustafa Kemal Atatürk, founder of the Turkish republic, was born in 1881. And a few hundred metres east of the Archeological Museum, at the edge of the 19th-century "New Town", is the **Yeni Cami** or "New Mosque" – an Art Nouveau folly erected by the Doenme (more properly, Ma'min). This crypto-Judaic sect, originally followers of the false 17th-century "messiah" Sabbatai Zvi, were disproportionately prominent in Ottoman industry and built many grand mansions in this area. Outwardly, though, they espoused Islam, and were consequently expelled in 1923.

By contrast, there are few tangible traces of Thessaloníki's Jewish past, thanks to the 1917 fire and the Nazi desecration of cemeteries and synagogues in 1943. Only the Art Deco **Monastiriot synagogue** ❻, near the Ministry of Northern Greece, survived the war. Centrepiece of the vast central market – which extends to either side of **Aristotélous**, selling everything from wooden furniture to live poultry – is the covered **Modhiano** ❼, a fish, meat and produce-hall named after the Jewish family which established it. (Their former mansion, out beyond the Yeni Cami, now houses the Folklife Museum – currently shut for repairs.) Though only half-occupied today, the Modhiano still supports several authentic, atmospheric *ouzerí* in the west arcade. Close by, the Louloudhádhika Hamam or Flower-Market Bath was also known as the **Yahoudha Hamam** or Jewish Bath ❽; the Jewish clientele is gone, but the flowers are still outside, and a good fish taverna operates inside even as the building is being restored. In the same area, on Aghíou Miná, is the **Museum of the Jewish Presence** (open Mon–Fri 9.30am–1pm; entrance fee).

For an escape from the city, try a half-day excursion to **Panórama**, an affluent village 11 km (7 miles) to the east whose views justify its name; several *zaharoplastía* sell such Anatolian specialities as *salépi* (orchid-root drink), *dódurma* (Turkish ice cream) and *trígona*, triangular cream pastries. **Hortiátis**, 10 km (6 miles) north of here, has since ancient times supplied Thessaloníki with water, and retains some pines spared by arsonists, plus good tavernas. From either

point, you can on a clear day look southwest across the Thermaïc Gulf to glimpse the bulk of **Mount Olympus** (Ólymbos) to the southwest, the traditional separation-point between Macedonia and Thessaly.

Maps:
City 160
Area 158

Around Thessaloníki: Macedonian sites

Traces of the 4th-century BC Macedonian empire which once stretched as far as India are scattered in a broad arc west to southwest of **Thessaloníki**, at the edges of the current flood plains of the Áxios and Aliákmonas rivers. In ancient times the Thermaïc Gulf extended much further inland, but the silt-bearing rivers have pushed the contemporary shoreline east. All of these sites can be toured with your own transport in a full day out of Thessaloníki. **Dion**, just northeast of Mount Olympus (Ólymbos), was founded by Macedonian kings both as a military mobilisation grounds and a precinct holy to the Olympian gods just overhead; its ruins, which date largely from the Roman and Byzantine eras, were buried by an earthquake-triggered mudslide in the 5th century AD (site open daily 8am–5pm; museum open Mon 10.30am–5pm; Tues–Fri 8am–5pm; Sat–Sun 8am–2.30pm; entrance fee). Since 1990, well-preserved mosaics have been found here, the best – of Medusa – transferred to safekeeping in the village museum (same hours).

Pride of place in the archeological museum at Dion goes to a 1st-century BC pipe organ, unearthed at the ruins in 1992.

Modern **Verghína**, on the south bank of the Aliákmonas, was formerly **Aigai**, the first Macedonian capital, and remained the royal necropolis. The subterranean chamber tombs of Philip of Macedonia and three others, discovered in late 1977 with their treasures intact, have been transferred from Thessaloníki and are impressively displayed as they were found. More modest tombs and a summer palace, the **Palatítsa**, just up the hill (the Verghina sites are open

BELOW: Mount Olympus (Ólymbos), home of the gods.

*Édhessa's waterfall –
plunging over a
spectacular
escarpment – is
certainly worth
the detour.*

BELOW: mosaic of a
lion-hunt, Pella
museum.

Tues–Sun 8.30am–3pm; entrance fee). Some 18 km (11 miles) northwest on the far side of the river, **Véria** sits at one end of an escarpment running north to **Édhessa ❷**. Extensive Ottoman neighbourhoods of vernacular houses have been preserved here, liberally sprinkled with three-score tiny churches disguised as inconspicuous barns; the frescoed one of **Hristós** can be visited (open Tues–Sun 8.30am–3pm). Muslim monuments include a baths complex and two mosques; in the former Jewish quarter of Barboúti ravine, a reconstructed synagogue testifies to the community already established when Saint Paul preached here.

North of Véria, other imposing Macedonian tombs can be visited at **Lefkádhia**. Édhessa, some 43 km (27 miles) from Véria, is unlike any other Greek town, thanks to the numerous channelled rivulets that wind through it and then over its famous waterfall plunging off the escarpment. A path leads down the ravine, through cascade mist, past a cave in the cliffside; upstream, atop the bluff, is a Roman or Byzantine bridge serving the Via Egnatia. Édhessa's architecture is nothing special, but its streamside parks and wide pavements are good for strolling.

Pella, about a third of the way along the road back to Thessaloníki, was the Macedonian capital after the mid-4th century BC. From here, Philip II ruled a united Greece after 338 BC, and here also his son Alexander studied under Aristotle – and trained for his fabled campaigns in the Orient. Most of the imperial capital is yet to be unearthed, but the superb mosaics – some *in situ*, some in the site museum – of a lion hunt, Dionysus riding a panther, and other mythological scenes, more than justify a stop (for both, open Tues–Sun 8.30am–3pm; entrance fee).

East to Halkidhikí

Many roads lead east out of Thessaloníki. One leads initially north to the town of **Kilkís** and the Greek shore of **Lake Diráni**, then into the Strýmon river valley towards the only paved road crossing into Bulgaria at **Promahónas**. This route is also followed by the railway, which in this part of Macedonia traces incredible inland loops connecting relatively contiguous coastal points. Cynics assert that European contractors who built the railways for the Ottomans during the late 19th century were paid by the kilometre; in truth the sultan, having been at the wrong end of some Russian gunboat diplomacy in Constantinople, stipulated that the track was to be invulnerable to bombardment from the sea.

A more direct, northeasterly road leads to **Sérres ❸**, important since Byzantine times and still a prosperous provincial town. It was burnt down by the retreating Bulgarians in 1913 and has been largely rebuilt, but two Byzantine churches remain, much altered by war and restoration: 11th-century **Ághii Theodhóri** and 14th-century **Ághios Nikólaos**. A domed Ottoman building in the shady central square serves as a museum. Some 19 km (12 miles) north, in a wooded mountain valley, is another, more venerable foundation: the monastery of **Timiou Prodhromou**, where Yennadhios II, first patriarch after the Ottoman conquest of Constantinople, elected to retire and is entombed.

The busiest road east of Thessaloníki skirts the lakes of **Korónia** and **Vólvi** en route to Thrace, but a slightly less travelled one veers southeast towards **Halkidhikí**, a hand-like peninsula dangling three fingers out into the Aegean. Long a favoured weekend playground of Thessalonians, since the 1980s it has also seen ever-increasing foreign patronage, especially Hungarians and Czechs in search of sun, sand and sea on a cheap package or a few tanks of fuel.

Map, pages 158–9

TIP

The northeast has hotter summers and cooler winters than the rest of Greece. Best time to visit Halkidhikí is in June or early July, when the land is still green and the hills still covered in flowers.

BELOW: fisherman mending his nets, Sithonía peninsula, Halkidhikí.

Your table awaits... Kassándhra peninsula is the most developed of Halkidikí's three "fingers'; the east coast resorts here are the prettiest and the most sheltered.

BELOW: Petrálona Cave, where Neanderthal remains have been discovered.

Little is left to suggest the area's important role in classical times, when local colonies of various southern Greek cities served as battlefields during the first decade of the Peloponnesian War between Athens and Sparta. However, fossils and a half-million-year-old skull have been discovered in the **Petrálona Cave**, 50 km (31 miles) southeast of Thessaloníki, revealing the existence of prehistoric settlement (open daily 9am–7pm in summer; closes 5pm in winter; entrance fee).

At **Stághira** on the way to Áthos, a modern statue of Aristotle overlooks the Ierissos Gulf and the philosopher's birthplace, ancient Stageira. **Xerxes's Canal**, now silted up, was built around 482 BC across the neck of Áthos peninsula to help the Persians avoid the fate suffered in their previous campaign, when their fleet was wrecked sailing round Áthos cape. This and Xerxes's floating bridge over the Hellespont were considered by the Greeks to be products of Persian megalomania – "marching over the sea and sailing ships through the land." The medieval **Potídhea Canal** still separates the **Kassándhra** peninsula from the rest of the mainland and serves as a mooring ground for fishing boats.

The beautifully forested slopes of Mount Holomóndas cover the palm's rollingly hilly centre; **Polýghyros**, with a dull Archeological Museum, is the provincial capital, but **Arnéa** ❹ sees more tourists for the sake of its woven goods and well-preserved old houses. Kassándhra, the westernmost "finger", had little life before tourism – most inhabitants were slaughtered in 1821 for participating in the independence rebellion, and the land lay deserted until resettlement by post-1923 refugees from the Sea of Marmara. **Néa Potídhea** ❺ by the canal and **Haniótis** near the tip are probably your best bets for human-scale development on a generally oversubscribed bit of real estate.

Sithonía, the middle finger, is greener, less flat and less developed; the **Mount Áthos** monasteries owned much of it before 1923, so again there are few old villages, apart from rustic **Parthenónas**, just under Mount Ítamos. The adjacent clutter of **Néos Marmarás** and the mega-resort of **Pórto Karrás** are exceptions to the rule of ex-fishing villages converted slowly for tourism with ample campsites and low-rise accommodation. **Toróni** and **Aretés** on the west coast are still relatively unspoiled, while nearby **Pórto Koufó**, landlocked inside bare promontories, is a yachter's haven. **Kalamítsi beach** on the east coast has an idyllic double bay, although **Sárti** further north is the main package venue.

Following the coast north past **Pyrgadhíkia** fishing hamlet brings you to the base of **Áthos**, the easterly "finger", whose pyramidal summit rises in solitary magnificence across the gulf to the east. Several resorts, including the beach-fringed islet of **Ammouliani** and cosmopolitan **Ouranópoli**, grace Áthos, but sun, sand and sea are not the main attractions here.

Mount Áthos

The fame of Áthos derives from its large monastic community, today nearly 2,000 strong. In past ages these monks earned it the epithet "holy", now an intrinsic part of the Greek name: **Ághion Óros**, the Holy Mountain. Its Christian history begins with the arrival of hermits in the mid-9th century, roughly 100 years before the foundation of the first monastery. Peter the Athonite, perhaps the most famous of these early saints, is supposed to have lived in a cave here for some 50 years.

The first monastery, **Meghístis Lávras**, was founded in AD 963 by St Athanasios, a friend of the Byzantine emperor, Nikiforos Fokas. Thereafter, foundations

Map, pages 158–9

TIP

Four-day permits to visit Mount Áthos can be obtained from the Ministry of Foreign Affairs in Athens, or the Ministry of Macedonia and Thrace in Thessaloníki. You must also have a letter of recommendation from your embassy or consulate.

BELOW: sunrise behind the Holy Mountain.

TIP

The most spectacular Áthos monastery is **Símonos Pétra**, built into a sheer cliff with vertiginious drops on three sides. Tenth-century **Meghístis Lávras** has the finest frescoes – but book at least two months in advance for a high-season stay.

BELOW: Símonos Pétra monastery.

multiplied under the patronage of Byzantine emperors who supported them with money, land and treasures; in return these donors are still prayed for, and imperial charters zealously guarded in the monastery libraries.

The 20 surviving monasteries are all coenobitic, a rule in which monks keep to strict regulations under the direction of an abbot, or *igoúmenos*. Property is communal; meals are eaten together in the *trapezaría* or refectory. All monasteries observe a Greek liturgy except for the Russian **Pandelímonos**, the Serbian **Hilandharíou** and the Bulgarian **Zográfou**; all adhere to the Julian calendar, 13 days behind the Gregorian, and all (except for **Vatopedhíou**) keep Byzantine time, reckoned from the hour of sunrise or sunset. Many monks prefer to live in smaller, less regimented monastic communities, the *skítes* and *kelliá* which are dotted around the peninsula but still dependent on the main monasteries. A few choose to live like hermits in an *isyhastírion*, a rough, unadorned hut or a cave, perched precipitously on a cliff edge.

In the 1970s, Áthos was perhaps at its nadir, with barely a thousand monks – many of limited educational and moral attainment – dwelling in dilapidated monasteries. Since then, a renaissance has been effected. The Holy Mountain's claims to be a commonwealth pursuing the highest form of spiritual life known in the Orthodox Christian tradition appear to have struck a chord, and the quality and quantity of novices from every corner of the globe (especially Russia, following the collapse of communism) is on the rise. Many buildings have also undergone much-needed restoration.

The number of pilgrims to Áthos has grown, too, even though the appropriately Byzantine process of obtaining an entry permit is expressly designed to discourage the frivolous and the gawkers. Only genuine religious pilgrims need

NO FEMALES ALLOWED

Áthos is probably most famous for the ávaton edict, promulgated in 1060 by Emperor Constantine Monomahos, which forbids access to the Holy Mountain to all females more evolved than a chicken (although an exception seems to have been made for female cats, which are kept to control the rodent population).

How did this come about? Revisionists point to prior chronic hanky-panky between monks and shepherdesses; the religious claim that the Virgin, in numerous visions, has consecrated lush Áthos as Her private garden – and women would simply be an unnecessary temptation. Over the years, many women have tried to gatecrash in disguise, only to be ignominiously ejected; a variety of women's groups in Greece and abroad have now taken up the issue.

A more serious challenge was posed in 1998 when the (female) Foreign Ministers of Sweden and Finland threatened to refuse to sign a decree upholding the Mount's "special status", since it contravenes one of the EU's most cherished laws: freedom of movement (Greece is one of 11 EU states signing the Schengen Accord, set up to abolish border controls amongst member-states by the year 2000). The Áthonite authorities have, nonetheless, vowed to resist all attempts to change the Holy Mountain's single-gender character.

apply; or at least that is the ideal. For – as always – political if not doctrinal strife is never far from the Holy Mountain. Most of the monks are born Greek, into a culture of intrigue (this is Macedonia, after all). Slavic novices and pilgrims have complained, since 1990, that they are discriminated against vis-à-vis Greeks. Entire bodies of monks have departed from, or been evicted from, particular monasteries in stormy disputes with abbots or Greek civil authorities. Traditionalists decry, as elsewhere in Greece, the bulldozing of paths and the burning of the previously virgin forests, otherwise sold as timber to finance ongoing renovations – much of it in highly brutalist style.

You must phone or fax most monasteries to reserve space in guest-quarters often full to bursting, and once there put up with the squealing of other guests' mobile phones. After decades of somnolence, Áthos matters again to the world, which has shown up in force. Only time will tell if the Mountain can defend itself against the world.

Eastern Macedonia

North of Áthos, the coast road threads through several resorts on the Strymonic Gulf, popular with Thessalonians and Serrans, before crossing the **Strýmon** itself at ancient Amphipolis. Scant ruins remain of this city, a Thracian settlement colonised by Athens in 438 BC, top a bluff protected on three sides by the river. Most passers-by content themselves with a glimpse from the river bridge of the **Lion of Amphipolis**, a colossal statue reassembled from fragments from the 4th- and 3rd-century BC. On the east bank, the road forks: a faster but less scenic coast highway, or the inland road along the base of Mount Pangéo via **Eleftheroúpoli**, threading through picturesque, slate-roofed villages.

Map, pages 158–9

The 40-sq-km (15-sq-mile) area which makes up the theocratic republic of Mount Áthos is officially a part of Greece, but it is governed by a "Holy Superintendency" of abbots, who are elected annually.

BELOW: the Russian Pandelímonos monastery on Mount Áthos.

The boom days are over, but Kavála still supports a tobacco-growing industry.

BELOW: the aqueduct at Kavála.

Both routes converge on **Kavála** , Macedonia's second city; as Neapolis, it was an important stop on the Via Egnatia, and a port for ancient Philippi. Well into the 1920s Kavála was a major tobacco-curing and export centre, though today the harbour sees more passenger ferries en route to Thássos and the north Aegean than it does commercial traffic. A mansion from the tobacco boom days houses the **Folk and Modern Art Museum**, featuring the Thássos-born sculptor, Polýgnotos Vághis (open Mon–Fri 8am–2pm; Sat 9am–1pm; entrance fee). The treasures in the modern Archeological Museum include tomb finds from both Avdira and Amphipolis.

Overnighting is not a priority in most people's minds – hotels tend to be noisy and overpriced – but the medieval walled **Panaghía** quarter, southeast of the harbour, merits a leisurely stroll up to the hilltop citadel, tethered to the modern town by a 16th-century aqueduct. Start along **Poulídhou**, passing a clutch of restaurants favoured by locals, arriving soon at the gate of the **Imaret** – a sprawling domed compound, allegedly the largest Islamic public building in the Balkans. Originally an almshouse and hostel, it reopened in the early 1990s after years of dereliction as an uncontestably atmospheric restaurant-bar.

Some 14 km (8½ miles) northwest, ancient **Philippi** – although named for Philip II – contains little that is Macedonian. From the acropolis, where three medieval towers rise on the ruins of Macedonian walls, you have extensive views of the battlefield which made Philippi famous. Here in 42 BC, the fate of the Romans hung in the balance as the republican forces of Brutus and Cassius, participants in the assassination of Julius Caesar in 44 BC, confronted the armies of the latter's avengers, Antony and Octavius. Upon their defeat, both Cassius and Brutus committed suicide; the Battle of Actium in 31 BC saw the final struggle between the two victors.

Roman ruins, mainly to the south of the highway, include foundations of both the forum and palaestra, plus a well-preserved public latrine in the southwest corner of the grounds. Philippi is reputedly the first place in Europe where St Paul preached the gospel. He arrived in AD 49, but offended the local pagans and was thrown into prison (a frescoed Roman crypt now marks the site). In AD 55, however, he got a better reception from the congregation later addressed in his *Epistle to the Philippians*. By the 6th century Christianity was thriving here, as the remains of several early basilica-churches testify (daily except Mon 8.30–3pm; entrance fee).

Driving east from Kavála, you soon cross the Néstos river, the boundary between Macedonia and Thrace, at the apex of its alluvial plain, a vast expanse of corn and tobacco fields. Some beautiful scenery along the Néstos Gorge can best be seen by train, or the old highway, between **Dhráma** and **Xánthi**

Thrace – and its Muslims

Ancient Thrace covered much of present-day Bulgaria and European Turkey, as well as the Greek coastal strip between the Néstos and Évros rivers. Greek colonisation of the coast from 800 BC onwards often led to conflict with the native Thracian tribes. The Via Egnatia spanned the area, leaving scattered Roman and, later

Byzantine fortifications. Later, Thrace was overrun and settled by both Slavs and Ottomans. It was eventually and messily divided between Bulgaria, Turkey and Greece, between 1913 and 1923, following various wars. Although a traumatic population exchange between Turkey and Greece occurred in 1923, the Muslim inhabitants of the Greek part of Thrace were allowed to remain in return for protection granted to 125,000 Greek Orthodox living in Istanbul. (Today the Greeks in Istanbul have been reduced to a few thousand, whereas the population of Muslims of Thrace has increased slightly to about 130,000.)

Map, pages 158–9

An ethnic Turkish minority dwells principally in Xánthi, **Komotiní** ⓫ and the plains southeast of the two cities; gypsies who adopted Islam and the Turkish language are also settled here. Another Muslim minority, the Pomaks, live in the Rodhópi range above Xánthi and Komotiní; descended from medieval Bogomil heretics, they speak a Slavic language and traditionally cultivate tobacco on mountain terraces.

The open-air **Saturday market** at Xánthi, just 53 km (33 miles) from Kavála, makes a good introduction to the region's Muslim demographics. Turkish and Pomak women favour long, dull overcoats and plain-coloured yashmaks (headscarves), now gradually being replaced by more stylish grey or brown coats and printed scarves. The gypsy women stand out in their colourful *shalvar* bloomers, their scarves tied behind the ears. Many men still wear burgundy-coloured velvet or felt fezzes, or white skullcaps. By night, the numerous, state-of-the-art bars and cafés along nearby **Vassilísis Sofías** do a roaring trade, thanks to students from the University of Thrace.

Xánthi became a prosperous commercial and administrative centre during the 19th century, thanks to tobacco. Renowned masons were brought from

BELOW LEFT:
Pomak women in Xánthi market.
BELOW:
a priest stocks up.

Map, pages 158–9

Epirus to build merchants' mansions, tobacco warehouses and *hans* (inns). The *hans*, large square buildings around a central courtyard, were resting-spots and trade-centres near the marketplace. One of the old mansions at the base of the old town has become a **Folk Museum** (open Mon, Wed, Fri, Sat 11am–1pm & 7–9.30pm, Tues, Thurs, Sun 11am–1pm; entrance fee). Further uphill lie the minarets and houses of the Turkish quarter – complete with numerous satellite dishes for tuning into Turkish-language TV.

At Komothiní, 56 km (35 miles) east of Xánthi via the bird-stalked lagoon of **Vistonídha** and the water-girt monastery of **Ághios Nikólaos**, Muslims constitute nearly half of the population. It's less immediately attractive than Xánthi, but here too is an old bazaar of cobbled lanes (Tuesday is the busiest day), complete with tiny shops, 14 functioning mosques and old-fashioned coffeehouses where old men chat quietly in Turkish or play with their *tespih* beads. A **Folk Museum** just off the central park displays local embroidery, costumes and metalwork (open Mon–Sat 10am–1pm; entrance fee); the **Archeological Museum** keeps finds from such Thracian sites as **Avdira**, south of Xánthi, and **Maroneia**, south of Komotiní (open Tues–Sun 8.30am–3pm; entrance fee).

Avdira itself does not repay a visit in its bedraggled state, though it nurtured two major philosophers: Democritus, who first expounded atomic theory, and the sophist Protagoras to whom is attributed the maxim "Man is the measure of all things." Odysseus legendarily called at Maroneia after leaving Troy for his return to Ithaca, procuring a sweet red wine which later saved him and his companions from the cyclops Polyphemus. Trapped in his cave, they plied Polyphemus with the wine, and then as he slept poked his single eye out with a red-hot brand and escaped by hiding under his sheep's bellies. A cave north of the sparse cliff-top site retains the name of **Polyphemus's Cave**; more rewarding, perhaps, is the medieval village of **Marónia**, preserving a few wooden mansions, and the tiny beach of Platanítis below, with a good fish taverna.

The road from Komotiní zigzags 65 km (40 miles) through barren hills before coming down to the rather drab port of **Alexandhroúpoli** ⑫, gateway to Samothráki island. It's wisest to press on into the valley of the Évros River, especially if you're a bird-watcher. The delta, east of the Roman spa of Traianopolis, is excellent for waterfowl, while the **Dhadhiá Forest Reserve**, a successful venture of the World Wildlife Fund for Nature, shelters black and griffin vultures. In between you can pause at **Féres** for the sake of its 12th-century church, **Panaghí Kosmosótira**, whose lofty, five-domed interior is generally open.

North of the turning for Dhadhiá, the first town of any size is **Souflí** ⑬, once famous for silk production. Corn fields have now replaced the mulberry trees whose leaves once nourished the silkworms, and only a small museum commemorates the vanished industry. **Dhidhymótiho**, 30 km (18½ miles) further upstream, has a Byzantine fortress at the old town's summit, and an abandoned mosque on the square whose features speak of Seljuk (and earlier) prototypes. From here, most traffic is bound for Turkish **Edirne**, whose graceful minarets are just visible from the Greek border town of Kastaniés. ❑

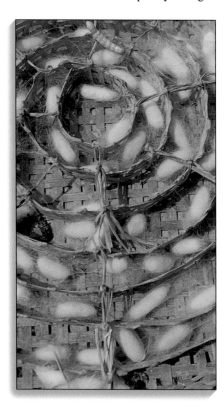

BELOW: the silk trade was once the mainstay of Souflí's economy.
RIGHT: icon, Dhionisíou monastery, Mount Áthos.

EPIRUS AND NORTHWEST MACEDONIA

Map, page 178

A spectacular mountain region of limestone peaks, wooded valleys and traditional stone villages, the northwest also offers a pristine national park where bears and wolves still roam

Epirus (Ípiros in Greek) and **western Macedonia** (Makedhonía) are worlds apart from the azure, sun-bleached Greece of the coasts. Their characters are determined by the limestone peaks and and deep river gorges of the Pindos (Píndhos) range, and by the lakes which spangle the borderlands with Albania and FYROM. The highest winter precipitation in mainland Greece ensures that forests are shaggy and the rivers foaming; isolation resulting from both mountains and climate fostered the growth of medieval, semi-autonomous villages built by traders and craftsmen returning from abroad. Local stone and wood has been transformed into imposing houses, with street cobbles, walls and roof slates blending in a uniform grey which, far from being depressing, is a classic example of harmonious adaptation to environment.

In antiquity, this was considered the limit of the civilised world; few ruins have been unearthed besides shadowy oracles at Dodona (Dhodhóni) and Ephyra. The Romans and Byzantines had scarcely more time for this rugged terrain south of the Via Egnatia, even though during the 13th and 14th centuries the Despotate of Epirus extended from the Ionian Sea to Thessaloníki. It sheltered the Angelos dynasty branch of Byzantine nobility, expelled from the imperial capital by the Fourth Crusade of 1204. They left behind intriguing churches around Árta, joining earlier masterpieces at Kastoriá.

Like the rest of northern Greece, Epirus and west Macedonia were only incorporated into the modern state in March 1913, some 80 years after the end of the independence war.

Eclipse – and renaissance?

In the 20th century, the remoteness which once protected the area undermined its continued vigour. The ravages of World War II and subsequent civil war, along with poor communications, the breakdown of traditional livelihoods and apparently punitive government neglect, spurred massive emigration, particularly to North America, Germany and Australia. By the 1970s, many Epirot and western Macedonian villages were in an advanced state of physical and social decline. Many houses were left to decay (or repaired shoddily), while others sheltered an ever-dwindling population of the economically inactive elderly, and perhaps their grandchildren. But since the early 1980s, matters have slowly changed. The government has acted to further integrate the region into the national economy, most spectacularly with good roads. Emigration has slowed and occasionally – thanks to tourism, subsidies for logging or grazing and better

PRECEDING PAGES: Dodona (Dhodhóni) amphitheatre. **LEFT:** Ali Pasha, despot of Epirus. **BELOW:** Mikrí lake, Préspa.

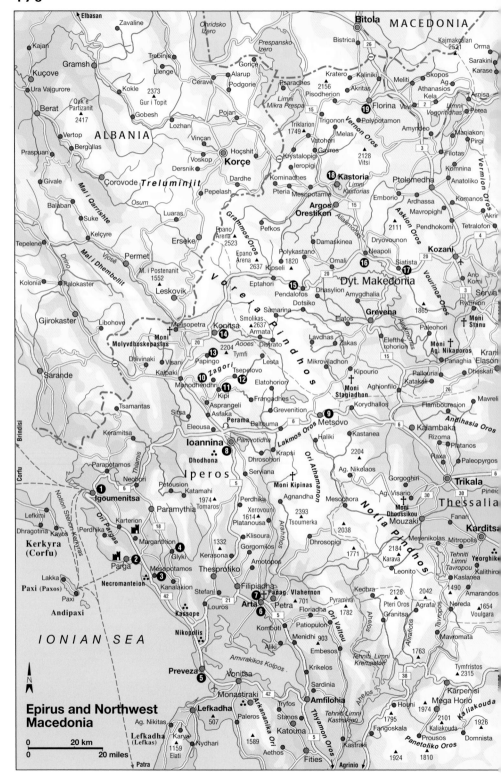

Epirus and Northwest Macedonia

infrastructure – even been reversed. Attitudes towards village life have softened, with traditional architecture and methods now viewed less as stumbling blocks to economic prosperity and more as cultural heritage to be preserved.

The core issues of this new era are most visible in the Zagóri district of Epirus. Preservation codes, and low-interest loans or outright subsidies, have led to the restoration of many buildings, so that entire villages are now preserved as homogeneous traditional settlements. Simultaneously, old roads are being paved and new ones bulldozed, often right over cobbled mule paths, giving access to the tiniest villages and most distant pastures. Yet because of the nature of tourism here (*see also Hiking in the Pindos, pages 192–3*), Zagóri is one of the few places in Greece where the number of walking trails is at least stable if not growing, thanks to a recent EU-funded program to clear and mark half-forgotten routes between points of interest.

However, as throughout Greece, a prize as rewarding for tourists as Zagóri has inevitably become the focus of ongoing battles between conservationists, developers and those engaged in pre-touristic enterprises. Roads to serve logging tracts and the high pastures scar the landscape, as does the national power corporation's reservoir at the sources of the Aóös river. Yet in the late 1980s, not a few herders and villagers allied themselves with urban mountaineers, local tourism personnel, international ecologists and even the European Kayaking Federation to halt a scheme promoted by Ioánnina-based interests for a second dam on the lower Aóös, plus various ski-lifts and roads which would have ruined the national park at the heart of Zagóri.

Low-impact, high-quality tourism – specifically bijou accommodation in some of the many restored houses – has been successfully promoted, particularly

Map, page 178

ABOVE: *tsarouchia* shoe, part of the Epirots' traditional costume.
BELOW: Kónitsa bridge, Zagóri.

in the gateway villages for the park, where the inhabitants have clearly seen that their bread is buttered on the side of the conservationists. Something similar is afoot in western Macedonia in the Prespa basin, on Greece's northwestern border with Albania and the Former Yugoslav Republic of Macedonia (FYROM). This is an extraordinary habitat, particularly for waterfowl, notably pygmy cormorants and two species of pelican, but also for a unique trout and a hardy breed of small cattle. The society for the protection of Prespa operates two information centres, one in Aghios Yermanos and the other on the shore of Megali Prespa lake in Psaradhes. In early 2000 the entire Prespa basin was declared a Balkan park by the governments of Albania, FYROM and Greece. The extraordinary bird life is most active in the spring.

Coastal Epirus

The modern port of **Igoumenítsa** ❶ at the very northwestern corner of Greece is the third-busiest in the country after Pátra and Piraeus (Pireás), a turnstile sort of place where an enforced halt should be avoided at all costs. Far more rewarding is the coastal road south, which after 39 km (24 miles) reaches the 11-km (7-mile) side road for **Párga** ❷, Epirus's main coastal resort, and deservedly so for the sake of its fine beaches, tiered houses and dominant Norman-Venetian castle. From the 15th to the late 18th centuries this was the Serene Republic's lone stronghold in Epirus, peopled by Souliot Orthodox Christians in constant conflict with their Muslim neighbours, as well as a small community of Jews who lived from the export of citrons to Europe for Jewish liturgical use. The British acquired it in 1814 and soon ceded it to the rapacious Ali Pasha of Ioánnina; the townspeople were compensated for their property and evacuated to Corfu. Párga

ABOVE: the local goat's cheese makes a tasty snack.
BELOW: plenty of winter rain keeps Epirus green.

now enjoys 100 percent hotel occupancy (mostly from package tours) from late June through to August, though out of season it still makes an atmospheric stop.

Some 22 km (14 miles) southeast, near **Mesopótamos** village ❸, lies the **Necromanteion of Ephyra** (open daily 8am–3pm), the venerable oracle of the dead described by Circe in the *Odyssey*. Today the **Ahérondas river** (one of the rivers leading to Hades) has silted up the surrounding agricultural plain, but in Homeric times it was a suitably mysterious, tree-fringed island in a lagoon. Supplicants entered the sanctuary via a maze of corridors and were then lowered by a pulley into a vaulted underground chamber to experience whatever spectral hoax the resident priests had concocted. Just inland, closer to its source, the Ahérondas squeezes through a spectacular gorge.

From the village of **Glykí** ❹, a side track signposted for the "*Skála Dzavélainas*" dead-ends at the *skála*'s start: a spectacular 90-minute path down to the river bed and up into the realm of the Souliots, a tribe never completely subdued by the Ottomans. From Glykí, continue south another 30 km (19 miles) to the combined side turning for **Zalóngo** and ancient **Kassope**. The former, a mountain-top monastery of little intrinsic interest, was witness to a Masada-like incident in 1806 which has since become a staple of Greek nationalist legend (every schoolchild knows the story): trapped by Ali Pasha's forces, several dozen Souliot women fled to a nearby pinnacle, where – rather than submit to the enemy – they danced into thin air clutching their children. An incongruous modern sculpture celebrates their defiance.

Nearby Kassope (always open) is less visited and eminently rewarding, a minor Hellenistic city whose jumbled ruins are matched by a fine view over the Ionian Sea and Lefkádha island. No such paeans apply to the artificial Roman

Map, page 178

TIP

The hill-top ruins of ancient Kassope make a glorious vantage-point from which to watch the sunrise. If you're tempted, a daily bus from Préveza makes the trip at 6am.

BELOW: Kónitsa priest, Epirus.

TIP

During the summer, Préveza makes a good base for visiting the Ionian islands, with frequent hydrofoil connections – though schedules often change at random.

city of **Nikopolis**, some 15 km (9 miles) south and 600 m (2,000 ft) below, which promises much from the sheer scale of its ruins but offers little up close. The nearby **Amvrakikós Gulf** was the classical Actium, where Octavian defeated Anthony and Cleopatra in 31 BC prior to styling himself the Emperor Augustus – and ordering the impractical founding of Nikopolis.

The gulf abuts the northern limits of **Préveza** ❺, once a sleepy, shabby provincial capital, now spruced up, partly to cater for tourists in transit between charter arrivals at **Áktion airport** and the fine beaches to the north, or on Lefkádha. In the old bazaar, more characterful than Párga's, a clutch of restaurants still offer the gulf's famous sardines, and summer nightlife is loud and varied – including, if what the posters say is true, one of the last traditional shadow-puppet theatres in Greece.

Some 50 km (31 miles) over on the far side of the gulf lies **Árta** ❻, ancient Ambracia; later, it was the seat of the Despotate of Epirus, and retains a legacy of churches from that era. Most notable is the enormous, cubic **Panaghía Parigorítissa**, which dates from the late 13th century and betrays some Italian influence in its palazzo-like exterior. High in the dome, supported by a gravity-defying cantilever system, floats a magnificent mosaic of the Pandokrátor (Christ in Majesty), the finest on the mainland after Daphni near Athens, despite damage from World War II bombing.

In the citrus groves around the town lie other late Byzantine churches and monasteries, the most beautiful of which is **Panaghía Vlahernón** ❼ in **Vlahérna** village, 6 km (4 miles) to the north. Despot Michael II added the domes in the 13th century, and is thought to be entombed inside; the caretaker here will lift a section of carpet to expose a section of fine floor mosaic.

BELOW: a graceful bridge at Árta.

Ioánnina

Map, page 178

Lining the shores of **Lake Pamvótis** (Pamvotídha), glittering below the stark face of **Mount Mitsikéli, Ioánnina ❽** has been one of Greece's great cities for over a thousand years: a beacon of Hellenic culture, a traders' entrepôt and, in the 19th century (its last glorious epoch) the capital of the infamous Ali Pasha. Nicknamed "the Lion of Ioánnina", this maverick Albanian Muslim tyrant broke away from the Ottoman Empire and established an autonomous "duchy". Today, the town remains one of Greece's liveliest provincial centres.

Unlike most large Greek centres, Ioánnina's history does not predate early Christian times, when an earthquake blocked the natural drainages of the surrounding plain, thus creating the lake. Its name derives from an early church of St John the Baptist, long since vanished. Then, after the Latin conquest of Constantinople in 1204 and the establishment of the Despotate of Epirus, the town grew in size and importance as refugees from "The City" swelled its population. It surrendered to the Ottomans in the 15th century; in 1788 Ali Pasha designated this city of 35,000 inhabitants (large for that time) his headquarters.

Ioánnina's layout is testimony to Ali's dubious legacy. While he left behind the city's most distinctive monuments (its mosques and the redoubtable walls of the **Kástro**), his artillery also blasted much of it to the ground resisting the siege of the sultan's troops in 1820. This, along with a postwar penchant for large apartment blocks, has given rise to the relentlessly modern Ioánnina which lies outside the old town.

ABOVE: museum pieces, Aslan Pasha Mosque.
BELOW: that's life.

The wide expanse of central **Platía Pýrrou**, joined to the plazas of **Akadhimías** and **Dhimokratías** and lined by various public buildings, makes an obvious starting-point for a city tour. Just east of Dhimokratías stands the **Archeological Museum** (open Tues–Sun 8.30am–3pm; entrance fee), home to an fine collection of bronzes and tablets inscribed with questions for the Dodona oracle.

Except for a few trendy bars off Pýrrou, and a couple of cinemas with good first-run fare, this area is no longer the main nocturnal hub of Ioánnina. That has shifted downhill along Avéroff towards the Kástro, past stalls selling the famous local *bougátsa* (custard or cheese pie), to take better advantage of the town's setting. More state-of-the-art café-bars cluster at the far end of **Ethnikís Andistásis**, facing the lake, and around **Platía Mavíli**, on the opposite side of the citadel. On summer nights, the latter – better known as **Mólos** – throbs with townspeople strolling past vendors selling roast corn, *halvás* and bootleg tapes of local clarinet music, all from gas-lit pushcarts.

Kástro, the five-gated, walled precinct of various Epirot despots including Ali Pasha himself, best conjures up Ioánnina's colourful past. A tangle of alleyways rises to a fortified promontory jutting out into the lake; at the lower corner looms the **Aslan Pasha Mosque**, now home to the **Popular Art Museum** (open summer: Mon–Fri 8am–3pm, Sat–Sun 9am–3pm; winter: daily 9am–3pm; entrance fee) with its diverse collection of Epirot costumes, jewellery and Judaeo-Islamic relics.

One of Ali Pasha's most infamous exploits – involving Kyra Frosini, the beautiful Greek mistress

The monastery of Ághiou Nikoláou Filanthropínon, near the island-village of Nissí, is worth a visit for its vivid frescoes.

of Ali's eldest son – is supposed to have taken place near the mosque-museum. In the most common variant of the tale, Ali punished the girl for resisting his advances by having her and 17 female companions tied up in weighted sacks and dropped in the lake. Racist-kitsch oleograph-postcards of the incident are still sold, depicting wild-eyed "Turks" and swooning Greek maidens and inscribed "Kyra Phrosyne Drown" with ungrammatical finality.

At the summit of the citadel looms the **Fetiye Tzami** (Victory Mosque) and one of Ali's restored palaces – today an indifferent **Byzantine Museum** (open Tues–Sun 8.30am–3pm; entrance fee). The former treasury nearby makes an appropriate showcase for displays on the city's traditional silver industry.

After defying the sultan for three decades, Ali finally met his end on the islet of **Nissí**, on the far side of the visibly polluted lake (motor boats make the trip from Mólos all day until 11pm). A small house in the grounds of **Ághios Pandelímon** monastery was his last hideout; here, trapped on the upper floor by a Turkish assassin, Ali was shot through the floorboards, then decapitated; his head was sent to Istanbul as a trophy.

Monasteries with more peaceful histories, and a fine island loop walk, lie in the opposite direction. Nearest Nissí village, **Ághiou Nikoláou Filanthropínon** contains vivid late-Byzantine frescoes, some depicting unusually gruesome martyrdoms; others by the entrance depict ancient sages such as Plutarch, Aristotle and Thucydides. Several tavernas in the village serve fresh frog legs and fish.

Worthy diversions

Some 20 km (12 miles) south of Ioánnina lies **Dodona** (Dhodhóni), Epirus's main archeological site, nestled in a valley at the foot of Mount Tómaros. Homer

called it "wintry Dodona", stressing Epirus's alpine atmosphere; Herodotus says its oracle (the oldest in Greece and until the 4th century BC, the most important), was begun by a priestess abducted from a similar one at Egyptian Thebes. Zeus – considered resident in the trunk of a holy oak tree – was worshipped here, priestesses deciphering the rustlings of the leaves which were the god's sacred pronouncements.

The carefully restored **amphitheatre**, dating from the 3rd-century reign of King Pyrrhus, has a capacity of 17,000 spectators – always far too large for the needs of the little town which existed here from 1000 BC until early Byzantine times. It is still used for performances (open Mon–Fri 8am–7pm, Sat–Sun 8.30am–3pm; entrance fee).

The road northwest out of Ioánnina leads to **Zagóri**, the mountainous heart of Epirus. If you're heading northeast into Thessaly from here, you can partially make up for missing Zagóri with a halt in **Métsovo ❾**, 58 km (36 miles) from Ioánnina. On this route you'll pass **Pérama** (open daily 8am–8pm; entrance fee), one of Greece's most spectacular caves, on the outskirts of Ioánnina. Then, after a long ascent towards **Katára Pass** ("Curse Pass") – the only permanently open road across the central Pindos – Métsovo appears in a ravine below. It ranks as the Vlach "capital", famous for its imposing houses, handicrafts, cheeses and the traditional costumes still worn by some older inhabitants.

Aside from the wonderful painting covering all the interior walls of the medieval monastery of **Ághios Nikólaos**, a short walk below town, the only other "sight" is the **Arhondikó Tosítsa Museum** (daily except Thurs, 8.30am–1pm and 4–6pm; guided tours only; entrance fee), its reconstructed interior displaying fine woodwork and textiles.

Map, page 178

ABOVE: exhibits in the Arhondikó Tosítsa Museum, Métsovo.
BELOW: Dodona's theatre.

Unlike so many Greek mountain villages, Métsovo is thriving: local worthies who made their fortunes abroad have set up endowments to encourage local industry, such as the nearby ski resort, whose clients periodically fill the dozen or so hotels – of a better standard than most in Ioánnina. And while many of the souvenirs pitched at coach tours are bogus – notably imported Albanian rugs – locally sold food is not: the red *katóyi* wine, cheese, salami and *trahanás* (sourdough soup-grain) all make excellent purchases.

The Zagorohória

Zagóri forms a culturally and geographically distinct region of Epirus comprising 46 villages – the **Zagorohória** – lying in an area bounded by the Métsovo-Ioánnina-Kónitsa highway and the Aóös river. Because of the region's infertility, local men emigrated to major commercial centres in eastern Europe during the Ottoman era, subsequently returning to their homeland with considerable wealth. This allowed locals to hire a representative to send taxes to the sultan directly rather than suffer from tax-farmers, securing a large measure of autonomy.

Zagóri's villages differ markedly: the east is populated largely by Vlachs (more properly, Arouman), a people rooted in Greece since antiquity, speaking a Romance language and living as transhumant shepherds and caravan-drovers. Fierce resistance to the Germans meant all the eastern villages were burnt down in early 1944, and crudely rebuilt. The western and central villages show more of a Slav/Albanian influence in place names and architecture; happily, most survived the war unscathed and today constitute one of Greece's showpieces.

The Zagorian landscape is dramatically varied, embracing sheer rock faces, limestone dells, dense forests, upland pasture and deep canyons. The **national**

BELOW: time for a gossip at a Métsovo bus stop.

park at its core, comprising the **Víkos Gorge** and lower reaches of the Aóös, was established partly to protect a dwindling population of bears, lynx, wolves and birds of prey. Yet even in the remotest corners there are signs of man: a belfried, post-Byzantine monastery; a graceful, slender-arched bridge from the Ottoman period; a clan of shepherds grazing flocks in the high meadows.

Map, page 178

Central Zagóri is best reached by the side road some 14 km (9 miles) out of Ioánnina, prominently marked for the Víkos Gorge. **Vítsa** village has some fine traditional houses, a wonderfully shaded central square, one of the oldest churches in the region (**Ághios Nikólaos**), and the easiest trail access to the floor of the gorge. Just up the road, more frequented **Monodhéndhri** ❿ supports two tavernas offering hearty local cuisine, while the photogenic basilica of **Ághios Athanásios** flanks the classic path descending to the gorge. For the less committed, either the new, rather gaudy *kalderími* (cobbled path) to the eagle's-nest eyrie of **Aghía Paraskeví monastery**, or the 7-km (4-mile) drive up to the **Oxiá overlook**, will afford breathtaking views.

From the junction below Vítsa, the easterly main road passes the turning for exquisite **Dhílofo** on its way to the major villages of **Kípi** ⓫, **Kapésovo** and **Tsepélovo** ⓬. Kípi lies nearest to a much-photographed cluster of 18th- and 19th-century packhorse bridges, the most famous of which is the three-arched Plakídha span. East of Kípi, **Negádhes** is known for its frescoed basilica, one of the best examples of the Zagorian style, while higher up and to the north perches Kapésovo, with a rural museum in its enormous old school, and yet another trail down to the canyon.

ABOVE: dramatic Víkos Gorge.
BELOW: old stone houses and cobbled streets are a feature of the Zagorohória.

This village also marks the start of a one-hour path incorporating the most amazingly sinuous of all Zagorian *kalderímia*, ending at **Vradhéto**, the highest – and formerly desolate – village in the area, now renovated and enjoying a renaissance. Continue on foot for about 40 minutes and you'll reach **Belóï viewpoint**, more or less opposite Oxiá. Twelve kilometres (7 miles) further, the paved road from Kapésovo arrives at Tsépélovo, flanked by rural monasteries and crammed with more mansions.

Back on the Ioánnina-Kónitsa highway, you'll pass through **Kalpáki**, where in the early winter of 1940–41 the Greeks halted the Italian invasion, rolling troops back into the snowy Albanian mountains for a season of hell. Just beyond, a 19-km (12-mile) side road heads east to the focus of most Zagorian tourism, the paired **Pápingo** villages ⓭, **Megálo** and **Mikró**. In recent years they've become quite fashionable, especially during the peak holiday season, but there's no denying their superlative setting at the foot of several 600-m (2,000-ft) high *pýrghi*, the outriders of **Mount Gamíla**. This massif (the heart of the national park) offers fine hiking, most notably to newt-filled **Dhrakólimni** (Dragon Lake).

The icy **Voïdhomátis river** drains out of the lower Víkos 5 km (3 miles) short of the Ioánnina-Kónitsa highway. Here, the largest packhorse bridge in Zagóri spans the Aóös where it exits some narrows to a vast floodplain. A 90-minute walk along the southern bank leads below forested, steep slopes to the **Stomíou Monastery**, magnificently perched on a cliff.

Kastoriá's fur trade began in the 17th century, when beavers still lived in its lake (Kastoriá means "place of the beaver"). Now these are extinct locally, and fur is imported.

BELOW: the majestic Pindos mountains.

Kónitsa ⓮ itself offers a fine view of the floodplain; an earthquake in 1996 and massive shelling during the civil war put paid to any real architectural distinction here. For that, head 23 km (14 miles) west to the monastery and namesake village of **Molyvdhosképastos**, just where the Aóös enters Albania. The monastery's early 14th-century church betrays a Serbian influence with its high, stovepipe dome and barrel-roof nave. Early in the 1990s it was reinhabited by some rather zealous monks, who encourage your conversion on the spot.

Due east of Kónitsa looms 2,637-m (8,651-ft) **Mount Smólikas**, roof of the Pindos and second summit of Greece after Mount Olympus (Ólymbos). From several of the Vlách villages along the Aóös, trails lead up towards the peak and yet another "Dragon Lake".

Northwest Macedonia

The 105-km (65-mile) road from Kónitsa to Neápolis is the single paved connection between Epirus and west Macedonia. It follows the valley of the **Sarandáporos river** upstream, between Smólikas and Mount Grámmos, site of the final battles of the civil war, passing the occasional blue-painted graffito *"Eleftheria Yia Vória Ípiros!"* ("Freedom for Northern Epirus!") – an expression of lingering irredentist sentiment for the Albanian portion of Epirus, home to roughly 100,000 remaining Greek Orthodox.

You officially enter Macedonia just before **Pendálofos** ⓯, the only place of any importance or appeal en route. Its fine stone houses – still in the Epirot style – straggle across the ravines which give the town its name ("Five-hills").

At **Neápolis** ⓰, the road divides: north to Kastoriá, southeast to **Siátista** ⓱. Perched on a bleak ridge some 20 km (12 miles) from the fork, this small town is noted for its fine 18th-century mansions or *arhontiká* – the residences of the *arhons*, or leading citizens – offering a glimpse into the self-contained society that flourished here during late Ottoman times. Then a wealthy centre for fur-trading, tanning, winemaking and a stopping-point for caravans on the trade route to Vienna, Siátista declined when commercial networks changed after Greek independence.

Start with the **Nerantzópoulos mansion** on Platía Horí, whose warden has the keys to other interesting structures such as the **Manoússi, Kanatsoúli** and **Poulikídhou residences**. Visiting these will give you a good background for nearby Kastoriá, another town which prospered from the fur trade.

Returning north, the road follows the upper valley of the **Aliákmonas river**, the longest in Greece, whose 300-km (185-mile) course arcs from the Albanian border to the Thermaic Gulf. Soon you reach the **lake of Orestiádha**, or Kastoriá, almost divided in half by the eponymous town built on a peninsula. On the town's southern outskirts lies a significant military cemetery, the last resting place of government troops who were killed during the battle for Grámmos-Vítsi, which brought an end to the civil war. In the town itself, a lake-side plaza named after General James Van Fleet serves as a reminder that American equipment and advisers guaranteed a royalist victory over communist insurgency.

A Byzantine county town

Map,
page
178

Despite extensive wartime damage, aggravated by thoughtless modernization in recent decades, **Kastoriá ⑱** remains one of northern Greece's more appealing towns. No less than 54 surviving medieval churches – many erected as private chapels by rich furrier families – indicate its past as a Byzantine provincial centre and fur factory. The fur trade still continues, however, nowadays the furs come not from locally trapped animals but from pelts imported from Scandinavia and Canada

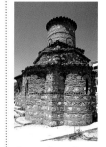

The half-dozen truly Byzantine specimens here represent some of the finest provincial art Greece has to offer, showing strong folk and Slav influences. You can see the best of them in a single morning, starting at the worthwhile **Byzantine Museum** (open Tues–Sun 8.30am–3pm; entrance fee) with its good icon collection (the warden here also has control of the keys to most of the churches), and working your way south to the **Karyádhis quarter**, with its fine old mansions.

Triple-aisled **Ághii Anárghyri** – built in 1018 by Emperor Basil II – sits at the northeast edge of town, overlooking the lake. If it's still shut for restoration and fresco-cleaning, be content with admiring the fine exterior brickwork. Nearby **Ághios Stéfanos** is also closed at present, but it is the second-oldest (10th-century) church in town, again with intricately geometric masonry and an unusual women's gallery inside. South of the museum, tiny **Panaghía Koumbelidhikí** is unmistakable with its disproportionately tall, drum-shaped dome, the only one in town, painstakingly rebuilt after Italian bombing in 1940. Interior frescoes are undergoing maintenance, but a highly unusual Holy Trinity, complete with bearded God, can be viewed in the barrel vaulting.

ABOVE: Byzantine church, Kastoriá. **BELOW:** with its lake-side setting, Kastoriá is one of northern Greece's prettiest towns.

Map, page 178

Continuing south and downhill, the extensive frescoes of the single-aisled basilica **Ághios Nikólaos Kasnítsi** are the best-preserved in Kastoriá; female saints predominate in the narthex, which long served as the women's section, while the image of the Virgin in the Assumption on the west wall is curiously reversed right-to-left. Finally, the **Taxiárhis tis Mitropóleos** is the oldest (9th-century) surviving church, with a later (14th-century) fresco of the Virgin Platytera adored by archangels in the apse.

In the low-lying Karyádhis (Dóltso) district, inland from the southern lakefront, stand the restored **Natzís** and **Immanouíl** *arhontiká*, of the same style and era as those in Siátista. Admission can be gained from the keeper of the **Folklore Museum** (open daily 10am–noon and 3–6pm; entrance fee), lodged in the Aïvazís Mansion on nearby **Kapetán Lázou**. From here, a narrow lake-shore lane heads 2½ km (1½ miles) east to **Panaghía Mavriótissa** monastery, now in ruins apart from two Siamese-twin churches – one 11th-century, the other 14th, both with fine frescoes. Peacocks strut, providing a fine view for the diners who patronise the adjacent lake-view restaurant.

To the Préspa Lakes and east

Some 36 km (22 miles) north of Kastoriá, following a branch of the Aliákmonas, is the side road to the Préspa Lakes basin, an atmospheric backwater where the frontiers of Greece, FYROM and Albania meet. There are two lakes: **Mikrí** Prespa, shallow and reedy, lying mostly in Greece, and deeper, reed-free **Megali** Prespa, shared by Albania, FYROM and Greece. Mikrí Prespa is the nesting ground for two endangered species of pelicans and numerous other birds, and the entire Prespa basin has been designated as a Balkan park by Albania, FYROM, and Greece. The surrounding hills are a haven for animals such as bears and wolves, though you will be lucky to spot them.

The best single target in the region is **Ághios Yermanós**, which has a visitor centre, high-quality lodging and two frescoed Byzantine churches. **Psarádhes**, the only Greek village on **Megáli Préspa**, also has an information centre and more tourist facilities and offers the opportunity to take a highly worthwhile boat excursion to the painted cave-church of **Panaghía Eleoússa**. Mikrí's islet of **Ághios Ahíllios** has an evocatively ruined 10th-century basilica.

The main road leading east – full of curtained Mercedes piloted by rich Albanians – passes through nondescript **Flórina ⓭**, then on towards Thessaloníki, alongside more lakes. Most notable is **Lake Vegoritídha**, whose two shoreline villages have restaurants and simple accommodation.

On the northern horizon you will notice **Mount Vóras** (Kaïmáktsalan), scene of a fierce, two-year battle during World War I between Serbs and Greeks on one side, Germans and Bulgarians on the other – neither the first nor the last campaign conducted hereabouts. Indeed, this area saw little peace during the first half of the 20th century, when the Macedonian Struggles (1900–08), the Balkan Wars (1912–13), World Wars I and II, and the civil war spelled out a narrative of strife equalled in few parts of the globe. ◻

Map,
page
178

HIKING THE PINDOS RANGE

*A hiking loop passes through several different ecological
habitats, and connects some of the most beautiful
villages of this northwestern region*

Vast tracts of wilderness, a varied landscape and a complex network of trails make this region a joy for hikers – and one not overcrowded by overseas standards. The North Pindos (Píndhos) offer many rewarding routes, from strenuous, multi-day high-level treks to various interconnected day-hikes through forest and fields. Visitors reliant on a car or public bus for exploration will find strolling the region's traditional villages rewarding.

Although the local trail system is extensive, it is unevenly maintained and waymarked (but improving, usually with painted or metallic diamonds). Thus a good map and compass, a specialist trekking guide (*see Further Reading, page 374*), a keen sense of direction, an ability to obtain and double-check trail information from villagers and shepherds, and a good sense of humour are necessary here. Pindos weather can change rapidly with little warning, so rain gear and a tent are essential – the latter also because indoor accommodation often fills up fast. Overnight trekkers should purchase two to three days' worth of food-stuffs in Ioánnina, as the stock in village shops remains quite limited.

The hiking loop outlined below begins and ends in the Pápingo villages where there is plentiful (if slightly pricey) accommodation, as well as reliable taver-nas and a regular (not daily) bus service. It has the disadvantage of being the most popular Pindos itinerary.

BELOW: an alpine
stream, North
Pindos.

Mikró Pápingo–Astráka Hut

This mountain refuge (visible from Megálo Pápingo) is staffed from May to October; 3–3½ hours (water available at regular intervals), 900-m (3,000-ft) ascent. Spend the balance of the day with a short walk from Astráka col to Dhrakólimni, an alpine tarn at 2,050m (6,300 ft) altitude, northwest of the 2,497-m (8,192-ft) Gamíla peak. Ideal site for views and picnics; 1 hour each way. Overnight at the refuge, or camp on turf just south of the seasonal Xiróloutsa pond (15-minute path descent to the east of the col en route to Dhrakó-limni: spring water available).

Astráka Hut/Xiróloutsa–Tsepélovo

A day-long hike between Astráka and Gamíla, through alpine meadows, the head of the Mégas Lákkos gorge and, finally, a steep descent; net altitude loss 850m (2,700 ft), 5–7 hours depending on pace. Water is scarce, so plan accordingly; overnight at Tsepélovo (five hotels and other smaller inns, but reservations required during July/August).

Tsepélovo–Kípi

The newly-renovated direct Kípi–Tsepélovo trail descends south from Tsepélovo, crosses the Vikákis ravine on an old bridge, and then adopts the south bank, high above the stream bed. Kípi (4½ hours) has two inns; if they're full, continue north by path 45 minutes to Koukoúli, and thence briefly by road to Kapésovo, with another inn. Kapésovo marks the start of the hairpin *kalderími* to Vradhéto, and also has trail access to the Víkos Gorge.

Kípi/Kapésovo–Vítsa–Monodhéndhri

From Kípi a marked route enters the upper end of the Víkos gorge, crossing it by the Mitsíou bridge and ascending a stair-*kalderími* to Vítsa (2 hours), with three inns and an evening taverna. A trail partly shortcuts the road up to Monodhéndhri (3 hours, a 300-m/1,000-ft climb from Kípi), with several more inns and two tavernas.

Monodhéndhri–Pápingo via Víkos Gorge

A signposted, well-renovated *kalderími* takes you to the usually dry bed of the Víkos (45 minutes). A fairly strenuous path marked as the O3 route negotiates the length of the canyon, on its true left bank after the first few minutes. At the intersection of Víkos Gorge and the side canyon of Mégas Lákkos (2½ hours, best lunch stop), a potable spring flows (unreliable after August). Continue through thick forest, then open pasture, before reaching the movable sources of the Voïdhomátis river (4½ hours from Monodhéndhri) which well out of the base of the Astráka *pýrghi*. Bearing left on an obvious cobbled path leads to Vitsikó (Víkos) village (45 minutes, 1 inn); the O3 route crosses the river, heading up and right, reaching Mikró Pápingo within 2 hours, for a day's total of 6½ hours; 100m (330 ft) net elevation loss, but plenty of sharp grades. Just over a hour above the Voïdhomátis, there's a signed side trail left for Megálo Pápingo. ❑

TIP

August is the peak month for hiking the Pindos, and thus worth avoiding. June is a better bet, with lingering snow patches to lend interest.

BELOW: tranquil Dhrakólimni, the dragon lake.

CENTRAL GREECE, THE SPORADES AND ÉVVIA

A region rich in temples and monasteries, from Delphi – mythical centre of the ancient world – to the dramatic Metéora peaks. And the cosmopolitan Sporades are only a stone's throw away

Map,
pages
198–9

The main reason people usually visit the region of central Greece known as **Roúmeli** is to visit the classical site at Delphi. This is an excellent reason, for Delphi is like no other ancient site, combining a unique wealth of monuments from all over the country with physical beauty. The drive takes just over two hours from Athens over good roads. The usual route is by turning off the national road at Thebes and continuing past Livádhia up into Mount Parnassus through Aráhova to Delphi. The modern city of **Thíva** (Thebes) ❶ has been built on the site of the ancient city, so there is little to be seen of the ancient Thebes so prominent in Greek myth and history. If you are a purist on these matters, the ancient palace has been excavated and the small museum is very good (open Tues–Sun 8.30–3pm; entrance fee). The next main town, **Livádhia** ❷, from the word for "plain" was a major power base for the Crusader states in the 13th and 14th centuries until it was captured by the Ottomans. The central square is still a bustling place, lined with grill- and sandwich-shops. Nearby, a Turkish bridge spans the waters gushing from powerful springs, the site of an ancient oracle. The impressive ruins of a medieval castle rise above.

After Livádhia, the road begins to rise into the foothills of Mount Parnassus. The turn to the left for **Dístomo** village and the **Monastery of Ósios Loukás** – dedicated not to St Luke the Evangelist, but to a 10th-century holy man named Luke – is clearly marked. The smaller **Church of the Virgin** (on the left) here was built in the 10th century; the larger, 11th-century **Church of Ósios Loukás** has some wonderful mosaics and frescoes, recently restored. The site commands a wonderful view down the valley.

The village of **Aráhova** ❸ is well up into the mountain, and beautifully situated. As you will see from the many rugs and weavings on display along the narrow main street, Aráhova is pretty tourist-oriented, favoured by Athenians who have holiday homes here for the nearby ski-slopes.

Delphi

The ancient site of **Delphi** ❹ is about another 8 km (5 miles) further on, tucked right under the cliffs. This is the place which – of all others in Greece – visitors have found most memorable, ever since its excavation at the end of the 19th century. Abrupt crags rise to the sky as hawks soar above. The site involves steep climbs with, as their reward, the continual glimpsing of new angles, and further treasures.

The first site on the right-hand-side of the road is the **Castalian Spring** (open daily; free). Parts of the

PRECEDING PAGES: narthex fresco, Megálo Metéoron monastery. **LEFT:** Roussánou monastery clings to a Metéora crag. **BELOW:** the *tholos* at Delphi.

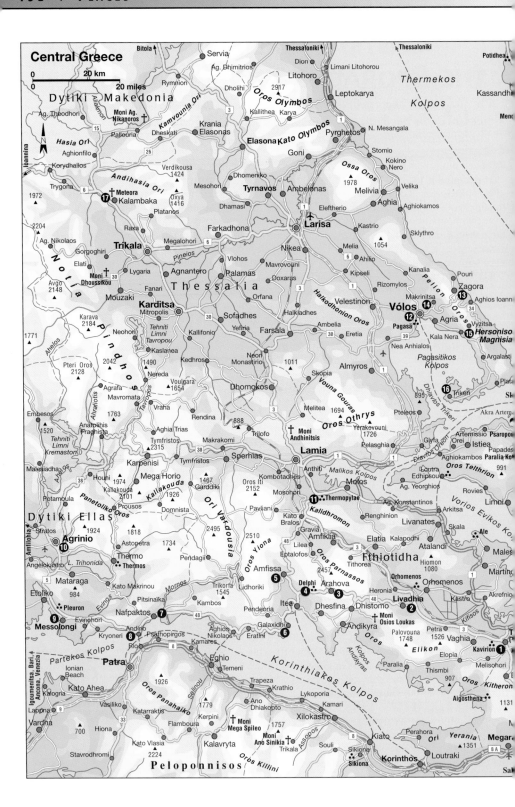

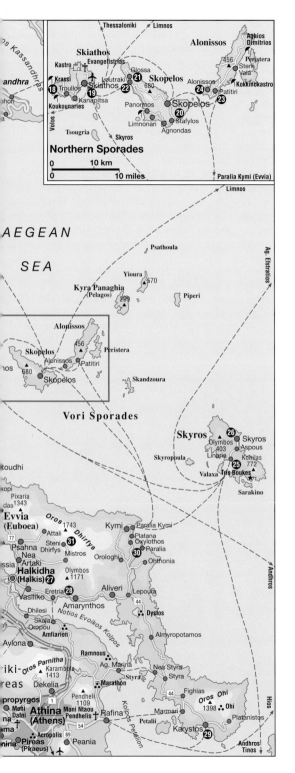

older, rectangular fountain right next to the road date to the 6th century BC, although the thin marble slabs on the floor are Hellenistic or early Roman. The large, rudimentary-looking fountain cut from the rock further in the cleft may date from the same era.

Before the spring, across the road at a lower level to the left, is the **gymnasium** area, complete with a long straight track and a round bath. Further left, towards Aráhova, and down, is the **Athena Pronaia Sanctuary**. Pronaia means "before the temple" and it is through this sanctuary that ancient visitors first passed. The remains here date from the 7th century BC (the early Temple of Athena) up to a 2nd-century AD base for a statue of the Roman emperor Hadrian. The most interesting, and striking, building here is the circular *tholos*, built in the late 4th century BC (open daily 8.30am–3pm, free).

The main site is the **Sanctuary of Apollo**, above the road past the Castalian Spring (open daily 8.30am–3pm). Most of the ruins after the ticket booth are Roman, but inside the sanctuary with its 5th-century BC base for the Corcyrean bull there are earlier monuments.

The top sights

For the modern visitor the highlights are the late 6th-or early 5th-century **Athenian Treasury** just after the first turn on the path; the **Athenian *stoa*** just before the path's second turn, this time to the left; and the **Temple of Apollo**.

The Athenian *stoa*, today with three Ionic columns and the lower segment of a fourth column before a polygonal wall, was a roofed area protecting souvenirs from the Athenian defeat of the Persian invaders. The Persian emperor Xerxes had constructed a floating bridge of ships to bring his army across the Hellespont into Europe. After the Persians were defeated at the Battle of Salamis in 480 BC the Athenians collected the cables used to tie the ships together and the prows of some of the ships, and displayed them here.

The Temple of Apollo on the site is the sixth temple which is supposed to

It was pronounced at Delphi that Oedipus would kill his father and marry his mother – thereby giving the world its most tragic hero and Freud his Oedipus complex.

BELOW: Delphi's Temple of Apollo.

have been built here, although of the first three there is only literary evidence. The fourth was Doric, built in the late 7th century BC; it was destroyed by fire. The fifth temple, also Doric, was completed late in the 6th century BC, and destroyed by earthquake. The sixth temple (what you see today) was built in the 4th century BC. The god Apollo, son of Zeus and Leto, was associated with the finer things in life: music, art, philosophy, law, medicine, archery – and prophecy, which was his main function here.

The oracle of Delphi consisted of several steps. The god Apollo would speak to a woman appointed to be the *Pythia*, who would hear the god's answer only when she was in a trance. Her words, in turn, could be understood only by the priests who interpreted them for the supplicant, often ambiguously, for a fee.

The small **theatre** above the Temple of Apollo was completed only in the 2nd century BC. It seats 5,000 people, has marvellous acoustics and a wonderful view down over the sanctuary. The stadium, 200 m (650 ft) long, is worth the somewhat steep walk. There are twelve rows of seats on the north side of the stadium and six rows of seats, now mostly fallen down the hillside, on the south side. You will easily find the starting and finishing lines, limestone blocks, with grooves cut for the runners' toes.

The 470 BC bronze statue of the charioteer is the most famous inhabitant of the **Delphi Museum**, but there are many other things to see. The massive early 6th-century Kleobis and Biton statues are of two young men the gods rewarded by having them die young in their sleep. The almost life-size silver bull – also dating to the 6th century BC – is the largest surviving ancient sculpture made of precious metal. The 6th-century Naxian sphinx used to guard the Temple of Apollo, and stood over 11m (36 ft) high on its column.

Also in this room are the friezes from the Siphnian Treasury showing scenes from the Trojan War and the battle between the gods and the giants (open daily, 8.30am–3pm).

Ámfissa, Galaxídhi, and Náfpaktos

Below Delphi, a seemingly endless plain of olive trees stretches north to the medieval capital of **Ámfissa ❺**, famous for its sheep's bells and olives. The town has a fine early 13th-century Frankish castle. To the south, the road goes down to the port town of **Itéa**. It is obvious that bauxite was loaded on to ships here for years, but if you keep on going you will reach the beautiful little port town of **Galaxídhi ❻**. Local shipowners prospered in the 18th and 19th centuries, building some fine old mansions, but eventually losing the competition with steamboats. There are some comfortable hotels, and a few good seafood restaurants and bars along the narrow harbour.

The very pretty coastal road winds on to **Náfpaktos ❼**. If you are driving and are not watchful you can pass right by, but the round little harbour here was once of major importance. The Ottomans used it as a base before heading out to defeat in the naval battle of Lepanto (which is what the Venetians called Náfpaktos), at the hands of an allied Christian armada commanded by John of Austria in 1571. An Ottoman chronicler records, "The Imperial fleet encountered the fleet of the wretched infidels and the will of God turned another way." For all its reputation, however, the battle had little significance because the Ottomans were so powerful at the time that they rebuilt their fleet within a year. It is well worth the climb up from the toy-like Venetian harbour, past little gardens, to the almost impregnable castle above.

Cervantes, then a crewman on a Spanish ship, lost his left arm to a cannonball at the Battle of Lepanto, fought at Náfpaktos in 1571.

BELOW: the little port town of Galaxídhi has a lovely setting.

From Náfpaktos, one can take a very indirect detoured route to Delphi by the old upland road along the slopes of **Mount Yióna**, as beautiful as the coast road and more hazardous. On the way, the stone village of **Lidhoríki** is near the birthplace of General Makriyánnis, a fighter in the War of Independence whose memoirs are the best insight into the mind of old Roúmeli. Here is a chance to breathe the air and stretch your legs before going on past the shining waters of the **Mórnos reservoir**, which helps to supply Athens with water. Stark rocks are intermittently set off by green valleys dotted with cattle; mountain fauna such as hawks (and occasionally eagles) and rock thrushes are noticeable.

Messolóngi, Agrínio, and the west coast

Continuing from Náfpaktos towards the west coast, the landscape is flatter and not as interesting. After **Andírio ❽**, the landing point for ferry boats from **Río** across the gulf of Kórinthos, the road climbs into the hills and passes by the ancient city of Calydon (of the mythological Calydonian boar hunt) where there are virtually no remains to be seen, and then winds down along the plain to the city of **Messolóngi ❾**, where Lord Byron died in 1824. The town had been under attack by the Turks since 1822. In 1825 the final siege was undertaken by 25,000 troops against 5,000 defenders. After a year of full siege, almost the entire population, soldiers and civilians, broke out of the town but were cut down in the mountains. Only 1,500 of the 9,000 people who broke out reached safety. The few townspeople who remained in town fired their own magazines, killing themselves and many Turkish attackers.

The entrance to the town through the Venetian wall is known as the **Gate of the Sortie**, constructed by King Otho where the inhabitants broke out of the

ABOVE: fortification, Náfpaktos harbour.
BELOW: Náfpaktos waterfront.

siege. To the right is the **Garden of Heroes**, with a tumulus covering the bodies of the unnamed defenders; the tomb of the Greek commander, Márkos Vótsaris; and a statue of Byron, beneath which the poet's heart is buried.

From Messolóngi the main road goes through the wild **Klisoúra gorge** by **Agrínio** and on to **Amfilóhia** at the southernmost point of the **Amvrakikós Gulf**, tobacco country much of the way. If you are going to Préveza and up the west coast of Epirus, a more interesting and far more beautiful route is to turn off the main highway after Messolóngi and go through **Etolikó, Neohóri, Astakós, Mýtikas**, and **Páleiros** to **Vónitsa**. The farming country between Etolikó until shortly before Astakós is quite pleasant, and from then on until Páleiros the road runs by the sea. The only drawbacks to this road are potholes and free-ranging pigs, cows, sheep and goats.

North from Thermopylae to Vólos

In antiquity, **Thermopylae** ⓫ was a narrow passage between the cliffs and the sea, although today silt from the nearby river has moved the coastline almost 5 km (3 miles) away. In 480 BC the Spartan king Leonidas held the pass for three days against a vastly larger Persian army until the Persians outflanked the defenders by using another mountain pass. Leonidas dismissed most of the Greek fighters, but fought with 400 Thespians and 300 Spartans until they were overwhelmed. A glorified statue of Leonidas now stands on the site, across the road from the grave mound for the Greek dead. Just beyond are the hot sulphur springs (Thermopylae means "hot gates") after which the pass is named.

One's first impression of **Vólos** ⓬ is that some giant took an accordion made of Athens, Piraeus (Pireás), Thessaloníki and all their outlying suburbs, and

Jason, who set out in the famous ship Argo to find the Golden Fleece, began his journey in Iolkos, an ancient site on the outskirts of Vólos.

BELOW: Vólos is one of the oldest port cities in Greece.

Orchards of cherry and apple spread out on the terraced hillsides below Mount Pélion. Look out for delicacies like these bottled fruits in the local village shops.

compressed it. This busy modern port is one of the fastest-growing industrial centres in the country – but there is a lovely promenade along the quay, and the harbour reminds one of island harbours more than big city ports. Running down to the sea are numerous narrow streets in whose arcades are hidden some great little *ouzerís*. Like most important Greek port cities, Vólos has an incredibly long history, dating back to Neolithic times (about 4600–2600 BC); the **Archeological Museum** here is worth exploring (open Tues–Sun 8.30am–3pm; entrance fee).

Mount Pélion

The mythological explanation for the mountains which circle the great Thessalian plain is wonderfully imaginative. Huge creatures called Titans or Giants (depending on whose version of the story you read – Homer, Hesiod, Ovid, Virgil) vied with each other to dominate the new gods, Zeus and Poseidon. What modern scientists call earthquakes, ice flows or tectonic plate-shifts, were simply credited to the Titans. It was they who tried to pile Pélion on Ossa, and both mountains on top of Olympus to reach the heavenly realm of the gods.

Mount Pélion was the land of the centaurs. These celebrated beings had the legs and bodies of horses (indicating the importance of the horse in the development of civilisation) and the arms and heads of men, and they were the teachers of many of the major heroes, including Achilles.

Intriguingly, the entire Pélion region was a main centre of learning in Greece throughout the 17th and 18th centuries. Many of the important secretaries and governors of provinces in the Austro-Hungarian Empire, in the sultan's inner circle and even a few in the Russian court were educated on Mount Pélion. Not much remains of this grandeur, but **Zagorá** ⓭, the largest village, still boasts

BELOW: traditional "Pélion-style" house, Makrinítsa.

an excellent library and **Makrinítsa** , about 19 km (12 miles) from Vólos, has preserved the highest concentration of 18th-century "Pélion-style" houses. Probably the original reason for the place becoming such a nursery of Greek erudition was its lush water supply, and its inaccessibility to the Turks.

The northeast facing beaches, where Mount Pélion crashes into the sea, are very beautiful, with their creamy Caribbean sand – real sand – and sea more turquoise and filtered purple than any photograph can convey. Sea-fashioned caves and hidden coves like Mylopótamos will lure you down the many steps at Tsangaráda or the twisty road that ends up at the resort of **Ághios Ioánnis**. You will need a number of days to see all the villages nestled on the slopes of Mount Pélion: do not miss **Miliés**, and **Vyzítsa**  (one of Pélion's most beautiful villages with cobblestone streets and houses on a par with Makrinítsa's to the north), **Ághios Lavréndis**, dedicated to folk art, or **Trikéri** , an isolated fishing village, to the south.

Metéora

Suddenly, as you round a bend in the dull road from Tríkala to Kalambáka, towering rock formations rise before you – the **Metéora** . Some of the most extraordinary monasteries in the world cling to these massive rocks, whose name derives from the verb *meteorízo*, to suspend in the air. Few places in Greece are so intensely visual. The strange outcroppings of rock, which once supported 24 monasteries, defy description. Most geologists hold to the theory that they were created by millions of years of erosion by the **Piniós river** as it split the Pindos (Píndhos) range to the west of the Thessalian plain from that of Mount Olympus (Ólymbos) and Mount Ossa in the east.

Map, pages 198–9

ABOVE: fresco, Megálo Metéoron. monastery.
BELOW: Ághios Stéfanos monastery.

Willows, planes and laurels border the Piniós River which cuts through the Vale of Témbi, making it a delightful place to hike. You can also take a boat-trip through the gorge.

BELOW: a priest on Skiáthos.

Whoever was the first hermit to scale a pinnacle – Andronikos or Athanasios, depending upon which of the various histories you may read – you can only marvel at how long it took to get stone by stone, brick by brick, board by board up to those heights with a basket and a rope ladder. The largest of the monasteries, the **Megálo Metéoron** – also known as Metamórphosis, or Transfiguration – took three centuries to complete after it was founded around 1356. **Ághios Stéfanos** (now run by nuns) was completed at the end of the 1300s.

Of the 24 monastic communities that flourished until the last part of the 17th century (their heyday was the 14th and 15th centuries), 18 are in ruins, and only six are inhabited and open to visitors. Clockwise, the visible monasteries are: **Ághios Nikólaos**, built around 1388 with a small chapel containing frescoes by the monk Theofánes of the Cretan School (*circa* 1527); Megálo Metéoron, looked after by a few monks of the St Basil order with a valuable collection of manuscripts dating from the 9th century and ancient icons displayed in the old refectory; **Varlaám**, with 16th-century frescoes by Franco Catellano (partly restored in 1870) and an old windlass, now used only for lifting supplies but formerly used for elevating monks as well; **Aghía Triádha** (Holy Trinity) which is approached by approximately 139 difficult steps chiselled out of the rock; and Ághios Stéfanos, with a renovated chapel and small museum displaying ecclesiastical robes, icons, manuscripts and similar treasures.

The **Vale of Témbi**, oblivious of time and armies, remains the same welcome lushness of cool and green as it has been for thousands of years. Even the encroachments of tourism have not changed the beautiful Piniós River which cuts the 10-km (6-mile) pass between Mount Olympus (Ólymbos) and Mount Ossa, although the steps down to the river are packed with souvenir shops. It was here in the Vale of Témbi that Daphne called for help in escaping the ardent Apollo. Her prayer was answered when she was turned into a laurel tree, which Apollo took as his sacred plant.

The Sporades: Skiáthos

The scythe of **Koukounariés** ⓲ is used as evidence on thousands of postcards that the Aegean can produce the kind of beach normally associated with the Caribbean. Propriety would prevent as many postcards from featuring **Krassí** (colloquially "**Banana Beach**") because it caters for nudists. The fact that no one cares whether bathers at Banana Beach strip off or not is typical of the easy-going, relaxed nature of the people of **Skiáthos** as a whole. The island has beaches for all occasions, not least because some among the supposed 60 will always be sheltered wherever the wind is coming from.

Koukounariés and Banana are near-neighbours at the end of the twisting, busy 18-km (11-mile) coast road from **Skiáthos Town** ⓳; there are dozens of beaches along it and several more beyond it, many with a taverna or at least a kiosk selling drinks and sandwiches. A path leading down from the road usually promises a beach at the end; with luck it won't be as crowded as Koukounariés. Round-the-island boat trips pass the rocky and otherwise inaccessible northern shoreline where the only human construc-

tion is the **Kástro**, the abandoned 16th-century capital once connected to the rest of the island by a single drawbridge. For 300 years the islanders huddled on this wind-buffeted crag, hoping the pirates would pass them by. During the last war Allied soldiers hid out there, waiting for evacuation. Nowadays it is an obligatory stop for the excursion caïques after they have dipped into three technicolour grottoes and dropped anchor at **Lalária**, a cove famous for its smooth, round stones, and before proceeding to a beach taverna for lunch.

A moped or hired car – or perhaps a mule and a desperate craving to get away from it all – would be necessary to follow the unpaved roads looping through the mountains. They provide stunning views as well as the chance to pop into monasteries which, with Kástro, are more or less the only buildings of historic interest. Of these, the grandest and closest to town is **Evangelistrías**, with **Kéchrias** and **Kounístra** also pilgrimage-worthy should the beaches pall.

The bluff above the under-used beach at the end of the very busy airport runway has produced fragments suggesting a prehistoric settlement, but neither it nor the rest of the island has ever been properly excavated. Fires set by the Nazis destroyed most of the pretty prewar town. But the port makes up in liveliness what it may lack in architectural merit. In fact, its nightlife is probably the most important consideration after the beaches for the type of visitor which Skiáthos Town attracts in intimidating numbers in August.

The preferences of the fast-living set change constantly, but it is not difficult to spot which places are in vogue, whether one's preference is for beer and blues, wine and Vivaldi, or tequila and fifties Rock. The lights are brightest but also the tackiest along **Papadhiamántis**, the road which bisects the two hills on which the town stands, and along the *paralía* or waterfront. The atmosphere

Map, pages 198–9

BELOW: Skiáthos Town's extremely lively nightlife belies its size.

is a bit classier and quieter around **Polytehníou** and the cobbled alleys above the port. Expect restaurants (with international flavours as well as Greek) rather than tavernas, and be prepared to pay accordingly, especially along the seafront. To the fury of taxi drivers and the regular bus operators, the tavernas out of town lay on special transport from the main dock.

The permanent population of 5,100 also includes an expatriate colony in lovely houses on the **Kanapítsa peninsula**. The fact that they want nothing done to improve the deplorable state of the access road says something, as do doubts about the new – and larger – airport terminal building. The island hardly needs to be able to admit more visitors than already arrive between mid-July and mid-September. Skiáthos has many devotees who return year after year – they know better and adjust their timing to suit.

Skópelos

Skópelos's distinguished past is not so much demonstrated by prominent historical sites as by the exceptionally fine houses in **Skópelos Town ⓴**, a handsome amphitheatre around a harbour lined with bars and tavernas under mulberry trees. The island escaped earthquakes and Nazi vindictiveness and is therefore the most "authentic" and traditional of the three northern Sporades (Skýros being in a class by itself). Slate roofs, wooden balconies, hand-painted shop signs and flagstone streets give it a serenity and dignity rarely found in Skiáthos in season. On the other hand, beaches are not the island's forte. It has far fewer than Skiáthos and Alónissos – mostly on the south and west coasts – though nudists are welcomed at **Velanio** just beyond the family beach at **Stáfylos** (where the king's tomb was found).

ABOVE: fishermen on Skópelos mend their nets.
BELOW: picking salad greens (*hórta*) on Skiáthos.

As compensation, Skópelos offers forested hills for spectacular walks to 40 monasteries and 360 churches, 123 of which are tucked among the houses above the port, which in turn is crowned by a Venetian castle planted on ancient foundations. **Glóssa ㉑**, the island's other town, is something of an oddity in that the people who live there have a pronounced dialect which, together with houses whose features are not like other island architecture, suggests that they immigrated from Thessaly. They seem to have made themselves welcome; other islanders refer approvingly to their "exaggerated hospitality". The main road on the island runs between the port of **Loutráki ㉒**, where Glóssa used to stand before it moved up the mountain for safety's sake, and Skópelos Town. It is an attractive run which includes a number of hamlets, beaches and **Panórmou Bay**, where there are a few remains of a city which probably existed in 500 BC. Now yachts park in one of its fjord-like inlets and tavernas ring its shores.

Alónissos

On the hill above **Patitíri ㉓**, the last port on the Vólos–Ághios Konstantínos ferry and hydrofoil routes, is the **Hóra** (also called **Alónissos Town ㉔**), the former capital destroyed by an earthquake in 1965. This compounded the blow the islanders had already suffered when all their grapevines withered and died from phylloxera only a few years earlier. Alónissos seems to have been ever thus: the previous capital, Ikos, the name by which the island as a whole was known in classical times, literally disappeared when the ground on which it stood toppled into the sea.

The submerged remains of the capital, off **Kokkinókastro** beach, are an important part of a Marine Conservation Park which may be explored with a

Map, pages 198–9

Around 30 endangered Mediterranean monk seals – the largest colony left in the Aegean – live on the deserted islets north of Alónissos. Much of the area is consequently off-limits to both tourists and fishermen.

BELOW: the harbour, Skópelos Town.

snorkel but not with scuba tanks (this is a general rule in the Aegean to prevent pilfering and damage). The way the island has adjusted to its unrealised potential and bad luck is something for which many visitors should be grateful. Its people are laid-back and charming, its atmosphere cheerful and unpretentious. It is also the least developed of the Sporades, a much quieter island surrounded by an interesting collection of islets. Some of them are off-limits to tourists and fishermen alike, protected areas within the Marine Park reserved for the endangered monk seal and other rare fauna. **Yioúra**, for example, is home to a unique breed of wild goat and also has a cave that is full of stalactites and stalagmites. It and **Pipéri** may not be visited but caïques leave Patitíri on calm days for excursions to the closer islets of **Peristéra** and **Kýra Panaghía**, where sheep flocks roam and there are a couple of monasteries to glimpse.

In the absence of proper roads (apart from the one to **Stení Vála**, which is the island's centre for research and protection of the Mediterranean monk seal), caïques are the most practical form of transport and there is a fleet of them waiting every morning at Patitíri to take bathers to the beach of their choice. The terrain is rugged and walking accordingly quite demanding, but exploring by motorbike is much safer here than it is on the winding gravel roads of Skiáthos and Skópelos.

The path from Patitíri up to the site of the 1965 earthquake looks and is steep, but the old town is served by a bus and is well worth a visit. Thanks largely to the efforts of foreigners who spied a bargain and bought up the old ruins, it is fast coming back to life. Boutiques are springing up in once-abandoned courtyards and there are several bars and tavernas commanding stunning views as well as providing restorative drinks and delicious food.

ABOVE: coffee-shop sign, Patitíri.
BELOW: Alónissos is the smallest and quietest of the northern Sporades.

Skýros

Skýros was probably two islands originally, the halves joining near where there is now a road linking **Linariá** ㉕, the main port, with the little village of **Aspoús** on the way to Skýros Town. The southern sector of the island is mountainous and largely barren, and visitors are unlikely to venture below **Kolimbádha** unless they are heading for **Pénnes** beach or the English poet Rupert Brooke's grave in an olive grove at Treís Boúkes. **Trís Boúkes** is about a 30-minute drive from Kolimbádha and Pénnes another 15 minutes more over a reasonably well-tended, wide dirt road.

The beaches at **Paghiá** and **Skloúka** just north of Kolimbádha are lined with a growing number of summer homes but have none of the appeal of the beaches in the northern half of the island. The real appeal of the southern part of the island is from the sea, for cliffs along most of the coast from Pénnes all the way around to **Ahílli Bay** near Aspoús fall straight down into the sea. These cliffs are inhabited by a few wild goats and seemingly innumerable Eleanora's falcons, which can be seen darting around the heights all the way over to Skýros Town. Excursions by boat can be arranged at the port of Linariá, where the Flying Dolphins and the island-owned ferry come in to land.

Skýros Town ㉖ is on the northern half of the island on the east coast, high above the long sand beach at the **Magaziá**. Life in the town is played out all along the meandering main street, which runs from the telephone exchange (OTE) past the raised, largely ignored square to the northern edge of town where the highly romantic statue of Rupert Brooke commands the view. A side street wanders up to the **kástro**, the old Byzantine/Venetian castle on the heights.

The beach below town runs from the Magaziá all the way down to **Mólos**,

Map, pages 198–9

BELOW: the fact that Brooke's memorial statue is a naked figure caused a local scandal when first unveiled.

A CORNER OF A FOREIGN FIELD ...

It was quite by chance that Skýros became the burial-place of the poet Rupert Brooke. When war broke out in 1914, Brooke at first thought of becoming a war corres-pondent, but soon changed his mind and decided to join up. He enlisted as a second lieutenant in the newly formed Royal Naval Division, and briefly saw action at the fall of Antwerp. In the spring of 1915, he arrived on the island of Límnos, where ships and men had begun massing in preparation for the ill-fated assault on Gallipoli.

Moúdhros Bay became so crowded that Brooke's detachment was ordered to wait instead off the bay of Trís Boúkes, in the far south of Skýros. Between manoeuvres, he and some fellow officers rested on shore in a small olive grove above the bay which, the others remembered, the poet particularly liked. Three days later he died of blood-poisoning on a hospital ship, aged 27; his fellow-officers buried him in the olive grove.

Brooke was subsequently beatified in the eyes of a nation mourning its youthful heroes, even though he never lived to see the horrors of trench warfare. Today, the site can be reached by caïque, on foot from Kolimbádha, or by taxi. There is also a memorial to Brooke in Skýros Town – a highly romanticised bronze statue of "Immortal Poetry".

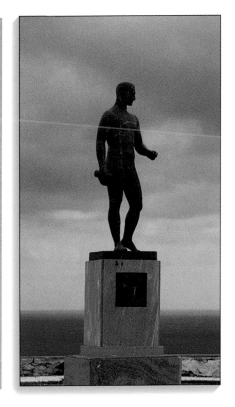

Map,
pages
198–9

with more stretches of beach – not as attractive – farther along the northeast coast near **Polýhri**. On the east side of the island there are pleasant sandy coves at Linariá just past the port and Péfkos. The central section of this part of the island is wooded, as is the northern coast from just past the airport down to the little bay of **Atsítsa** which has, as required, a small taverna by the water.

Évvia (Euboea)

Évvia, Greece's second-largest island (after Crete) is just off the coast of mainland Greece, looking on the map like a large jigsaw puzzle piece just slightly out of position. The island's main town, **Halkídha ㉗**, is close enough to the mainland for a small drawbridge and a new, far larger suspension bridge to make easy connection. Aristotle is supposed to have been so frustrated in trying to understand the tides here in the narrow channel, which are highly irregular and sometimes quite fast, that he jumped into the waters.

Halkídha is now an industrial town, but the **kástro** with its mosque and church of **Aghía Paraskeví** are worth visiting, as is the Archeological Museum in the new town. There is also a synagogue, built in the middle of the 19th century and still used by the very small but active Jewish Romaniote community. **Erétria ㉘** to the south is a crowded summer resort town where the ferries land from **Skála Oropoú** on the mainland. As with Halkídha, Erétria is a town to pass through, but the small **Archeological Museum** here is very good, although sadly it is rarely open.

ABOVE: statue in Halkídha town.
BELOW: the waterfront, Halkídha.

In general, the southern part of the island is drier and less green. The coastal road from Erétria is dotted with villages and summer homes until just before **Alivéri** where it turns inland. The turning for the south, notably the prosperous seaside town of **Kárystos ㉙** is at **Lépoura**. From here the main road goes through the hamlet of **Háni Avlonaríou**, with the large and unusual 14th-century church of **Ághios Dhimítrios**, before continuing through often beautiful hilly farmland to drop down on the east coast to **Paralía** (or Stómio) ㉚ where a small river reaches the sea. The wide new road then runs along the shore through **Platána** to the harbour at **Paralía Kými** and the boat to Skýros. North of Halkídha the small village of **Stení ㉛** on the slopes of **Mount Dhírfys** is a favourite goal for Athenians seeking clean air and grill restaurants. **Límni** on the west coast is a pretty and convenient 19th-century town, although the beaches are unimpressive.

A long stretch of truly outstanding beach lies farther north, after the ancient but still functioning baths at **Loutrá Edhipsoú**, from **Gregolímano** and **Ághios Yeórghios** all the way around the triangular point of the peninsula. The east coast is mountainous, with rocky shoulders dropping sharply down to the sea, but there are a few beaches worth seeking out. They include **Angáli** beach, **Paralía Kotsikiás**, **Psaropoúli** beach, and **Elliniká** beach, of which the last is the smallest and prettiest.

The famous bronze statue of Poseidon poised to throw a spear, now in Room 15 of the National Museum, was found in the sea off **Cape Artemesion** on the northern coast in 1928. ❑

Island Hopping

The pleasures of travelling from one island to another using Greece's inter-linking ferry routes are numerous. There is the never-ceasing view – a bas-relief pattern in blue of low, mysterious mountains. A chance to mingle with the Greeks themselves who pile on board with food, children and, as often as not, a *bouzoúki* or two. Plus, a unique opportunity to visit other islands not on the itinerary – 15 minutes closely observing a port from the top deck can reveal much about a place and its people.

To travel the ferries wisely, it helps to remember three basic facts. First, ferry journeys can be long. Second, they can be frustrating. If your ship reaches the island you want in the middle of the night, it is your responsibility to wake up and get off. Seasoned island-hoppers travel with an alarm clock. However, a hasty departure in darkness has deposited more than one independent traveller on the wrong island altogether.

Third, weather is a factor. The wind called the *meltémi* is a fact of Greek life, although recent reports indicate that the famous *El Niño* has weakened it somewhat. Don't bank on it. When the winds are too strong the ships are delayed or kept in port. If you are relying on the ferries to get you back to Athens for your flight home, leave at least one full day's leeway. Athens has its pleasures; missing your flight does not.

The best known ferry routes are the main Cyclades circuit (Santoríni, Íos, Náxos, Páros and Mýkonos) and the Argo-Saronic Gulf route (Aegina, Hydra, Póros). Another route is to the major Dodecanese islands; travelling between Rhodes, Kós, Kálymnos, Léros and Pátmos is easy. Less well known, and therefore more satisfying, are the western Cyclades islands (Kýthnos, Sérifos, Sífnos and Mílos) and three of the four Sporades islands (Skiáthos, Skópelos, Alónissos). These routes exist as much to serve domestic needs as they are to serve tourists and they operate all year round, albeit at a reduced

level. Both Rhodes and Kós in the Dodecanese are hubs for several satellite islands. And there are also the Ionian islands, where it is easy to travel among Lefkádha, Itháki, and Kefalloniá.

Bookshops in Athens sell a monthly guide called *Hellenic Traveling*, an expensive but good source of information about most sailings. A map is useful when studying it, for some of the listings give the name of the port rather than the name of the island.

In recent years the hydrofoils have been playing an increasing role in inter-island travel. They now go to all the islands mentioned above in much less time than is taken by the ferries. This is great, particularly if time is limited, but there are disadvantages. The hydrofoils are considerably more expensive and provide practically no view. Nor are hydrofoils immune to the weather, for they are less able to bear high waves than ferries. And they have been known to stay in port through a scheduled departure simply because there were not enough passengers to justify the trip. There is no way to escape the uncertainties. ❏

RIGHT: unless you do your research, it's easy to miss a connection or end up on the wrong island.

THE ISLANDS IN BLOOM

The Greek islands are at their most bountiful in spring and early summer, when every hillside and valley is decorated with glorious colour

Greece in spring is a botanist's dream and a gardener's despair. Some 6,000 species of wild plant grow in Greece and the islands, and in the spring (March to May) visitors may enjoy a magnificent cornucopia of flowers and fragrances.

Hillsides resemble giant rock gardens, while brilliant patches of untended waste ground outdo northern Europe's carefully tended herbaceous borders with ease. Winter rains, followed by a bright, hot, frost-free spring, produce a season's flowers compressed into a few, spectacular weeks before the summer's heat and drought become too much. By late May or June the flowers are over, the seeds for next year's show are ripening, and greens are fading to brown to match the tourists on the beaches.

SUMMER SURVIVAL

Except in the cooler, higher mountains, most plants go into semi-dormancy to survive the arid summer. The first rains of autumn, which could be in early September, but may be late November, tempt a few autumn bulbs into flower but also initiate the germination of seeds – plants that will grow and build up strength during the winter in preparation for the following spring when their flowers will again colour in the waiting canvas of the hills and valleys.

The richness and diversity of the flora are due in part to the islands' location between three continents – Europe, Asia and Africa – partly to the Ice-Age survival in temperate Greece of pre-glacial species, and partly to the wonderful variety of habitats. Limestone, the foundation of much of Greece, is a favoured home for plants, providing the stability, minerals, water supply and protection they need.

▷ **THE HILLS ARE ALIVE**
Sunshine, colour and quantity mark the spring flowering of the islands, as here in the mountains of Crete in mid-April.

△ **A GOOD REED**
Not bamboo – but it has similar uses. The giant reed (*Arundo donax*) can even be made into pan-pipes.

▽ **CUP OF MANY COLOURS**
Ranunculus asiaticus is an unlikely buttercup, with poppy-sized flowers in shades of white, pink, orange, red – and occasionally yellow.

▽ **SCARLET MEMORIAL**
The startling reds of *Anemone coronaria* mark the arrival of spring and in myth represent the spilt blood of the dying Adonis.

▽ **HANDY BUSH**
The long flowering period of the native oleander makes it popular in garden and as an ornamental roadside crash-barrier.

BEETLES, BEES AND BUTTERFLIES

△ FIRE FENNEL
According to legend, fire was brought to earth by Prometheus hidden in the smouldering stem of a giant fennel (*Ferula communis*).

▽ NATURAL FOOD
Wild artichokes are painfully spiny to prepare for the pot, but their flavour is much prized by Greek country folk over the spineless cultivated variety, and their market price increases accordingly.

The profusion of flowers and plants provides food for an equal profusion of insects. Butterflies are conspicuous from spring to autumn, including the lovely swallowtail (*above*) whose colourful caterpillars feed on the leaves of common fennel. Its larger, paler and more angular relative, the scarce swallowtail, despite its name, is even more abundant.

Look for clouded yellows and paler cleopatras, reddish-brown painted ladies and southern commas, white admirals, and a myriad of smaller blue butterflies.

Butterflies, bees and day-flying hawkmoths tend to go for flowers with nectar, while beetles and flies go for the pollen. Some bugs even use the heat accumulated in the solar cup of many flowers in order to warm up their sex lives.

The leaves of plants feed armies of insect herbivores, which themselves are eaten by more aggressive insects. Some of the omniverous Greek grasshoppers and crickets are as happy munching through a caterpillar, or even another grasshopper, as the grass it was sitting on.

Map, page 218

THE IONIAN ISLANDS

Lushest of all the Greek island chains, the Ionians offer superb beaches, great natural beauty and a distinct culture – including a graceful Venetian influence in the local architecture

During the 8th and 7th centuries BC, wanderers from Corinth settled on the most northern of the Ionians, bringing with them a distinct culture. Two centuries later, Corfu's secession from Corinth brought about the beginning of the Peloponnesian War. Subsequently, the Ionians have had many warrior landlords – including Napoleon – but it was the long period of Venetian rule (1396–1797) which has left the most indelible mark on the islands.

A heavy rainfall makes the Ionians among the greenest of Greek island chains. Olive groves and vineyards are reminders that agriculture, rather than tourism, still claim a part in the economy. However, this same unsettled weather has dampened many a traveller's holiday; from mid-September until mid-May, rains can wash out any beach outing quite without warning.

Corfu (Kérkyra)

The **Old Port**, where the ferries from the mainland dock, and the **Old Fort** (dating back to the 8th century) are both in the north of **Corfu Town** (Kérkyra Town) ❶, while Kanóni, overlooking the picturesque **Pondikoníssi** island, is in the south. In between lie beautiful Italianate buildings with narrow streets, small squares, churches, leather shops, restaurants, ice-cream stands, grocery stores, jewellery stores and all the regular stores and bakeries of a busy people.

BELOW: brightly painted doorway, Corfu Town.

The 16th-century **New Fort** is in better shape than the Old Fort. Traditionally, a large, open esplanade was kept between the Old Fort and the town so attackers would have no cover. Today the esplanade, or **Spianádha**, gives the city a wide field of green on which the locals play cricket, a legacy of Corfu's years as a British protectorate (1830–64). The two graceful 18th- and 19th-century apartment buildings facing the green are known as the **Listón**, a reference to those people listed high enough socially to walk beneath the arcades. The 16th-century church of **Ághios Spyrídhon**, the island's guardian saint (many local men are named Spýros), lies in the streets behind.

Whatever else you may do in Corfu Town, don't miss the **Archeological Museum**'s gorgon's-head pediment, which once decorated a 6th-century BC Temple of Artemis in the ancient city of Paleopolis. There is nothing else like in it archaic Greek art (open Tues–Sun 9am–3pm; entrance fee).

Kontokáli, now serving the tourist trade, lies on the coast north of Corfu Town, which is filled all along the bay with hotels, restaurants and shops. The best beach along this stretch is the farthest, at **Barbáti**, before the mountains drop more sharply down to the sea. The small beach at **Nissáki** ❷ has crystal clear aquamarine water; the coastline which stretches northeast from here is particularly beautiful. **Kassiópi** is one of the busier resorts, with a ruined Angevin castle on the headland, several wonderful pebble beaches and many discotheques and bars.

Along the northern coast, **Aharávi** appears as an unappealing crossroads on the main road, but the village closer to the sea is quiet and pleasant. **Ródha** and **Sidhári** are full-tilt tourist development without judgement. However, there are some quiet beaches in the northwest below the attractive village of **Perouládhes**; the resort of **Ághios Stéfanos ❸** is also enjoyable.

If you rent a car, the roads in the hills around **Mount Pandokrátor** can be idyllic, with views over cypresses towering dark green over silver-green olive trees. The narrow, winding roads can be dangerous.

The most famous beaches are on the west coast, beginning with the wide bay of **Ághios Yeórghios**. The hamlet of **Kríni** leads to the 13th-century Angevin castle of **Angelókastro**, after which appear the beautiful double bays of **Paleokastrítsa ❹**, once idyllic, now swamped with visitors. The smaller bay of **Ermónes** is upmarket; **Glyfádha** and **Ághios Górdhis** are highly developed, highly popular long stretches of sandy beach. Best-known of the sights along the east coast of the island is the pretentious **Achilleion** (near **Gastoúri** village), built in the late 19th century for the Empress Elisabeth of Austria.

Benítsis ❺ on the southeastern coast below Corfu Town is heavily developed, with an active night life. **Messongí** is more pleasant and, farther on, Boukáris even more so in that it has only a few restaurants and hotels and a decent stretch of undeveloped coast. The big (British) package tour centre is **Kávos** on the east coast near the southernmost tip of the island. If you are an unredeemed adolescent, go here; otherwise, stay clear.

The Greeks call these west coast islands the Eftanísa – the seven isles. But as Kýthira, the seventh isle, lies off the southern tip of the Peloponnese, it remains quite isolated from the others.

BELOW: a cricket match on the Spianádha, Corfu Town.

Paxí (Paxos)

Paxí is hilly and green with rugged cliffs and some good beaches interspersed with groves of olive trees. Do not miss the pretty town of **Gáios ➏**, or the beautiful little horseshoe bay at **Lákka ➐**, with a Byzantine church and two beaches. **Longós** on the eastern coast is a pretty village with some good tavernas, near **Gastoúri** village, but better swimming is at the adjacent **Levrehió** beach. **Andipaxí** islet has two tavernas open during the summer.

Lefkádha (Lefkas)

Lefkádha can only be reached by road over a floating drawbridge across the Lefkádha canal. **Lefkádha Town ➑**, which faces the canal, has safe mooring for yachts.

Much of the island's olive groves and vineyards are along the protected east coast, which has some fine calm-water beaches all the way through **Lygiá** and **Nikiána** down to the tourist boom-town of **Nydhrí ➒**, on the northern edge of deeply indented **Vlyhós Bay**.

On the south coast, the most dramatic cove is the narrow bay of **Sývota**. **Vassilikí ➓**, over the mountain, has a fine little harbour and a good long beach, the goal for many windsurfers. Boats leave from here for the sharply pointed **Sappho's Leap** peninsula and the lovely west coast beaches beyond.

Ághios Nikítas on the north coast is a tiny fishing village now utterly overwhelmed by the summer crowd; avoid it in high season. From **Ághios Ioánnis** on the north coast, there is a continuous stretch of beach all the way past the old windmills and around the shallow saltwater lake known as the **Yíra** to a lighthouse on a canal, near the 14th-century Santa Maura fort.

Itháki (Ithaca)

Most boats dock at the main town, **Vathý ⓫**, at the end of a deeply inset bay. The town was badly damaged by an earthquake in 1953, but much has been rebuilt in the old style. **Arethoúsa's Spring**, the **Cave of the**

Nymphs and ancient **Alalkomenes**, all associated with Odysseus, are near Vathý. The route across the isthmus and along the coast to the villages of **Léfki** and **Stavrós** in the northern half of the island is particularly beautiful.

Stavrós ⓬ is a pleasant but undistinguished town above the nearby **Pólis** beach. Remains of the island's oldest settlement are on **Pelikáta hill** here, but for the most beautiful view on the island, go on past the little hill-village of **Exoghí** to the chapel. Another road from Stavrós leads to the village of **Platrithiás**, which also has Mycenaean remains.The two lovely little port villages of **Fríkes** and **Kióni** are ideal but very popular places to stay.

Kefaloniá (Cephalonia)

Kefaloniá is the largest and most mountainous of the Ionian islands. **Mount Énos**, at 1,628m (5,340 ft), is the highest mountain in the Ionian islands, and covered, reasonably enough, in Cephalonian fir. The west coast of the island below **Argostóli ⓭** has some wonderful beaches beginning at **Lássi ⓮** and continuing all the way down the coast. Sea water flows into the unusual so-called "swallow holes" (*katavóthres*) near Argostóli, reappearing on the east coast near Sámi at **Karavómylo**. Although now just a trickle, before the disastrous 1953 earthquake the flow was strong enough to power flour mills. The ruins of the island's Venetian capital, **Ághios Yeórghios**, are well worth seeing.

Numerous fish farms line the road along the east side of the Argostóli Gulf; the west coast is not particularly inviting, either. **Lixoúri** can be reached by ferry from Argostóli. Built since the 1953 earthquake, the town itself is rather dull, but it has some comfortable hotels and restaurants. Skip the first beach to the south, **Lépedha**, for **Mégas Lákkos** and **Xi**, beautiful stretches of red sand

There was an old man of Corfu/Who never knew what he should do/So he rushed up and down/Till the sun turned him brown/That bewildered old man of Corfu.

–EDWARD LEAR

BELOW: Fiskárdho.

Map, page 218

backed by cliffs. Between them is **Kounopétra**, the huge boulder that used to rock on its bed until the 1953 earthquake set it still. There is a fine beach pebble at **Petaní** in the northwest part of this peninsula.

The beautiful beach at **Myrtosá** is on the east side of the Gulf of Myrtos (when the swell is high, treat the undertow with considerable respect). The village of **Ássos** rests on the isthmus leading to a large hill which rises sharply out of the sea; on the summit is a large 16th-century Venetian fort. But the island's most famous resort is the small port of **Fiskárdho** ⓯, tightly packed in high season. There are wonderful small beaches, many of them with cypress trees, all around this northern part of the island, along with **Melissáni**, an underground lake with part of the roof open to the sky – when the sun shines down on the waters, the colours are magnificent.

Also worth a visit is **Drogarátis Cave**, just west of Sámi, with its weirdly shaped stalactites and stalagmites. And along the coast from Sámi down to **Póros**, the mountain drops steeply to the sea creating innumerable small coves – incomparable, but accessible only by boat.

Zákynthos (Zante)

Zákynthos is another island of green mountains and plains, Venetian architecture, stunning beaches and both good and bad tourist development. Much of the harbour-town of **Zákynthos** ⓰ was rebuilt after the 1953 earthquake in the same style; it may appear like a movie-set but the Venetian atmosphere is far more pleasant than concrete. The 17th-century church of **Ághios Dhionýsios**, the island's patron saint, is on the left of the harbour as your boat approaches, while the 14th-century church of **Ághios Nikólaos tou Mólou** is on the right.

The **Museum of Post-Byzantine Art** here has some superb 17th-and 18th-century paintings (open Tues–Sun 8.30am–3pm; entrance fee).

Most visitors go to the long white sands of **Laganás Bay**, where there is an agglomeration of hotels, restaurants and bars, fast-food joints and discos. However, the explosive development at **Laganás** ⓱ is relatively new. For centuries. the beaches here have been nesting-grounds for Loggerhead turtles (*Caretta caretta*). The Sea Turtle Protection Society patrols the beach to protect the nests and operates an information booth to tell visitors about these beautiful creatures which may startle you as you swim. A long stretch of isolated beach nearby has been bought by the Greek World Wide Fund for Nature to keep undisturbed for turtle-nesting.

The beaches on this island defy superlatives. The southern peninsula below Zákynthos Town past **Argási** ⓲ has some wonderful stretches along the east coast, culminating in **Yeráki** ⓳ at the southern tip. This is also a turtle-nesting ground, so visitors cannot stay on the beach after sunset. At **Kerí** ⓴, on the southwest peninsula, there are incomparable views of the sea; the coast above Kámbi has **Shipwreck Cove**, where an old wreck rests in the sand between towering cliffs; On the northern tip of the island is the **Blue Grotto** – sun on the clear water here reflects an iridescent blue on the cave walls. ❑

RIGHT: cushions have all sorts of uses on Corfu.
BELOW: Shipwreck Cove, Zákynthos.

ISLANDS OF THE SARONIC GULF

Map, page 224

Often viewed as little more than suburbs of Athens and Piraeus, these pine-cloaked isles offer a surprising range of attractions – differing not just from the mainland, but from each other as well

Athens and the islands of the Saronic Gulf are often lumped together in guidebooks. There is sense in this since many Athenians frequent these islands at weekends, while during the summer the islands become veritable extensions of the more fashionable Athenian neighbourhoods. Yet this view of the Argo-Saronic islands doesn't take into account their separate identities. They are islands, not suburbs. Each has its own character and deserves more of our attention.

Salamína (Salamis)

Salamína is best known for an ancient naval battle (480 BC) in which outnumbered Athenian ships routed the enormous Persian fleet – the ships being the "wooden walls" which the Delphic oracle had predicted would save Athens. Pride of the island is the 17th-century **Faneroméni Monastery** on the Voudoro peninsula, just 6 km (4 miles) from the capital, **Salamína Town ❶**.

The island is decidedly not posh. Rather, the appeal is that it is relatively undeveloped and can be reached so quickly, just a few minutes' ride across from Pérama to the port town of **Paloúkia ❷**. Most of the inhabitants live in Salamína (also called **Kouloúri**), which has an archeological and a folk museum. Boats also leave regularly from **Piraeus** (Pireás) **❸** harbour for **Selínia**, **Peráni**, and the little port of **Peristéria ❹** on the east coast. The pleasant village of **Eándio** on the west coast has a good hotel.

Aegina (Éghina)

Aegina is close enough to be within easy reach from the mainland and far enough to retain its island identity. About an hour and a half by ferry from Piraeus – or half an hour by Flying Dolphin hydrofoil – it has had little trouble attracting visitors. Long a favourite Athenian retreat, the island remains more popular among weekend smog-evaders than foreign tourists or Greeks from elsewhere. The main produce is pistachio nuts, sold all along the harbour street.

Shaped on the map like an upside-down triangle, the island's southern point is marked by the magnificent cone of **Mount Óros**, the highest peak in the Argo-Saronic islands, visible on a smog-free day from Athens's Acropolis. The island's centre and eastern side is mountainous; a gently sloping fertile plain runs down to the western corner where **Aegina Town ❺** overlays in part the ancient capital of the island.

Aegina Town has several 19th-century mansions constructed when the first Greek president, Ioánnis

LEFT: morning coffee. **BELOW:** checking the catch of the day in Hydra harbour.

Kapodhístrias (1776–1831), lived and worked here. The **Archeological Museum** in the centre of the town displays a number of interesting artefacts from the island's history (open Tues–Sun 8.30am–3pm; entrance fee). The modern harbour, crowded with yachts and caïques, is next to the ancient harbour, now the shallow town beach north of the main quay, towards the ancient site of **Kolóna**.

Kolóna, meaning "column", is named after the one conspicuously standing column of the **Temple of Apollo**. The temple (Doric, six columns by 12, built in 520–500 BC) was superseded by a late Roman fortress, fragments of which survive on the seaward side. Although from the sea the position of the temple looks unimpressive, the view from the hill is very pleasant. There is a small museum on the site, and the reconstructed mosaic floor of an ancient synagogue (open daily: 8.30am–3pm; single entrance fee for both site and museum).

The island's most famous ancient site is the **Temple of Aphaia**, in the northeast, above the often packed summer resort town of **Aghía Marína**. The temple stands at the top of a hill in a pine grove commanding a splendid view of the Aegean. Built in 490 BC in the years after the victory at Salamis, it has been called "the most perfectly developed of the late Archaic temples in European Hellas". The only surviving Greek temple with a second row of small superimposed columns in the interior of the sanctuary, it is quite beautiful, one of the most impressive ancient temples you will see (open Mon–Fri 8.30am–7pm, Sat–Sun 8.30am–3pm; entrance fee).

On the way to the temple you will pass by the modern **Monastery of Ághios Nektários**, the most recent Orthodox saint, canonised in 1961. Across the ravine from the monastery is the ghostly site known as **Paleohóra** ("old town"), built in the 9th century as protection against piracy. Abandoned in 1826 after Greek

ABOVE: the Temple of Aphaia was built in 490 BC.
BELOW: Aegina's pistachio groves.

independence, most of the 38 churches left standing are in utter disrepair, but you can still see the remains of several frescoes.

The west coast of the island is quite gentle, with a good sandy beach at **Marathóna**, but better reasons to head out here are to enjoy a meal in one of the many fish tavernas along the harbour at **Pérdhika** ❻, or to go on by hired boat to swim at the beautiful beach on the tiny uninhabited island of **Moní**.

Angístri

Angístri is the small island facing Aegina Town. The larger boats stop at **Skála**, while the smaller ones stop at the more attractive **Mýlos**. The island is not much developed but there are several hotels. The most attractive beach is near the lake on the southwestern coast by the small islet of **Dhoroúsa**.

Póros

The island of Póros is separated from the Peloponnese by a small passage of water – the word *póros* in Greek means "passage" or "ford". As your boat turns into the ford from the northern entrance, the channel opens ahead and lovely **Póros Town** ❼ comes into view. Almost landlocked, it is one of the most protected anchorages in the Aegean: your first glimpse will be of white houses and bright orange rooftops with the clock tower on top of the hill. Póros can be reached not only by ship and Flying Dolphin but also (with considerably more effort) by driving via the **Isthmus of Corinth** to **Epídhavros** (Epidauros) and then down to the coast at **Dhryópi** and little **Galatás** ❽ across the channel.

Although a number of hotels have been built on the island and prominent Athenians have owned vacation houses here for decades, it has never been as

In the 7th century BC, Aegina became a leading maritime power, thanks to its strategic position; its silver coins – known as "tortoises" – became common currency in most of the Dorian states.

BELOW: Póros Town is built on a hill, with the highest point at the centre.

Plumbing

A scribbled note behind the bathroom door warned: "Greek loos are dodgy. Throw your paper in the bin provided." Another notice, in another place, was more to the point: "Don't put anything down the toilet you haven't consumed first." It's a sobering thought after *kalamária* and a few *oúzos*.

In Greece, all things lavatorial are a snare and a delusion. Greek plumbing is the eighth wonder of the world – you wonder how it works at all. Everyone has a plumbing experience to relate.

Seasoned Grecophiles know all about the no-paper rule, thus avoiding clogging, flood and hysterics from landladies. They also know that it's a good idea to carry tissues or napkins nabbed from taverna tables, just in case. Cramped cubicles at the back of Kostas's, Yorgos's or Charis's seldom bear close inspection with overflowing bins, floors awash and no loo roll. In extremis the brand-name cry of "Softex" is a nationally recognised distress signal.

Squat-over loos are common, especially if they are public conveniences. You might even come across a hole in the floor over the sea for instant and natural flushing. Brace yourself: some toilets can be grim. For reasons known only to themselves – fear of lavatory seats? Aids scares? – some Greeks prefer to ignore the pan altogether and use the floor instead. And that's just in the Ladies.

In the main, toilet facilities in most tavernas and restaurants are adequate with soap, towels and the ever-present bottle of *hloríni*. And you can be sure that even in the poorest of village *pensions*, the *tó loutró* (bathroom) will be sumptuously decorated. The matching suite is essential, especially if your lodgings are eventually to become a dowry for a lucky daughter. The fact that there's rarely a shower-tray, just a hole in the uneven floor down which water refuses to drain (you have to urge it along with your loo brush), or that the door won't shut because it's been warped by all the water and the posh fittings have all gone rusty, seems neither here nor there.

"Can we drink the water?" is a normal tourist question. "Where can we find the water?" is a specifically Greek inquiry. Lack of fresh water is a problem for many islands, so be prepared to get by with bottled, and wait patiently for the water-boat to arrive.

When the boat comes in there's usually a mad scramble with hosepipes as families fill up their wells, jugs, and containers. You may find you have to make daily trips to the pump or village tap as well. Some islands like Hálki in the Dodecanese have Heath Robinson water systems relying on a spaghetti junction of bewildering pipework. The natural water supply is brackish, but every now and then it can be switched over to fresh for a virtual feast of salt-free washing.

"Save water: shower with a friend," one taverna sticker advised. In the Dodecanese a yachtie almost got lynched by furious villagers for doing his washing at the communal fresh-water tap – so be warned, and pursue cleanliness accordingly. Most countries take good old H_2O for granted, but in arid Greece in high summer, water is a precious commodity and conservation is the key. ❏

LEFT: fresh water is scarce on the islands, so be prepared to pursue cleanliness accordingly.

fashionable as Hydra or Spétses (chiefly because the beaches are fewer and not as good), but during summer it gets every bit as crowded as Aegina.

In 1846 a Greek naval station was established on the northwest side of Póros, on the peninsula just before the narrow stream separating a small section of Póros Town from the main part of the island. When the station moved to Salamína in 1878, the site was used as a school; it is now used for training naval cadets. This area contains several fine family mansions with well-tended gardens and can be a refreshing place to stroll on a hot summer afternoon.

The main sight on Póros is the **Monastery of Zoïdhóhos Pighí** (Virgin of the Life-Giving Spring) beautifully situated on a wooded hillside (20 minutes from town by bus). Only a few monks still live there today. Noteworthy is a wooden, gold-painted iconostasis dating from the 19th century.

In front of the monastery a road encircling the heights to the east climbs through the pine-woods to the ruins of the **Sanctuary of Poseidon** in a saddle between the highest hills of the island. The temple was excavated at the turn of the century and little remains, but its setting is rewarding.

The sanctuary was the headquarters of the Kalavrian League, an association of several towns that included Athens as well. The Athenian orator Demosthenes, who had opposed the imposition of Macedonian rule over Athens, sought refuge in the sanctuary after an Athenian revolt following the death of Alexander the Great was quelled by Antipater, Alexander's successor in Macedonia. When Demosthenes was found, he took poison but stepped outside the sanctuary before dying so he would not defile holy ground.

Ancient **Troizen** (Damalas) is about 8 km (5 miles) from Galatás across the straits on the Peloponnese. The mythological Greek hero Theseus is supposed

Map, page 224

ABOVE: All aboard!
BELOW: the *Flying Dolphin* hydrofoil calls at Póros.

to have grown up here before he went off to Athens to become king. The rock he is said to have raised to prove his strength is still here, next to the Sanctuary of the Muses. Theseus is also meant to have returned to Troizen in his old age, providing Euripides with the plot for his famous play, *Hippolytus*, about the young queen Phaedra who unjustly accused Theseus's son of having violated her. Modern drama is held in the **Devil's Gorge** just above the site. For peace, go to the **Lemonódhasos**, a beautiful grove consisting of some 2,000 lemon trees, about half an hour's walk on the other side of Galatás.

Hydra (Ídhra)

The island of Hydra – once Ydrea, "the well watered" – now appears as a long, barren rock. But the harbour and the white and grey stone buildings which make up the town are still lovely; they have drawn the artistic and the fashionable since the 1950s and many, many more ever since. It is one of the few places in the country that has reined in the uncontrolled growth of cement construction, thus keeping its beauty.

The heart of the island is its harbour-town, also called **Hydra ❾**. All around the picturesque bay white houses climb the slope, accented by massive grey *arhontiká* (mansions built by the shipping families who made fortunes in the 18th and 19th centuries), many of them designed by architects from Venice and Genoa. Along the quay are the colourful shops of the marketplace, with the clock tower of the 18th-century **Monastery of the Panaghía** in the centre; much of the stone used to build it was taken from the ancient Sanctuary of Poseidon on the island of Póros. The harbour itself, girded by a little thread of a breakwater, forms a crescent, its two ends flanked by l9th-century cannons.

ABOVE: weathered fruiterer's sign, Hydra Town.
BELOW: waterfront traffic, Hydra Town.

The town has many good tavernas and restaurants, as well as highly popular bars and discotheques. Yet the higher reaches and the hills beyond remain surprisingly untouched, charming and full of Greek colour. Narrow alleys and steep staircases lead from one quarter to the next. The uniformity of white walls is broken again and again by a century-old doorway, a bright blue window frame, a flight of striking scarlet steps, or a green garden fence. **Mandhráki ⓾**, northeast of town, has the only sand beach, but the southwest is more interesting. A wide path goes along the coast to **Kamíni** and to **Vlychós**, with its early 19th-century arched stone bridge. There are some good tavernas in both places, and water-taxis available if you've had too much good fish and wine.

Spétses

Spétses is the southernmost of the Argo-Saronic Gulf islands. In antiquity it was known as Pityousa, "pine tree" island, and it is still by far the most wooded of the group. Tourist development here is more extensive than on Hydra but less than on either Póros or Aegina, and in recent years responsible planning has helped keep the island's charm.

Although **Spétses Town ⓫** has its share of bars and fast-food places, the Paleó Limáni (Old Harbour) still radiates a gentle grace. The 18th-century *arhontiká* you see in this part of the town are now the property of wealthy Athenian families who return to the island every summer.

Like Hydra, Spétses' heyday was the late 18th century, when mercantile trade made it wealthy; also like Hydra, it became a centre of activity during the Greek War of Independence, offering its merchant fleet of over 50 ships for the Greek cause. The island is distinguished for being the first in the archipelago to revolt

ABOVE: A splash of Greek colour, Hydra
BELOW: Spétses' Old Harbour.

Map, page 224

Map, page 224

Privately owned Villa Yasemía, near Aghía Paraskeví, is the original of magical Bourani in John Fowles' 1966 novel, The Magus.

RIGHT: an unusual sight: an empty Spétsiot café.
BELOW: island life is mirrored in Spétses Town.

against Ottoman rule in 1821 and the fortified main harbour, still bristling with cannons, now forms one of the town's focal points, the **Dápia**.

Bouboulína, Greece's national heroine of the Greek War of Independence, was a Spétsiot woman who took command of her husband's ships after he was killed by pirates off the North African coast. She contributed eight of the 22 Spétsiot ships which blockaded the Turks in Náfplio (Nauplion) for more than a year until the garrison surrendered in December 1822.

In the September before Náfplio surrendered, an Ottoman fleet attempted to lift the blockade by threatening Spétses. The fighting was indecisive but the Ottoman fleet eventually withdrew. They were encouraged to leave by fezzes being placed on the asphodel plants that grew in masses along the shore (from a distance the fezzes swaying in the wind looked like men, presumably armed).

This great victory is celebrated annually, every 22 September, by a *panayíri* focused on the church of the **Panaghía Armáta** on the lighthouse headland close to the Old Harbour. A mock battle is staged, a Turkish flagship made out of cardboard is burned in the middle of the harbour and there follows a display of fireworks.

Although after the War of Independence Spétses' fleet declined with the emergence of Piraeus as the main seaport, the traditions of shipbuilding continue unabated. The small **museum** in the imposing 18th-century *arhóntikó* of Hatziyánni Mexí, a major shipowner in the late 18th century, contains coins, costumes, ship models, weapons and other memorabilia from the island's past including the bones of the famous Bouboulína. The house in which she lived is behind the Dápia (open Tues–Sun 8.30am–2.30pm; entrance fee).

Outside the town to the northwest is **Anargýrios and Korghialénios College**, a Greek impression of an English public school. John Fowles taught here and memorialised both the institution and the island in his 1966 novel *The Magus*. The school no longer operates and the buildings are used only occasionally as a conference centre or for special programmes. This section of town is less posh than the Old Harbour, and has some fine small tavernas.

The town beach by the church of **Ághios Mámas** and the small beach in the Old Harbour are not as nice as the beautiful beaches of **Aghía Marína, Ághii Anárghyri, Aghía Paraskeví** and **Zogeriá**, going around the wooden southern coast of the island from the east to the west. In addition, there are various beaches opposite Spétses on the Peloponnesian coast, of which the most accessible is at **Kosta**. For those who enjoy water-skiing, **Pórtohéli** with its protected bay provides the perfect setting.

Spétses also has excellent ferry and hydrofoil links to Náfplio, Árgos, Epídhavros, Mycenae and to the southern town of Monemvasía. During the summer months when the Ancient Drama Festival is held in Epídhavros, a trip to one of the performances there is a delight. Yet an evening walk in the Old Harbour or in the woods of Ligonéri, a ride in a horse-drawn carriage from the Dápia to Aghía Marína, and an (expensive) trip by water-taxi for an evening meal at Ághii Anárghyri are only a few of the pleasures that Spétses itself provides. ❑

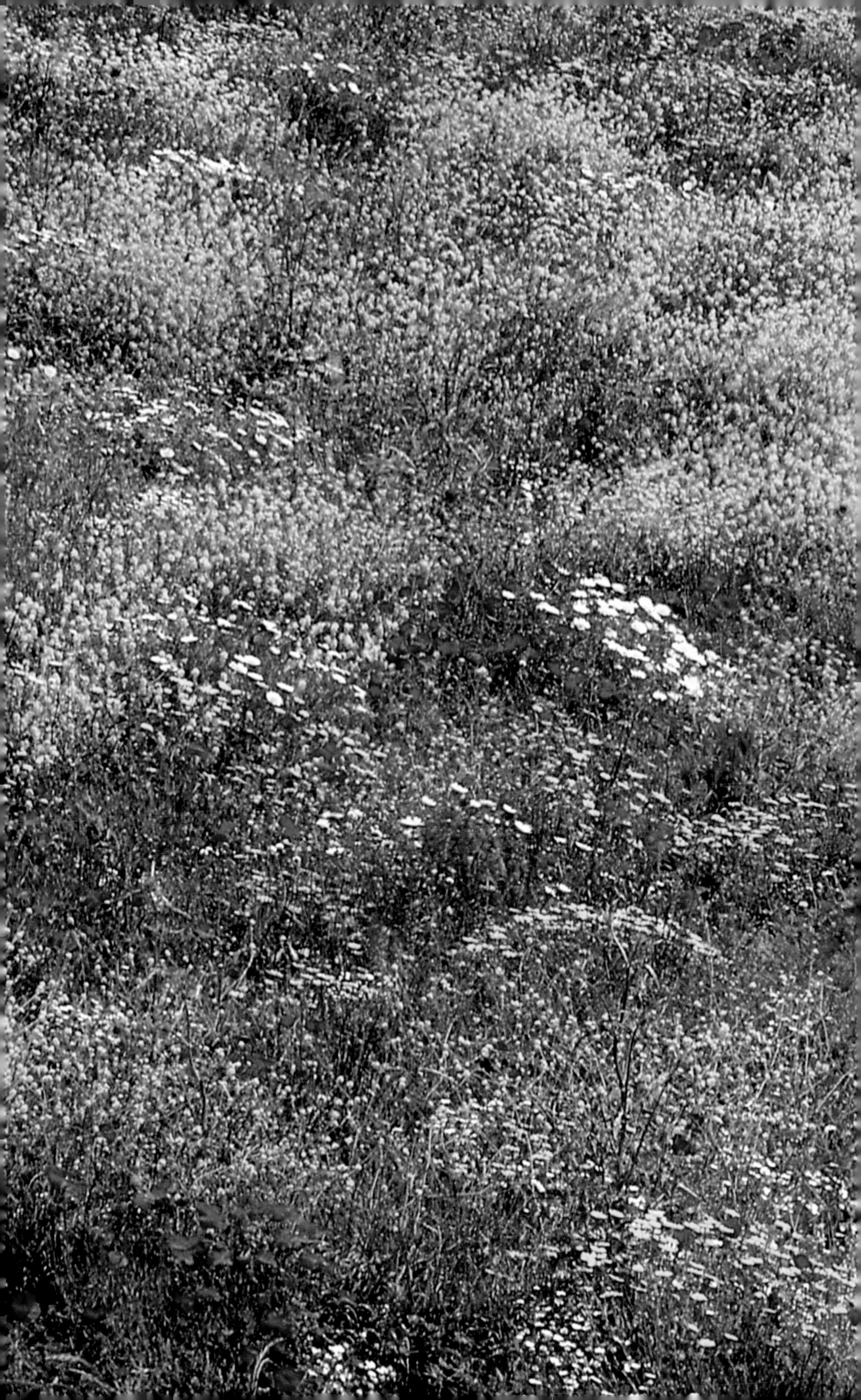

THE PELOPONNESE

Map, page 236

Steeped in ancient history – from the first Olympic stadium to Agamemnon's Mycenae – the southern provinces also offer fine beaches, turquoise-coloured bays, and the wild and unspoilt Máni

The Peloponnese (Pelopónnisos) takes its name from the legendary hero *Pelops*, plus the Greek for island, *nísos*, although it is seldom thought of as an island. Driving over from Attica (Attikí), it's easy to miss the little isthmus – riven by the Corinth Canal, lending some credence to the "island" tag – joining the Peloponnese to the mainland. The area's medieval name was the Moreás, now rarely used; it derives either from an abundance of mulberry trees (*mouriá*) or more probably from the mulberry-leaf shape of the peninsula.

Korinthía: key to the Moreás

By an administrative quirk, Korinthía province in the northeast includes a bit of the geographical mainland northeast of the canal; 13 km (8 miles) beyond the spa resort of Loutráki lies the **Perahora Heraion**, with an archaic **Hera temple** and a *stoa*. Another important ancient sanctuary, venue for the quadrennial Isthmian games, can be found at **Isthmía** on the southwest side of the canal; the Roman baths here retain extensive floor mosaics of sea creatures real and imaginary, while the site **museum** (hours uncertain at present) features vivid *opus sectile* panels portraying harbour scenes, Nile bird life and revered ancient personalities. The canal itself, dug between 1882 and 1893, is obsolete in our era of mega-container ships, but a few freighters and tour ships still squeeze through its 23-m (75-ft) width, to the delight of spectators up on the bridge gangway.

Ancient **Corinth**, 4 km (2½ miles) southwest of modern **Kórinthos ❶**, could not help but prosper through domination of trans-Isthmian haulage in pre-canal days. The Hellenistic city was razed in 146 BC by the Romans in reprisal for resistance, but refounded a century later as capital of Greece. What remains, despite devastating earthquakes in AD 375 and 521, is the most complete imperial Roman town plan in Greece. Corinth's well-deserved reputation for vice and luxury predictably exercised Saint Paul when he arrived in AD 52 for an 18-month sojourn.

A typically Roman obsession with plumbing is evident: there are the graphically obvious latrines off the marble-paved **Lehaion Way**, the still-functioning **Lower Peirene Fountain** at its end, and the ingenious **Glauke Fountain**, its four cisterns hewn from a monolith and filled by aqueduct (site open summer: 8am–7pm; winter: 8am–5pm; entrance fee).

Of the earlier Greek city, only seven columns from a Doric **Apollo Temple** still stand, though the site museum – despite a selective 1990 burglary – retains a generous collection of late archaic pottery and some intricate Roman-villa mosaics from Corinth's glory years (same hours as site, but closed Mon). Rather more evocative, however, is the nearly impregnable

PRECEDING PAGES: spring wildflowers.
LEFT: tradition lives on at Olympia's stadium.
BELOW: traditional tower-house, the Máni.

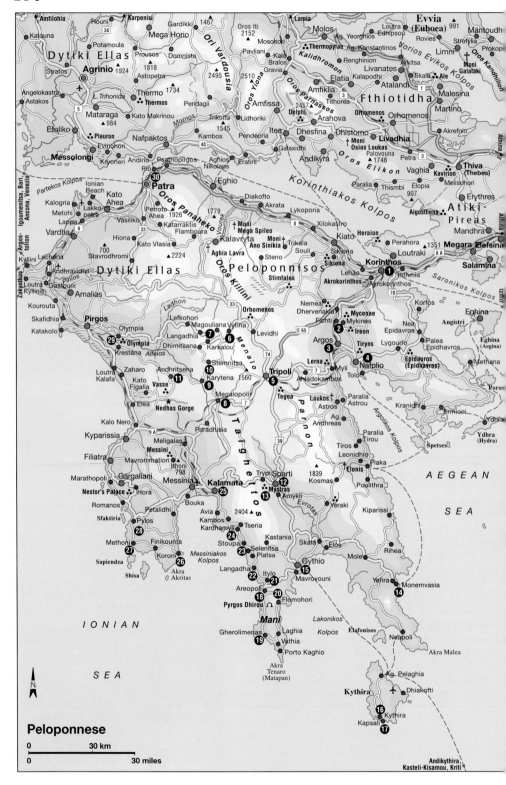

Peloponnese

0   30 km

0   30 miles

acropolis of **Acrocorinth** (open daily except Mon 8.30am–3pm; free), long the military key to the peninsula and necessarily held by every occupying power. Enter via the gentler west slope through a set of **triple fortifications** to find yourself amidst weedy desolation; little is left of the Ottoman town here, evacuated after Greek rebels took it in 1822. Most sieges, however, were successfully resisted thanks to the **Upper Peirene Fountain**, a subterranean affair near the southeast corner of the ramparts. At the very summit stand foundations of an **Aphrodite Temple**, reputedly once attended by 1,000 sacred prostitutes; the view all around is quite marvellous, stretching up to 60 km (40 miles) in every direction.

The wide tollway to Trípoli forges southwest from modern Kórinthos. Near **Dhervenákia**, exits lead west 8 km (5 miles) to ancient **Nemea**, yet another shrine with its own biennial games. You can see the stadium where these – supposedly inaugurated by Hercules, slayer of the Nemean lion – were held, but the most enduring landmarks are three surviving Doric columns of a 4th-century **Zeus Temple**; its fellows, toppled by Byzantine vandals, lie all about like so many giant sausage-slices. The site (open Tues–Sun 8.30am–3pm; entrance fee) occupies the floor of a bucolic valley; surrounding vineyards produce the grapes for the full-bodied Nemea red wines, some of Greece's best.

The word "currant" derives from the word "Corinth" – a reference to the city's long-established trade in currants, still one of Greece's most successful exports.

Argolídha: Mycenaean cradle

The old highway enters the Argolid plain at modern **Mykínes** ❷, a village devoted to citrus and tourism; adjacent stands ancient **Mycenae**, a fortified palace complex covering an easily defendable, ravine-flanked ridge. Mycenae gave its name to an entire late Bronze-Age era – and made the reputation of a German self-taught Classical scholar (and self-made millionaire), Heinrich

BELOW: the Corinth Canal was finished in 1893.

Map, page 236

Schliemann. From 1874 to 1876 he excavated here, relying on little other than intuition and the literal accuracy of Homer's epics. Greek archeologists had already revealed the imposing **Lion Gate** of the citadel, but the rich tomb finds Schliemann made, now in the National Museum of Athens, amply corroborated Mycenae's Homeric epithet "rich in gold". These days, revisionists point to Schliemann's sloppy excavating techniques and economy with the truth – the gold death mask which prompted his boast "I have gazed upon the face of Agamemnon" is now dated to 300 years earlier – but the dedicated amateur did scoop the experts in the greatest archeological trove of the century.

At the site itself, little remains above waist height inside the perimeter walls of the palace, though a rather alarming secret stairway descends to a siege-proof cistern in the northeast corner. Outside, however, are two burial chambers of unsurpassed ingenuity: the *tholos* tombs dubbed, rather speculatively, the **Treasury of Atreus** and the **Tomb of Clytemnestra**, also known as "beehives" after the manner of their construction (open daily 8am–5pm; entrance fee).

Ancient Argos

The road across the Argolid plain divides at **Árgos ❸**, capital of Argolídha province and a major agricultural centre. Tomatoes and citrus – the latter introduced by American advisers after World War II – are king; the modern town itself is of little interest apart from its **Archeological Museum** (open Tues–Sun

ABOVE: Heinrich Schliemann.
BELOW: the Lion Gate at Mycenae.

8.30am–3pm; entrance fee). But just south, beside the Trípoli-bound road, sprawl the ruins of **ancient Argos**, one of the oldest Greek settlements; most notable is the huge, steeply raked theatre (open all hours; free). From here, walk up to the Frankish castle atop Lárissa hill, site of the ancient **acropolis**, for a view nearly on a par with Acrocorinth's. To the northwest is **Mount Kyllíni**, snow-capped in season. Ahead, beyond a foreground of orchards and the occasional cannery, you can make out Mycenae and the low hillock of ancient Tiryns en route to Náfplio (Nauplion), stacked up against the promontory on the far side of the Argolid gulf.

Just over halfway to Náfplio from Árgos loom the 13th-century BC ruins of Homer's "wall-girt" **Tiryns** (open summer: daily 8am–7pm, winter: daily 8am–5pm; entrance fee), another royal palace complex. The site, an 18-m (60-ft) bluff rising from an ancient marsh, was not as naturally defensible as its neighbour, Mycenae, so the man-made fortifications – originally twice their present height – were necessarily more involved. Massive masonry blocks reaching 3 cubic m (100 cubic ft) each were joined in mortarless walls termed "Cyclopean", after the only beings thought capable of manoeuvring them. No heraldic lions over the entry-gate here, and no beehive tombs; but Tiryns satisfies enough with a **secret stairway** to the westerly postern gate, and – near the southeast corner – a corbel-ceilinged **gallery**, its walls polished smooth by the millennial rubbings of sheltering sheep.

Náfplio ❹, rising in tiers at the southeast corner of the valley, is more than a little mirage-like, for the well-preserved Old Town retains an elegance a world away from scruffy, utilitarian Árgos just 12 km (7

miles) to the northwest. The tottering neoclassical architecture, pedestrian-friendly marble streets and interlocking fortresses date mostly from the second Venetian occupation of 1686–1715, and subsequent Ottoman reconquest; the fortified rock here had been a pivotal point in their struggles for control of the Aegean from the 15th century onward. Between 1829 and 1834 Náfplio served as the country's first capital, but today it's a laid-back place, despite playing a role as an upmarket resort; it even stays busy in winter, thanks to Athenian weekenders.

Map, page 236

Náfplio is overawed by **Akronafpliá**, four separate fortresses of various ages just overhead, plus, on an easterly hill, the sprawling, early 18th-century **Palamídhi**, whose meandering curtain-wall encloses seven self-contained bastions designed to withstand the strongest artillery of the era. Yet its Venetian garrison capitulated with barely a fight in 1715 to the Ottomans, who in turn surrendered to the Greek rebels after a more protracted siege in 1822. Just under 900 steps lead up from the Old Town to the summit – and more eyefuls of the Argolid (open Mon–Fri 8am–4.45pm, Sat–Sun 8.30am–2.45pm; entrance fee).

Some 27 km (17 miles) east of Náfplio, **Epidauros** (Epídhavros) is visited for the sake of its magnificent 4th-century BC **amphitheatre**, whose perfect acoustics tour guides perpetually demonstrate with coins dropped on the orchestra floor. Because it lay buried until the late 19th century, the theatre masonry survived the ages relatively unscathed, and restoration has been minimal.

The theatre is just one part of a vast sanctuary to the healing demi-god Asklepios; its ruins, being re-excavated, extend to the northwest. The most accessible bits are the classical **stadium**, its stone benches and starting line still visible; the monumental gateway and stretch of buckled pavement, part of the sacred way to

ABOVE:
the fort-island of
Boúrtzi, Náfplio.
BELOW:
climbing amongst
the ruins at Náfplio.

the port (today's beach resort of **Paleá Epídhavros**), and the *tholos*, a circular, originally domed structure with a concentric maze in the foundations thought to contain serpents (sacred to Asklepios) or to be the venue for a priestly initiation rite (open summer: daily 7.30am– 7pm; winter: daily 8am–5pm; entrance fee).

The closest village to the site is **Lygourió**, which formerly lived mainly from its extensive olive groves but which now hosts most of the tourist traffic which comes for the summer festival of ancient drama. Performances by both Greek and international theatre companies take place by night in the ancient theatre, with special buses from Athens and Náfplio laid on for ticket-holders.

Heading west from Náfplio, you can avoid re-entering Árgos by using the beachfront road along the gulf, joining the highway to Trípoli at **Lerna** (modern **Mýli**), where Hercules slew the Hydra.

Arkadhía: Arcadian idylls

The modern 1970s highway – though not the 1990s toll expressway – leaves the flatlands of fragrant citrus at Mýli to enter gorges culminating in the high, pear- and apple-planted uplands around **Trípoli ❺**, capital of Arkadhía province. The name Trípoli recalls the three ancient towns of **Tegea**, **Mantineia** and **Palladium**, the latter an undistinguished Roman-imperial foundation. Mantineia, north of modern Trípoli, retains much of its ancient walls, and a reputation for excellent modern wine, while Tegea to the south offers the tumbled ruins of the **Temple to Athena Alea** in the middle of modern Aléa village.

Trípoli (then Tripolítza) was the Moreán capital in Ottoman times, but was burnt during the war of independence. Aside from a few fine neoclassical buildings, restaurants and a lively market, there's little here to interest casual tourists.

ABOVE: Arcadian landscape.
BELOW: the classical theatre at Epidauros.

The north-bound, toll-free road skirts the base of forested, blade-like **Mount Ménalo** via the handsome villages of **Levídhi** and **Vytína** ❻, the latter a popular "hill station" for Greeks. Beyond Vytína, towards Ilía, the most logical and compelling halt is **Langádhia** ❼, its famous masons responsible for sturdy stone houses teetering on a slope above the gorge of the name. But the main attraction of montane Arkadhía lies due west of Trípoli, accessible either from the Megalópoli road or a turning south between Vytína and Langádhia. **Megalópoli** ❽ itself, saddled with pollution-belching power plants, is a shabby modern successor to **ancient Megalopoli**, an artificial classical township abandoned within two centuries of inauguration, leaving only the largest amphitheatre in Greece to mark its passing.

Map,
page
236

Dubbed – hyperbolically – the "Toledo of Greece", thanks to its evocative castle and houses overlooking a kink in the **Alfiós River**, **Karýtena**'s ❾ sleepy demeanour belies a tumultuous history. Established as the seat of a Frankish barony during the 13th century, it was later retaken by the Byzantines, who endowed Karýtena with three churches and an arched bridge over the Alfiós. Both bridge and town figure on one side of the 5,000-drachma note; the beturbanned Independence War chieftain, Kolokotrónis, glares out from the other, for he successfully resisted a long Ottoman siege here in 1826.

Heading north along the paved road towards Dhimitsána, you'll travel roughly parallel to the east flank of the **Loúsios Gorge**: a short route, but in terms of concentrated interest one equalled by few other parts of the Peloponnese. At **Ellinikó** village, a dirt track descends into the canyon, emerging at the medieval Kokkorás bridge and the Byzantine chapel of **Ághios Andhréas**. Nearby are the excavations of ancient **Gortys**, an *asklipeion* or therapeutic centre; the archi-

ABOVE: ready for the hike, Langádhia village.
BELOW: Arcadian beehives.

Taking it easy in the mountain village of Vytína, a popular "hill station" for Greek tourists.

BELOW: time seems to have stood still in little Dhimitsána, an 18th-century Arcadian merchant town.

tectural highlight here is an peculiar round structure, thought to be a bath-house.

Stemnítsa , further along the paved road, has been officially renamed **Ipsoúnda** but the Slavic name remains more popular; it's an atmospheric, introverted place in a hidden cirque, with imposing mansions looking only at each other. A single jewellery shop recalls the former silver-smithing industry. Near the head of the Loúsios valley, **Dhimitsána** sprawls engagingly over a saddle demarcated by the river, its skyline graced by four belfries. The mansions here, like Stemnítsa's, date from its mercantile golden age, the 1700s.

Dhimitsána also marks one end of the hiking route threading the gorge; the path proper begins in **Paleohóri** hamlet, following red-and-white blazes and diamonds with the legend "32". The first significant stop is **Néa Filosófou monastery** on the west bank, with late 17th-century frescoes including Jesus walking on the Sea of Galilee; shortly beyond, 10th-century **Paleá Filosófou** monastery is largely ruined and almost indistinguishable from its cliff-side surroundings. Finally, where the path divides (the west-bank option leads to Gortys), you should recross the river for the most spectacular monastery of all: 11th-century **Aghíou Ioánnou Prodhrómou**, one of those martin's-nest-type monasteries which the Greek Orthodox Church loves to tuck into cliff faces. It is, however, a tiny place, with limited facilities for male pilgrims, so try to budget enough daylight time to hike onwards by trail to Stemnítsa.

From Karýtena a westerly road follows the Alfiós, past its co-mingling with the Loúsios, to **Andhrítsena** , roughly halfway between Megalópoli and the sea. Resolutely traditional shops and a morning produce market in the central square recall the village's historical status as a major entrepôt. Today, however, it seems scarcely touched by the steady trickle of tourist traffic passing through

to the 5th-century temple of **Apollo Epikourios** at **Vassai** (Vásses), 14 km (9 miles) south. Although the most intact ancient shrine in Greece, it's unlikely to enchant in its present condition – concealed by a colossal, guy-wired tent and fully exposed to winter frosts, it's estimated to be literally coming apart at the seams (open daily 8am–sunset; entrance fee). More rewarding for many is the **gorge of the River Nédhas** a few kilometres south, just below the modern village and ancient ruins of **Figalia**, whose citizens originally built the temple in gratitude for Apollo having lifted a plague.

Map, page 236

Lakonía: ancient Spartan heartland

As you descend the 60-km (37-mile) road from Trípoli to modern Spárti, the long ridge of **Mount Taïghettos** with its striated limestone bands looms into sight on the right. Ahead stretches the olive-and-citrus-rich floodplain of the Evrótas river, belying the stereotypical image of ancient Sparta as a harsh, "spartan" place (the province's name, Lakonía, also lives abroad as "laconic" – supposedly the distinguishing characteristic of the classical natives).

Spárti ⑫, the modern successor to ancient Sparta, is a dreary place redeemed only by some attractive squares and neoclassical facades, vestiges of a bout of Bavarian town planning in 1834. Stop, if you do at all, for the excellent **museum** and traces of an **ancient acropolis**. The museum (open Tues–Sun 8.30am–2.30pm; entrance fee) is particularly rich in late Roman floor-mosaics from local villas, and eerie votive offerings from the **sanctuaries of Apollo** at Amýkles and **Artemis Orthia** on the acropolis – where youths were flogged until they were bloody to honour the goddess. At the acropolis itself, however, 700 m (½ mile) northwest of town, not much remains aside from a badly eroded

In 1821, the local Archbishop of Dhimitsána, Yermanós, called for an uprising against the Turks, after which all of Arkadhía was liberated.

BELOW: taking provisions to the monastery.

Entrance to the Mitrópolis cathedral, Mystrás. The city was destroyed by the Turks in 1460, but the last inhabitants left only when King Otto founded modern Spárti in 1834.

BELOW: Mystrás' Perívleptos church has some superb frescoes.

theatre and the sparse remains of the Byzantine church of **Ághios Níkon**. What little the Spartans built was appropriated for the construction of Byzantine **Mystrás** , 6 km (4 miles) west (open daily summer: 8am–7pm; winter: 8.30am– 3pm; entrance fee). A romantically ruined walled town, clinging to a conical crag and topped by a castle, Mystrás' name is a corruption of *mezythrás*, the Greek for "cream-cheese maker" – thought to be a reference to this cheese's traditional conical shape.

Originally founded by the Franks in 1249, Mystrás grew to a city of 20,000 souls under the Byzantines, becoming the capital of the Morean despots after 1348. Until the Ottomans took over in 1460, it flourished as a major cultural centre, attracting scholars and artists from Serbia, Constantinople and Italy to its court. The latter's influence is evident in the brilliantly coloured (and remarkably well-preserved) frescoes which adorn Mystrás' churches – uniquely in Greece, these are as crammed with extraneous figures, buildings and landscapes as any Italian painting of the time. Architecturally, the churches are a composite of three-aisled-basilica ground plan and domed cross-in-square gallery, making them airily well-lit by Byzantine standards. Proto-Renaissance sensibilities (and the Frankish wives of most of the despots) inspired belfries and colonnaded porticoes. It is easy to see why Mystrás is regarded as the last great Byzantine architectural outpouring before the onset of the Ottoman era.

Perívleptos church contains a complete cycle of frescoes depicting the *Dodekaeorton* or twelve major feasts of the church, with such light touches as children playing in the Entry to Jerusalem. Nearby **Pandánassa**, the newest church built in 1428, has a typically Gothic exterior as well as vivid frescoes within, the best of these neck-craningly high. By contrast, the oldest of the

churches, the **Mitrópolis** or cathedral, is resolutely conservative in structure, notwithstanding awkward domes added later; here frescoes include a complete cycle of Christ's Miracles. The **Vrondóhion** monastic complex harbours yet another 14th-century church, the more daring **Afendikó**, the weight of its six domes borne by a system of piers below and colonnaded gallery above. Sea monsters bob in the Baptism fresco, while above the altar, apostles marvel at a mandorla of ascending Christ.

Map, page 236

Mystrás has a miniature "echo" in **Gheráki** (25 km/16 miles east of Spárti), of which few have heard and fewer still bother to visit. Although an ancient town (Geronthrai) existed here, its masonry has been liberally recycled into the half-dozen churches scattered about. Gheráki's fortified **acropolis** is less spectacular than that at Mystrás, and closes early (open daily 8.30am–2.30pm; entrance fee); if time is limited, find the key-keeper by the post office (8am–2pm) who will open up four frescoed churches in and around the modern village.

Completing the trio of Lakonian Byzantine towns is **Monemvasía** ⓮, 94 km (58 miles) southeast of Spárti. Like Mystrás, it's a fortified double town, clinging to a limestone plug rising 350m (1,150 ft) from the sea and inevitably nicknamed the "Gibraltar of Greece" – although the "Dubrovnik of Greece" would be an equally apt term for the tile-roofed, wall-encased lower town on the south slope. Supporting 50,000 souls in its heyday as a semi-autonomous city-state, Monemvasía prospered by virtue of its fleets and handy location, halfway between Italy and the Black Sea. Never taken by force, it did surrender, if necessary, to prolonged siege – no food could grow on the rock, though enormous cisterns provided water. Nearby vineyards produced the famous Malvasia sweet wine – similar to Madeira, and known as Malmsey or Malvoisie in the west –

ABOVE: fortified Monemvasía clings to a crag overlooking the sea.
BELOW: a peaceful corner of Monemvasía cemetery.

Cherries for sale, Monemvasía lower town. In medieval times, food supplies were the rock-city's weak point; everything had to be imported from the mainland.

BELOW:
Marathoníssi islet at Gýthio.

but local production ceased by the 15th century. Following the opening of the Corinth Canal, Monemvasía lost all commercial and military significance.

The lower town, within its 900-m (½-mile) circuit of Venetian walls on three sides, is invisible as you cross the causeway until the massive west gate (closed to vehicles) suddenly appears. Immediately above the gate perches the house in which prominent poet Yánnis Rítsos was born in 1909; one wonders what the conservative locals made of his forthright Marxism and bisexuality. On his death in 1990 he was buried in the nearby cemetery, with one of his poems chiselled on the gravestone in lieu of religious sentiment.

Linked by a maze of tunnels, arcades and cul-de-sacs at the end of steep, cobbled lanes, many of the lower-town houses have been bought up and restored by wealthy Athenians and foreigners. Masoned steps zig-zag up the cliff face overhead to the older, upper town, first settled and fortified in the 6th century AD but abandoned since the early 1900s and now utterly ruined. The sole exception to the desolation is atmospheric 14th-century **Aghía Sofía** church with its 16-sided dome, poised at the edge of the northerly cliff and the first point in Monemvasía to catch the sunrise.

Gýthio ⓫, 47 km (29 miles) southeast of Spárti, is a port town on the ferry routes to Kýthira and Crete, a holiday resort in its own right and a deceptively congenial gateway to the austere Máni. The quay is lined by tiled vernacular houses and pricey fish tavernas; across the Lakonian Gulf the sun rises over **Cape Maléa** and Mount Taïghettos is glimpsed one last time on the north. In ancient times Gýthio served as Sparta's port, and provided purple murex for dying Roman togas; until recently it exported acorns used in leather tanning. There are few sights, apart from a Roman amphitheatre and the historical

museum in the **Tzanetbey Grigorákis Tower-House** (open daily 9.30am–5pm; entrance fee) on **Marathoníssi** islet (ancient Kranae) tied to the mainland by a causeway. It was here that Paris and Helen legendarily spent their first night together, and so launched a thousand ships.

Map, page 236

Kýthira – bridge to Crete

The island of **Kýthira**, two hours' sail offshore (although much closer to Neápolis port on Cape Maléa), sees at least one ferry boat daily; the habitually rough crossing is ameliorated by one's arrival at the sparkling new (1996) harbour at **Dhiakófti**. Essentially a bleak plateau slashed by well-watered ravines, the island forms part of a sunken land-bridge between the Peloponnese and Crete. It is very much an in-between sort of place, with a history of Venetian and British rule like the other Ionian isles with which it, in theory, belongs – although it is now lumped administratively with the Argo-Saronics. Architecturally, it's a hybrid of Cycladic and Venetian styles with an Australian accent, courtesy of remittances from the 60,000-odd locals who headed Down Under in the 1950s.

The island does not put itself out for visitors: accommodation is dear and oversubscribed, and good tavernas thin on the ground. Yet Kýthira seems increasingly popular as a trendy haunt, thanks to regular hydrofoils and flights from Athens. **Kýthira town** ⑯ is also one of the finest island capitals of the Aegean, with medieval mansions and Venetian fortifications.

Far below, **Kapsáli** ⑰ is the yacht and alternative hydrofoil berthing, though better beaches are found on the east coast – as far as the fishing anchorage of **Avlémonas**. There are more castles to be found there and at **Káto Hóra**, just above **Aghía Sofía cave**, the principal west-coast attraction;

According to classical mythology, the island of Kýthira was the birthplace of Aphrodite, the beautiful goddess of love.

BELOW: Kapsáli village harbour, Kýthira.

the ghost village of **Paleohóra** in the northeast was the capital from 1248 to 1537, when it failed the pirate-proof test.

The Máni – home of Greece's hard men

TIP

To see the best examples of the distinctive Maniot tower-houses, head for the villages of Váthia, Kítta, Nómia and Flomohóri.

An arid, isolated region protected by Taïghettos' southern spur, the Máni was the last part of Greece to espouse Christianity (in the 9th century), but made up for lost time by erecting dozens of small country chapels. Little grows beside stunted olive trees, though in September an extra dash of colour is lent by hedges of fruiting prickly pears. "Outer" or **Éxo Máni** (Ítylo northwest to Kalamáta) is more tourist-friendly, fertile and better watered; "Inner" or **Mésa Máni**, south of a line connecting Ítylo with Gýthio, has the more noteworthy churches on the west shore, and tower-studded villages sprouting from the sheer east coast. But extreme conditions have prompted wholesale depopulation, and the villages here only fill during the autumn hunting season.

From Gýthio, the main road into the Máni passes the castles of **Passavá** and **Kelefá**, the sole Ottoman attempts at imposing order locally, before arriving at **Areópoli** ⑱, main market town and tourist base of the Inner Máni. Formerly Tsímova, stronghold of the Mavromihális clan, it was renamed for the god of war after independence, in recognition of its contribution to the independence struggle. Two churches, both 18th-century, distinguish it: **Taxiárhis** with its campanile and zodiacal apse reliefs, and frescoed **Ághios Ioánnis**.

Some 8 km (5 miles) south, just off the west-coast road towards **Cape Mátapan** (Ténaro), the caverns at **Pýrgos Dhiroú** are the sole organised tourist attraction in the Máni; visits are partly by boat along a subterranean river, and queues can be long. Between here and Gheroliménas lie more than half-a-dozen

BELOW: shepherd and his flock in the Máni – a peaceful scene which belies the area's belligerent history.

FEUDS IN THE MÁNI

While there may be some truth to Maniot claims that they are descended from the ancient Spartans, more cruicial to the region's medieval history was the arrival during the 13th to the 15th centuries, of refugee Byzantine nobility. These established a local aristocracy – the Nyklians – which formed competing clans, as in Scotland only they had the right to erect tower-mansions.

Poor farmland and a fast-growing population spurred not just piracy and banditry, but complex vendetta between clans. Blood feuds could last for years, with sporadic truces to tend crops; women, who delivered supplies, were inviolate, as were doctors, who treated the wounded impartially. Combatants fired at each other from neighbouring towers, raising them as high as five storeys so as to lob rocks onto their opponents' flat roofs. The vendettas generally ended either with the annihilation or utter submission of the losing clan. Rather than rule the Máni directly, the Ottomans encouraged the feuding in the hopes of weakening any concerted rebellions, appointing a Nyklian chieftain as *bey* to represent the sultan.

The office passed between rival clans, but under the last *bey*, Pétros Mavromihális, the clans united, instigating the Greek independence uprising on 17 March 1821.

frescoed Byzantine churches; unfortunately, most are permanently locked, and hunting for the warden in Areópoli can be time-consuming. Two of the best, at Áno Boularí, are also the easiest to access. Apply in the Gheroliménas post office for the key to **Ághios Stratigós**; nearby **Ághios Pandelímon** – scandalously doorless and unroofed – has the earliest (10th-century) frescoes around, with figures of saints Pandelímon and Nikítas in the apse. **Gheroliménas** ❿ itself, 20 km (12 miles) from Areópoli, can offer tavernas and accommodation, but not much else – it dates only from 1870. The 35 ridgetop tower-houses of dramatic **Váthia**, 10 km (6 miles) further east, have become photogenic synonyms for the Máni; many have now been restored as upmarket accommodation.

The main tarred road out of Gheroliménas loops along the eastern shore via **Lághia** (famed for its broad-based, tapering towers and purple-marble quarries) and **Flomohóri** ⓴ (with the highest towers and pebbly **Kótronas** beach below) before re-emerging at Areópoli. Just across the ravine dividing Inner Máni from Outer is bluff-top **Ítylo** ㉑, lushly set and – unlike so many of its neighbours – relatively prosperous; below the village lies the frescoed monastery of **Dhekoúlou**, and the beach resort of **Néa Ítylo**.

The caves at Pýrgos Dhiroú get very busy in high season; to preserve the magic, try to get there early.

The pride of **Langádha** village ㉒, 14 km (9 miles) north, is the central 11th-century church of **Ághios Sótiros**, whose frescoes still await uncovering and restoration; continguous **Plátsa** and **Nomitsís** between them have four more Byzantine chapels. Tourism takes over at the picturesque fishing port of **Selenítsa** (Ághios Nikólaos); nearby **Stoúpa** ㉓ has two sandy bays and plenty of facilities as well. **Kardhamýli** ㉔ ranks as the premier resort before Kalamáta, offering among its charms a long pebble beach, a late-medieval acropolis and some good walking just inland.

BELOW: Váthia, one of the best-preserved Maniot villages.

Kalamáta is best known for its prosperous export trade in large, shiny black olives. They are excellent with oúzo.

BELOW: St Andrew's church, Pátra.

Messinía: the Peloponnesian banana belt

Kalamáta can also be approached directly from Spárti via the spectacular 60-km (37-mile) road which crosses Mount Taïghettos, good hotels and eateries strategically dotting the way. On the Lakonian side, near **Trýpi** village, is the **Keiádhas**, an abyss where the ancient Spartans supposedly hurled their sickly or malformed babies. **Kalamáta** ㉕ itself has only just recovered from a devastating 1986 earthquake which left half the population homeless; despite subsequent emigration it's still the biggest town hereabouts (40,000 people), with an attractive seafront, some lively untouristed *tavérnes* and its famous shiny-black olives to recommend it.

Most visitors to Messinía province have their sights set on the low southwesterly promontory ending in **Cape Akrítas**, with its fine beaches and balmy climate. Prime target is **Koróni** ㉖, founded by Venice in 1206 to guard the sea lanes between the Adriatic and Crete. The castle here still shelters a few houses, orchards and pine groves, but a convent occupies most of it. The town outside the walls (built since 1830) has weathered tourism well, its vernacular houses with their wooden balconies still lining the steep stair-streets. **Zánga beach**, one of the best in the Peloponnese, extends for 3 km (2 miles) west.

Methóni ㉗, another "eye of Venice" lying 35 km (22 miles) west, grew wealthy after 1209 from the pilgrim trade to Palestine. Its sprawling castle, lapped on three sides by the sea, combines military architecture of various eras: beyond the Venetian sea-gate, a Turkish octagonal tower overlooks two islets, while a French arched bridge of 1828 spans the Venetian moat. Little remains of the medieval town inside, however, and the modern village outside the walls is not nearly as attractive as Koróni's, nor is the beach.

Pýlos **㉘**, 12 km (7 miles) north, is another somewhat lacklustre town; despite its pleasant setting on huge, landlocked **Navaríno Bay**, what life there is seems confined to the immediate environs of **Platía Tríon Navárhon**, the main square. The bay has seen two momentous naval battles: in 425 BC, when the Athenians bested the Spartans off **Sfaktiría island**, and in October 1827, when a combined French, Russian and English armada sunk Ibrahim Pasha's Ottoman fleet, thus guaranteeing Greek independence. The three allied admirals are honoured by an obelisk in their namesake square. For beaches you'll have to head for the north end of the bay, just off the main road to the Bronze-Age **Palace of Nestor**, discovered in 1939 and now protected by a synthetic roof.

Map, page 236

Ilía: Olympia and the Cape

From pretty **Kyparissía**, north of Nestor's Palace, it's a pleasant coastal drive to the site of ancient **Olympia ㉙**, where the Kládheos river meets the Alfiós. The sanctuary here was in use for two millennia as a religious and athletic centre; of all the Hellenic competitions associated with shrines, the Olympic Games, held every four years at the late-summer full moon, were the most prestigious, and the pan-Hellenic truce declared for their duration was honoured by the various city-states on pain of stiff fines. Although the first verified games were held in 776 BC, the **Áltis**, a sacred forest at the base of Krónio hill, was consecrated to pre-Olympian deities as early as the second millennium BC.

The most salient monuments are the **Palaestra** training centre, whose courtyard colonnade has been re-erected; the **workshop of Phidias**, the celebrated sculptor (identified by a cup found with his name inscribed); the archaic **Hera temple** with its dissimilar columns; the enormous **Zeus temple**, now reduced to column sections; and the **stadium** with its 192-m (630-ft) running course and surviving vaulted entrance (open summer: daily 8am–7pm; winter: Mon–Fri 8am–5pm, Sat 8.30–3pm; entrance fee).

ABOVE: the Olympics return to Greece in 2004.
BELOW: Hermes in the site museum, Olympia.

In the **site museum**, pride of place goes to the relief pediments recovered from the Zeus temple debris, now on display in the central hall (open summer: Mon 12.30–7pm, Tues–Sun 8am–7pm; winter: daily, 8.30am–3pm; entrance fee).

Aháïa: Pátra and its hinterland

Entering Aháïa province along the coast north of **Kyllíni**, sample the enormous, 7-km (4-mile) beach of **Kalogriá** and the swamps (plus umbrella-pine dune forest) just behind. This, one of the largest wetlands in the Balkans, has yet to gain significant protection as a wildlife reserve; go now before the developers scare off the incredibly rich birdlife.

Pátra ㉚, 38 km (24 miles) further, is Greece's third-largest city, and principal port for ferries to Italy and select Ionian islands. With its fearsome traffic, anonymous postwar architecture and lack of beaches, it's hardly the ideal spot for a quiet holiday retreat; only the ancient **acropolis** (with an originally Byzantine castle) seems peaceful. But linger at Carnival time to witness Greece's best observance, with parades, floats and conspicuous attendance by students and the gay community. ❑

THE CYCLADES

Home to some of the most breathtakingly beautiful – and popular – islands in all Greece, the Cyclades offer buzzing beaches, good nightlife and a wealth of ancient sites

For many people the Cyclades *are* Greece; other island chains are mere distractions from this blue Aegean essence. Inhabited as early as 6000 BC, by the third millennium a fascinating island culture flourished here, with fine arts and crafts and lively commerce – as anyone who visits the excellent Goulandrís Museum of Cycladic Art in Athens will appreciate (*see page 152*).

Of the 56 islands, 24 are inhabited. There are two basic ferry routes: the first, eastern and central, takes in elegant Ándhros and religious Tínos, includes Mýkonos, Páros and Náxos – the backpackers' (and everyone else's) beat – calls briefly at undeveloped islets like Dhonoússa and Iráklia, and concludes in spectacular Santoríni. The second, western, arches by Kýthnos, Sérifos, Sífnos and Mílos; these are somewhat less popular, with different cultural attributes. Off both ferry routes, Kéa attracts Athenian weekenders.

Ándhros

Ándhros was settled centuries ago by Orthodox Albanians (a few still speak Albanian); their stone huts of the north contrast with the whitewash and red tile of the other villages. The port town, **Gávrio**, is only that. **Batsí ❶**, 6 km (4 miles) south, is a pleasant Cycladic "fishing" town: whitewash, cafés, beaches, packaged tours, and development at the outskirts. On the east coast, **Ándhros Town (Hóra) ❷** remains remarkably unspoiled. The prize exhibit in the **Archeological Museum** (open Tues–Sun, 8.30am–3pm; entrance fee), indeed in all Greece, is the famous Hermes of Ándhros, a 2nd-century copy of Praxiteles' statue.

South of the Paleópolis/Hóra road is the most spectacular of Ándhros's 13 Byzantine monasteries, **Panáhrandou** (Wholly Immaculate) ❸; 1,000 years old, it still retains ties with Constantinople.

Ándhros has many beaches; the easiest to get to are **Nimbório** just south of the port, the string of lovely strands between Gávrio and Batsí, and **Yiália** (near Steniés, north of Ándhros town) – plus a number of beautiful and remote coves such as **Ághios Péllos**.

Kéa

Kéa-bound boats leave from the mainland port of Lávrio, some 50 km (30 miles) from Athens, and land at **Korissía**, locally called **Livádhi**. The main town, **Ioulís (Hóra) ❹**, rides a rounded ridge overlooking the island's northern reach, a site chosen for its inaccessibility from foreign marauders. The famous **Lion of Kéa**, a smiling, maneless beast almost 6m (20 ft) long, is a 15-minute walk northeast of Hóra. Carved from grey granite; it is probably early archaic.

The jagged west coast has many sandy spits, several impossible to reach. **Písses** and **Koúndouros** are just

Map, pages 256–7

PRECEDING PAGES: church domes at a village, Santoríni. **LEFT:** windmill, Mýkonos Town. **BELOW:** Little Venice, Mýkonos.

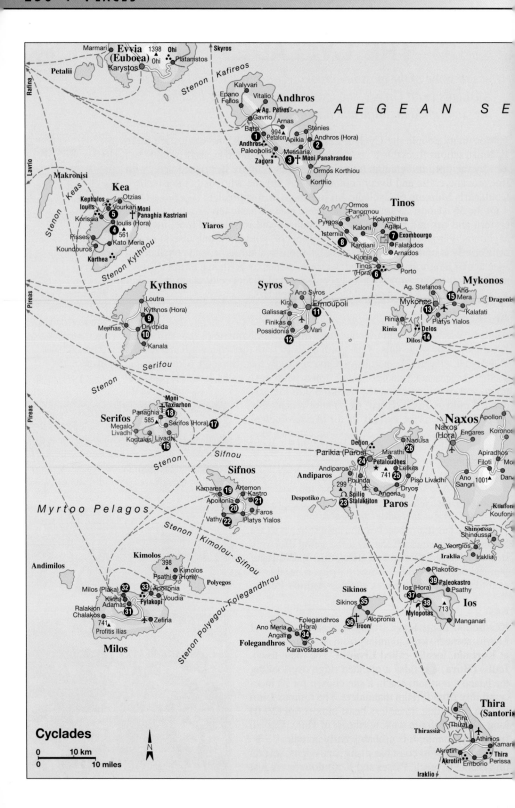

Cyclades

0   10 km
0   10 miles

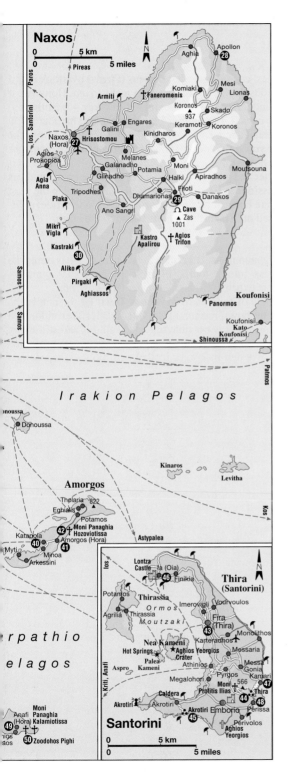

two of the resorts which have sprung up to accommodate the Athenian escapees. Close to Korissía is **Vourkári ❺**, with **Aghía Iríni** church, a Minoan excavation, and an ancient road.

Tínos

Tínos receives many thousands of tourists – but they are mostly Greeks here for the church, the **Panaghía Evangelístria** (Our Lady Annunciate). In 1823, the nun Pelaghía dreamt of an icon; it was duly unearthed and the church built to house it. The icon's healing powers have made **Tínos Town** (**Hóra**) ❻ the Lourdes of Greece. Women fall to their knees upon arrival, and crawl painfully to the church. Healing miracles often occur.

For a reminder of the Ottoman conquest, visit the peak of **Exómbourgo ❼**, 643m (2,110 ft), with its ruined fortress (Tínos was the last island to fall to the Turks, in 1723). **Kolymbíthra** in the north is Tínos's best beach. **Ághios Sóstis**, near Pórto on the south coast, is also a decent stretch of beach.

Of the monasteries to see, the abandoned **Katapolianí**, near **Istérnia** ❽ is exceptional. **Kardianí**, the village southeast of Istérnia, is Tínos's most spectacularly set – though arcaded **Arnádos** gives it competition.

Kýthnos

After iron mining operations ceased, Kýthnos lost its prime source of income. Foreign tourism has not supplemented it, but Athenian tourism has helped. **Mérihas** on the west coast has the biggest choice of accommodation. In summer, a "taxi-boat" runs from here to **Episkopí**, **Apókrisi**, and **Kolóna** beaches. **Kýthnos town** (**Hóra**) ❾ 6 km (4 miles) northeast of Mérihas, is exquisite. The town's streets are spanned by wood-beamed arches joining two sides of one house. Rock pavements are decorated with fish, stylised ships and flowers.

Above **Loutrá** (5 km/3 miles east from Hóra), at Maroúla, excavations have revealed the earliest known Cyclades settlement – dating from before 4500 BC. A stream bed splits **Dryopída** ❿ (the

medieval capital) into two; the chambered Katafíki cave here is linked in legend with the Nereids.

Sýros

Sýros remains the Cyclades' capital, but when Piraeus (Pireás) overtook it as a trade centre in the late 1800s, it was cut off from the mainstream. However, it retains excellent inter-island ferry links and useful – if low-key – facilities.

Shipyards dominate the capital, **Ermoúpoli** ⓫, but behind the harbour a few grace-notes appear: the area called **Ta Vapória** ("the ships"), uphill from the shopping streets, is where you'll find many 19th-century neoclassical mansions (a few doubling as cheap hotels).

The island's south is softer and greener than the thinly populated north and has good beaches, namely **Possidonía** ⓬ and **Vári** as well as Fínikas. Up the west coast, **Galissás** and **Kíni** are emerging resorts. During the Colonels' rule, political prisoners were interned on **Yiáros**, the empty island to the north.

Mýkonos

Mýkonos has made itself glamourous. Otherwise unprosperous, it has turned its rocky, treeless ruggedness into a tourist-pleasing package that works – incidentally making it more expensive than most other Greek islands.

Summer draws thousands of tourists to **Mýkonos Town** ⓭ to sample the celebrated bars, transvestite shows, restaurants serving Lobster Thermidor, and the fur and jewellery shops. Yet it is possible to eschew all this and still enjoy a visit. For one thing, the town is the prettiest and most solicitously preserved in the Cyclades, with its wooden balconies loaded with flowers, red-domed

ABOVE: Octopus being dried.
BELOW: pilgrims come from all over Greece to worship on Tínos.

chapels and billows of whitewash. The odd-shaped **Paraportianí** (Our Lady of the Postern Gate) is probably Greece's most photographed church.

Little Venice, a row of buildings hanging over the sea at the north, is the least frenetic part of town. The **Folklore Museum** (open Mon–Sat, 5.30–8.30pm; Sun 6.30–8.30pm; entrance fee) and the **Archeological Museum** (open Tues–Sun, 8.30am–2.30pm; entrance fee), at different ends of Mýkonos's quay, are full of interesting objects. Caïques also depart from here for **Delos** ⓮, the sacred island that is the centre of the Cyclades (in myth Mýkonos was Delian Apollo's grandson – *see also page 267*). Or one can strike inland to **Áno Merá** ⓯ 7 km (4 miles) east, the only real village, which is largely unspoilt by tourism.

Mýkonos is famous, indeed notorious, for its all-night bars and all-day beaches. For bars, you must inquire – the scene changes all the time. For beaches, **Paradise** is straight nude, **Super Paradise** gay nude, and both are beautiful; **Kalafáti**, reached via Áno Merá, is quiet; **Platýs Yialós** and **Psárrou** popular with families. And the reservoir lake in the island's centre attracts thousands of migrating birds.

Sérifos

A long tail of land slashes out to enclose **Livádhi** ⓰, Sérifos' harbour. With a half-dozen each of tavernas, hotels and disco-bars, this is a pleasant place to stay, with good beaches on either side. **Sérifos Town (Hóra)** ⓱ clings to the mountain above which gives it a precipitous beauty – and spectacular views.

The road is paved as far as the fortified Byzantine **Taxiárhon Monastery** ⓲ to the island's extreme north. The scenic walk there from Áno Hóra's main

ABOVE: Pétros the pelican, mascot of Mýkonos Town.
BELOW: Paradise beach, Mýkonos.

Map, pages 256–7

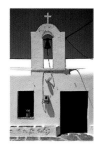

square takes about an hour and a half, via the village of **Kállisto**. The rustic villages of **Galáni**, **Pýrgos** and **Panaghía** focus the magnificent valley beyond the Taxiárhon. You can cross this valley by one of two footpaths around the hill that bisects it, or stick to the road.

Sérifos abounds in beaches, most accessible only on foot and so unspoiled. **Megálo Livádhi** in the southwest is the island's second port (buses cross to it in the summer only). Once a mining centre, it is now rather forlorn.

Sífnos

Sífnos was and is a potter's isle. In the flawlessly pretty harbour, **Kamáres** ,
in Fáros, Platýs Yialós, and especially isolated Hersónisos, potters still set out long racks of earthenware to dry in the sun. Weaving and jewellery-making are the other crafts; there are fine examples of local weaving in the folklore museum in **Apollonía** ❷⓪, the capital (a notice on the door tells you where to find the curator). Connected to Apollonía, **Artemónas** (the towns are named for the divine twins Apollo and Artemis) is Sífnos's richest town, with mansions and old churches. The oldest community, however, is **Kástro** ❷①, the former capital, perched 100m (300 ft) above the sea and 3 km (2 miles) to the east of Apollonía.

Sífnos's south shore settlements make tranquil beach-side bases. A paint-blazed footpath leads from **Kataváti** just south of Apollonía to **Vathý** ❷②, a potter's coastal hamlet provided with a road only in 1993. Vathý's most visually stunning feature is the **Taxiárhis** (Archangel) **Monastery**, poised as though ready to set sail. But Sífnos's most beautiful spot may well be **Hrysopighí** (Golden Wellspring) **Monastery**, built in 1653 on an islet reached by a small footbridge. No longer in monastic use, basic rooms can be rented in summer.

ABOVE: sugar-cube church, Sífnos.
BELOW: stepping through the clear, bold tones of the Cyclades.

Andíparos

Once, 5,000 years, ago this small, pretty island was joined to Páros. A narrow channel now separates the two, plied by frequent car ferries and excursion boats bringing visitors to its famous cave, **Spílio Stalaktitón** (the Cave of the Stalactites) . Though cement steps lessen the adventure, the cave's primordial beauty still stuns. Buses run from **Andíparos Town** to the cave; if you choose to walk, it will take about two hours.

Andíparos is only 11 km by 5 km (7 miles by 3 miles), so there are no impossible distances. Good beaches and bars have lured to Andíparos some of Páros's former business. **Ághios Yeórghios**, on the south coast, has two tavernas, and faces the goat island of **Despotikó**. South of the cave the **Faneroméni chapel** stands alone on a southeastern cape.

Páros

If you arrive at this heavily trafficked island in August, expect to sleep either under the stars or expensively. The cheaper rooms go fast, though in the evening they are empty – everyone is taking in the famous nightlife of **Parikía**, Páros's capital. Parikía is as pretty as Mýkonos, but not so labyrinthine. The four main things to see here are the beautiful 6th-century **Ekatontapylianí church** (Our Lady of a Hundred Doors), the **Archeological Museum** (open Tues–Sun, 8.30am–2.30pm; entrance fee), the ancient **cemetery** (next to the post office), and the Venetian **Kástro** in the centre of town, built wholly of classical marbles.

Léfkes, the Turkish capital, is the largest inland village. There are several 17th-century churches, the two most prominent edged with an opaline-blue wash. In beautiful **Náousa**, on the north coast, the little harbour's colourful

ABOVE: detail of Ekatontapylianí church, Páros.
BELOW: putting Náousa in the frame, Páros.

Flowering shrubs adorn the old houses climbing up the hillsides in Náxos Town. Náxos is the most fertile island of the Cyclades chain.

BELOW: unfinished entrance to the Temple of Delian Apollo, Náxos.

boats seem to nudge up right against the fishermen's houses. Though the village has become fashionable, with upmarket boutiques and restaurants, the harbour is still sacrosanct.

In the west is the much-visited **Valley of the Butterflies**, or **Petaloúdhes**, a big well-watered garden with huge trees. The black and yellow butterflies – moths actually – are colourful and countless in early summer. A big road goes there, but no bus. The bus does, however, go to **Poúnda**, from where the small ferry to Andíparos leaves.

Náxos

Náxos is the largest and most magnificent of the Cyclades, and its **Hóra (Náxos Town)** a labyrinthine chaos of Venetian homes and castle walls, post-Byzantine churches, Cycladic to medieval ruins and garden restaurants. The former French School, built into the ramparts, now houses the **Archeological Museum** (open Tues–Sun, 8.30am–3pm; entrance fee). Níkos Kazantzákis, who wrote *Zorba the Greek*, studied here when it was a school. On an islet to the north of Hóra's ferry dock, a colossal free-standing marble door frame marks the entrance to the never-completed **Temple of Delian Apollo** of 530 BC.

On the northern shore of Náxos is the resort town of **Apóllon** ㉘, a one-time hippie enclave. A huge 6th-century BC *kouros* – probably bearded Dionysos – lies on the hillside above the settlement, abandoned when the marble cracked.

Filóti ㉙, on the slopes of Mount Zás, is Náxos's second-largest town. If you are there for the three-day festival (from 14 August), don't bother trying to stay sober. The Trageá valley, from Filóti to **Halkí**, is all olive trees, amid which are several Byzantine churches – numerous walks are possible here.

It is only in the last ten years that Náxos has become known for its beaches. Some of the best in the Cyclades are on the west coast, facing Páros. **Ághios Yeórghios** south of the port is most popular. **Aghía Ánna**, partly nude, is a good beach for rooms; **Mikrí Vígla** beyond it has a good taverna; and the furthest south **Kastráki ⓾**, offers blissful solitude.

Map, page 256–7

Mílos

Mílos is a geologist's paradise. Snaking streams of lava formed much of the island's coastline, thrusting up weirdly shaped rock formations; it has also always been extensively mined, once for obsidian, now for bentonite, perlite and china clay, amongst others. Gaping quarries disfigure the landscape.

Mílos has graciously adapted to the thin stream of tourism it receives, concentrated in **Adhamás ⓿**, the port, and Apollónia, a fishing village in the northeast. Inside the **Aghía Triádha** church in Adhamás, Cretan-style icons dominate; Cretans refugees founded the town in 1853.

The island's capital, **Pláka** (also called **Mílos**) **⓫**, has both an **Archeological Museum** (open Tues–Sun, 8.30am–3pm; entrance fee) and a **Folklore Museum** (open Tues–Sat, 10am–1pm and 6–8pm; Sun 10am–1pm; entrance fee). A hike to the **Panaghía Thalássitra** (Mariner Virgin), the chapel above Pláka (follow signs for Anna's Art Dresses), and the old **Kástro** walls gives splendid views.

Southwest of Pláka lies the verdant **Vale of Klíma**, on whose seaside slope the ancient Milians built their city. A marble plaque marks the spot where a farmer unearthed the Aphrodite of Mílos (Venus de Milo) in 1820. Below lies one of the island's prettiest villages, **Klíma**, with brightly painted boathouses lining the

When the original Venus de Milo was unearthed on the island in 1820, both arms were still intact. They were "amputated" during her clumsy removal from the island by the French.

BELOW: the tiny, barren island of Folégandhros.

Urn from the site at Akrotíri on Santoríni. The largest Minoan city outside Crete, it was destroyed in a volcanic eruption in 1500 BC – at first, archeologists thought they'd found Atlantis.

BELOW: lovely Ía village, Santoríni.

shore. Further down the road from Pláka to Adamás are the only **Christian catacombs** in all Greece. Carved into the hillside, they are the earliest evidence of Christian worship in the country.

Ten km (6 miles) northeast from Adamás lies the rubble of the ancient city of **Fylakopí**, whose script and art resemble the Minoan. It flourished for a thousand years after 2600 BC. **Apollónia** ㉝, a restful base in the northeast, is a popular resort with a tree-fringed beach. It is a good starting point for several short walks that give the full measure of Mílos's strange volcanic beauty.

Folégandhros

Despite its tiny size – 32 sq km (12 sq miles) populated by barely 500 people – Folégandhros's role in very recent history has not been insignificant: many Greeks were exiled here during the country's 1967–74 military rule.

There are buses to the capital, **Folégandhros (Hóra)** ㉞, a magnificently sited medieval town with an inner **kástro** high above the sea. **Hrysospiliá**, the "golden cave" near Hóra, gapes over the sea. It is rich with stalagmites and stalactites. Excavations show this was a place of refuge in the Middle Ages.

The island's second village, **Áno Meriá**, comprises stone houses and farms; the surrounding hills are dotted with chapels.

Síkinos

Although connected to Piraeus and other Cyclades twice or thrice weekly by ferry, and by caïque to Íos and Folégandhros in summer, rocky Síkinos so far seems to have shrugged off tourism. It also escapes mention in the history books for long periods of time, but there are antiquities and churches to be seen.

The three beaches, **Aloprónia** (also the port), **Ághios Nikólaos** and **Ághios Yeórghios** to the north face Íos. From Aloprónia harbour it is an hour's hike (or regular bus ride) to **Síkinos Town** ㉟, which consists of the simple village (**Hóra**) and the medieval **Kástro**, with its wonderful village square arranged for defence. The abandoned convent of **Zoödóhos Pighí** sits above.

Síkinos is a sparse island with few obvious diversions. One site of note, the **Iroön** ㊱, stands on what was once thought to have been a temple to Apollo; this is now reckoned to be an elaborate Roman tomb, incorporated into a church during medieval times.

Íos

A tiny island with few historic attractions, Íos is not devoid of natural beauty or charm. The harbour is one of the Aegean's prettiest. The hilltop Hóra, capped by a windmill, blazes with the blue domes of two Byzantine churches. Its layout and the palm trees that flank it look almost Levantine.

But ever since the 1960s, Íos has drawn the young and footloose, and this is its defining characteristic. Most nightlife shifts constantly about the little capital town, **Hóra** (also called **Íos**) ㊲. Indeed, after the sun sets, Íos resembles a downmarket, younger Mýkonos. At around 11pm, beach stragglers break the quiet ready for night-time revels (a bus runs regularly between beach and harbour via Hóra). Once ensconced inside a bar, they could be anywhere in the western world, with few Greeks in sight. However, Íos also has many good swimming beaches, including the nude beaches north of the harbour. People still sleep on the beach at **Mylopótas** ❸, although this is now less common. There are summer caïques to **Manganári bay** in the south and **Psáthy** in the east.

Beyond the church are the remains of **Paleokástro** ❹, an elevated fortress containing the marble ruins of what was the medieval capital. At a lonely spot toward the northern tip, behind the cove at **Plakotós**, is a series of prehistoric graves, one of which the islanders fiercely believe belongs to Homer, who is said to have died en route from Sámos to Athens.

Amorgós

A spine of mountains – the tallest is Krikelas in the northeast, at 822m (2,696 ft) – precludes expansive views here unless you're on top of them. The southwesterly harbour town of **Katápola** ❿ occupies a small coastal plain, while the elevated **Hóra** (or **Amorgós town**) ❶, accessible by a regular bus service, centres on a 13th-century Venetian castle. Hóra has no less than 40 churches and chapels – including one that holds only two people, the smallest church in Greece.

The island's two most famous churches are outside Hóra. **Ághios Yeórghios Valsamítis**, 4 km (2 miles) southwest, is on a sacred spring; this church's pagan oracle was finally closed only after World War II. Half an hour east of Hóra, spilling from a jagged cliff like milk from a jug, the 11th-century Byzantine monastery of the **Panaghía Hozoviótissa** ❷ – one of the most beautiful in Greece – is home to a revered icon of the Virgin from Palestine.

Map, page 256–7

ABOVE: alternative transport, Amorgós.
BELOW: Firá perches high above the sea.

Map on page 256–7

Below the monastery, **Aghía Ánna** beach beckons. To the southwest lie secluded coves for bathing and sunning; a line of windmills edges the ridge above. The north of the island is characterised by high-perched villages, excepting **Eghiális**, a small anchorage with accommodation and good beaches nearby.

Santoríni

Entering the bay of Santoríni on a boat is one of Greece's great experiences. Broken pieces of a volcano's rim – Santoríni and its attendant islets – form a multicoloured circle around a bottomless lagoon that, before the volcano's eruption (*circa* 1500 BC), was the island's high centre. The Atlantis legend, so it is thought, begins here.

Thíra (or Thera) is the island's ancient and official name. Greeks, however, prefer its medieval name, Santoríni, after Saint Irene of Salonica, who died here in 304. **Firá** , the capital, sits high on the rim, its white houses (many barrel-vaulted against earthquakes) blooming like asphodels.

To the east of Firá, the land smooths out into fertile fields. A few bare hills push up again in the southeast. On one of them sits **Ancient Thíra**, inaccessible for safety reasons; founded in the 9th century BC. **Akrotíri** in the south, a Minoan town preserved in volcanic ash like Pompeii, continues to be excavated, but if you want to see the beautiful frescoes and pots found there you must – to the locals' chagrin – go to Athens' Archeological Museum.

Though Firá is most developed, many other places offer plentiful accommodation. **Ía (Oía)**, on the island's northernmost peninsula, is perhaps Greece's most photographed village. Nearby, beautiful cave houses, rented out by the National Tourist Organisation (EOT), are a local speciality. Each year, there are also more places available to stay and eat in **Kamári** and **Périssa**, busy resorts on the east coast. Périssa has the main campsite. Both have roasting hot black pebble beaches. They make a good starting point from which to climb to Ancient Thíra, if you don't take a taxi or bike.

Some boats put in below Firá at **Skála Firá**, from where you ascend by donkey, by funicular or by foot up the stone stairway. But most put in at **Athiniás**, 10 km (6 miles) further south.

Anáfi

Fewer than 300 people live on Anáfi today, surviving mainly by fishing and subsistence farming. Summer tourism, mostly German, has boosted the economy only slightly, and the island makes few concessions. It is served by a twice-weekly caïque from Santoríni and several ferries from Piraeus.

The south-facing harbour, **Ághios Nikólaos**, has rooms available in summer. A short bus ride or half-hour walk up, the main town, **Hóra** (or Anáfi) offers a wider choice, and life in the streets has so far been unaltered by tourism. **Zoödóhos Pighí Monastery** was erected over the ancient shrine to Apollo in the island's southeast corner. Extensive courses of marble masonry in its walls are believed to be remnants of the old temple. Above the monastery soars the smaller monastery of **Panaghía Kalamiátissa**, high on a pinnacle that is Anáfi's most distinctive feature. ❏

BELOW: fish face.

Ancient Delos

Minuscule Delos, southwest of Mýkonos, is heaven for archeologists. Extensive Greco-Roman ruins occupying much of the island's 4 sq km (1.5 sq miles) make Delos the equal of Delphi and Olympia.

Sufferers of *mal de mer* should remember, before setting forth, that the island is "windy and waste and battered by the sea". The voyage may be only 45 minutes but, as the caïque heaves and shudders, it can seem 10 times that long. Dedicated travellers are advised to forego breakfast.

It was on Delos that Leto, pregnant by Zeus, gave birth to the twins Apollo and Artemis. (Artemis was actually born on the adjacent islet of Rheneia, nine days after Apollo – surely a difficult delivery!) Delos – then a floating rock – was rewarded when four diamond pillars stretched up and anchored it in the heart of the Cyclades.

Most of the ruins occupy two arms of a right angle. Your first sight (southern arm) is of the theatre and various domestic buildings. To the left is the sanctuary to which pilgrims from all over the Mediterranean came with votive offerings and sacrificial animals.

For nearly a thousand years, this sanctuary was the political and religious centre of the Aegean, and host to the Delian Festival, held every four years and, until the 4th century BC, Greece's greatest religious gathering. The Romans turned it into a grand trade fair, and made Delos a free port. It also became Greece's slave market, where as many as 10,000 slaves were said to be sold daily. But by the start of the Christian era, the island's power and glory were on the wane; soon afterwards, it fell into disuse.

Follow the pilgrim route to a ruined, monumental gateway leading into the Sanctuary of Apollo. Within are three temples dedicated to Apollo – and one to Artemis – and the remains of a colossal marble statue of the god. Close by is the Sanctuary of Dionysios, with several Dionysic friezes and phalli standing on pedestals – including a marble phallic

bird, symbolising the body's immortality. Continue to the stunning Lion Terrace, where five archaic (and seemingly anorexic) lions squat, ready to pounce. Below this is the Sacred Lake, and a palm tree which marks the spot of Apollo's birth.

Most visitors delight in that part of Delos which was occupied by artisans rather than gods. Their houses, close to the port, are a regular warren, separated by narrow lanes lined by 2,000-year old drains, with niches for oil-burning street-lamps. The main road leads to the theatre, which seated 5,500. It is unimpressive, but there are superb views from the uppermost of its 43 rows. Close to the theatre are grander houses surrounded by columns and with exquisite mosaics.

From here, a gentle stroll leads to the summit of Mount Kínthos (110 m/368 ft), from which the views of the ruins and the Cyclades are memorable. Finish off your tour by descending first past the grotto of Hercules, and then stopping at the Sanctuaries to the Foreign Gods. In classical times practically the entire Levant traded here, under the tutelage of shrines erected to their divinities. ❑

RIGHT: one of the lean Lions (carved in the 7th century BC) which guard Delos' Sacred Lake.

THE NORTHEAST AEGEAN

While the cosmopolitan eastern islands of Sámos, Híos and Lésvos once played a leading role on the world's stage, the scattered isles of the far north are still relatively untouched by tourism

Map, page 270

The islands of the northeast Aegean have little in common other than a history of medieval Genoese rule. The northerly group, comprising Thássos, Samothráki, and Límnos, has few or no connections with the outh Aegean; indeed Thássos belongs to the Macedonian province of Kavála, nd Samothráki to Thracian Évros. This close to the mainland, and with a short ummer season, the Greeks' own affection for these convenient islands takes recedence over foreign package tourism.

Lésvos, Híos and Sámos to the southeast once played leading roles in antiquity, colonising across the Mediterranean and promoting the arts and sciences, hough little tangible evidence of ancient glory remains. All three islands served s bridges between Asia Minor and the rest of the Hellenic world and were, in act, once joined to the coast of Asia Minor until Ice Age cataclysms isolated hem; Turkey is still omnipresent on the horizon, a mere 2 km (1 mile) distant cross the Mykale straits at Sámos. Politically, however, the two countries are ften light-years apart, something reflected in absurdly inflated fares for the hort boat trip across.

hássos

ust seven nautical miles from mainland Macedonia, nountainous and almost circular Thássos is essenially a giant lump of marble, mixed with granite and chist, crumbling into white beach sand at the island's nargins. Along with numerous illegal ones scarring he landscape, Greece's largest legal marble quarry rovides employment for many; the cut slabs, lying tacked or being trucked about, are a common sight. n antiquity, gold, silver, and precious stones were lso mined here.

Ferries and hydrofoils for Thássos leave regularly rom **Kavála**; there are also ro-ro services for drivers rom **Keramotí** further east. Bus services around the coastal ring road are adequate, though most visitors ent motorbikes – Thássos is small enough for a long-lay tour – or cars. The east and south coasts have the etter beaches; the west coast has access to most nland villages. Honey, candied walnuts, and *tsípouro*, he northern Greek firewater, are favourite souvenirs.

Thássos's past glory as a wealthy mining town and egional seafaring power is most evident at the harbour capital of **Liménas** (or Thássos Town) ❶, where ubstantial remnants of the ancient town have been excavated; choice bits of the ancient acropolis overead are nocturnally illuminated. The biggest area, ehind the picturesque fishing harbour, is the *agora*; he nearby **Archeological Museum** is due to open ome time in 2000.

LEFT: Lésvos festival-goer.
BELOW: celebrating Easter lunch, Panaghía, Thássos.

Beginning at the **Temple of Dionysos**, a path permits a rewarding walking tour of the ancient walls and acropolis. First stop is the Hellenistic **theatre** (currently shut for re-excavation); continue to the medieval **fortress**, built by a succession of occupiers from the masonry of an Apollo temple. Tracing the course of massive 5th-century BC walls brings you next to the foundations of an Athena temple, beyond which a rock outcrop bears a **shrine of Pan**, visible in badly-eroded relief. From here a vertiginous "secret" stairway plunges to the **Gate of Parmenon** – the only ancient entry still intact – at the southern extreme of town.

The first village clockwise from Liménas, slate-roofed **Panaghía ❷** is a busy place where life revolves around the plane-tree-filled square with its four-spouted fountain. **Potamiá ❸**, further down the valley, is less architecturally distinguished; visitors come mainly for the sake of the **Polýgnotos Vághis Museum** (open Tues–Sat 9am–1pm, summer also 6–9pm, Sun 10am–2pm; entrance fee), featuring the work of the locally born sculptor. Beyond, the road plunges to the coast at Potamiá Bay. **Skála Potamiás**, at its south end, is all lodging and tavernas, with more of that to the north at **Hryssí Ammoudhiá**; in between stretches

Thanks to frequent forest fires during the 1980s and early '90s, Thássos is now three-quarters denuded of its original pine forest, which survives only in the northeast.

a fine, blond-sand beach. There are even better strands at **Kínyra**, 24 km (15 miles) from Liménas, but most one-day tourists schedule a lunch stop at the several tavernas of **Alykí** hamlet ❹, architecturally preserved owing to adjacent ruins: an ancient temple, and two atmospheric Byzantine basilicas.

Rounding the southern tip of Thássos, you pass three beach resorts at **Astrídha**, **Potós** and **Pefkári**; only the former remains attractive, Potós in particular is an overbuilt package dormitory. At **Limenária** ❺, now the island's second town, mansions of the departed German mining executives survive; more intriguingly perhaps, it's the start-point for a safari up to hilltop **Kástro**, the most naturally pirate-proof of the inland villages. Beyond Limenária, there's little to compel a stop.

Theológos ❻, actually reached from Potós, was the island's Ottoman capital, a linear place where most houses have walled gardens. **Mariés** sits piled up at the top of a wooded valley, just glimpsing the sea; by contrast **Sotíros** enjoys phenomenal sunsets, best enjoyed from its central taverna shaded by enormous plane trees. Of all the inland settlements, **Megálo Kazazvíti** (officially **Megálo Prínos**) ❼ has the grandest *platía* and the best-preserved traditional houses, snapped up and restored by outsiders; ground-floor windows still retain iron bars, reminders of pirate days.

Samothráki (Samothrace)

Samothráki raises forbidding granite heights above stony shores and storm-lashed waters, both offering poor natural anchorage. Homer perched Poseidon atop 1,611-m (5,000-ft) **Mount Fengári**, the Aegean's highest summit, to watch the action of the Trojan War to the east. Over time, the forest cover has receded

ABOVE: island cottage industry: tomatoes, drying in the sun.
BELOW: tourist fatigue on the ferry from Thássos.

ABOVE: May Day wreath, Samothráki doorway.
BELOW: Límnos's volcanic soil produces excellent fruit and vegetables.

from the now-barren peak, where modern climbers – on rare occasions – still have the same view, extending from northwestern Turkey to Mount Áthos.

Fengári (Mount Moon) and its foothills occupy much of the island, with little level terrain except in the far west. Tourism is barely developed, and the remaining islanders prefer it that way; in its absence the permanent population has dipped below 3,000, as farming can support only so many. Certainly an overpriced car-ferry from Alexandhroúpolis on the Thracian mainland does not help matters – you may as well sail from Kavála for roughly the same price. Boats, and occasional hydrofoils, dock at **Kamariótissa**, the functional port where rental vehicles are in short supply; only the west of the island has paved roads, and a rudimentary bus service. **Samothráki (Hóra)** ❽, the official capital 5 km (3 miles) east, is more rewarding, nestled almost invisibly in a circular hollow. A cobbled commercial street serpentines past sturdy, basalt-built houses, many deserted. From outdoor seating at the two tavernas on Hóra's large *platía*, you glimpse the sea beyond a crumbled Byzantine-Genoese fort at the edge of town.

Samothráki's other great sight is the **Sanctuary of the Great Gods**, tucked into a ravine some 6 km (4 miles) from Kamariótissa along the north-coast road. From the late Bronze Age until the coming of Christianity, this was the major religious centre of the Aegean. Local deities of the original Thracian settlers were easily syncretised with the Olympian gods of the later Aeolian colonists, in particular the *Kabiri*, or divine twins Castor and Pollux, patrons of seafarers – who needed all the help they could get hereabouts.

The sanctuary ruins (open Tues–Sun 8.30am–3pm; entrance fee) visible today are mostly late Hellenistic, and still eerily impressive if overgrown. Obvious monuments include a partly re-erected temple of the second initiation; the odd, round **Arsinoeion**, used for sacrifices; a round theatral area for performances during the summer festival; and the fountain niche where the celebrated Winged Victory of Samothrace (now in the Louvre) was discovered.

Some 6 km (4 miles) further east, hot springs, cool cascades and a dense canopy of plane trees make the spa hamlet of **Thermá** ❾ the most popular base on the island, patronised by an uneasy mix of the elderly infirm and young bohemian types from several nations. Hot baths come in three temperatures and styles – including outdoor pools under a wooden shelter – while cold-plunge fanatics make for **Gría Váthra** canyon to the east. Thermá is also the base camp for the climb of Mount Fengári, a six-hour round-trip.

Villages south of Hóra see few visitors, though they lie astride the route to **Pahiá Ámmos**, the island's only sandy beach. From **Lákoma** village ❿, it's about 8 km (5 miles) by rough dirt track to the beach, where a single seasonal taverna operates. Beyond Pahiá Ámmos, you can walk to smaller **Vátos** nudist beach, but you'll need a boat – or to drive completely around Samothráki – to reach the gravel beach of **Kípi** in the far southeast.

Límnos

Nowhere in the Aegean does legend match landscape so closely as here. In mythology, Zeus cast hapless Hephaistos from Mount Olympus (Ólymbos) onto Límnos with such force that the fall lamed him permanently. The islanders rescued the god to revere him as a fire deity and patron of metallurgy, an understandable allegiance given the overtly volcanic terrain of Límnos. Hephaistos re-established his forge here; now-solidified lava crags in the west oozed forth as late as the classical period, reassuring Limnians that Hephaistos was at work.

Map, page 270

BELOW: the rooftops of Aghiássos village on Lésvos.

Dominating the approaches to the Dardanelles, Límnos has been occupied since Neolithic times, and always prospered as a trading station and military outpost, rather than a major political power. The Greek military still controls nearly half the island's extent, including half of the huge airport, belying an otherwise peaceful atmosphere. The volcanic soil dwindles to excellent beaches, or produces excellent wine and a variety of other farm products; surrounding seas yield plenty of fish, thanks to periodic migrations through the Dardanelles.

Most things of interest are found in the port-capital, **Mýrina ⑪**, or a short distance to either side – luckily, since the bus service is appalling. Volcanic stone has been put to good use in the older houses and street cobbles of Mýrina, while elaborate Ottoman mansions face the northerly town beach of **Romeïkós Yialós** with its cafés; the southerly beach of **Tourkikós Yialós** abuts the fishing port with its seafood tavernas. Public evidence of the Ottoman period is limited to an inscribed fountain, and a dilapidated mosque behind a supermarket, both near the harbour end of the single, long market street. Festooned engagingly over the headland above town, the ruined *kástro* is worth climbing up to for sunset views.

The road north from Mýrina passes the exclusive **Aktí Mýrina** resort en route to good beaches at **Avlónas** and **Ághios Ioánnis**. In the opposite direction lie even better ones at **Platý** and **Thános**, with tiered namesake villages on the hillsides just above; continuing southeast from Thános brings you to **Nevgátis**, acknowledged as the island's best beach. Mýrina's admirably presented Archeological Museum (open Tues–Sun 8.30am–3pm; entrance fee) holds finds from the island's major archeological sites: **Kabeirio** (Kavírio), **Hephaistia** (Ifestía) and **Polyochni** (Polyóhni). These are all a long trip away in the far east of Límnos, and of essentially specialist interest.

ABOVE: garden urn in Plomári, Lésvos's second town.
BELOW: traditional café, Aghiássos, Lésvos.

Sadder relics of more recent history flank the drab port town of **Moúdhros ⑫** – two Allied cemeteries maintained by the Commonwealth War Graves Commission. During World War I, Moúdhros was the principal base for a disastrous Gallipoli campaign; of about 36,000 casualties, 887 are interred outside of Moúdhros on the way to **Roussopoúli**, while 348 more lie behind the village church at **Portianoú ⑬**, across the bay.

Ághios Efstrátios (Aï Strátis)

A tiny wedge of land south of Límnos, Ághios Efstrátios is doubtless the most desolate spot in the northeast Aegean – all the more so since a 1967 earthquake devastated the single village. Owing to junta-era corruption, reparable dwellings were bulldozed and the surviving inhabitants (nearly half were killed) provided with ugly, pre-fab replacement housing on a grid plan. This, plus two dozen surviving buildings, is all you see if you disembark the regular ferries stopping here on the Rafína-Límnos-Kavála route, or (in summer) the small Límnos-based ferry. Still, this does mean that none of the several beaches (within 90 minutes' walk to north or south) is likely to contain another soul.

Lésvos (Mytilíni)

Greece's third-largest island, measuring 70 by 40 km (44 by 24 miles) at its extremities, remote, fertile Lésvos is the antithesis of the *nisáki,* or quaint little

islet. Between far-flung villages lie 11 million olive trees producing 45,000 liquid tonnes of oil a year. Shipbuilding, carpentry, *oúzo*-distilling, and pottery remain important, but none rival the olive, especially since it complements the second industry, tourism. Nets to catch the "black gold" are spread in autumn.

Early inhabitants were related to the Trojans; in *The Iliad* the Achaeans punished Lésvos for siding with Troy. Natives were later supplemented by Aeolian colonists, who in a convoluted topography created by two penetrating gulfs founded six city-states, the most important being Eressos, Mithymna, Antissa and Mytilene. Although they vied for political supremacy, Lésvos developed a uniform culture, nurturing such bards as Terpander and Arion well before Alcaeus and Sappho in the 6th century pushed lyric poetry to new heights, while their contemporary Pittacus (no friend of aristocrats like Alcaeus or Sappho) initiated democratic reforms.

With its thick southern forests and idyllic orchards, Lésvos was a preferred Roman holiday spot; the Byzantines considered it a humane exile for deposed nobility, while the Genoese Gateluzzi clan kept a thriving court here for a century. To the Ottomans it was "The Garden of the Aegean," their most productive, strictly governed and heavily colonised Aegean island. Following 18th-century reforms within the empire, a Christian land-owning aristocracy developed, served by a large population of labouring peasants. This quasi-feudal system made Lésvos fertile ground for post-1912 Leftist movements, and its habit of returning Communist MPs since the junta fell has earned it the epithet "Red Island" among fellow Greeks.

The years after 1912 also saw a vital local intelligentsia emerge, but since World War II Lésvos's socio-economic fabric has shrunk considerably with

Map, page 270

The ancient city-state of Eressos in western Lésvos is thought to be the birthplace of the poetess Sappho; it has subsequently become something of a place of pilgrimage for gay women from all over the world.

BELOW: the harbour at Mytilíni.

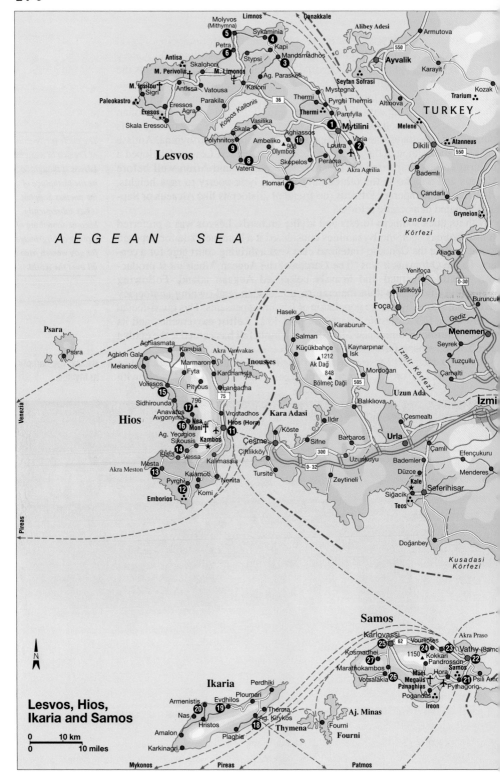

Lesvos, Hios, Ikaria and Samos

emigration to Athens, Australia and America. However the founding here in 1987 of the University of the Aegean brought hope for a cultural revival.

Map, page 276

Mytilíni ❶, the capital (its name a popular alias for the entire island), has a revved-up, slightly gritty atmosphere, as befits a port town of 30,000; it is interesting to stroll around, though few outsiders stay. Behind the waterfront, assorted church domes and spires enliven the skyline, while **Odhós Ermoú**, one street inland, threads the entire bazaar, from the fish market to a clutch of excellent – if pricy – antique shops. Behind the ferry dock is the **Archeological Museum** (open Tues–Sun 8.30am–3pm; entrance fee) featuring Hellenistic mosaics and some interesting grave *stelae*.

More noteworthy are a pair of museums in **Variá ❷**, 4 km (2½ miles) south of town. The **Theóphilos Museum** (open Tues–Sun 9am–1pm and 4.30–8pm; entrance fee) contains over 60 paintings by locally born Theóphilos Hazimihaïl, Greece's most celebrated naive painter. The nearby **Thériade Museum** (open Tues–Sun 9am–2pm and 5–8pm; entrance fee) was founded by another native son who, while an avant-garde art publisher in Paris, assembled this collection, with work by the likes of Chagall, Picasso, Rouault and Léger.

The road running northwest from Mytilíni follows the coast facing Turkey. **Mandamádhos ❸**, 37 km (23 miles) from Mytilíni, offers a surviving pottery industry and, at the outskirts, the enormous **Monastery of the Taxiárhis** with its much-revered black icon. At **Kápi** the road divides; the northerly fork is wider, better paved and more scenic as it curls across the flanks of **Mount Leptétymnos**, passing by the handsome village of **Sykaminiá ❹** (12 km/7 miles more). You descend to sea level at **Mólyvos ❺**, linchpin of Lésvos tourism and understandably so: the ranks of sturdy tiled houses climbing to the medieval cas-

ABOVE: Mytilíni castle.
BELOW: the harbour at Mólyvos.

A painting in the Theóphilos Museum, Variá. A wandering tramp, Theóphilos painted murals to earn a crust. After he died in 1934, his naive paintings became internationally known.

BELOW: mural in the cloisters of the Perivolís Monastery.

tle are an appealing sight, as is the stone-paved fishing harbour. Its days as a bohemian artists' and alternative activities colony are over, however, with package tourism dominant since the late 1980s. **Pétra** ❻, 5 km (3 miles) south, accommodates the overflow on its long beach, while inland at the village centre looms a rock plug crowned with the **Panaghía Glykofiloússa** church. At its foot the 18th-century **Vareltzídena Mansion** (open Tues–Sun 8.30am–3pm; entrance fee) is worth a look, as is the frescoed church of **Ághios Nikólaos**.

From Pétra, head 17 km (10 miles) south to the turning for **Límonos Monastery**, home to small ecclesiastical and folklore museums, before continuing west towards the more rugged half of the island, with its lunar volcanic terrain. Stream valleys foster little oases, such as the one around **Perivolís Monastery**, 30 km (19 miles) from Limónos (daily 8am–7pm), decorated with wonderful frescoes. Beyond 10 km (6 miles), atop an extinct volcano, the **Monastery of Ipsiloú** contemplates the abomination of desolation – complete with scattered trunks of the "Petrified Forest", prehistoric sequoias mineralised by volcanic ash.

Sígri (90 km/56 miles from Mytilíni), a sleepy place flanked by good beaches, is very much the end of the line, though lately an alternate ferry port; most prefer **Skála Eressoú**, 14 km (9 miles) south of **Ipsiloú**, for a beach experience, in particular numerous lesbians come to honour Sappho, who was born here.

Southern Lésvos, between the two gulfs, is home to olive groves rolling up to 967-m (3173-ft) **Mount Ólymbos**. **Plomári** ❼ on the coast is Lésvos's second town, famous for its *oúzo* industry; most tourists stay at pebble-beach **Ághios Isídhoros** 3 km (2 miles) east, though **Melínda** 6 km (4 miles) west is more scenic. **Vaterá** ❽, whose 7-km (4-mile) sand beach is reckoned the best

on the island, lies still further west; en route, you can stop for a soak at the restored medieval spa outside **Polyhnítos ❾**, 45 km (28 miles) from Mytilíni.

Inland from Plomári, the remarkable hill village of **Aghiássos ❿** nestles in a wooded valley under Ólympos. Its heart is the major pilgrimage church of **Panaghía Vrefokratoússa**, which comes alive for the 15 August festival, Lésvos's biggest. Local musicians are considered among the island's best.

Map, page 276

Psará

Only about 350 inhabitants remain on melancholy Psará, its bleakness relieved only by occasional fig trees and one cultivated field in the west. Besides the lone port village, there's just one deserted monastery in the far north. Six beaches lie northeast of the port, each better than the preceding, though all catch tide-wrack on this exposed coast. A few tourists trickle over from Híos, either on the thrice-weekly Miniotis Line ferry from Híos Town, or a summer-only caïque from Volissós of similar frequency; ferries call rarely from Sígri on Lésvos.

Híos (Chíos)

Although the island had been important and prosperous since antiquity, the Middle Ages made the Híos of today. The Genoese seized control here in 1346; the Justiniani clan established a cartel, the *maona*, which controlled the highly profitable trade in gum mastic. During their rule, which also saw the introduction of silk and citrus production, Híos became one of the wealthiest and most cultured islands in the Mediterranean. Local prowess in navigation was exploited by 150 ships calling here annually; Christopher Columbus apocryphally came to study with Híot captains prior to his voyages.

BELOW: scraping resin off the mastic trees, Híos.

A STICKY BUSINESS

The mastic bushes of southern Híos (Chíos) are the unique source of gum mastic, the basis for many products before petroleum was refined. It was popular in Constantinople as chewing-gum, and allegedly freshened the breath of the Sultan's concubines. The Romans made mastic toothpicks to keep their teeth white and prevent cavities; Hippocrates praised its therapeutic value for coughs and colds; and lately practitioners of alternative medicine make even more ambitious claims on its behalf.

In the 14th and 15th centuries, the Genoese set up a monopoly in the substance; at its peak, the trade generated enough wealth to support half-a-dozen *mastihohoriá* (mastic villages). However, the coming of the industrial revolution and the demise of the Ottoman empire was the end of large-scale mastic production.

Today, smaller amounts are generated in a process which has not really changed since ancient times. In late summer, incisions made in the bark weep resin "tears", which are scraped off and cleaned. Finally, the raw gum is sent to a central processing-plant where it is washed, baked and formed into "chiclets" of gum. Some 150 tons are produced annually, most of it exported to France, Bulgaria and Saudi Arabia for prices of up to $35 a kilo.

In 1566 the Ottomans expelled the Genoese, but granted the islanders numerous privileges, so that Híos continued to flourish until March 1822, when poorly armed agitators from Sámos convinced the reluctant Hiots to participate in the independence uprising. Sultan Mahmut II, enraged at this ingratitude, exacted a terrible revenge; a two-month rampage commanded by Admiral Kara Ali killed 30,000 islanders, enslaved 45,000 more, and saw all settlements except the mastic-producing villages razed. Híos had only partly recovered when a strong earthquake in March 1881 destroyed much of what remained and killed 4,000. Today Híos and its satellite islet **Inoússes** are home to some of Greece's wealthiest shipping families.

Its catastrophic 19th-century history ensures that **Híos Town** or **Hóra** ⓫ (population 25,000) seems at first off-puttingly modern; scratch the ferroconcrete surface, however, and you'll find traces of the Genoese and Ottoman years. The most obvious medieval feature is the **Kástro**; moated on the landward side, it lacks a seaward rampart, destroyed after the 1881 quake. Just inside the impressive **Porta Maggiora** stands the **Justiniani Museum** (open Tues–Sun 9am–3pm; entrance fee), a good collection of religious art rescued from rural churches. Off a small nearby square is the Muslim cemetery with the tomb of Kara Ali – he of the massacres, blown up along with his flagship by one of Admiral Kanarís's fireboats in June 1822. Further in lies the old Muslim and Jewish quarter with its derelict mosque and overhanging houses; Christians had to settle outside the walls.

Heading south from Hóra you pass through **Kámbos**, a broad plain of high-walled citrus groves dotted with the imposing sandstone mansions of the medieval aristocracy, standing along narrow, unmarked lanes. Many were destroyed by the earthquake, while a few have been restored as accommodation or restaurants. Irrigation water was originally drawn up by *manganós* or waterwheel; a few survive in ornately paved courtyards

The onward road heads southwest towards mastic-producing southern Híos, with its 20 villages known as the *mastihohoriá*, built as pirate-proof strongholds by the Genoese during the 14th and 15th centuries. Laid out on a dense, rectangular plan, their narrow passages are overarched by earthquake buttresses, with the backs of the outer houses doubling as the perimeter wall.

Pyrghí ⓬, 21 km (13 miles) from Hóra, is one of the best-preserved villages; most façades are incised with black-and-white geometric patterns called *xystá*. A passageway off the central square leads to the Byzantine **Ághii Apóstoli** church, decorated with later frescoes. In the back alleys, tomatoes are laboriously strung for drying in late summer by teams of local women. Some 11 km (7 miles) west, **Mestá** ⓭ seems a more sombre, monochrome labyrinth, which retains defensive towers at its corners; several three-storeyed houses have been restored as accommodation. Such quarters are typically claustrophobic, though, and guests will appreciate the nearby beach resorts of **Kómi** (sand) and **Emboriós** (volcanic pebbles).

With your own car, the beautiful, deserted west coast with its many coves is accessible via **Véssa**, ⓮

ABOVE: stringing tomatoes on Híos. **BELOW:** a typical example of *xystá* decorations on a house in Pyrghí.

the paved road eventually taking you to castle-crowned **Volissós** in the far northwest. To either side of this half-empty village are the island's finest beaches – and visible scars from a series of 1980s fires which burnt two-thirds of Híos's forests. Between **Kastélla** and **Elínda** bays, a good road snakes east uphill to **Avgónyma** ⓰, a clustered village well restored by returned Greek-Americans. Just 4 km (2½ miles) north perches almost-deserted, crumbling **Anávatos** ⓱, well camouflaged against its cliff; from here in 1822, 400 Hiots leapt to their deaths rather than be captured.

Some 5 km (3 miles) east, the monastery of **Néa Moní** (open daily 8am–1pm and 4–8pm; 4–6pm winter) forms one of the finest surviving examples of mid-Byzantine architecture, founded in 1049 by Emperor Constantine Monomachus IX on a spot where a miraculous icon of the Virgin had appeared. It suffered heavily in 1822 and 1881, first with the murder of its monks, plus the pillage of its treasures, and then with the collapse of its dome. Despite the damage, its mosaics of scenes from the life of Christ are outstanding.

Ikaría and Foúrni

This narrow, wing-shaped island is named for mythical Ikaros, who supposedly fell into the sea nearby when his wax wings melted (the Greek Air Force adopted him as a patron, apparently impervious to the irony). One of the least developed large islands in the Aegean, **Ikaría** has little to offer anyone intent on ticking off four-star sights, but appeals to those disposed to an eccentric, slightly Ruritanian environment. For three brief months after 17 July 1912, when a certain Dr Malahias declared the island liberated, it was an independent republic, with its own money and stamps. In later decades, Ikaría served as a place of exile

Map, page 276

ABOVE: detail from the Byzantine Néa Moní, Híos.
BELOW: a remote chapel on remote Ikaría island.

Composer and former communist Míkis Theodhorákis, best known for the film-score for **Zorba the Greek**, *was held in a concentration camp on Ikaría during the Greek civil war.*

for hundreds of communists; the locals thought they were the most noble, humanitarian folk they'd ever met, and still vote Communist in droves – not quite what Athens intended.

Ághios Kírykos is the capital and main southerly port, its tourist facilities geared to the clientele at the neighbouring spa of **Thermá**. Taxis are far more reliable than the bus for the 41-km (25-mile) drive over the 1,000-m (3,300-ft) **Atherás** ridge to **Évdhilos**, the north-facing second port. Another 16 km (10 miles) takes you past **Kámbos**, with its sandy beach and ruined Byzantine palace, to the end of the asphalt at **Armenistís**. Here only do foreigners congregate, for the sake of excellent beaches – **Livádhi** and **Mesaktí** – just east, though the surf can be deadly. **Nás**, 4 km (2½ miles) west, is named for the *naos* or temple of **Artemis Tavropolio** on the banks of the river draining to a popular pebble cove. **Yialiskári**, a fishing port 4 km (2½ miles) east, is distinguished by its photogenic jetty chapel.

There are few bona fide inland villages, as the proud Ikarians hate to live on top of each other, and keep plenty of room for orchards between their houses. Above Armenistís are four hamlets lost in pine forest, collectively known as **Rákes**; at **Hristós**, the largest, people cram the café-bars all night, sleep until noon, and carry belongings (or store potent wine) in hairy goatskin bags. The surrounding countryside completes the hobbit-like image with vertical natural monoliths and troglodytic cottages for livestock made entirely of gigantic slate slabs. Dirt roads are abysmal, especially towards the south coast, where the few hamlets are easier reached by boat.

Foúrni, one of a mini-archipelago of islets southeast of Ikaría, lives from its thriving fishing fleet and boatyards; seafood dinners figure high in the ambitions

BELOW: the beach at Kokkári, Sámos.

of arriving tourists, who mostly stay in the main, surprisingly large port town. A road links this with **Ághios Ioánnis Hryssóstomos** in the south and idyllic **Hryssomiliá** in the far north, the only other villages, but path-walking (where possible) and boat-riding are more relaxing ways of getting around. Best of many beaches are at **Kámbi**, one ridge south of port, or at **Psilí Ámmos** and **Kálamos** on the north.

Map, page 276

Sámos

Almost subtropical **Sámos**, with vine terraces, cypress and olive groves, surviving forests of black and Calabrian pine, hillside villages, and beaches of every size and consistency, appeals to numerous package tourists. A half-dozen wildfires since 1986 have not yet done for its natural beauty, and only the east has been thoroughly commercialised; impassable gorges, the Aegean's second-highest mountain and beaches accessible only on foot hold sway in the far west.

From the immense harbour mole at heavily commercialised **Pythagório** ㉑, constructed by Classical slaves, and scarcely changed, you can watch majestic Mount Mykale in Turkey change colour at dusk. The port's shape suggested a frying-pan, hence Tigáni, the town's former name – perhaps too prophetic of what it's become: a casserole of lobster-red Scandinavians fried in suntan-oil. The authorities changed the name in 1955 in honour of native son Pythagoras.

The 1,040-m (3,200-ft) **Evpalínio Órygma** (Eupalinos' Tunnel, open Tues–Sun 9am– 2.30pm), an aqueduct built during the rule of the brilliant but unscrupulous tyrant Polykratis (538–522 BC), cuts through the hillside northwest of town. It is one of the technological marvels of the ancient world; surveying was so good that two work crews beginning from each end met with no verti-

ABOVE: sponges for sale, Pythagório harbour.
BELOW: sprucing up a fishing-boat, Pythagório.

The archeological museum in Vathý has a rich trove of finds from the ancient Sanctuary of Hera, just west of Pythagório.

cal error and a horizontal one of less than 1 percent. You can visit much of it, along the catwalk used to remove spoil from the water channel far below.

The ruins of what was once a vast, grandiose **Sanctuary of Hera** – one re-erected column and sundry foundations – lie 8 km (5 miles) to the west of Pythagório, past coastal Roman baths and the airport (open Tues–Sun 8.30am–3pm; entrance fee).

Vathý or Sámos Town ㉒, built along an inlet on the north coast, is the main port, founded in 1832. Tourism is less pervasive here, though many do call at the excellent **Archeological Museum** (open Tues–Sun 8.30am–3pm; entrance fee), with a rich trove of finds from the Sanctuary of Hera. In pride of place is a 5-m (16-ft) high, nearly intact *kouros*, the largest ever found. The small-objects collection (in a separate wing) confirms the temple's Middle Eastern slant of worship and clientele: orientalised ivories, and locally-cast griffin's heads.

Áno Vathý, the large village clinging to the hillside 2 km (1 mile) southeast, existed for two centuries before the harbour settlement; a stroll will take you through steep cobbled streets separating 300-year-old houses, their overhanging second stories and plaster-lath construction more akin to the architecture of northern Greece and Anatolia than the central Aegean.

First stop of note on the north-coast road (12 km/7 miles) is **Kokkári** ㉓, a former fishing village now devoted to tourism. The original centre is cradled between twin headlands, while windsurfers launch themselves from the long, westerly pebble beach. Overhead loom the wooded crags of **Mount Ámbelos** (1,150 m/3,800 ft); paths go up directly from behind Kokkári, while cars climb a road just past **Avlákia** to thriving little **Vourliótes** ㉔, with several tavernas on its photogenic square. **Vrondianí monastery**, 3 km (2 miles) east, co-hosts the

island's liveliest festival (7–8 September); some 20 minutes' walk below Vourliótes, the hamlet of **Pnáka** has a powerful spring and another taverna.

The coastal highway continues west, sometimes as a sea-level corniche route, to **Karlóvassi** , 34 km (21 miles) from Vathý. It's a sprawling, somewhat dishevelled place, little touristed and lumped into four districts. **Néo**, the biggest, houses post-1923 refugees and sports cavernous, derelict warehouses down by the water, vestiges of the leather-tanning trade which thrived here before 1940. **Meséo** is more villagey, as is **Áno** or **Paleó**, lining a green valley behind the sentinel church of **Ághia Triádha**. **Limín**, just below Áno, has most local tourist facilities, including a ferry service.

The shore west of here has some of Sámos's best beaches, including sand-and-pebble **Potámi**, visited by most of Karlóvassi at weekends. Beyond here, you must walk to a pair of remote, scenic beaches at **Seïtáni**. **Karlóvassi** lies roughly halfway around an anticlockwise loop of the island; head south, then east through an interior dotted with small villages of tiled, shuttered houses and stripey-domed churches.

At **Ághii Theodhóri** junction, choose southwest or east. The former direction takes you through **Marathókambos** and its port to **Votsalákia**, Sámos's fastest-growing beach resort; better, more secluded coves lie further west along the road curling around the base of **Mount Kérkis** (1,437 m/4,725 ft), which forms the west end of the island. It's usually climbed from **Evangelístria convent** on the south or **Kosmadhéï** on the north – either way a full day's outing. Returning to Pythagório, schedule stops in **Pýrgos** for a can of local honey, and just below **Mavratzéï**, at the monastery of **Megális Panaghías**, with the best frescoes on Sámos, dating from after 1586. ❏

Map, page 276

BELOW: the narrow, cobbled streets of Áno Vathý, Sámos.

THEODOR ELIA[…]

FRANKFURT A/M

TH. ELIADIS · ELIADIS

PLAKAT-FABRIK
WÜSTEN & KORNSAND, FRANKFURT A/M.

Die Sch[…]

1. Ein Schwamm-Taucher, welcher von einem Haifisch verschlungen wird.
2. Ertrunkener Taucher, weil er Tau und Ballaststein verloren.
3. Schwamme-Sammler.
4. Taucher, das Zeichen zum Aufziehen gebend.
5. Taucher, die Wurzeln eines grossen Schwammes ausziehend.
6. Taucher, der die Besinnung verloren hat und ertrinken muss.
7. Zu Hilfe eilender Taucher.
8. Taucher, welcher sein Tau verloren hat und nach oben zu schwimmen versucht.
9. Zu Hilfe eilender Taucher mit Tau und Stein.
10. Taucher, im Moment des Aufziehens.
11. Taucher, welcher Tau und Stein verloren, mit Hilfe der Ankerkette heraufgezogen wird.
12. Ta[…] Ob[…]
13. und[…]
15. Ta[…] gri[…]
16. Ta[…]

SCHWAMM-GROSSHANDLUNG
EIGENE SCHWAMM-FISCHEREI auf der SPORADE-INSEL KALYMNOS.

THE DODECANESE

An archipelago with enormous range, from holy Pátmos to busy Kós, from wild Kárpathos to resort-studded Rhodes – where the legacy of the Crusaders and the ancients is still much in evidence

Greek place-names are often revealing of history, and the word "Dodecanese" (*Dhodhekánissos*), a new name by Greek standards, is no exception. Over four centuries of Ottoman rule they were known as the Southern Sporades, a name still appearing on older maps. During this period, smaller, more barren islands here were granted considerable privileges – in effect being invited to live by their own wits – though larger, more fertile Rhodes and Kós were more strictly governed, and colonised by Muslims. But after the establishment of an independent Greece in 1830, and periodic armed hostilities between it and the Ottoman Empire, such privileges were gradually withdrawn. The 12 larger islands (*dhódeka nissiá* in Greek) submitted a joint objection against these infringements in 1908; the protest failed, but the new name stuck, although there are, depending on how one counts, 14 or even 18 inhabited isles in this chain, spread in an arc along the Turkish coast.

In 1912 the Italians took this group, subsequently renamed the "Italian Islands of the Aegean". The Fascists, in particular, were busy colonialists, erecting numerous distinctive edifices, planting eucalyptus, building roads and imposing their language and culture on public life; any local born before 1928 will still be able to converse in Italian. In late 1943, Germany assumed control here after the Italian capitulation, and in turn surrendered the islands to the British two years later. Finally, in early 1948, the Dodecanese were united with Greece to become the country's southeastern-most, and most recent, territorial acquisition. Today the islanders live – as they always have – largely off the sea, which has brought them a novel catch of vital importance to the local economy: tourists.

Rhodes: cultural beacon

The best-known of the Dodecanese islands, Rhodes (Ródhos) is endowed with a balmy climate and a wealth of monuments. Ancient Rhodes originally consisted of three city-states: Kameiros, Ialyssos and Lindos. Following Athenian attacks, they decided to unite, founding Rhodes Town at the island's northeast tip, separated from Asia Minor only by 13-km (7 mile) strait. Fortifications were completed by 408 BC, and the town laid out on a grid plan.

Well-defended by its daring fleet, and strategically positioned, Rhodes prospered as a trading-station and led a charmed life despite fickle alliances, as the moment suited, with Athens, Sparta, Alexander the Great, or the Persians. Under Alexander, Rhodes forged links with the Ptolemies, so the Rhodians refused to fight the Egyptians alongside King Antigonos. After Alexander's death, Antigonos sent his son, Demetrios Polyorketes, along with 40,000

PRECEDING PAGES: a 19th-century advertisement for Kálymnian sponges. **LEFT:** windmill on Kárpathos. **BELOW:** Mandhráki harbour, Rhodes New Town.

men to attack the city in 305 BC. He failed after a year-long siege; the leftover bronze military hardware was melted down to make the island's most famous landmark, the 31-m (102-ft) Colossus of Rhodes, a representation of Apollo. A beacon to passing ships and monuments, it stood at the harbour entrance for nearly 70 years before it fell to the ground during an earthquake in 226 BC.

Legend has it that the Colossus stood with one foot on either side of Mandhráki harbour entrance. But to do so it would have to have been over 10 times its original size – an impossible architectural feat.

The city emerged from the siege with prestige and prosperity enhanced, eclipsing Athens as the cultural beacon of the east Mediterranean until unwisely acting above its station by trying to reconcile the warring Romans and Macedonians. Rome retaliated in 168 BC by effectively making Rhodes a Roman vassal; involvement in the Roman civil wars a century later saw Rhodes sacked by Cassius and its fleet destroyed. After Octavius's victory in 42 BC and the establishment of imperial Rome, Rhodes regained some autonomy, and again served as a finishing-school and sybaritic posting for officialdom, but its glory days were over. In late Roman and Byzantine times the island endured second-rate status, prone to Barbarian raids.

Early in the 14th century, the Knights of St John – expelled from Palestine and Cyprus – settled on Rhodes, ejecting its Byzantine rulers. They proceeded to occupy and fortify virtually all of the Dodecanese, rebuilding Rhodes Town's rickety Byzantine city walls and acting as a major irritant to the sultan with their depredations on Ottoman shipping. Finally, in spring 1522, Süleyman the Magnificent landed an army of 100,000 on Rhodes to end the problem; Rhodes's second siege was shorter and more conclusive than the first, but only just. The Knights resisted valiantly, but finally were forced to surrender; 180 survivors concluded honourable terms of surrender and sailed off to exile on Malta on New Year's day, 1523.

BELOW: Palace of the Grand Masters.

Island resorts

Despite still-visible damage from Allied shelling in 1945, the **City of Rhodes ❶** is one of the architectural treasures of the Mediterranean, a remarkably complete walled medieval town. The **ramparts** themselves (one-hour tours only; Tues, Sat, 2.45pm; entrance from gate beside Palace of the Grand Masters) give a good perspective over the palm-and-minaret-studded lanes. At the northwest summit stands the **Palace of the Grand Masters ❷** (open Mon 12.30–7pm, Tues–Fri 8am–7pm, Sat–Sun 8am–3pm; entrance fee), hastily reconstructed by the Italians after its destruction by an 1856 ammunition explosion. From outside, the better-restored **Street of the Knights (Ippotón) ❸**, where the chivalric order once housed its members by language, leads downhill to the badly labelled **Archeological Museum ❻** (open Tues–Sat 8.30am–6pm, Sun 8.30am–3pm; entrance fee), the **Byzantine Museum ❹** opposite (open Tues–Sun 8.30am– 3pm; entrance fee), with its exhibits of local icons and frescoes, and the ethnographic **Decorative Arts Collection** (Tues–Sun 8.30am–3pm; entrance fee). Despite a small resident Turkish minority, Ottoman monuments are not highlighted except for the wonderful, still-functioning **Turkish Baths ❺** (sporadic hours); the arcaded synagogue in the former Jewish quarter can also be visited.

Líndhos ❷, 44 km (27 miles) south along the east coast, is the other big tourist magnet. Settled early thanks to its fine natural harbour – the only one aside from **Mandhráki** at Rhodes Town – its strong acropolis holds a scaffolded Hellenistic Athena temple and a Knights' castle. Clustered below is the late-medieval village of imposing mansions built by local sea-captains; with its barren surroundings, the place has always lived from the sea. Italian, German and British bohemians first rediscovered Líndhos in the 1960s, attracted by the pellucid light, but its role as an artists' colony has long since been replaced by one as a package-tour dormitory; midsummer visits are not recommended.

Second of the Dorian city-states, **Kámeiros**, 33 km (20½ miles) down the windswept west coast, merits a visit for being a perfectly preserved classical townscape, without the usual later accretions; unlike old Líndhos, it was abandoned shortly after 408 BC (Tues–Sun 8.30am–3pm; entrance fee). Not so ancient **Ialyssos** (open Tues–Fri 8.30am–6pm, Sat–Sun 8.30am–3pm; entrance fee), 12 km (7½ miles) southwest of town, better known for its appealing medieval monastery of **Filérimos**, now well-restored after being damaged during World War II.

Most of the island is easiest reached by rental car. Knights' castles at **Monólithos ❸** and **Kritiniá**, beyond Kameiros, make suitable targets, along with the village of **Siána ❹** in between, all these points under the shadow of 1,215-m (3,986-ft) **Mount Attávyros**, summit of Rhodes. The best Byzantine monuments in the interior are the frescoed church of **Ághios Nikólaos Foundouklí**, just below 798-m (2,618-ft) **Profítis Ilías**, and the recently reinhabited monastery of **Thári** with its 14th-century frescoes, lost amidst unburnt pine forest halfway between Líndhos and Monólithos. Better beaches on the more sheltered

ABOVE: detail of harbour wall, Mandhráki harbour, Rhodes.
BELOW: the Athena Temple, Líndhos.

Maps:
City 290
Area 292

east coast include **Tsambíka ❺**, huddled below a giant volcanic promontory, and **Agáthi ❻**, just north of Feraklós castle and **Haráki** port **❼**. Inland, **Eptá Pighés ❽** is an enduringly popular oasis, its reservoir an Italian legacy. Beyond the Líndhos promontory, still-excellent beaches are much emptier; there are few specific sights aside from the wonderfully frescoed 11th-century church at **Asklipío** village **❾**, which lies just after Thári.

Kárpathos

The most dramatic way to arrive at Kárpathos is by ship from Rhodes. After several hours' journey on often rough seas, the island appears with its imposing summit-ridge. Some, though not all, boats stop at **Dhiafáni ❿**, the northerly port which only received a jetty in 1996. By daylight, onward passengers have the time to get acquainted with Kárpathos. Its eastern shore drops steeply to the sea, baby pines sprouting from slopes recovering from huge 1980s blazes which denuded the north; occasionally, the cliffs relent at large, white, empty beaches.

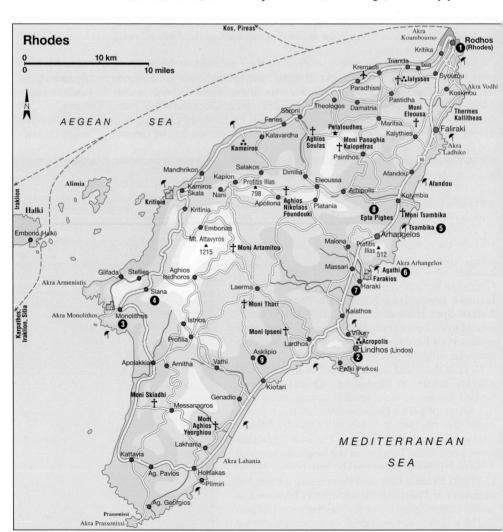

After these first impressions, the main port of **Pigádhia ⓫** is inevitably a disappointment, with very little to recommend it other than its fine setting; it dates only from the 19th century. This lack of distinction also has to do with Kárpathos's status as a backwater since ancient times; neither the Knights nor the Ottomans bothered much with it, leaving it to the Genoese and Venetians, who called it Scarpanto.

Maps, pages 292, 294

Getting back to a beach is likely to be a top priority; an excellent one stretches immediately north for 3 km (1¾ miles) along **Vróndi Bay**. More secluded ones, visible on the ferry ride in, prove close up to have aquamarine water and white-sand or pebble shores of Caribbean calibre, guarded by half-submerged rock formations. The best of these are **Appélla**, **Aháta** and **Kyrá Panaghía**, accessible either on small-boat excursions or overland – though Kárpathiot roads are appalling and hire-cars expensive. The west coast is far more exposed, but at remote **Lefkós**, a series of three bays tucked in between headlands, there are excellent beaches and a growing resort to attend them.

Most villages are well inland and high up, the standard medieval strategy against pirates, of whom Kárpathos had more than its fair share. The wealthist settlements are a trio – **Apéri ⓬**, **Óthos** and **Voládha** – just south of cloud-capped Mount Kalilímni (1,215 m / 3,986 ft), plus **Menetés ⓭** near the airport, all studded with traditional and contemporary villas.

The source of the wealth seems initially mysterious, since there is little fertile lowland, industry is non-existent, and mass tourism began only in the late 1980s. In fact, Kárpathos lives largely off remittances from seamen and emigrants (mostly in the United States); this economy has profoundly affected local culture, architecture and attitudes. It has deliberately slowed the development of

ABOVE: traditional door-knocker, Líndhos.
BELOW: Ólymbos village, Kárpathos.

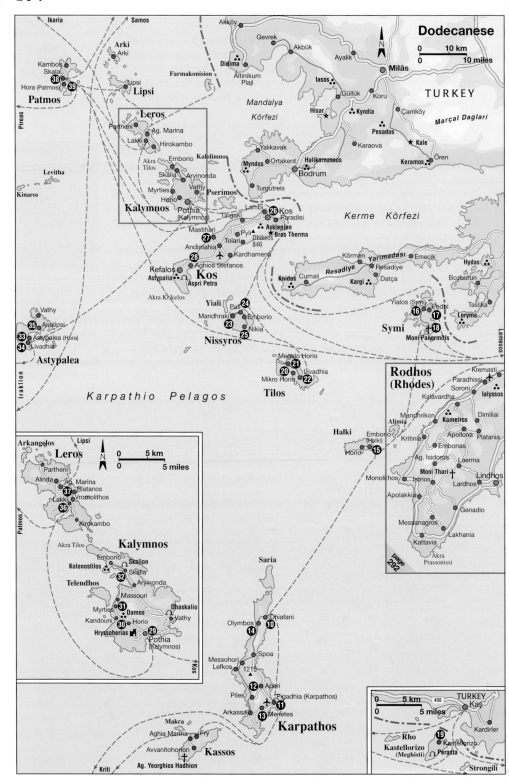

Dodecanese

0   10 km
0   10 miles

Ikaria   Samos   Akköy   Gevrek   Akbük   Ayalik   N
Arki
Arki   Didima   Altinikum   Iasos   Milâs
Kambos   Farmakonisi   Plaji   Güllük   Koru   TURKEY
Skala   38
Hora (Patmos)   39   Lipsi   Lipsi   Mandalya   Hisar   Kyndia   Çamköy   Marçal Daglari
Patmos   Körfezi   Pesados   Kale
Leros   Karaova   Keramos   Ören
Partheni   Ag. Marina   Yalıkavak   Ortakent   Halikarnassos
Levitha   Lakki   Hirokambo   Myndos   Bodrum
Akra   Emborio   Katolimnos   Turgutreis
Kinaros   Tilos   Skalia   Aryinonda   Pserimos
Myrties   Vathy
Horio   Pothia   Lambi   26   Kos
Kalymnos   (Kalymnos)   Lingaki   Paradisi   Kerme Körfezi
Mastihari   Pyli   Asklepion
27   Tolari   Dhikeos   Brus Therma
Andimahia   Kardhamena   846
28   Körmen   Yarimadasi   Emecik
Kefalos   Aghios Stefanos   Resadiye   Hydas
Astypalia   Kos   Knidos   Cumali   Resadiye   Bozburun
Aspri Petra   Kargi   Datça
Akra Krikelos   Yiali   Pali   24   Yialos (Symi)   Pedhi   Taslika
Vathy   Mandhraki   Emborio   16   17   Loryna
35   Analipsi   23   Nikia   Symi   18
33   Astypalea (Hora)   Nissyros   25   Moni Panormitis
34   Livadhia
Astypalea   Megalo Horio   21
20   Livadhia
Mikro Horio   22   Rodhos   Kremasti
Karpathio Pelagos   Tilos   (Rhodes)   Paradhissi
Soroni   Ialyssos
Kalavardha
Halki   Alimia   Manchrikon   Kameiros   Dimiliai
Emborio   Apollona   Platania
(Halki)   Kritinia   Embonas
Horio   15   Ag. Isidoros   Lzerma
Moni Thari   Lindhos
Monolithos   Istrios   Lardhos
Apolakkia   Genadio
Arkangelos   Lipsi   Messanagros   Lakhania
Leros   N   0   5 km   Kattavia   Akra
0   5 miles   page   Prassonissi
Partheni   292
Alinda   Ag. Marina   37   Platanos
Lakki   Vromolithos
36
Xirokambo
Akra Tilos   Kalymnos
Emborio   Skalion   Saria
Kolonostilos   Skalia
Telendhos   32   Aryinonda
Massouri
Myrties   31   Dhaskalio
Kandouni   Damos   Horio   Vathy   TURKEY
Hryssoherias   30   Olympos   Dhiafani   0   5 km   400   Kaş
29   Pothia   14   10   0   5 miles
(Kalymnos)   Messohori   Spoa   Kardirler
Lefkos   1215   Rho
Piles   12   Aperi   Kastellorizo   19   Kastellorizo
Pigadhia (Karpathos)   (Meghisti)   Perasta
Arkassa   Menetes   11   Strongili
Makra   13   Karpathos
Aghia Marina   Fry
Avvanitohorion   Kassos
Kriti   Ag. Yeorghios Hadhion

Pireas   Iraklion   Pireas   Iraklion   Lemesos   Kos

tourism – you won't find cultivated smiles or servile behaviour on Kárpathos – and, paradoxically, also enhanced the position of women who stayed behind. Overseas values have also left their mark on house-building, though even the most vulgar modern pile may sport a date of construction, the owner's initials and a traditional emblem, perhaps a mermaid or double-headed Byzantine eagle. In its original form, the vernacular Kárpathiot house consists of a single, mud-floored space appropriately divided; to one side a raised wooden platform or *dhórva*, where the bride's dowry linen, festival clothing and mattresses are kept, the latter rolled out at night.

In the centre, a wooden pole – the "pillar of the house" – upholds the ceiling, and to complete the symbolism a painting or photograph of the couple is pinned to the pole under their wedding-wreath – a custom perhaps developed to acquaint children with chronically absent fathers. The walls are decked with shelves and plate-racks, containing hundreds of kitsch and near-kitsch ornaments: not local handicrafts, but assorted ethnic dolls, gaudy pottery and other baubles collected by Kárpathiot sailors on their wanderings. Even modern, multi-room villas will still model their *salóni* on this pattern.

Many Dodecanese islands are matrilineal (as opposed to matriarchal); on Kárpathos it's merely more evident, at least in the northernmost villages of **Ólymbos ⑭** and Dhiafáni, where the women still wear traditional clothes, whereas the well-travelled men have worn Western clothes for as long as anyone can remember. The women's pantaloons, aprons, head-kerchiefs and boots are still locally made, but this everyday costume is completed by Irish wool scarves and (unfortunately) imported sequins and embroidery, much of it Chinese and Bulgarian. Festival dress is rather more colourful and includes a

Map, page 294

ABOVE: swathes of bougainvillea brighten Ólymbos village.
BELOW: traditional dress in Dhiafáni.

gold-coin collar, the number of coins signalling a girl's wealth to prospective suitors.

Two of the most renowned festivals – Easter and Assumption Day – are still celebrated with special verve at Ólymbos, draped over its windswept ridge. It has long been something of a honeypot for anthropologists academic and amateur owing to its relict Dorian dialect, aforesaid costumes, music, and communal ovens. But conventional tourism has been as warping – and rescuing – here as outside subsidies have been elsewhere on the island; the last of several windmills stopped working as a real accessory to life late in the 1970s, but two were restored as functioning museum-pieces a few years later.

Just southwest of Kárpathos, **Kássos** is its bleak satellite, devastated by a massacre in 1824 and totally dependent ever since on seafaring. **Hálki**, about halfway between Dhiafáni and Rhodes Town, is another bare speck of limestone enlivened by the colourful port of **Emborió** ; formerly home to sponge-fishers, most of it was restored in the late 1980s and is now packed from April to October with upmarket package tourists.

Sými

Sými lies northeast of Rhodes, between the outstretched claws (as it were) of Turkey's Datcá Peninsula. Though still retaining a portion of its former forests, it's nearly waterless, and dependent on cisterns or tanker-boats, which has limited tourism. Most day-trippers come to see the photogenic harbour-settlement, which at the end of the 19th century supported a greater population (25,000) than Rhodes. Prosperity was based on sponge-diving, for which the island long held the Ottoman monopoly, and the related industry of caïque-building.

TIP

If you decide to buy a natural sponge as a souvenir of Sými, make sure to ask for one that has not been bleached. Bleach is used to make the sponge look more inviting, but it also weakens the fibres.

BELOW: on Sými, fresh vegetables often have to be imported from larger islands.

Map, page 294

Although the Italian takeover of both the Dodecanese and the Libyan coast (where the sponges were harvested) failed to break the Greek hold on the sponge industry, World War II and the rise of synthetic sponges rang down the curtain on an era; the privations of the war years scattered the population to Rhodes, Athens and overseas, and today fewer than 3,000 call **Yialós** (the quayside settlement) ⑯ and **Horió** (the hillside village) home. Some caïques are still fashioned in the Haráni boatyards, but the sponges sold from Yialós's souvenir-stalls are mostly imported from Florida and the Philippines.

Sými's self-government during the Ottoman period was typical of "infidel" communities providing a desirable commodity, who were generally left to themselves as long as they paid a yearly tribute-tax (in Sými's case, a boatload of sponges for the sultan's harem). Two *dhimoghérondes*, or municipal elders, were elected for one-year terms each 25 January: one presided over the local council and outstanding judicial matters, and managed relations with the Ottoman bureaucracy, while the other managed the community revenues. The number of (male) voters was unlimited, although they had to be over 21 and under 80, literate, of sound mind, with their taxes paid up and no penal sentence pending; the local council was elected initially by acclamation in assembly, but by secret ballot after 1902.

Pédhi ⑰, the valley south of Horió ridge, is the only arable patch of Sými, thanks to a few wells; there's a small waterside hamlet, too, and some scraps of sand beach. Emborió bay, north of Yialós, offers an artificial beach, a Byzantine mosaic floor and a small catacomb complex. But most of the island's beaches are pebbly, and accessible only by arduous hikes or boat excursions; the favourites are **Marathoúnda**, **Nanoú** and **Ághios Vassílios**. Among rural monasteries, the most artistically distinguished is **Mihaïl Roukouniótis**, due west of town, with its vivid 18th-century frescoes. But it's the gargantuan **monastery of Mihaïl Panormítis** ⑱ in the far south which – handy to the sea-lane in from Rhodes – gets the most visitors; a small museum, a large pebble courtyard and a sombre memorial to resistance fighters executed here in 1944 are the main sights.

ABOVE: hospitality awaits in Yialós.
BELOW: many of the sponges sold in Yialós are imported from Florida.

Kastellórizo (Meghísti)

Kastellórizo, some 70 nautical miles east of Rhodes in the shadow of Anatolia, has similarly come down in the world. At the turn of the 19th century, this limestone dot on the map had a population of over 10,000, thanks to the best natural harbour between Piraeus (Pireás) and Beirut and the schooner fleet based here. But the fleet was sold rather than motorised; the island was heavily shelled during World War I while occupied by the French, then rocked by a 1926 earthquake and a 1944 munitions blast, which together destroyed three-quarters of the houses.

Most "Kassies" emigrated postwar to Rhodes and west Australia; with just 200 clinging to life in a virtual ghost town, the Americans even tried to convince Greece to cede the island to Turkey in 1964, in return for limited hegemony in Cyprus.

In the end, it was pleasure-yachting and a movie (*Mediterraneo*, filmed here in 1990) that probably

saved Kastellórizo from desolation; a flood of Italian tourists has revived its fortunes, along with a recent airport and other government subsidies. There are no beaches and little to see other than rural monasteries, an ancient acropolis, a tiny castle-with-museum and a sea-cave entered only by boat. But the social scale of **Kastellórizo Town**  is cosy, and the nightlife surprisingly lively.

Níssyros is nick-named the "Polo Mint island", thanks to its clusters of white cube houses and its hole in the middle – the hissing crater of Polyvótis volcano.

Tílos and Níssyros

Seahorse-shaped Tílos, north of Hálki and west of Rhodes, is the least maritime of these islands; with fertile volcanic soil and sufficient ground water, the islanders instead made Tílos the granary of the Dodecanese. Since the late 1980s, discerning tourists have appeared, attracted by tranquillity, some fine beaches and good hiking opportunities. Historically there were just two villages, imaginatively named **Mikró Horió** (Little Village, in the east) , and **Megálo Horió** (Big Village, in the west) , continually at odds with each other; Mikró was abandoned after World War II in favour of **Livádhia** , the port and main tourist resort. The rivalry supposedly ended with the election, in late 1998, of a single municipal council – the only sensible solution for a permanent population of 350.

The crags above the plains hide seven small castles of the Knights of St John, as well as several medieval chapels. **Éristos** in the west is the largest and best beach; inland extends a great *kámbos* planted with citrus, the whole surveyed by Megálo Horió. In the far west, **Ághiou Pandelímona** is the main monastery, and venue for the principal festival (26–27 July, annually).

Round Níssyros, between Tílos and Kós, is not merely "volcanic", as it's often described, but actually *is* a volcano – a dormant one that last erupted in 1933. Accordingly, what water exists here is sulphur-tainted, but the island is

BELOW: seeking the shade on Tingáki beach, Kós.

paradoxically green with oaks and almond-trees, plants which love volcanic soil. **Mandhráki ㉓**, the port and capital, is attractive with its close-packed houses overawed by **Panaghí Spilianí**, installed in the inevitable Knights' castle, and the even more imposing remains of the 7th-century BC Doric citadel just south. **Páli ㉔** is the alternate port for fishermen, just east of the mineral-water spa which has been refurbished with EU funds; you don't come to Níssyros for beach life, but on the east coast **Líes** and **Pahiá Ámmos** are more than decent.

There are two inland villages: **Emborió**, virtually abandoned and bought up by outsiders, and the more thriving **Nikiá ㉕** in the southwest, at the edge of the volcanic caldera, created in 1422 when the (originally much taller) island blew its top. Coach-tours of tourists based in Kós visit periodically, but otherwise the lifeless crater-floor, with its hissing steam-vents and sulphurous smell, is likely to be deserted,

Map,
page
294

Kós

The second-largest Dodecanese island in population, **Kós** is also third-largest in size, after Rhodes and Kárpathos. It follows the lead of Rhodes in most things: a shared history, give or take a few years; a similar Knights' castle guarding the harbour, plus a skyline of palms and minarets; and likewise an agricultural economy displaced by tourism. However, Kós is much smaller than Rhodes, and much flatter – amazingly so – with only one mountain, **Dhíkeos**, rising sharply from the southeast coast; the margin of the island is fringed by excellent beaches, most easily reached by motorbike or even pushbike.

An earthquake in 1933 devastated most of **Kós Town ㉖**, but gave Italian archeologists a perfect excuse to excavate comprehensively the ancient city.

ABOVE: don't forget those postcards ...
BELOW: Kós Town.

Look out for traditional handicrafts such as these brightly coloured embroidered cushions in the Old Bazaar in Kós Town.

BELOW: cool shades and contrasting colours ...

Hence much of the town centre is an archeological park, with the ruins of the Roman *agora* (the eastern excavation) lapping up to the 18th-century **Loggia Mosque** and the millennial **Plane Tree of Hippocrates**, not really quite old enough to be coeval with the great ancient healer. The western digs offer covered mosaics and the colonnade of an indoor running-track; just south stand an *odeion* and the **Casa Romana**, a restored Roman villa with more mosaics and murals (open Tues–Sun 8.30am–3pm; entrance fee).

The Italian-founded **Archeological Museum** has a predictable Latin bias in exhibits, though the star statue a purportedly of Hippocrates, father of medicine, is in fact Hellenistic (open Tues–Sun 8.30am–3pm; entrance fee). Hippocrates himself (*circa* 460–370 BC) was born and practiced here, but probably died just before the **Asklepion**, 4 km (2½ miles) southwest of town, was established. The site (open Tues–Sun 8.30am–3pm; entrance fee) impresses more for its position overlooking the straits with Turkey than any structures, their masonry thoroughly pilfered by the Knights to build their enormous castle, which – unlike the one at Rhodes – was strictly military.

Between the Asklepion and Kós Town, pause at **Platáni**, roughly halfway, to dine at one of two excellent Turkish-run tavernas; as on Rhodes, most local Muslims have chosen to emigrate to Turkey since the 1960s. There was a small Jewish community here too, wiped out like the Rhodian one in 1944, leaving behind only the marvellous Art Deco synagogue by the town *agora*.

The road east of town dead-ends at **Brós Thermá**, enjoyable hot springs which run directly into the sea. West of town are the package resorts of **Tingáki** and **Marmári** with long white beaches, and the less frantic **Mastihári ㉗**, with a commuter boat to Kálymnos. In the far southwest, facing Níssyros, are the

most scenic and sheltered beaches, with names like "**Banana**" and "**Magic**"; at nearby **Ághios Stéfanos** ㉘, twin 6th-century basilicas are the best of several early Christian monuments. The Kéfalos headland beyond saw the earliest habitation of Kós: **Pétra cave**, home to Neolithic man, and classical **Astypalia**, birthplace of Hippocrates, of which only the little theatre remains.

On the western flank of Mount Dhíkeos, the Byzantines had their island capital at old **Pýli**, today a jumble of ruins below a castle at the head of a spring-fed canyon. Closer to the 846-m (2,776-ft) peak cluster the appealing villages collectively known as **Asfendhioú**, in the forested north-facing slopes looking to Anatolia. At **Ziá**, taverns seem more numerous than permanent inhabitants, and are especially busy at sunset and after. **Asómati**'s vernacular houses are slowly being bought up and restored by foreigners.

Kálymnos

First impressions of Kálymnos, north of Kós, are of an arid, mountainous landmass with a decidedly masculine energy to the main port town of **Póthia** ㉙. The now almost-vanished local sponge industry has left ample evidence behind: Kálymnian *salónia* laden with huge sponges and shell-encrusted amphoras, souvenir shops overflowing with smaller sponges, and, more ominously, various crippled old men.

In the old days, divers used to sink themselves by tying heavy stones to their waists. Holding their breath, they scraped off the rock-fixed sponges spied from the surface; they could usually get two or three before they had to resurface for air. Better divers could dive 40 fathoms deep before the "machine" was introduced late in the 19th century. The "machine" is the local term for the first

Map, page 294

So many Kálymniots emigrated to Darwin, Australia, in the 1950s and 60s that the Australian-Greek taxi-drivers there now simply call it "Kálymnos".

BELOW: ... are a feature of Kálymnos' architecture.

diving apparatus, a rubber suit with a bronze helmet connected to a long rubber hose and a handpowered air-pump. The diver was let out on a long cable and given enough air-hose for his final depth, where he could stay a long time owing to the constant air supply.

Too long, as it soon turned out – compressed air delivered to divers at the new, greater depths bubbled out of solution in their bloodstream as they rose, invariably too rapidly. The results of this nitrogen embolism – informally known as "the bends" – included deafness, incontinence, paralysis and often death. By the 1950s the physiological mechanism was understood and the carnage halted, but it was too late for hundreds of Kalymnian crewmen.

To the northwest loom two castles: **Hryssoherías**, the Knight's stronghold, and the originally Byzantine fort of **Péra Kástro**, above the medieval capital of **Horió** ㉚, still the island's second town. Most visitors stay at the beach resorts on the gentler west coast between **Kandoúni** and **Massoúri**, with **Myrtiés** ㉛ the most developed of these, and also the port for the idyllic islet of **Télendhos**. The east coast is harsh and uninhabited except for the green, citrus-planted valley extending inland from the fjord of Vathý, and for the towns of **Kéfala** in the far southwest, and **Skalía** ㉜ in the far north.

ABOVE: spit-roasted lamb makes a succulent lunch in Myrtiés, Kálymnos.
BELOW: Astypálea, seen through the vaulting of a Genoese castle.

Astypálea

Lonely, butterfly-shaped **Astypálea**, stuck out on a subsidised ferry line between Kálymnos and the Cyclades, would be probably more at home among that archipelago. The Knights didn't make it this far; the Venetians are responsible for the fine castle at the summit of **Astypálea Town (Hóra)** ㉝, the most dazzling Dodecanese hill-village aside from a namesake on Pátmos. Houses

Map, page 294

with colourful wooden *poúndia* (balconies with privies) adorn the steep streets; until this century, there was also a separate hamlet inside the upper castle. Hóra aside, however, Astypálea is rather bleak, with only a few good beaches to the southwest (**Tzanáki**, **Ághios Konstandínos** and **Vátses**) plus a few more like those at **Marmári** and **Stenó** along the island's narrow middle. Most travellers stay at the uninspiring port of **Skála**, at more congenial **Livádhi** ❸ to the west, or at **Análipsi** in the island's centre.

Léros and Lipsí

Léros, with its half-dozen deeply indented bays, looks like a jigsaw puzzle-piece gone astray; the deepest inlet, that of **Lakkí**, sheltered an important Italian naval base from 1923 onward, and from here was launched the submarine that toppled the Greek battleship *Elli* in Tínos harbour on 15 August 1940.

Today the main ferry port, **Lakkí Town** ❺, is bizarre, an Art Deco experiment, built by the Italians, far too grand for the present token population; now the institutional buildings, reminders of colonial subjugation, seem neglected. The local atmosphere is not cheered by the presence of three asylums for handicapped children and mentally ill adults. The substandard conditions in all of these prompted an uproar in Greece and elsewhere in Europe when exposed by the press in the late 1980s.

The rest of Léros is more inviting, particularly **Pandéli** with its waterfront tavernas, just downhill from the capital of **Plátanos** ❻, draped over a saddle culminating in a well-preserved Knights' castle. South of both, **Vromólithos** has the best easily accessible car-free beach on an island not known for good sand. **Ághia Marína**, beyond Plátanos, is the hydrofoil harbour, and like Pandéli it

TIP

If you fancy getting away from it all, the tiny islet of Maráthi, Lipsí's neighbour, has a decent beach and just two tavernas which rent out rooms. During the summer, ferries from Pátmos stop here daily.

BELOW: a country chapel, Léros.

Map, page 294

offers good tavernas. **Álinda**, north around the same bay, is the oldest established resort, with a long beach.

Lipsí, the small island just north, has like Tílos awakened to tourism since the 1980s. A patchwork of well-tended farms, the island's fertile appearance is deceptive – there is only one spring, and up to four times the impoverished local community have emigrated since the 1950s. All facilities are in the single port town, built around the best natural harbour; smaller bays, with beaches, are found at **Katsadhiá** in the south and **Platýs Yialós** in the northwest.

Pátmos

Pátmos has been indelibly linked to the Bible's Book of Revelations (Apocalypse) ever since tradition placed its authorship here, in AD 95, by John the Evangelist. The volcanic landscape, with its strange rock formations and sweeping views, seems suitably apocalyptic.

Skála ㊲ is the port and largest village, best appreciated late at night when crickets serenade and yacht-masts are illuminated against a dark sky. By day Skála loses its charm, but all island commerce, whether shops, banks or travel agencies, is here. Buses leave regularly from the quay for the hilltop **Hóra** ㊳, but a 40-minute cobbled path short-cutting the road is preferable.

Just over halfway stands the **Monastery of the Apocalypse** (open daily 8am–2pm, Mon, Tues, Thurs, Sun 4–6pm; free), built on the grotto where John had his Revelation. A silver band on the wall marks where John laid his head to sleep; in the ceiling is a great cleft through which the divine voice spoke.

Hóra's core, protected by a huge, pirate-proof fortress and visible from a great distance, is the **Monastery of St John the Theologian** (same hours), founded in AD 1088 by the monk Hristódhoulos Latrenos. A photogenic maze of interlinked courtyards, stairways, chapels and passageways, it occupies the site of an ancient temple to Artemis. The **Treasury** houses Greece's most impressive monastic collection outside Mount Áthos; priceless icons and jewellery are on display, though the prize exhibit is the edict of Emperor Alexios Komnenos granting the island to Hristódhoulos. The **Library**, closed to all but ecclesiastical scholars, contains over 4,000 books and manuscripts.

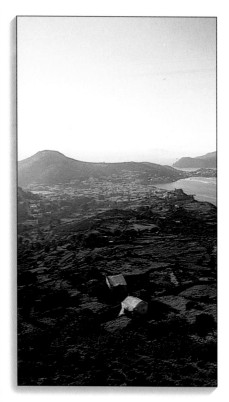

BELOW: Skála port and the serene bay of Pátmos.
RIGHT: an absorbing image, Sými.

Away from the tourist-beaten track, Hóra is pregnantly silent, its thick-walled mansions with their pebble courtyards and arcades the preserve of wealthy foreigners. Short-term rooms are thus hard to come by, but there are a few good tavernas and, from **Platía Lótzia** in the north, one of the finest views in the Aegean, taking in at least six islands on all but the haziest of days.

The rest of the island is inevitably anticlimactic, but the beaches are good. The biggest sandy one is **Psilí Ámmos** in the far south, accessible by boat trip or a half-hour walk from the road's end. Beaches north of Skála include **Melóï**, with a good taverna and outdoor cinema; **Agriolivádhi**; **Kámbos**, popular with Greek families; isolated **Livádhi Yeranoú**, with an islet to swim to; and finally **Lámbi**, sprinkled with irresistible, colourful volcanic pebbles. ❏

CRETE

With its mountains and beaches, ancient ruins and lively modern culture, the country's biggest island is for many the quintessential Greek island

Map, pages 308–9

Megalónissos (Great Island) is what Cretans call their home, and "great" refers to far more than size. It can certainly be applied to the Minoan civilisation, the first in Europe and the core of Cretan history. Visitors by the thousand pour into the ruins of Knossós, Festós, Mália and Zákros, before heading towards one of the scores of excellent beaches. With two major airports, Crete cannot be classified as undiscovered, but through its size and scale it manages to contain the crowds and to please visitors with widely divergent tastes. While a car is essential for discovering the best of the island, car hire is, unfortunately, comparatively expensive.

For more than half the year, snow lies on the highest peaks which provide a dramatic backdrop to verdant spring meadows ablaze with flowers. This, as botanists and ornithologists know well, is by far the best time to visit. The former arrive to view more than 130 species which are unique to the island, while the latter are thrilled by more than 250 types of birds heading north. It is in spring that the island is redolent with sage, savoury, thyme, oregano – and dittany, the endemic Cretan herb. Bathing in an infusion of dittany is rumoured to increase sexual desire.

Crete, much more than other Greek islands, is a place both for sightseeing and for being on the beach. Minoan ruins are the major magnets, but there are also Greek, Roman and Venetian remains, and a score of museums. There are hundreds of Byzantine churches, many with rare and precious frescoes. If the church is locked; enquire at the nearest café. Even if you don't track down the key, you will enjoy the encounter with local people.

LEFT: hiking along the Samariá Gorge.
BELOW: Iráklion harbour and the Koúles fortress.

Iráklion (Heráklion)

The capital of Crete since 1971, **Iráklion ❶** has nearly a third of the island's population and is Greece's fifth-largest city. Although it vaunts the highest per capita income of any Greek city, this wealth does not show in the civic infrastructure. Indeed, much of Iráklion is a building site, thanks to a tendency to spend money on starting buildings without sufficient capital for completion.

Most tourists head for the Minoan site of **Knossós ❷** (open daily 8am–7pm, except Saturday afternoons; entrance fee; *see also pages 318–19*). To fully comprehend the site and its contents, this should be combined with a visit to the outstanding **Archeological Museum ❹** (open daily 8am–7pm, except Monday mornings; entrance fee) . The tourist office is almost next door, and both are moments from the cafés and restaurants of **Eleftherías** (Freedom) **Square ❸**.

Iráklion's other major attractions are from the Venetian era, testifying that this was Crete's most

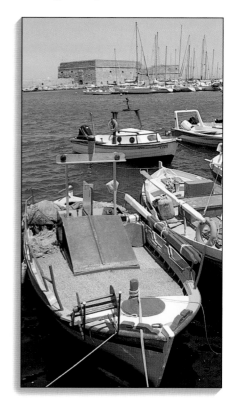

prosperous period in historical times. Head seawards to the old harbour and visit the **Venetian** *arsenali* (covered boat-building yards) 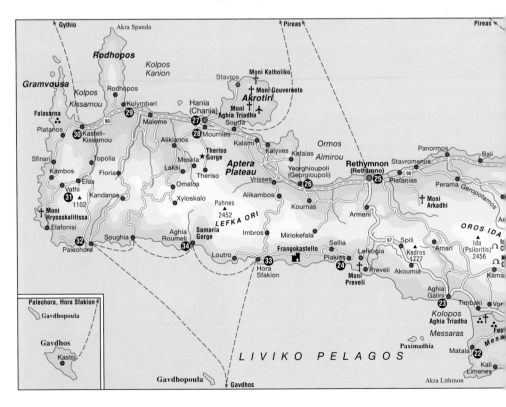 and the restored **Koúles fortress** (open Mon–Sat, 8am–6pm; Sun 10am–3pm; entrance fee) whose three high-reliefs of the Lion of St Mark confirm its provenance.

A few minutes to the west of the old harbour on S. Venizélou is the **Historical Museum** with collections from early Christian times onwards (open Mon–Sat, 9am–2pm; entrance fee). Head towards the city centre and the upmarket cafés of **Venizélou** (also Lion or Fountain) Square which takes its popular names from the stylish 17th-century **Morosíni fountain** and guardian marble lions. Overlooking the square is the handsome, rebuilt, Venetian *loggia* (city hall), flanked by the churches of **Ághios Márkos** and **Ághios Títos**. Since 1966, when it was returned from St Mark's in Venice, the skull of St Titus, St Paul's apostle to Crete and its first bishop, has been housed in Ághios Títos.

Walk south through the "market street", redolent with tantalising smells, jammed with people and resonant with decibels, but now very touristy (the true city markets take place in Iráklion's suburban streets) and then west to the Icon Museum (open Mon–Sat, 9am–1pm; entrance fee), housed in the small church of **Aghía Ekateríni**. It contains some exquisite icons, six of them by the 16th-century master, Mihaíl Damaskinós.

Challenging but rewarding is a circumambulation of the 15th-century **city walls**, in their day the most formidable in the Mediterranean. They stretch for nearly 4 km (2½ miles) and in parts are 29 m (95 ft) thick. En route, pause a moment at the tomb of the great Irákliot author and iconoclast **Níkos Kazantzákis** to enjoy the spectacular views.

Walk Iráklion's Venetian walls and you will reach the tomb of local author Níkos Kazantzákis, of Zorba the Greek fame. His epitaph reads: "I believe in nothing, I hope for nothing, I am free."

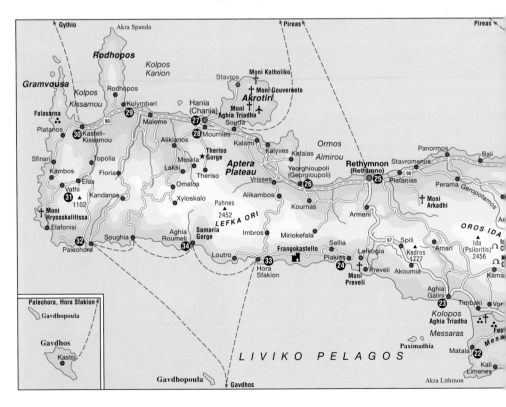

In and around the village of **Arhánes** ❸, 12 km (8 miles) south of Knossós, are three churches with interesting frescoes and icons, and three Minoan sites. Evidence suggests that when the **Anemóspilia** temple was destroyed, by an earthquake, a priest was in the ritual act of sacrificing a youth. Such conjectures have outraged some scholars as much as Níkos Kazantzákis's books outraged the established Orthodox Church.

A steep climb from Arhánes (allow one hour) leads to the summit of **Mount Yioúhtas** (811m/2,660 ft), from where you can admire the panorama while griffin vultures soar overhead. Resembling a recumbent figure, said to be Zeus, the mountain top has a Minoan peak sanctuary, a 14th-century chapel, and caves in which Zeus is buried. Perhaps this proves the truth of the aphorism that "all Cretans are liars" because to most Greeks, Zeus is, after all, immortal.

Týlissos ❹, 13 km (8 miles) southwest of Iráklion, possesses three well-preserved small palaces or large villas (open daily 8.30am–3pm; entrance fee) and is one of the few present-day villages to retain its original pre-Hellenic name. Twenty km (13 miles) further west on the same road, the village of **Anóghia** ❺ is a weaving and embroidery centre. Many locals wear native dress but this is no stage setting: Anóghia has a long tradition of resistance and revolt – the village was razed in 1944 – and its men and women are among the fiercest and bravest in Crete.

From Anóghia the road climbs to the magnificent **Nída plateau** from where it is a 20-minute uphill stroll to the **Idean Cave** which was the nursery, if not the birthplace, of Zeus. Here the infant god was hidden by the Kourétes, who clashed their weapons to drown the sound of his cries, while the nymph Amalthée fed him goat's milk. Strong walkers might wish to push on to the summit of **Mount Psilorítis**, at 2,456m (8,060 ft) the highest point on Crete.

Map, page 310

TIP

It's usually possible to arrange for a taxi driver to drop you off somewhere and pick you up a few hours later. Alternatively, you can negotiate a private sightseeing tour.

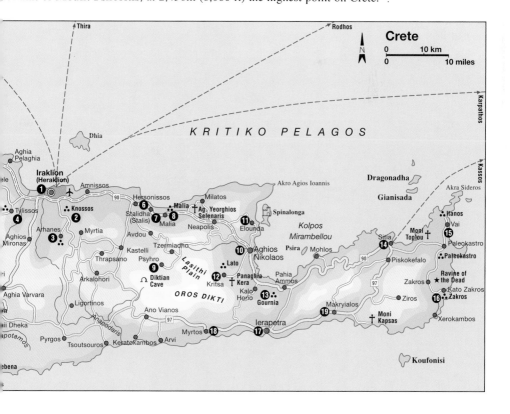

The Diktian Cave, supposedly the birthplace of Zeus. His father, the Titan Kronos, had been told he'd be overthrown by a son, so he ate all his offspring. Only Zeus survived, as he was hidden here for protection.

East from Iráklion

Return to Iráklion and continue eastwards along the expressway for 24 km (15 miles), but then forget the "express". You have reached the Cretan Riviera – a stretch reminiscent of Blackpool or Coney Island – with the resorts of **Hersónissos** ⑥, **Stalídha** (Stális) ⑦ and **Mália** ⑧. It is neither elegant nor ethnic: bars, heavy rock, pizzerias and fast food abound. However, the beaches are among the best and busiest.

The **Palace** at Mália (open Tues–Sun, 8.30am–3pm; entrance fee), traditionally associated with King Sarpedon, brother of Minos, is contemporary with Knossós. The ruins are not as extensive as Knossós or Festós, but even without reconstruction, they are more readily understood. The remarkable number of store-and workrooms suggests a wealthy country villa more than a palace. Recent excavations have unearthed the **Hrysólakkos** (Golden Pit) from the proto-palatial period (2000–1700 BC), an enormous necropolis with numerous gold artefacts.

From either Mália or Hersónissos, twisting mountain roads lead up to the **Lasíthi Plain**, 840 m (2,750 ft) above sea level and 57 km (36 miles) from Iráklion. This fertile and impeccably cultivated land supports a cornucopia of potatoes and grain crops, apples and pears. However, rare is the day and lucky the visitor who sees the unfurled sails of the 10,000 wind-pumps that irrigate the rich alluvial soil. **Psyhró** ⑨ is the starting point for the giant **Diktian Cave**, another birthplace of Zeus.

Onwards to **Ághios Nikólaos** ⑩, 69 km (43 miles) from Iráklion, invariably abbreviated by tourists to "Ag Nik". Magnificently situated on the Gulf of Mirabello and overlooked by the eastern mountains, this was once the St Tropez

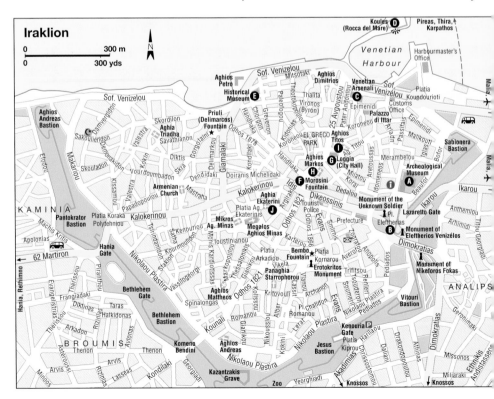

of Crete. Here, and at **Eloúnda** ⓫ (10 km/6 miles away), are some of the island's best and most expensive hotels, although Ag Nik does lack a decent beach, having built a football pitch over its best one. Hotels, discos and cafés cluster around Ag Nik's **Mandhráki** harbour and small "bottomless" lake. The nearby island of **Spinalónga**, an isolated leper colony until 1957 (the last in Europe), with a ruined Venetian fortress and poignant memories, is readily reached from Ag Nik by boat.

Clinging to the hillside 11 km (7 miles) from Ag Nik is **Kritsá** ⓬, said to be the home of the best weavers on the island. Their brilliantly coloured work hangs everywhere – for sale – complementing the flowers and contrasting with the whitewashed homes that line the narrow village alleyways. Immediately below is the church of **Panaghía Kerá**, Crete's greatest Byzantine treasure. The entire interior is an illustrated bible of 12th- to 15th-century frescoes. Until a few years ago Panaghía Kerá was a functioning church; with changing times it is now a museum with admission charges.

Leave Ag Nik and head east. After 19 km (12 miles), **Gourniá** ⓭ (open Tues–Sun, 8.30am–3pm; entrance fee), the remains of the streets and houses of a Minoan town, is spread over a ridge that overlooks the sea. In spring, when the site is covered with a riot of flowers and filled with their perfume, even those bored with old stones will be delighted to be here.

Sitía ⓮, 70 km (44 miles) from Ag Nik, is a laid-back town which, to the delight of visitors and the chagrin of locals, has not yet hit the big time. Here are the almost obligatory Venetian fort, Archeological (open Tues–Sun, 8.30am–3pm; entrance fee) and Folklore Museums, and an unimpressive beach. After a further 24 km (15 miles) is **Váï** ⓯, renowned for its myriad palm trees,

Map, pages 308–9

ABOVE: the remains of the leper colony on Spinalónga island.
BELOW: bustling Ághios Nikólaos.

large sandy beach and tropical ambience. The palm trees are native, not from a desert island, and the beach is usually crowded.

Káto Zákros , 43 km (27 miles) from Sitía, is the fourth great Minoan site (open Tues–Sun, 8am–2pm; entrance fee), situated below the spectacular **Ravine of the Dead**, where caves were used for Minoan burials. The main dig has the customary central courtyard with royal, religious and domestic buildings and workshops radiating outwards; most date from the neo-palatial era (1700–1380 BC, the apogee of Minoan civilisation). Crete's eastern end is sinking below the water table, however, so they are often waterlogged.

Back at Gourniá, a flat road crosses the island to **Ierápetra** (35 km/22 miles from Ag Nik), the south coast's only large town and Europe's southernmost. Recently, Ierápetra has enjoyed a boom in both market gardening and in tourism, although it is hardly atmospheric; there is a promenade behind an average beach and a tiny Venetian fort. Fifteen km (9 miles) to the west lies the pretty village resort of **Mýrtos** , which takes advantage of mild weather to remain open throughout the winter. Eastwards 24 km (15 miles) from Ierápetra is the summer resort (and reasonable beach) of **Makrýialos** , from where a side road leads to the 14th-century **Kapsás Monastery** set snugly into the cliffs at a gorge entrance.

South from Iráklion

ABOVE: the mosque at Ierápetra.
BELOW: soaking up the sun on Váï palm beach.

Head south from Iráklion over the island's spine and you reach a breathtaking view of the Plain of Mesará, whose rich soil and benign climate make it an agricultural cornucopia. At the edge of the plain, 40 km (25 miles) from Iráklion is the village of **Ághi Dhéka** (Holy Ten) with its heavily restored medieval church; fragments from nearby Górtyn have been incorporated into its walls

Górtyn (Górtys) **⑳** is 1 km (½-mile) further. This was the capital of the Romans, who came to Crete in the 1st century BC to settle feuds but who stayed and conquered the island. Outstanding are the Roman *odeon* and a triple-naved basilica, the latter by far the best-preserved early church in Crete, built to house the tomb of St Titus (daily 8.30am–3pm; entrance fee). But the most renowned artefacts are some stone blocks incorporated into the *odeon*. About 2,500 years ago a 17,000 character text, the Code of Górtyn, was incised on these – rules governing the behaviour of the people. The script is written in ox-plough manner – reading left to right along one line, then right to left along the next.

Those in search of more classical ruins, of health and of good swimming might wish, to turn off and drive south to **Léndas ㉑** (72 km/45 miles from Iráklion), before continuing to Festós. Nearby **ancient Lebéna** was the port for Górtyn, and its therapeutic springs made it a renowned sanctuary with a temple to Asklipiós, the god of healing. Traces of this, with mosaic floors and large baths, can be seen. **Festós** (Phaistos), Crete's second great Minoan site (open daily 8am–7pm; entrance fee), occupies a magnificent location 16 km (10 miles) west of Górtyn. State-rooms, religious quarters, workshops, storerooms and functional plumbing can all be identified; those purists who bristle at Knossós's reconstruction can let their imaginations run riot unhindered here.

Next, on to **Mátala ㉒**, 70 km (44 miles) from Iráklion. The resort first gained renown when the sandstone caves in the cliffs around the small sandy beach became home to the world's hippies; Joni Mitchell wrote a song about it. The scenic 30-minute walk south to Red Beach is highly recommended, though **Kómmos** beach to the north is much larger and has a recently excavated Minoan site. The larger south coast resort of **Aghía Galíni ㉓** also lies on the Gulf of

Map, pages 308–9

ABOVE: church bells at Mátala resort.
BELOW: a glorious spread of Cretan wildflowers.

Mesará, though a little further west. The harbour, with a short wide quay and a tiny main street jammed with tavernas and bars, is enclosed within a crescent of steep hills covered with modest hotels. Further into western Crete, is **Plakías** ㉒, with its five large beaches and spectacular mountain backdrop, 112 km (70 miles) from Iráklion.

West from Iráklion

Back in Iráklion, an oleander-lined expressway runs west towards Réthymnon. Leave the new road 25 km (16 miles) from the capital to arrive in **Fódhele** (Phódele), a small village rich in orange-trees and locally made embroidery. A restored house here is said to be the birthplace in 1545 of Dhomínikos Theotokópoulos, better known as **El Greco**. Fódhele's fame may be fleeting for the latest word is that El Greco was probably born in Iráklion.

At Stavroménos or Plataniás, just before Réthymnon, turn southeast for the beautifully situated **Arkádhi Monastery** (80 km/50 miles from Iráklion), Crete's most sacred shrine. If the elaborate 16th-century western façade of the church seems familiar, it is because it is on the 100-drachma note.

Réthymnon (Réthimno) ㉓, which prides itself on being Crete's intellectual capital, has an intact old town with a small, picturesque Venetian harbour; the quayside – choc-a-bloc with colourful fish restaurants – is guarded by an elegant lighthouse. To the west is the immense ruined **Fortétsa**, said to be the largest extant Venetian castle, with excellent views (open daily, 9am–4pm; entrance fee). The town's other attractions – the **Rimóndi Fountain**, the **Archeological Museum** (open Tues–Sun 8.30am–3pm; entrance fee) and the **Neradzés Mosque** – all lie between the harbour and the fortress. Venetian houses

ABOVE: Arkádhi Monastery – Crete's most sacred shrine. **BELOW:** Byzantine chapel near El Greco's "birthplace", Fódhele.

ICONS AND EL GRECO

The artist El Greco (1545–1614), a Cretan native who studied under Titian, is best-known for his portraits and religious pictures painted in Rome and Toledo. His highly distinctive style anticipated modern impressionism by his use of cold white, blue and grey colour-schemes, and by his sacrifice of realism to emotional effect. His work also strikingly fuses Byzantine and Renaissance influences, a legacy of his early training as an icon-painter in Iráklion.

These beautiful and highly stylised pictures are not objects of idolatrous worship, but this was precisely the indictment of the so-called iconoclasts in the 7th and 8th centuries. In an effort to purify the religion they proceeded literally to deface thousands of icons throughout Byzantium. Intact pre-9th century icons are consequently very rare. The church of Aghía Ekateríni here has a fine collection of icons, including a group by Mihaíl Damaskinós, a contemporary of El Greco. Both artists are thought to have studied at the church, all that remains of the Mount Sinai Monastery School, founded by exiles from Constantinople after the fall of "the City".

Only one work by El Greco can be viewed on Crete – *View of Mount Sinai and the Monastery of St Catherine* in the Historical Museum (*for details, see page 308*).

with unexpected architectural delights line the narrow streets linking these sights, while minarets and overhanging wooden oriels give the place a Turkish-style raffishness.

Réthymnon and – to the west – Haniá are joined by an expressway and an old road. Leave the highway after 23 km (14 miles) to enter **Yeorghioúpoli** (Georgioúpoli) **㉖** at the mouth of the River Armyrós. This delightful, princely highway has a good long beach and a eucalyptus-shaded square.

Haniá (Chaniá) **㉗**, 59 km (37 miles) from Réthymnon, is Crete's second city and its capital until 1971. It is a larger version of Réthymnon and claims to be one of the oldest continuously inhabited cities in the world; its jewel is the outer **Venetian harbour**. Here, the quayside is wide and backed by character-ful, colourful old buildings whose reflections shimmer in the water. The ambience is of the Levant and this is *the* place for the *vólta* – the evening stroll. The **Archeological Museum** (open Tues–Sun 8.30am–3pm; entrance fee) occupies the church of the Franciscan Friary, one of the best-preserved and largest of a score of still-standing Venetian churches. The medieval synagogue has been wonderfully reconstructed.

Those with a sense of history will visit Mourniés and Thériso, villages south of Haniá. The house in which Eleuthérios Venizélos, father of the modern Greek nation was born, now a museum, is in **Mourniés ㉘**.

West from Haniá

The road west from Haniá hugs the coast, passing several busy small resorts that merge imperceptibly, before arriving at **Kolymbári ㉙**. Proceed westwards, passing memorable views of the plain of Kastéli and the Bay of Kísamos

ABOVE: olive-oil tins in Haniá's covered market make colourful souvenirs.
BELOW: Haniá's Venetian-built waterfront.

enclosed within the peninsulas of Rodhopoú and Gramvoúsa. The road makes a tortuous descent to the plain and to pleasant but rather characterless **Kastéli-Kissámou ㉚** (42 km/26 miles from Haniá).

Turn left at **Plátanos** and a twisting corniche leads after 44 km (28 miles) from Kastéli, to **Váthi ㉛** and several splendidly frescoed Byzantine churches. From Váthi a poor road through a ravine leads in a dusty 10 km (6 miles) to the **Hrysoskalítissa Convent**. The name means "Golden Stairway" and refers to one of the 90 steps descending from the terrace being made of solid gold (failing to perceive that step is considered proof that you have sinned). From here, a barely negotiable road terminates at the broad sands of **Elafonísi**, bordering a shallow lagoon. Wade across to the eponymous islet which has excellent beaches – possibly the best on the island – and you are at westernmost Crete.

Around the corner to the southwest lies **Paleóhora ㉜** (76 km/48 miles from Hanía), a self-contained resort that has a ruined castle and both sand and shingle beaches (the latter for windy days). **Hóra Sfakíon** (Sfakía) **㉝**, 75 km (47 miles) from Haniá, is the capital of the Sfakians, who epitomise the independent and unmanageable Cretans. A small, cliff-hanging, picturesque port with a brave past, its sole *raison d'être* today – but don't tell this to the Sfakians – is to transfer exhausted tourists returning by ferry from their Samariá Gorge excursion.

ABOVE: taking it easy in pretty Hóra Sfakíon.
BELOW: lunchtime blues in Hóra Sfakíon's little harbour.

The Samariá Gorge

Crete offers an exciting and spectacular walk through the **gorge of Samariá**, the longest (18 km/11 miles) in Europe. The walk starts by descending a steep stairway at **Xylóskalo**, 1,200m (3936 ft) above the sea, at the southern end of the vast Omalós plain, itself some 45 km (28 miles) tortuous drive from Haniá.

After about 10 km (6 miles), with most of the steeper descent over, the abandoned **village of Samariá** and its church come into view. Stop and admire the church's lovely 14th-century frescoes – an opportunity to regain your breath without loss of face. The going now gets tough and involves criss-crossing the river-bed (be warned: flash floods can occur and warden's warnings should be observed). As the gorge narrows, the walls soar straight upwards for 300–600 m (1,000–2,000 ft). Soon after passing the church of Aféndis Hristós, the **Sidheróportes** (Iron Gates) are reached; here the gorge – scarcely penetrated by sunlight – is little more than 3.5m (11 ft) wide. However, only a giant can, as sometimes claimed, stretch out and touch each side.

If you are overcome by exuberance and feel tempted to burst into song – don't. The park is under the strict aegis of the Haniá Forest Service which specifically forbids singing, among other activities. And all the while the elusive Cretan wild goat, the *agrími*, will be watching your efforts, though it is unlikely that you will see them. On the other hand, even the most innocent of botanists will be delighted by the gorge, while ornithologists have been known to spot bearded vultures overhead.

And so to old **Aghía Rouméli** and the church of the Panaghía. However, there is a further 3 km (2 miles) of hot and anticlimactic walking before celebrating with a longed-for swim or cold drink at new, coastal **Aghía Rouméli** ❸❹. Thus refreshed, the only practical exit from the gorge – other than retracing the same route – is by boat eastwards to Hóra Sfakíon or westwards to Paleóhora. There are no roads.

The gorge is open from about the beginning of May until the end of October (entrance fee). Allow four to six hours for the walk. ❑

Map, pages 308–9

ABOVE: cross-country transport, Samariá Gorge.
BELOW: a welcome sight for tired hikers: the ferry at Aghía Rouméli.

CENTRE OF EUROPE'S FIRST CIVILISATION

Until a century ago, the Minoan civilisation was little more than a myth. Now its capital is one of the largest and best restored sites in all Greece

Knossós is a place of questions, many unanswered. Many visitors to the site find the concrete reconstructions and repainted frescoes (often from very small existing fragments) aid comprehension. But for many, used to other, more recent, ruins that are clearly defensive or overtly religious, the site is mysterious. Can we hope to look back at fragments of a culture from 3,500 years ago and understand its imperatives and subtleties?

In legend, Knossos was the labyrinth of King Minos, where he imprisoned the minotaur, the human-bovine child of his wife Pasiphae. In reality, the role of the Minoan palace was probably not in the modern sense of a palace, but perhaps as an administrative and economic centre, unified by spiritual leaders.

Among the 1,300 rooms of the main palace were both the sacred and the commercial: lustral baths for holy ceremonies; store rooms for agricultural produce; workshops for metallurgy and stone-cutting. Nearby are the Royal Villa and the Little Palace.

Try to visit earlier or later in the day, to avoid the worst of the crowds, and to avoid being swept along by the flow. Look for the subtle architectural delights – light wells to illuminate the larger rooms; hydraulic controls providing water for drinking, bathing and flushing away sewage; drains with parabolic curves at the bends to prevent overflow.

Combine that with a midday visit to the archeological museum – to take full advantage of the air-conditioning inside the building.

△ **OVERVIEW**
The scale of the site is most apparent from the air – nearly 2 hectares (4 acres) of palaces ruled a population of perhaps 100,000.

▽ **EMPTY VESSELS**
Huge earthenware jars, *píthi*, were used to store grain, olive-oil, wine or water.
Similar jars are still made in a few Cretan villages today.

△ **CHAIR OF STATE**
The throne room, possibly court or council room, has gypsum throne flanked by benches, and frescoes of griffins. These may have symbolised the heavenly, earthly and underworldly aspects of the rulers.

CONTROVERSIAL EXCAVATIONS

△ **THE PLAY'S THE THING**
The theatre was used for plays and processions. An engineered road, one of the oldest in Europe, leads from here to the Little Palace.

▽ **ALL AT SEA**
The fresco in the Queen's apartments (which included an *en suite* bathroom) features dolphins, fishes and sea urchins.

◁ **BULL AND GATE**
A (replica) fresco depicting the capture of a wild bull decorates the ramparts of the north entrance, leading to the road to Knossos' harbour at Amnissos.

▽ **DILEMMA OF HORNS**
The famous double horns now sitting on the south facade were once regarded as sacred symbols, though perhaps this is an overworking of the bull motif of the site.

◁ **COLOUR CODING**
The South Propylon (pillared gateway) has near life-size frescoes of processionary youths, including the famous slender-waisted cup-bearer. In Minoan art, male figures were coloured red, female white.

In 1878 a local merchant, Mínos Kalokairinós, uncovered a fragment of the remains at Knossos, but the Turkish owners of the land prevented further excavation and even the wealthy German Heinrich Schliemann couldn't afford their asking price when he attempted to buy the site.

However, once Crete gained autonomy from the Turks at the turn of the century, the way was open for the English archeologist Arthur Evans (later knighted) to purchase the area and begin excavating. He soon realised that this was a major discovery. He worked at Knossós over a period of 35 years, though by 1903 most of the site had been uncovered.

Evans' methods of using concrete to reconstruct the long-gone timber columns, and to support excavated sections of wall have received much criticism. While these preserved some of the structure *in situ*, it also involved much interpretative conjecture on the part of Evans (pictured above with a 1600 BC steatite bull's head from the Little Palace).

Excavation continues to this day, under subtler management.

INSIGHT GUIDES

TRAVEL TIPS

CONTENTS

Getting Acquainted

The Place

Situation 39°N, 22°E
Area 131,950 sq km (50,950 sq miles), including around 25,050 sq km (9,670 sq miles) of islands
Capital Athens
Population 10.2 million. Greater Athens and Piraeus have a population of 4 million. Thessaloníki, the second-largest city and a university town, has nearly 1 million residents, and the most-populated island is Crete, with just over half a million inhabitants
Language Modern Greek
Literacy 95 percent
Religion Predominantly Greek Orthodox Christianity, with small minorities of Muslims, Catholics, evangelical sects and Jews
Currency Drachma
Weights and measures Metric
Electricity 220V, two-pin plugs (see also *What to Pack*)
International Dialling Code 30 (Athens: 1)
Time Zones Two hours ahead of Greenwich Mean Time. The clock is advanced one hour, from the last weekend in March to the last weekend in September, for extended daylight hours

Geography

Mainland Greece is made up of Attica, the Peloponnese, central Greece (more poetically known as Roúmeli), Thessaly, Epirus, Macedonia and Thrace. Its backbone is the Píndhos Range, extending from Roúmeli to the Albanian border in Epirus reaching its highest point at Smolikas, but the highest mountain is Olympus, straddling the border between Thessaly and Macedonia, at a height of 2,917m (9,570ft).

The coast is a series of so many coves and inlets that it runs to 15,000km (9,320 miles), and the Mediterranean reaches its deepest point at the 4,850m (15,912ft) Oinoussa Pit off the south coast of the Peloponnese.

The hundreds of islands that spill out into the Mediterranean and Aegean are divided into groups: the Ionian archipelago to the west, the Sporades in the central Aegean, the Cyclades and Dodecanese running out southeast from Athens, and the northeast Aegean islands just off the Turkish coast. The first and third-largest islands are Crete and Lésvos, both famous for their variety of flowers, though the flora throughout the whole of Greece is remarkable.

The People

Although about 40 percent of the country's population lives in Athens, the city is often called a village. Greeks rarely move far from their village roots, even though (with more and more young people moving to cities) chronic depopulation of the countryside has become a serious problem.

Even the most jet-setting businessman is home-loving and much of the Greeks' social life is centred round the family. Children are adored (and given more licence than you might allow your own!).

A nation of many passions, from football and basketball to politics, which can be very partisan, the Greeks love nothing better than discussing the meaning of life. If you strike up a conversation in a taverna, expect to while away an hour or two – especially during election time, when the whole country buzzes with political fervour and speculation.

Government

Greece is a republic with a president, elected by parliament, who holds ceremonial executive power. The parliament has 300 elected members led by the prime minister.

King Constantine went into exile in December 1967 following the April seizure of power by the infamous colonels' junta, and the monarchy was abolished after a referendum held after the collapse of the dictatorship in 1974. Since then two parties, New Democracy (conservative) and PASOK (socialist) have taken turns at governing; PASOK has been in power since 1993, winning in both the 1996 and the, extremely close, 2000 elections under Kóstas Símitis.

Economy

About 23 percent of the land is arable, and the country produces fruit, vegetables, olives, olive oil, wine, currants, grain, cotton and tobacco. Its natural resources include the minerals bauxite, lignite and magnesite, and there is crude oil and marble. About 15 percent of the 4-million labourforce works in mining and manufacturing, producing textiles, chemicals and food products. Shipping is still an important source of revenue.

In 1981 Greece became the 10th member of the European Union, with full integration at the end of 1993; in early 1998 it subscribed to the ERM in preparation for the single currency, though its economy was not strong enough to be included in the first round of qualifying nations.

The late 1980s and early 1990s saw a huge rise in the cost of living throughout the country; a shock for anyone who remembers it as a "cheap & cheerful" destination. Although it is no longer the place for bargain-basement holidays, the drachma tends to devalue steadily against other currencies, at a rate slightly faster than the current domestic inflation of about 4 percent, so Greece remains good value for foreign travellers.

Seasonal Averages

- **January–March**
  6–16°C (43–61°F)
- **April–June**
  11–29°C (52–84°F)
- **July–September**
  19–32°C (66–90°F)
- **October–December**
  8–23°C (46–73°F)

Climate

The Greece seen in tourist posters is a perennially warm and sunny place – and it is, by European standards. But this picture does not do justice to the considerable climatic variety. The north and inland regions have a modified continental climate, so winters are quite cold and summers extremely hot. In Ioánnina, Trípoli and Kastoriá, for example, snow and freezing temperatures are not uncommon. In the mountain regions, winters are even more inclement.

The southern islands, the coastal Peloponnese and the Attic Peninsula conform more to the traditional Mediterranean image: a long, warm season of rainless, sunny days extending roughly from early May to mid-October. But here too the winters are cool, with rain falling in unpredictable spells between November and April.

In general, late spring (late April–June) and autumn (September–early October) are the best times to visit. During these periods, you will find mild to warm temperatures, sunny days and fewer tourists. Throughout July and August Greece is at its sultriest and most crowded. Still millions of tourists seem to prefer the heat and the company, choosing this busiest period for their holiday.

Business Hours

All banks are open from 8am to 2pm Monday to Thursday, closing at 1.30pm on Friday. In heavily visited areas, however, you may find banks open additional late-afternoon hours and on Saturday mornings for currency exchange. Convenient ATM's are now becoming increasingly available.

The schedule for business and shop hours is more complicated. Business hours vary according to the type of business and the day of the week. The main thing to remember is that businesses generally open at 8.30am and close on Monday, Wednesday and Saturday at 2.30pm. On Tuesday, Thursday and Friday most businesses close at 1.30pm and reopen in the afternoon from 5pm to 8.30pm.

You'll soon learn that schedules are very flexible in Greece (both in business and personal affairs). To avoid disappointment, allow ample time when shopping and doing business. That way, you may also enter into the Greek spirit of doing business, in which a good chat can be as important as the matter of business itself.

Religion

The Greek Orthodox Church still exerts enormous influence on contemporary life, both in mainland Greece (including Athens) and the islands. Sunday is the official day of rest, and even in mid-season in some tourist areas, shops and activities are suspended. Excursion boats from island to island, for example, might well be running to schedule, but what no one bothers to point out is that nothing on the destination island will be open when you arrive. Always enquire beforehand when planning anything on Sundays.

The most important holiday in Greece is Easter, celebrated by the Greek Orthodox calendar and usually a week or two to either side of Catholic Easter. It is advisable to find out before booking a spring holiday exactly when Easter is, as services, shops and even flights experience disruptions during the weeks before and after Easter.

On 15 August, the Assumption of the Virgin Mary, many places hold a *paniyiri* (celebration) to mark the reception of the Panaghía (as she is in Greek) into heaven. Greeks make pilgrimages from all over the country to Tínos in the Cyclades where the icon of the Panaghía Evangelístria is said to work miracles. Pilgrims flock to Pátmos too, where St John is said to have written the book of Revelations. The most colourful festival of the Virgin, however, takes place on 15 August in the hillside town of Ólymbos on the island of Kárpathos, where the women wear brilliant traditional dress and the *paniyiria* can last for days.

Nearly every day is a cause for celebration for someone in Greece. Instead of marking birthdays, Greeks have *yiortés*, name days, which celebrate Orthodox baptismal names. When the day commemorates a popular name-saint like John or Helen, practically the whole nation has a party. You'll hear locals say: "Yiortázo simera" (I'm celebrating today). To which you may reply: "Hrónia pollá" ("many years", in other words, many happy returns).

Siesta

Siesta is observed throughout Greece, and even in Athens the majority of people retire behind closed doors between the hours of 3pm and 6pm. Shops and businesses close, and it is usually impossible to get much done that day until late-afternoon or early evening. Driving motorbikes and scooters is often prohibited through residential neighbourhoods.

This provides a wonderful respite in even the noisiest of tourist towns, and is the ideal time to take a nap or extend a leisurely lunch into the afternoon. Anyone with a strong constitution and protective clothing will be rewarded if they choose this time to visit otherwise-busy archeological sites (a few of which stay open after 3pm): crowds have usually considerably diminished.

Planning the Trip

Visas and Passports

Citizens of EU nations have unlimited visitation rights to Greece; your passport will not be stamped upon entry or exit. With a valid passport, citizens of the United States, Canada, Australia and New Zealand can stay in the country for up to three months with no visa necessary. To stay longer, you must obtain a permit from the Aliens' Bureau in Athens (173 Alexandras Avenue, tel: 64 21 616). Citizens of other countries should contact the nearest Greek embassy or consulate about visa requirements

Public Holidays

The Greeks like their festivals and celebrate them in style, so most business and shops close during the afternoon before and morning after a religious holiday.

● **1 January** New Year's Day
● **6 January** Epiphany
● **Moveable** Clean Monday (First Day of Lent)
● **25 March** Evangelismós/ Annunciation
● **1 May** Labour Day
● **Moveable** Good Friday
● **Moveable** Orthodox Easter, Easter Monday
● **Moveable** Pentecost Monday/Aghíou Pnévmatos (50 days after Easter)
● **15 August** Assumption of the Holy Virgin
● **28 October** "Ohi" Day, National Holiday
● **25 December** Christmas Day
● **26 December** Gathering of the Virgin/Sýnaxis tis Theotókou.

Customs

There are no official restrictions on the movement of goods within the European Union, provided the goods were purchased within the EU. It is no longer necessary for EU nationals to exit Customs through a red or green channel.

Duty-paid goods

If you buy goods in Greece for which you pay tax, there are no restrictions on the amounts you can take home. EU law has set "guidance levels", however, on the following:

• **Tobacco** 800 cigarettes, or 400 cigarillos, or 200 cigars or 1kg of tobacco.
• **Spirits** 10 litres
• **Fortified wine/wine** 90 litres
• **Beer** 110 litres
If you exceed these amounts you must be able to prove the goods are for personal use.
Duty-free goods If you buy goods duty-free the following restrictions still apply:
• **Tobacco** 200 cigarettes, or 100 cigarillos, or 50 cigars, or 250g of tobacco.
• **Alcohol** 1 litre of spirits or liqueurs over 22 percent volume, or 2 litres of fortified, sparkling wine or other liqueurs.
• **Perfume** 60cc of perfume, plus 250cc of toilet water.

There are no restrictions on the amount of currency you can take into Greece.
   Visitors arriving with stereo equipment and cameras may be required to have such items recorded in their passports. This is to prevent the sale of untaxed luxury items to Greek nationals. Officials may check to make certain you leave with whatever you brought. Note as well that it is considered a grave and punishable offence to remove antiquities, no matter how small, from Greece. You will also not be allowed to depart with over 10,000 drachmas in Greek currency. There are also restrictions on the amount of foreign currency you take out of the country if you convert

unused drachmas back into your own currency.

Health

Greece has few serious diseases apart from those that you can contract in the United States or the rest of Europe. Citizens of the United States, Canada and United Kingdom do not need any immunisations to enter the country.

Insurance

British and EU residents are entitled to free medical treatment in Greece as long as they carry an E111 form (obtainable from post offices). Provision is not of the highest quality, however: medical staff may not even know what an E111 form is so you could have a battle on your hands obtaining free provision, plus you will be admitted to one of the lowest-grade state hospitals and have to pay for your own medicine. So it is advisable to take out private medical insurance. You will have to pay for treatment, so you must keep receipts for any bills or medicines you pay for to make a claim. If you plan to hire a moped in Greece, you will have to pay a supplement to cover you for accidents.

Hazards

Nearly half the stray dogs in rural areas* carry echinococcosis (treatable by surgery only) and kala-azar disease (leismaniasis), a protozoan blood disease spread by sandfleas. Mosquitos can be a nuisance in some areas of Greece, but repellents are readily available in pharmacies.
   On the islands, baby pit vipers and scorpions are a problem in spring and summer. They will not strike unless disturbed, but do not put hands or feet in places (such as drystone walls) that you haven't checked first. If you swim in the sea, beware jellyfish whose sting is usually harmless but can swell and hurt for days. On beaches, it is worth wearing sandals to avoid sea urchins (little black cushions on rocks that can embed their tiny spines into unwary feet).

Water

The drinking water in Greece is safe, though occasionally brackish on certain islands; spring water in the mountains is universally available – collect it in a canteen rather than buying plastic bottles.

Money Matters

The Greek national currency is the dhráhma (drachma in English), which comes in coins of 1, 2, 5, 10, 20, 50 and 100dr, plus notes of 50, 100, 200, 500, 1000, 5,000 and 10,000dr. Amounts under 10dr are virtually worthless, especially since the devaluation of March 1998, and such coins – and the 50dr note – are approaching extinction.

An unlimited amount of foreign currency and travellers' cheques may be brought into Greece. All banks and most hotels are authorised to buy foreign currency at the official rate of exchange fixed by the Bank of Greece. Though it's safer to carry most of your currency in travellers' cheques, it is also worth carrying a limited sum in US dollars or pounds sterling. On those occasions when you can't find a place to cash cheques, there will usually be a shop or post office interested in changing drachmas for these currencies.

Credit cards

Many of the better-established hotels, restaurants and shops accept major credit cards. The average pension or *tavérna* does not, however, so be sure to enquire if that is how you intend to pay. You will find that most brands of card are accepted by the numerous autoteller machines, upon entry of your PIN number. For example, the National Bank of Greece takes Mastercards; the Commercial Bank serves Visa; and the Alpha Credit Bank accommodates Visa and American Express cardholders. You will find that this is the most convenient and least expensive way of getting funds, and many of the machines operate around the clock.

Drugs and Medicines

Greek pharmacies stock most over-the-counter drugs, and pharmacists are well trained (including to supply medicine that might be prescription-only elsewhere). So you should have no problem obtaining most medicines (except in remote areas and islands). Generally, they are expensive, however, so if you have space it's worth packing hayfever tablets, painkillers, indigestion tablets and anti-fungal sprays. Check labels carefully, though, as codeine (a key ingredient in some painkillers such as Panadol and Solpadeine) is banned in Greece.

Greek authorities take the unauthorised use of drugs very seriously indeed; this is not the country in which to store cannabis. Homeopathic and herbal remedies can be bought in larger towns.

Photography

Although Greece is a photographer's paradise, taking photographs at will is not recommended. Cameras are not allowed in museums, and you may have to pay a fee to take photographs or use your camcorder at archeological sites. Watch out for signs with a camera with a cross through it.

Prints can be processed just about anywhere in Greece, but slides are sent to Athens so wait until you get home to get them processed.

What To Pack

Clothes

If you visit Greece during the summer months, you will want to bring lightweight, casual clothing. Add a sweater or jacket to this and you will be prepared for the occasional cool night breezes. Lightweight shoes and sandals are ideal in the summer, but you will also need a pair of comfortable walking shoes that have already been broken in. If you plan to do any rigorous hiking in the mountains or on the islands, bring sturdy, over-the-ankle boots with a good tread; leather will be more comfortable in summer temperatures.

In general, both Greeks and tourists dine in casual dress. You will only need formal dress if you plan to go to fancy establishments, casinos, formal affairs and so on. If you visit Greece during the winter months, which can be surprisingly cold, bring the same kind of clothes you would wear during spring in the northern part of the United States or central Europe.

Sun protection

A hat, sun cream and sunglasses are also highly recommended for protection from the intense midday sun* (sun creams are widely available).

Dress codes

The Greeks will not expect you as a tourist to dress as they do, but scuffed shoes, ripped jeans or visibly out-of-date clothing are generally frowned upon.

In certain places and regions, you will encounter requirements or conventions concerning the way you dress. To enter a church, men must wear long trousers, and women, sleeved dresses. Often dresses or wraps will be provided at the church entrance if you do not have them. Not complying with this code will be taken as insulting irreverence.

Some specific areas have their own dress codes. On Mýkonos, for example, male and female tourists alike will shock no one by wearing shorts or a swimsuit in most public places. But this same apparel will be severely alienating in a mountain village in Epirus or Crete or in any other area that is less accustomed to tourists. The best approach is to observe what other people are wearing and dress accordingly.

Adaptors

220 AC is the standard household electric current throughout Greece. So non-switchable appliances from North America (shavers and hair dryers) require step-down transformers, which are difficult to get in Greece. Greek plugs are the standard round, two-pin European continental type, different from those in North America and the UK; plug adaptors for American appliances are easy to find, three-to-two-pin adaptors for UK appliances much less so, so these are best purchased before departure.

Universal plug

Greek basins rarely come with plugs, so if you want water in your sink a universal plug is essential.

Film

Although 35mm film is widely available, it is expensive and available in a limited range of film speeds, so it's wise to bring your own.

Torch

If you're planning a trip to one of the islands, well worth packing as walking back after the taverna can be tricky if there's no moon!

Toiletries

Most international brands are widely available, except on the smaller islands (where you may have trouble getting even basics such as tampons if there is no pharmacy in sight).

Getting There

By Air

Greece has good air connections with all five continents and is serviced by numerous international airlines. Charter flights generally operate from mid-April to the end of October, or into November on Rhodes and Crete. There are ways of flying in at a much lower cost than the standard airline fares (such as APEX, stand-by, last-minute seats or "bucket shop" tickets),

and you may want to familiarise yourself with the different possibilities, and their related advantages and disadvantages, before buying a ticket.

The great majority of airline passengers travelling to Greece make Athens Hellenikon Airport their point of entry, though the new airport being built at Spata should begin operating in time for the 2004 Athens Olympics. If you are flying with Olympic Airways you will arrive at the West Air Terminal. All other airlines service the East Air Terminal. Connecting the two terminals are taxi services and buses which depart every 20 minutes.

Between central Athens and Hellenikon there are various connecting services. A taxi ride from the West Terminal to Athens (Syntagma or Omónia squares) should cost approximately 2100dr and will take 25-40 minutes depending on traffic. From the East Airport, it should cost slightly more and will take slightly longer. There's

Specialist Operators

The Greek National Tourist Organisation (*see page 327*) provides a list of tour operators and specialist agents offering holidays in Greece.

● **Adventure/outward-bound breaks/holidays**
Trekking Hellas, 7 Filellinon Street, 10557 Athens
Tel: 1 33 10 323
Fax: 1 32 34 548
E-mail: trekking@compulink.gr

● **Archaeological tours**
American School of Classical Studies at Athens, 41e 72nd Street, New York, NY 10021
Tel: (212) 861 0302.
Led by curators of the British Museum:
British Museum Traveller, 46 Bloomsbury Street, London WC1B 3QQ
Tel: (020) 7323 8895
Fax: (020) 8580 8677.

● **Botanical tours**
Marengo Guided Walks, 17 Bernard Crescent, Hunstanton

PE36 6ER, UK
Tel: (01485) 532710
● **Cruises to ancient sites**
Swan Hellenic, 77 New Oxford Street, London WC1A 1PP
Tel: (020) 7800 2200
Fax: (020) 7800 2723
● **Historical/nature tours**
Filoxenia Tours, Sourdock Hill, Barkisland, Halifax, HX4 0AG, UK
Tel: (01422) 375999
Fax: (01422) 310340
● **Holistic health holidays**
Skyros Centre, 92 Prince of Wales Road, London NW5 3NE
Tel: (020) 7267 4424
Fax: (020) 7284 3063
E-mail; skyros@easynet.co.uk
● **Mountain cottages**
Greek National Tourist Organisation, 4 Conduit Street, London W1R
Tel: (020) 7734 5997
Fax: (020) 7287 1369
● **Walking holidays**
Explore Worldwide, 1 Frederick Street, Aldershot, GU11 1LQ UK

Tel: (01252) 344161
Fax: (01252) 315935
Ramblers' Holidays, PO Box 43, Welwyn Garden City, AL8 6PQ, UK
Tel: (01707) 331133
Fax: (01707) 333276
Waymark Holidays, 44 Windsor Road, Slough, SL1 2EJ, UK.
Tel: (01753) 516477,
fax: (01753) 517016.
● **Walking/cycling tours/mountain expeditions**
Sherpa Expeditions, 131a Heston Road, Hounslow, TW5 0RD, UK
Tel: (020) 8577 2717
Fax: (020) 8572 9788
www.sherpa-walking-holidays.co.uk
● **Wildlife/nature trails/horse riding holidays**
Peregrine Holidays, 40-41 South Parade, Summertown, Oxford, OX2 7JP, UK
Tel: (01865) 511642
Fax: (01865) 512583
E-mail: 106357.1754@compuserve.com

Route Planner

For a small fee the Automobile Association's European Routes Service will plan your route. The AA issues detailed itineraries for overland journeys, tailored to your needs and preferences, whether they be the quickest route to a certain destination or a drive without using motorways. A detailed printout provides information on places of interest and scenery as well as the roads. Tel: (0117) 930 8242.

a fee of 50dr per bag as well, plus supplements for leaving the airport, and at Christmas or Easter week.

The bus service is much cheaper and works well if you're not in a rush. Take bus 091 leaving about every 20 minutes, or every hour from midnight–6am for Syntagma and Omónia.

Between Piraeus and the East-West Terminals, bus 19 runs about hourly from 5am to 10.20pm to Aktí Tzelépi and then on to the main harbour in Piraeus. Both charge 200drs 5am–midnight, 400dr midnight–5am. The same journey by taxi will cost over 1500 drs.

By Sea

By far the majority of visitors entering Greece by sea do so from the west, from Italy. You can catch a boat to Greece from Venice, Ancona, Trieste and Bari, but the most regular service is from Brindisi. Daily ferry lines (less frequent in the low-season) connect Brindisi with the three main western Greek ports: Corfu, Igoumenítsa and Pátras. Corfu is a 9-hour trip; Igoumenítsa 11 hours; and Pátras 16 to 18 hours, depending on whether you take a direct boat or one that makes stops in Corfu and Igoumenítsa. The "Superfast" ferries introduced in between Ancona and Pátras offer an efficient 22-hour crossing, and daytime hydrofoils operate sporadically between Igoumenítsa and Brindisi.

Igoumenítsa is the ideal port of call for those setting off to see

central-western Greece. Pátras is best if you want to head directly to Athens or into the Peloponnese. Regular buses and trains connect Pátras and Athens (4 hours by bus, 5 hours by train). If you plan to take your car with you on the boat, you should definitely make reservations well in advance. Otherwise, arriving a few hours before the departure time should suffice, except during peak seasons when booking in advance is essential for seats or berths.

If you want to enter Greece from the east, boats run weekly between Haifa, Limassol, Rhodes and/or Crete, and Piraeus.

By Land

From Europe The most direct overland route from northwestern Europe to Greece is a long one:

Tourist Information

Australia & New Zealand Greek National Tourist Organisation, 51 Pitt Street, Sydney NSW 2000. Tel: (02) 9241 1663/4, fax: (02) 235 2174).

Canada 1233 Rue de la Montagne, Montreal, Quebec H3G 1Z2 Tel/fax: (514) 871 1535. 1300 Bay Street, Upper Level, Toronto, Ontario M5R 3KB. Tel: (416) 968 2220, fax: (416) 968 6533.

UK Greek National Tourist Organisation, 4 Conduit Street, London WIR 0DJ. Tel: (020) 7734 5997, fax: (020) 7287 1369.

United States, Head Office, Olympic Tower, 645 Fifth Avenue, 5th Floor, New York, New York 10022. Tel: (212) 421 5777, fax: (212) 826 6940. 168 North Michigan Avenue, Chicago, Illinois 60601. Tel: (312) 782 1084, fax: (312) 782 1091. 611 West Sixth Street, Suite 1998 Los Angeles, California 90017. Tel: (213) 626 6696, fax: (213) 489 9744.

Athens Airport

During the peak summer season it is impossible to walk through Athens Airport without tripping over sleeping bodies and rucksacks. These are either students using the airport as overnight accommodation, or passengers stranded here by cancelled or delayed flights. Delays are an inevitable part of flying to and from Greece, so come armed with food, water and a good book. All part of the fun.

3,000 km (1,900 miles) from London to Athens. It has always been a rather arduous and impractical travel option if you're just trying to get to Greece for a brief holiday; ongoing troubles in former Yugoslavia now mean even longer detours through Hungary, Romania and Bulgaria. Check with your local Greek tourist office or motoring organisation for the latest information before leaving.

There is also the option of making use of the one or two remaining, reputable bus lines that connect Athens and Thessaloníki with many European cities (taking 3.5 days to/from London, for example). The various trains you can take from northwest Europe will take about as long as the bus, cost considerably more, but fares include the Italy-Greece ferry crossing, and may get you to Greece feeling more intact.

From Asia via Turkey If you are travelling strictly overland to Greece from Asia you will pass through Istanbul and cross into Greece at the Évros River. The best way to do this is by car or bus. The road is good and the journey from Istanbul to Thessaloníki takes approximately 15 hours; several companies serve the route.

The train has the appeal of following the route of the old Orient Express, with better scenery than the road. But, unless you're a great rail fan, the travel time can be off-putting: 17 hours by the timetables, up to 19 hours in practice, including long halts at the border.

Practical Tips

BBC in Athens are: 3–7.30am GMT–9.41 (31 m), 6.05 (49 m), 15.07 (19 m); 7.30am–6pm GMT–15.07 (19 m); 6.30pm–11.15pm GMT–9.41 (31 m), 6.05 (49 m). Additionally, a plethora of private stations broadcast locally from just about every island or provincial town, no matter how tiny.

There are three state-owned and operated television channels (ET1 and ET2 in Athens, ET3 in Thessaloniki) and at least five private television channels (Antenna, New, Mega, Seven-X and Alpha). Often they transmit foreign movies and programmes with Greek subtitles rather than being dubbed. Several cable and satellite channels are also broadcast, including Sky, CNN and Super Channel.

Media

Print

Many kiosks throughout Athens and other resorts receive British newspapers either late the same night (in Omónia Square) or, more usually, the next day.

The daily (except Monday), four-colour *Athens News* (online at: athensnews.dolnet.gr) is interesting and informative, with both international and local news, particularly good for the Balkans, with complete TV and cinema progammes as well. *Atlantis*, Greece's English-language monthly, has articles on Greek politics, topics of interest and the arts. *Odyssey* is a glossy, bi-monthly magazine created by and for the wealthy Greek diaspora, somewhat more interesting than the usual airline in-flight mag.

If you are in Athens, *Athens Today* and *Now in Athens* (available from the National Tourist Information Organisation office) have general information about travel, museums, galleries and current musical performances.

Radio & TV Stations

ER 1 and ER 2 are the two Greek state radio channels. ER 1 is divided into three different "programmes". First (728 KHz) and Second (1385 KHz) both have a lot of Greek popular music and news, some foreign pop and occasional jazz and blues. Third (665 KHz) plays a lot of classical music. ER 2 (98 KHz) is much like the first two programmes.

The BBC World Service offers news on the hour (plus other interesting programmes and features). The best short wave (MHz) frequencies to pick up the

Postal Services

Most local post offices are open weekdays from 7.30am until 2pm. The main post offices in central Athens (on Eólou near Omónia Square and on Syndagma Square at the corner of Mitropóleos Street), however, are open weekdays and 7.30am–8pm, Saturday and Sunday 7.30am–2pm.

Postal rates are subject to fairly frequent change, so you'll do best to enquire at post offices. Stamps are available from the post office or from many kiosks (*períptera*) and hotels, which charge a 10–15 percent commission. Make sure you know how much it is to send a letter or postcard, though, as kiosk owners tend not to be up to date with latest international postal rates. Bear in mind that sending the attractive, large-format postcards costs letter-rate postage.

If you want to send a parcel from Greece, do not wrap it until a post office clerk has inspected it, unless it's going to another EU country, in which case you can present it sealed. Some post offices stock various sizes of cardboard boxes for sale in which you can pack your material, as well as twine, but you had best bring your own tape and scissors.

Letters can be sent Post Restante to any post office. Take your passport when you go to pick up mail.

Telecommunications

The easiest way to make telephone calls is to purchase a telephone card from a kiosk and use a phone booth. Cards come in three sizes: 100 units, 500 units and 1,000 units, with the largest ones representing the best value. Otherwise, you may find a telephone at a kiosk, for which you will pay 25 or 30drs. for a local call.

You can also make long-distance calls from any one of the many kiosks which have metered phones. However, a call from a kiosk will cost considerably more than from a cardphone, or from the new-style coin-op counter phones which take 10, 20 and 50dr pieces, often found in hotel lobbies and restaurants. Calls from hotel rooms typically have a 100 percent surcharge on top of the standard rates.

Many post offices offer fax services; and a growing number of cybercafés are also springing up in the larger towns.

With the proliferation of cardphones and mobile phones, branch

Embassies

All embassies are open from Monday to Friday, usually from 8am until 2pm.
- **Australia** 37 Dhimitríou Soútsou Street (tel: 64 50 404).
- **Canada** 4 Ghennadhíou Street (tel: 72 73 400).
- **Ireland** 7 Vassiléos Konstandínou Street (tel: 72 32 771).
- **New Zealand** (consulate 268 Kifissías Ave, Halándri, 68 74 701).
- **South Africa**: 60 Kifissiás Avenue (tel: 68 06 645).
- **UK** 1 Ploutárhou Street (tel: 72 72 600).
- **United States**: 91 Vasilíssis Sofías Avenue (tel: 72 12 951).

"Greek" Time

Beware Greek schedules. Although shops and businesses generally operate the hours indicated on page 323, there is no guarantee that when you want to book a ferry or buy a gift, the shop will actually be open. To avoid frustration and disappointment, shop and book things between 10am and 1pm Monday to Friday.

Since 1994 Athens has experimented with "straight" hours during the winter to bring the country more in line with the EU, but this appears to be discretionary rather than obligatory, with some stores observing the hours and others adhering to traditional schedules. Whether or not this will catch on and spread to the rest of Greece and the islands is anyone's guess.

The shops in Athens' Pláka district remain open until 10pm or longer to take advantage of browsers, and tourist shops throughout the country usually trade well into the evening in summer. But butchers and fishmongers are not allowed to open on summer evenings (although a few wink at the law), and pharmacies (except for those on rota duty) are never open on Saturday mornings.

sunbathing is often not sanctioned, so watch for signs forbidding it on beaches. The main rule-of-thumb is this: if it is a secluded beach and/or a beach that has become a commonly accepted locale for nude bathing, you probably won't be bothered by, nor offend, anyone.

The Greek Orthodox Church holds sway in Greece, so keep any unfavourable comments about churches or even Greek civil servants to yourself.

Strikes

Strikes and demonstrations are a way of life in Greece. Should there not be one in Athens while you're passing through, you should consider yourself lucky.

offices of the state phone service OTE have largely withdrawn their attended phone booths where you paid upon completion of a call. In the largest cities, the central OTE building may be open 7.30am to 10 or 11pm, occasionally around the clock, to sell cards for its inside booths; elsewhere you'll be lucky to find OTE open past 7pm, and occasionally they close as early as 3pm.

Although mobile phones are all the rage among well-heeled Greeks, you have to own a GSM phone to make a call.

Medical Treatment

For minor ailments your best port of call is a pharmacy. Greek pharmacists usually speak good English and are well-trained and helpful, and pharmacies stock a good range of medicines (including the Pill and morning-after Pill), though these are expensive.

If you need a pharmacy after hours or at weekends, you can find out which are open either by looking at the bilingual, Greek/English card posted in pharmacy windows (in big cities one or two will be open 24 hours a day), or by consulting a local newspaper.

There are English-speaking GPs in all the bigger towns and resorts, whose rates are usually reasonable. Ask your hotel or the Tourist Police for details.

Treatment for broken bones and similar problems is given free of charge in the state-run Greek hospitals. For more serious problems you must have private medical insurance as most hospitals outside Athens show little knowledge of Form E111, which entitles EU members to free treatment.

If you have a serious injury or illness, you are better off travelling home for treatment if you can. Greek hospitals lag behind northern Europe and the US in both their age and standard of care; the Greeks bring food and bedding when visiting sick relatives.

Etiquette

The Greeks are at heart a very traditional nation, protective of their families and traditions. So it essential to follow their codes of conduct.

Locals rarely drink to excess, so drunken behaviour is treated with at best bewilderment, at worse severe distaste.

Nude bathing is legal at only a few beaches (such as on the island of Mýkonos), but it is deeply offensive to Greeks. Even topless

Security and Crime

Greece is one of the safest countries in Europe. Crime is rare and the petty theft that does occur is more likely to have been committed by other tourists rather than locals. Greeks regularly leave cars and rooms unlocked and, although it is not advisable to do so, luggage left unattended will probably remain undisturbed. Even belongings left behind in a café will usually have been put aside for you to collect.

Tipping

Menu prices at most restaurants and tavérnes include service charge, so a tip is discretionary.

Emergency numbers

In Athens ring the following numbers for assistance:
● **Ambulance** 161
● **Police** 100
● **Tourist police** 171
Elsewhere, hotel staff will give you details of the nearest hospital or English-speaking doctor. Or contact the Tourist Police, who are always extremely helpful.

Help and Information

● **Tourist offices**
If you would like tourist information about Greece before or during your trip, write, call or visit the nearest Greek National Tourist Organisation, known as the GNTO, or EOT in Greek (*see page 327*). They provide information on public transport, as well as leaflets and details about sites and museums. There are 15 regional GNTO offices across the country, the largest of which is centrally located in Athens at Amerikís 2.
Tel: (01) 3310561/2.
There is also an information desk at the East Air Terminal which is open during the day and displays ferry sailings to the islands even when it is closed.

● **Tourist Police**
The Greek Tourist Police are often a mine of information too. Located in most large cities, they are a branch of the local police, and can be helpful in providing information about hotels as well as helping with a wide variety of travel questions.

When service has been particularly good, it is customary to leave an extra 5 percent or so in coins on the table for the waiters – in practice rounding up to the next multiple of a thousand drachmas on a bill.

Just as important as any such gratuity, however, is your appreciation of the food you eat. Greek waiters and restaurant owners are proud when you tell them you like a particular dish.

Women Travellers

Lone female visitors have to bargain for the Greek macho. In tourist areas, especially beach bars and discos, a few Greek men can be predatory: ignoring them, or a few firm, sharp words, is the best policy.

In remote areas, on the other hand, the Greeks are highly traditional and may find it hard to understand why you are alone. You will not be allowed into their all-male drinking cafés.

Travelling with Kids

Children are adored in Greece, with many families still highly superstitious about their welfare – don't be surprised to see kids with amulets pinned to their clothes to ward off the evil eye. So expect your own kids to be the centre of attention. You may have to put your foot down when shop owners offer things free or strangers are over-indulgent.

Getting Around

Public Transport

By air
Flying is considerably more expensive than travelling by boat, bus or train (three times more than a seat, just under double the price of a boat berth), though still reasonable when compared to the price of domestic flights in other countries. For example, the 45-minute jet flight between Thessaloníki and Athens costs about $80.

Greece's national airline, Olympic Airlines, has been having management and labour troubles for years. Strikes and working to rule have in the past caused some flights to be cancelled or delayed (a situation that shows no signs of changing), so do be as careful as

Left luggage

Airports There is a left-luggage facility opposite the Athens West Airport Terminal, but none at East Terminal.
Hotels Most hotels in Greece are willing to store locked suitcases for up to a week if you want to take any short excursions. This is usually a free service, provided you've stayed a night or two, but the hotel accepts no responsibility in the highly unlikely event of theft.
Commercial offices On the islands there are left-luggage offices in many harbour towns. For a small charge space can be hired by the hour, day, week or longer. Although contents will probably be safe, take valuables with you.

you can about your flight arrangements. You can book tickets, pay fares and collect timetables at any Olympic office, plus at numerous on-line travel agents.

Alternatively, a smaller carrier, Air Greece, is gaining popularity among Greeks for internal flights. They fly from Athens to Thessaloníki, Rhodes, Iráklion and Haniá in Crete and also Iráklion to Thessaloníki. The Air Greece head office is at Daidalou 36, Iráklion, Crete, tel: (081) 330/533 074. There is also an Athens office, tel: 325 5011/324 or 4457/960 0646.

Island flights are often fully booked over the summer, so reserve seats at least a week in advance.

By bus

A vast network of bus routes, called the KTEL, spreads across Greece; KTEL is a syndicate of bus companies whose buses are cheap, generally punctual and will take you to almost any destination that can be reached on wheels. Among Greeks it's a popular way of travelling, so you will have good company. KTEL buses on the more idiosyncratic rural routes often have a distinct personal touch. Many drivers decorate and treat the bus with great care. They are proud of it and how they drive it.

The most important thing to note about KTEL is that in larger cities there will be different bus stations for different destinations. Travelling from Thessaloníki to Halkidhikí, for example, you will leave from one station, and to Ioánnina, from another; Athens has two terminals, while Iráklion in Crete has three.

An additional bus service is provided by OSE, the state railway organisation. Their coaches run only along the major routes, but often dovetail usefully with the KTEL for times.

City buses: Despite an influx of new rolling stock, travelling by the regular Athens blue buses remains a fairly miserable way of getting around the city. They are usually crowded and hot, and the routes are a mystery even to long-time residents. However, they are eminently reasonable, at 100dr per ticket. Tickets, valid on trolleys as well, are sold individually or in books of 10, from specific news kiosks and special booths at bus and metro stations, and at various non-strategic points around the city. Most bus services run until just before midnight.

Separate services run to airports and seaports. The Express bus 091 goes from Omónia/Syntagma squares to both airports at regular intervals, with tickets 170–200dr depending on the time of day. The green bus 040 runs from Filellínon Street (near Synagma Square) to Piraeus 24 hours a day, every 20 minutes (every hour after 1am). An orange KTEL-Attica bus goes from 14 Mavromatéon Street, Pédio toú Áreos Park, to Rafína, and takes approximately 90 minutes.

Athenian Taxis

Taxis in Greece, especially in Athens, merit a guidebook to themselves. It may be that your taxi "experience" will figure among the most prominent memories of your holiday. The Greek taxi experience is best divided into three stages:

First: getting a taxi. It's nearly impossible at certain times of the day (especially before the early-afternoon meal). When you hail a taxi, try to get in before stating your destination. Drivers are very picky and often won't let you in unless you're going in their direction. If you have to say it, say it loudly and clearly (with the right accent) as they may otherwise just pass you by. If you see an empty taxi, run for it, be aggressive – or a quick Athenian will beat you to it.

Second: the ride. Make sure the meter is on when you start out, and not on 2 (double fare, only permitted from midnight to 5am, or outside designated city limits).

Once inside, you may find yourself with company. Don't be alarmed. It is traditional for drivers to pick up two, three, even four individual riders, provided they're going roughly in the same direction. In fact, as taxis are so cheap they can end up functioning as mini-bus services. Packed in with a Greek mother with overflowing shopping bags, a chic businessman and a bohemian university student, you may find yourself in the middle (literally) of interesting conversations. If you are alone you may end up chatting with an ex-seaman who tells you a few yarns from his days in the States, or perhaps with a driver who speaks no English at all.

Third: paying up. If you've travelled with company, make sure you aren't paying for that part of the trip that happened before you got in. You should pay the difference in meter reading between embarking and alighting, plus the 200dr minimum. Otherwise the meter will tell you the straight price which may be adjusted according to tariffs that should appear on a placard clipped to the dashboard. There are extra charges for each piece of luggage, for leaving an airport or seaport, plus around Christmas and Easter.

Some drivers will try to rip you off, especially if it seems you're a novice in Greece. If the price is high, don't hesitate to argue your way, in whichever language, to a normal price.

In recent years various radio taxi services have started up in Athens and most other larger towns. They can pick you up within a short time of your call to a central booking number. You pay more, but this is well worth it if you want a car at a busy time of day. They are the preferred strategy if you're laden with luggage and have a flight or boat to catch.

Ferry Timetables

In 1997 the GNTO finally had a stab at producing a comprehensive, impartial ferry timetable, *Greek Travel Routes* (from booking agents and GNTO offices). Whether they will continue with it is uncertain, but this timetable is far superior to the privately published *Greek Travel Pages* and *Hellenic Travelling* (from larger bookshops in Athens), which may not list firms that do not advertise.

Alternatively, tourist information offices supply a weekly schedule, and most offices hang a schedule in a conspicuous place so you can look up times even if the branch is closed. This should, however, not be relied on implicitly.

In general, for the most complete and up-to-date information on each port's sailings the best source is the Port Police (in Piraeus and most other ports), known as the *limenarhío*.

Be aware that when you enquire about ferries at a travel agent, they will sometimes inform you only of the lines with which they are affiliated.

Trolley buses: Though even less comfortable than the blue buses, Athens trolleys are marginally faster and more frequent, and serve points of tourist interest; number 1 links the centre of the city with the railway stations, numbers 5 and 9 pass the archeological museum, and number 7 does a triangular circuit of the central districts.

Trains

The best thing about rail travel in Greece is the price: it is even less expensive than taking the bus. Otherwise, the Greek rail service, known as OSE, is quite limited, both in the areas it reaches and frequency of departures. Greek trains are also fairly slow and, unless you are doing the Athens–Thessaloníki run overnight in a couchette, or the quickish run down to Pátra (where the station is virtually opposite the docks), you will probably find the bus more convenient.

You can speed things up by taking an Intercity express train for a considerable surcharge. If you're on a tight budget you can really cut costs by taking the train round-trip, in which case there is a 20 percent reduction. Students and youths under 26 are usually eligible for certain discounts; all the common railpasses are honoured in Greece, though you may still have to pay certain supplements and queue for seat reservations.

Metro: The new metro system opened at the end of January, 2000, suddenly making central Athens easily accessible, and the tickets are valid on many of the city's buses and trolleys. The old line between Piraeus and Kifissiá is clean and reliable; city-centre stops are at Thissíon, Monastiráki, and Omónia.

By Sea

It is hard to imagine a visit to Greece without a boat trip. Nearly every island in the Greek seas can be reached by one kind of boat or another, be it a large car ferry, small passenger boat or hydrofoil.

Ferries: Piraeus is the nerve centre of the Greek ferry network, and chances are you will pass through it at least once. In high season, routes are numerous and it is worthwhile looking around before purchasing your ticket. It is also advisable not to purchase your ticket too far in advance: very rarely do tickets for the boat ride actually sell out, but there are frequent changes to schedules so you may be left trying to get a refund.

In response to overloading scandals in 1996, mandatory, computerised ticketing for all boats was supposedly introduced in 1998, so it is no longer possible to purchase tickets on board as in the past.

when you purchase your ticket, get detailed instructions on how to find its berth – the Piraeus quays are long and convoluted, and when you climb aboard in Piraeus, be sure you are on the right boat.

All the above prompts this suggestion: be flexible when travelling the Greek seas. Apart from schedule changes, a bad stretch of weather can keep you island-bound for as long as the wind blows. Strikes too are often called during the summer, and usually last for a few days. However, when they do occur, advance notice is usually given in the news media.

If you are travelling by car, especially during the high season, you will have to plan much further ahead because during the peak season some lines are booked for car space many weeks in advance. The same caveats apply to booking a cabin for an overnight trip during summer.

Otherwise *gamma* class – also known as deck, tourist, or third – is the classic, cheap way to voyage the Greek seas. There is usually a seat of one sort or another – in community with an international multitude, singing with a guitar, passing a bottle around under the stars. And if the weather turns bad you can always go inside to the "low-class" lounge, the snack bar or a quiet hallway corner.

Hydrofoil: At the other end of the naval spectrum, you will find a scheduled hydrofoil service to many islands, whose network has expanded greatly in recent years. This is the executive way to island hop; hydrofoils are more than twice as fast as the ferries and about twice as expensive.

These connect Piraeus with most of the Argo-Sarónic region (Éghina, Póros, Ídhra, Spétses and many Peloponnese mainland ports as far as Monemvasía), as well as Vólos and Thessaloníki with the Northern Sporades (Alónissos, Skiáthos, Skópelos and so on) and resorts on the Pílion Peninsula. In the northeast Aegean, there are local, peak-season services between Thássos, Samothráki and the mainland, while in the Dodecanese all the islands between Sámos and

Rhodes, inclusive, are well served.

The most reliable and durable companies are:

Ceres Flying Dolphins, 8 Aktí Themistokléous, Piraeus.
Tel: 01/42 80 001
Fax: 01/42 83 526 (preferable, as the voice line is usually engaged)
Dodecanese Hydrofoils, Platía Kýprou, Mandhráki Harbour, Rhodes. Tel: 0241/24 000.

Private Transport

Cars

Having a car in Greece enables you to reach a lot of otherwise inaccessible corners of the country.

At the time of writing, EU-registered cars are no longer stamped into your passport upon entry to the country, can circulate freely, and are exempt from road tax as long as this has been paid in the home country. However, you are not allowed to sell the vehicle. Non-EU nationals will find that a bizarre litany of rules apply to importing cars, chief among them that you must re-export the car when you depart, or have it sealed by Customs in an off-road facility. Circulating, you are allowed an initial six-month period of stay, plus a nine-month extension if you find a guarantor, after which the car is again liable to sealing, or re-export for a minimum of six months before re-entry.

It is suggested that visiting foreign motorists have an international driver's licence (available only through the automobile club in your home country; ELPA in Greece has ceased issuing them), but in practice it is not required. Similarly, with the advent of the single European market, insurance Green Cards are no longer required, though you should check with your home insurer about the need for any supplementary premiums – many policies now include pan-European cover anyway.

Greek traffic control and signals are basically the same as in the rest of continental Europe. However, Greek driving has little in common with driving in Frankfurt or Oslo. Translate Zorba on wheels, if you will. Motorways speeds are routinely in excess of the nominal 100kph (62 mph) limits, and drivers overtake with abandon. A red light is often considered not so much an obligation as a suggestion, and drivers flashing lights at you means the opposite of what it does in the UK: here, it means "*I'm* coming through". Accordingly, Greece has the highest accident rate in Europe after Portugal, so drive defensively.

Despite all this, Greece has a mandatory seatbelt law, and children under 10 are not allowed to sit in the front seat. Every car must also carry a first-aid kit in the boot.

Both leaded and unleaded petrol are readily available throughout Greece, though filling up after dark can be difficult. Most garages close around 7pm and, although a rota system operates in larger towns, it is often difficult to find out which station is open. International petrol stations operated by companies like BP, Mobil and Shell take credit cards, but Greek ones often don't.

Motorcycles, Bicycles and Scooters

On most Greek islands and in many mainland tourist areas, you'll find agencies that rent small motorcycles, various types of scooters, 50cc and under, and even mountain bikes. On the smaller islands these are certainly the way to go.

They give you the freedom to wander where you will, and weekly rates are reasonable. For any bike of over 50cc, helmets and a motorcycle driving licence are both

Athens' Rush Hour

Drive at your peril in Athens during the rush hour. The twin perils of traffic jams and pollution reached such heights in the capital that a law was introduced: on even days of the month only cars with even-numbered licence plates are allowed in the centre; on odd days only those with odd-numbered plates. This has, unfortunately, done little to improve the congestion, noise and smog in Athens, as many families have two cars (one of each type of number plate) and alternate according to the day of the week.

Breakdowns

The Greek Automobile Association (ELPA) offers a breakdown service for motorists, which is free to AA/RAC members (on production of their membership cards). Phone 104 for assistance.

theoretically required, and occasionally these rules are enforced.

Before you set off, make sure the bike of whichever sort works by taking it for a test spin down the street. Brakes in particular are badly set, lights may need new fuses or bulbs, and spark-plugs get fouled – ask for a spare and the small wrench to change them. Otherwise, you may get stuck with a lemon or, worse, and be held responsible for its malfunctioning when you return it.

Reputable agencies now often furnish you with a phone number for a breakdown pickup service. Above all, don't take unnecessary chances, like riding two on a bike designed for one. More than one holiday in Greece has been ruined by a serious moped accident.

Cruises

Apparently one in six of all visitors to Greece embarks on an Aegean cruise. Cruises can range from 1-day trips to the Saronic Gulf islands, to 21-day packages on a "floating hotel" departing from Piraeus taking in Gibraltar and Morocco. Many people elect for the 7-day excursion, which offers an opportunity to see a couple of

Car Rental

Renting a car in Greece is relatively expensive in comparison with other European countries, owing to high insurance premiums and import duties. Prices vary according to the type of car, season and length of rental and do not include VAT at 18 percent. Payment can, and often must, be made with a major credit card. A full home-country driving licence and/or International Driving Permit is required and you must be at least 21 years old, sometimes 25.

In the UK and North America, you can book a car in advance through a major international chain such as Hertz or Avis. But there are many reputable, smaller chains, some particular to Greece, that offer a comparable service at lower rates. In Athens most are on Syngroú Avenue, or you can call:
European,
36-38 Syngroú Ave,
01/92 46 777
Reliable,
3 Syngroú Ave,
01/92 49 000
Just,
43 Syngroú Ave,
01/92 39 104

islands in the Cyclades, a few Dodecanese islands, and a stop-over in Turkey for good measure. Accommodation, prices and standards vary widely and it might be an idea to shop around for a good price.

Ticket agencies in Athens are the places to visit, with cruise opportunities prominently displayed in windows. (Although, if you have ever been at Mýkonos harbour when the ships arrive and watched the frantic preparations of shop managers adjusting their prices upwards, it may change your mind about a cruise entirely.)

The most comprehensive company is Royal Olympic Cruises, formed by the merger of Epirotiki and Sun Lines. It is accustomed to dealing with foreigners, and offers four-day, seven-day and 14-day cruises. Details can be found from any travel agent or by contacting Royal Olympic's headquarters at Aktí Miaoúli 18538, Piraeus, tel: 429 1000.

London-based Swan Hellenic

Cruises offer all-inclusive holidays on large luxury liners, with guest speakers instructing passengers on anything from archeology to marine biology. Swan Hellenic are at 77 New Oxford Street, London WC1A 1PP, tel: (020) 7800 2200.

Yacht Charter

Chartering a yacht is one of the more exotic ways of island-hopping in Greece. It is by no means cheap, although renting a boat with a group of friends may not far exceed the price of renting rooms every night for the same number of people.

Depending on your nautical qualifications and your taste for autonomy, you can either take the helm yourself or let a hired crew do so for you. There are over 1,000 yachts available for charter in Greece, all of which are registered and inspected by the Ministry of the Merchant Marine. For more information about chartering contact:
The Hellenic Professional Yacht

Owners' Association
43 Freattýdhos Street,
Zéa Marina, Piraeus.
Tel: 45 26 335.
The Greek Yacht Brokers and Consultants' Association
36 Alkyónis Street,
Paleó Fáliron, Athens.
Tel: 98 16 582.

Kaïkia

Apart from large and medium-sized ferries, most of which carry cars, there are swarms of small kaïkia (caiques) which in season offer inter-island excursions pitched mostly at day-trippers. Since they are essentially chartered by travel agencies, they are exempt from Ministry of Transport fare controls and can be very pricey if used as one-way ferries from, say, Sámos to Pátmos. The stereotypical transfer by friendly fisherman is, alas, a thing of the past; never comfortable at the best of times, it is now actually illegal – knowing this, skippers quote exorbitant prices if approached.

Spelling & Place Names

This book has employed a transliteration system which attempts to guarantee proper pronunciation by foreigners as much as it represents, letter for letter, the Greek alphabet in Roman characters. If you find a place name that is unfamiliar, check on more than one map or ask at a local ticket office if the destination has another name or spelling.

Some examples include:
● **Sýntagma Square** in Athens is also known as **Sindagma**, **Platía Syntágmatos** or (in English) **Constitution Square**.
● The island of **Lésvos** is known as **Lesbos**, **Mytilene**, or **Mytilíni**.
● **Corfu** can be called by its Greek name **Kérkyra**
● **Itháki** can be known by its English name **Ithaca**.

Where to Stay

How To Choose

There is a range of accommodation in Greece, from deluxe hotels to student hotels. Listed are a sample of different categories across the country.

On the islands and in many parts of the mainland, another kind of cheap lodging is renting private rooms (*dhomátia*). These are rented out by local residents at prices controlled by the tourist police.

In general, when looking for any kind of accommodation, local tourist offices or, in their absence, the Tourist Police, can be of considerable help. If you're in a fix, you can enquire at their office. If you'd like to make a reservation or arrangement in advance, call them and they'll often be able to help you out.

Hotels in Athens

$$$ Divani-Palace Acropolis
19–25 Parthenonos, Athens 11742
Tel: 922 9650
Fax: 921 4993
Luxurious hotel a few blocks down from the Acropolis, with swimming pool, restaurant and bar. Often has tour groups.

$$$ Grande Bretagne
Syntagma Square, Athens 10563
Tel: 330 0000
Fax: 322 8034
This is the grand old lady of Athenian hotels, the posh venue for innumerable political, cultural and society events. If you get in here on a package deal, fine, otherwise it is very expensive. Be sure your room faces the street, not the inner courtyard. The GB Corner is a wonderfully comfortable place for meals.

$$$ Park
10 Alexandras Avenue, Athens 10682
Tel: 883 2711–19
Fax: 823 8420
Across the street from the Pedion tou Areos park and conveniently near the National Archaeological Museum.

$$$ St Geroge Lycabettus
2 Kleomenous Street, Dexameni, Kolonaki, Athens 106 75
Tel: 729 0711–19
Fax: 729 0439
On the slopes of Lycabettus in the comfortable neighbourhood of Kolonaki with a fine view down over Athens towards the Acropolis. Small swimming pool on the roof.

$$$ Amalia
10 Amalias Avenue, Athens 10557
Tel: 323 7301–9
Fax: 323 8792
Not overly posh but a thoroughly comfortable place to stay near Syndagma Square.

$$$ Electra Palace
18 Nikodimou Street, Athens 10557
Tel: 324 1401–7
Fax: 324 1875
In Pláka with a roof bar and swimming pool with a sharply angled view of the Acropolis.

$$ Christina
15 Petmezá Street and Kallirói Avenue, Athens 11743
Tel: 921 5353
Fax: 361 8174
Comfortable hotel on the edge of the neighborhood of Koukaki.

$$ Plaka
7 Kapnikaréas Street, Athens 10556
Tel: 322 2096-7
Fax: 322 2412
The bright white lobby is impressive, as is the roof garden's wonderful view towards the Acropolis. In Pláka near the Roman agora.

$$ Achilleas
21 Lekka Street, Athens 10562
Tel: 323 3197
Despite the entrance off the street, this is good value. Completely renovated in 1995. Handy for both Pláka and Syndagma Square.

For details of the Greek Tourist Authority's hotel classification system see Hotel Categories on page 337.

Price Guide

Price categories are based on the cost of a double room for one night in the high season:
$$$ Expensive 35–60,000dr
$$ Moderate 12–35,000dr
$ Inexpensive under 5,000dr
– 12,000 dr

$$ Acropolis View
10 Webster Street, Athens 117422.
Tel: 921 7303–5
Fine small hotel on a quiet side street near the Herodes Atticus theatre, with some rooms and a rooftop bar facing the Acropolis. In the upper area of Koukaki.

$$ Athenian Inn
22 Charitos Street, Athens 10675
Tel: 723 8097
Quiet location three blocks from Kolonaki Square. Lawrence Durrell wrote in the guest book, "At last, the ideal Athens hotel, good and modest in scale but perfect in service and goodwill." This is still the case.

$$ Attalos
20 Athinas Street, Athens 10554
Tel: 321 2801–3
Fax: 324 3124
Two blocks from Monastiraki Square, friendly and attentive staff, good value. Athinas Street is busy during the day but quiet at night. Rooms are plain but clean. The roof garden has fine views of the city and Acropolis.

$$ Austria
7 Mousson, Athens 11742
Tel: 923 5151
Owned by an Austrian-Greek family, this hotel is near the Acropolis on a quiet street, with front rooms overlooking the park. The view of the Acropolis from the roof is marvellous. In the upper area of Koukaki.

$$ Museum
16 Bouboulinas and Tositsa, Athens 10682
Tel: 360 5611–3

Price Guide

Price categories are based on the cost of a double room for one night in the high season:
$$$ Expensive 35–60,000dr
$$ Moderate 12–35,000dr
$ Inexpensive under 5,000dr
– 12,000 dr

For details of the Greek Tourist Authority's hotel classification system see Hotel Categories on page 337.

Fax: 380 0507
Conveniently located one block from archaeological museum.
$$ Nefeli
16 Ypereidou Street, Athens 10558
Tel: 322 8044
Small, clean, well-run hotel in a quiet area of Plaka.
$ Pella Inn
Ermou and 1 Karaiskaki, Athens 10554
Tel: 321 2229
Family-run hotel between Monastiráki Square and the Thisseion trolley station. By no means posh, but clean and friendly. The upper floors facing Ermou Street have a wonderful view of the ancient Greek agora and Acropolis.
$ Tempi
29 Aiolou, Athens 10551
Tel: 321 3175
Low-budget alternative, three blocks north of Monastiráki Square. Because it is a pedestrian street, Aiolou is quiet at night. The rooms are clean and the staff friendly. Laundry room.
$ Marble House
35 A. Zinni Street, Athens 11741
Tel: 923 4058
Inexpensive, clean, friendly atmosphere. Two blocks from Syngrou Avenue and the Olympic Airlines office. No air-conditioning, but with powerful ceiling fans.
$ Hostel Aphrodite
12 Einardou Street, Athens 10440
Tel: 881 0589
E-mail: hostel-aphrodite@ath.
forthnet.gr
Clean, unpretentious and friendly, this small hotel is a good deal.

Slightly off the beaten track but conveniently near the trolley station in Victoria Square. They have a pleasant basement bar and an excellent deal on inter-island boat passes.
$ Student Inn
16 Kydathenaion, Athens 10558
Tel: 324 4808
Inexpensive rooms in Pláka.

Roúmeli & Thessaly

Arachova
$$ Xenia Hotel
Arachova, Viotia 32004
Tel: (0267) 31 230
Fax: (0267) 32 175
The standard "modern" large cement block construction, but conveniently located with parking in the village towards Delphi.

Delphi
$$$ Amalia
Apolonos, Delphi, Fokis 33054
Tel: (0265) 82 101
Fax: (0265) 82 290
The largest and most upmarket Delphi hotel, with swimming pool.
$$$ Vouzas
1 Pavlou & Friderikis, Delphi, Fokis 33054
Tel: (0265) 82 232
Fax: (0265) 82 033
The first hotel on the left as you enter the village, with fine views down over the olive-tree valley.
$$$ Xenia
Delphi, Fokis 33054
Tel: (0265) 82 151
Designed by one of the great leaders of modern architecture in Greece, now a bit faded but comfortable, with verandas and good views down the valley.

Galaxídhi
$$ Galaxídhi
11 Syngrou, Galaxidhi 33052
Tel: (0265) 41 850
Fax: (0265) 41 02 6
Family-run hotel with pleasant garden for breakfast, 60 metres/yards from the port.
$$ Ganymede
E. Vlami, Galaxidhi 33052
Tel: (0265) 41 32 8
Beautiful, and expensive small hotel

run by idiosyncratic owner, about 500 yards from the port.

Vólos
$$ Aigli
24 Argonafton, Volos 38333, Magnissia.
Tel: (0421) 25 69 1
Fax: (0421) 33 00 6
The best hotel in town, moderately expensive.
$$ Admyttos
5 Ath. Diakou, Volos 38333, Magnissia
Tel: (0421) 21 11 7
Medium-range reasonable.
$$ Philippos
9 Solonos, Volos 38333, Magnissia
Tel: (0421) 37 60 7
Fax: (0421) 39 55 0
Medium-range reasonable.

Makrinítsa
$$ Archontiko Mousli
Makrinitsa 37011, Magnissia
Tel: (0428) 99 22 8
$$$ Archontiko Xiradaki
Makrinitsa 37011, Magnissia
Tel: (0428) 99 25 0
$$ Archontiko Repana
Makrinítsa 37011, Magnissia
Tel: (0428) 99 54 8
All traditional mansions reworked as comfortable hotels.

Zagorá
$$$ Ta Archontiká tou Konstantinídi
Zagorá 37011, Magnissia
Tel: (0426) 23 391
Fax: (0426) 22 671
Wonderfully restored mansion with a lovely garden.

Tsangaráda
$$$ Kastaniés
Aghios Stefanos, Tsangaráda 37012
Tel: (0426) 49135
Fax: (0426) 49 16 9
Only five rooms. Luxurious, very comfortable, beautiful, with home-made bread and locally made jam served at breakfast.
$$ Konáki
Aghia Paraskevi, Tsangaráda 37012, Magnissia
Tel: (0426) 49 48 1
Pleasant and off the main road.

Aghios Ioánnis

This is a popular spot and you may well not find a room, despite the many hotels here. For assistance, phone the tourist office, tel: (0426) 32 218.

$$$ Aloe
Aghios Ioánnis 37012, Magnissia
Tel: (0426) 31 24 1
Fax: (0426) 31 34 1
By the water.

$ Anessis
Aghios Ioánnis 37012, Magnissia
Tel: (0426) 31 12 3
Fax: (0426) 31 22 3
Also by the water, but more reasonably priced.

Miliés

$$$ Archontikó Philipídi
Miliés 37010, Magnissia
Tel: (0423) 86 71 4
Refurbished traditional mansion.

$$$ Paliós Stathmós
Milies 37010, Magnissia
Tel: (0423) 86 42 5
Pleasant hotel converted from an old train station.

Vyzítsa

$$$ Archontikó Kóntou
Vyzítsa 37010, Magnissia
Tel: (0423) 86 79 3
Fax (In Athens): (01) 8065341
The only single rooms the Archontikó Kóntou has have bathrooms down the hall; the price for these rooms is 12,000dr (including obligatory breakfast charge of 1,000 dr).

$$$ Archontikó Vafeiádi
Vyzítsa 37010
Tel: (0423) 86 76 5
Fax: (0423) 86 04 5
The Archontikó Vafeiádi does not have single rooms.

Furnished Apartments in Athens

$$$ Andromeda
22 Timoléontos Vássou Street
Athens 11521
Tel: 646 6361–2, 643 7302–4

$$$ Ava
9 Lyssikrátous Street
Athens 10558
Tel: 323 6618

$$$ Lion
7 Evzónon Street

$$$ Archontikó Karayiannopoúlou
Vyzítsa 37010, Magnissia
Tel: (0423) 86 71 1
All comfortably refurbished traditional mansions. No single rooms.

Aghios Lavréndis

$$ Kéntavros
Aghios Lavréndis 38500, Magnissia
Tel: (0428) 96 22 4
Fax: (0428) 96 10 0
Small hotel in a quiet village.

Kalambáka

$$$ Amalía
Kalambáka 42200, Tríkala
Tel: (0432) 75 21 6
Large, fully equipped hotel with swimming pool. This is the most plush hotel in the area. No single rooms.

Kastráki

2km (about a mile) northwest of Kalambáki, a pleasant small village with several hotels and rooming houses.
$$ Kastráki
Patriarchou Dimitriou Street, Kastráki 42200, Tríkala

Athens 11521
Tel: 724 8722–4
$$$ Perli
4 Arnís Street
Athens 11528
Tel: 724 8794–8
$$ Egnatia
64 Trítis Septemvríou Street
Athens 10433
Tel: 822 7807

Tel: (0432) 75 33 5
Fax (0432) 75 33 5
New small hotel with beautiful view of both the rocks and the valley.
$$ Ziogas Rooming House
Kastráki 42200
Tel: (0432) 24 03 7
Beautifully cared for, less expensive.

Epirus & Northwest

Messolóngi
$$ Theoxenia
2 Tourlidos Street,
Messolónghi 30200
Tel: (0631) 22 49 3
Fax: (0631) 22 23 0
Large hotel 450 metres (500 yards) outside town on the water with bar and restaurant.
$$ Avra
5 Har. Trikoupi, Messológhi 30200
Tel: (0631) 22 28 4
Small hotel near the central square and restaurants.

Vonitsa
$$ Bel Mare
Vonitsa 30002, Aitoloakarnania
Tel: (0643) 22 39 4
Fax: (0643) 23 55 8

Hotel Categories

The Greek authorities have six categories for hotels. Ratings are not entirely logical, however: although the letters are supposed to represent the hotels' facilities, a swimming pool or tennis court could place an establishment in the A or Luxury bracket even though in every other respect it

has indifferent facilities.

The following general principles apply, though:
Luxury, A and B class hotels all have private bathrooms. Most C-class hotels have bathrooms, while D and E-class rooms sometimes come with bathroom but will more likely just have a

shower. E may not even have that.
Luxury and A-class hotels must have a bar and restaurant and offer a full choice of breakfasts. B and C class will provide a buffet breakfast in a separate dining room, but classes below that will often offer little better than a bread roll, jam and coffee.

Medium-sized hotel on the shore near the castle.

Ioánnina

$$ Galaxy
Platía Pyrrou
Tel: (0651) 25 05 6
Fax: (0651) 30 27 4
Comfortable and quiet (a rarity here), mountain views from the balconies, but you pay for the privilege.
$$ Kamares
Zalakósta 74
Tel: (0651) 79 34 8
An old mansion restored as an inn, situated in a quiet neighbourhood near the citadel.

Métsovo

$ Athens/Athenai
Near Central Plaza
Tel: (0656) 41 33 2
The first hotel in Métsovo (1925), and one of the first in the province, the converted en-suite rooms represent an unbelievable bargain; excellent ground-floor restaurant (see p. 355) completes the feel of a good French country inn.
$ Bitounis
Main street
Tel: (0656) 41 21 7
Fax: (0656) 41 54 5
More luxurious digs, managed by energetic, English-speaking brothers long resident in London.

Zagóri

$$ Pension Koulis
Megálo Pápingo
Tel: (0653) 41 13 8
The original village inn, converted in 1993 to en suite rooms; if you're off to the mountains, the Hristodhoulos family here can book you into the Astráka mountain hut.
$ O Dhias
Mikró Pápingo
Tel: (0653) 41 25 7
Another excellent renovated inn, more purpose-built than Koulis; the proprietor is again trekker-friendly, as mountaineering is the main enterprise hereabouts.

Párga

$$ Galini
orchard at edge of Párga

Tel: (0684) 31 5 81
Fax: (0684) 32 2 21
Quite possibly the largest rooms in Epirus, renovated early in the 1990s. Come off-peak season; otherwise the hotel – and town – are swamped by package tours.

Kastoriá

$ Xenia Limnis/Xenia du Lac
Platía Dhexamenís
Tel: (0467) 22 5 65
Fax: (0467) 26 3 91
Most of the Xenia chain is not especially recommendable; this, by far the quietest and still one of the more comfortable hotels in town, is an exception. It's just opposite the worthwhile Byzantine Museum.

Northeast

Litóhoro

$$ Myrto
Aghíou Nikláou
Tel: (0352) 81 39 8
Fax: (0352) 82 29 8
Reckoned the best and quietest of several hotels in the "gateway" to Mt Ólymbos, and not overpriced.

Édhessa

$$ Katarraktes
Near the cascade
Tel: (0381) 22 30 0
Fax: (0381) 27 23 7
The best in Édhessa, with an unbeatable location.

Sithonia

$ Haus Sakis
Toróni
Tel: (0375) 51 26 1
The Teutonic name tips you off to the predominant clientele. Rooms are decent and the ground-floor restaurant is surprisingly good.

Ammouliani

$ Gripos
Ághios Gheórghios beach,
Ammouliani islet,
Áthos peninsula
Tel: (0377) 51 04 9
Certainly the most characterful inn in Halkidhikí, with its antique-furnished, terracotta-tile-floored rooms and huge balconies. The

owner farms pheasants and serves *mezédhes* by the pool – not that you really need it, with one of the best beaches in northern Greece on your doorstep.

Olymbiádha

$$ Liotopi
Tel: (0376) 51 36 2
Fax: (0376) 51 25 5
Quiet, garden-set hotel at the south end of this low-key coastal resort, with the twin attractions of Próti Ammoundhiá beach and ancient Stageira, Aristotle's birthplace, close by.

Kavála

$$ Esperia
Erythroú Stavroú 44
Tel: (051) 22 96 21
Fax: (051) 22 06 21
Most Kavála hotels are pricey and noisy; this one's affordable, and has both double-glazing and air conditioning.

Fanári Beach, Thrace

$$ Fanári
Tel: (0535) 31 30 0
Fax: (0535) 31 38 8
Overnighting in either Xánthi or Komotiní appeals to few and is expensive in any event; this reasonable hotel, equidistant to both, is the ideal solution.

Alexandhroúpoli

$$ Lido
Paleológou 15
Tel: (0551) 28 80 8
Enormous, en suite rooms on a quiet street, even though the building is over 30 years old, make this a good choice.

Dhadhiá

$ Ecotourism Hostel
1km (about half a mile) beyond Dhadhiá village
Tel: (0554) 32 26 3
Run by the visitors' centre for the WWF's Dhadhiá Wildlife Refuge, each of the well-furnished en suite rooms has been given bird names rather than numbers. An essential base if you hope to rise early enough in summer to catch the local raptors soaring.

Thessaloníki

$$$ Makedonia Palace
Meg. Alexandrou Street,
Thessaloníki 54640
Tel: (031) 83 75 20–9
Fax: (031) 83 79 48
Just 600 metres (550 yards) from
the city centre. All rooms have a
balcony are there are specially
designed business rooms available.
All luxury facilities.

$$ Capitol
8 Monastiríou Street,
Thessaloníki 54629
Tel: (031) 51 62 21
Fax: (031) 51 74 53
Superior first-class hotel situated in
the heart of Thessaloníki noted for
its grill room.

$$$ Electra Palace
5a Aristotélous Square,
Thessaloníki 54624
Tel: (031) 23 22 21/30
Fax: (031) 23 59 47
Another central hotel with luxury
facilities. The architecture reflects a
Byzantine style.

$$ Capsis
18 Monastiríou Street
Thessaloníki 54629
Tel: (031) 52 13 21–9
Fax: (031) 51 05 55
In the city centre. This hotel offers
all the usual luxury facilities
including a roof garden, gym,
swimming pool and sauna.

$$ Metropolitan
65 Vassilísis Olgas and Fleming
Streets, Thessaloníki 54642
Tel: (031) 82 42 21 [8 lines]
Fax: (031) 84 97 62
Olympic Airways bus stop in front of
the hotel, all first-class facilities.

$$ Palace
12 Tsimiskí Street,
Thessaloníki 54624
Tel: (031) 257 400
Good value, enormous rooms,
underpriced for its class.

$$ Philippion
Kedhrinós Lófos, Thessaloníki
5 km from the city centre
Tel: (031) 20 33 20–22
Fax: (031) 21 85 28
Located in the forest of Seih Sou,
5 km (3 miles) from the centre of
Thessaloníki and 15 minutes' from
the airport (free shuttle bus to/from
the city). Excellent terrace view.

$$ Victoria
13 Langádha Street,
Thessaloníki 54629
Tel: (031) 52 24 21–5
Fax: (031) 51 28 92
Located in the commerical district
near the international fair and its
conference centre, museums and
ancient monuments.

$$ ABC Hotel
41 Angeláki Street,
Sindriváni Square
Thessaloníki 54621
Tel: (031) 26 54 21 [5 lines]
Fax: (031) 27 65 42
In the centre, close to the
International Fair. All rooms have
been recently renovated.

$$ Amalia
33 Ermoú Street,
Thessaloníki 54624
Tel: (031) 26 83 21
Fax: (031) 23 33 56
A bit overpriced, but reputable.

$$ Continental
5 Komninón Street,
Thessaloníki 54624
Tel: (031) 22 89 17
Fairly quiet Art Deco building,
somewhat erratic service.

$$ Esperia
Olympou 58, Thessaloníki
Tel: (031) 26 93 21
Fax: (031) 26 94 57
Recently refurbished, double
glazing, hill views.

$$ Park
81 Íonos Dhragoúmi Street,
Thessaloníki 54630
Tel: (031) 52 41 21–4
Fax: (031) 52 41 93
Modern and sterile, but comfy
rooms some with sea view.

$$ Pella
65 Íonos Dhragoúmi Street,
Thessaloníki 54630
Tel: (031) 52 42 21–4
Fax: (031) 52 42 23
In the heart of Thessaloníki. Very
good, popular with archaeologists
and older tourists.

$$ Telioni
16 Aghíou. Dhimitríou Street,
Thessaloníki 54630
Tel: (031) 52 78 25/6
Situated in the centre of the city. All
rooms have colour TV and private
bath. Cafeteria-bar and breakfast
buffet.

Price Guide

Price categories are based on
the cost of a double room for one
night in the high season:
$$$ Expensive 35–60,000dr
$$ Moderate 12–35,000dr
$ Inexpensive under 5,000dr
– 12,000 dr

For details of the Greek Tourist
Authority's hotel classification
system see Hotel Categories on
page 337.

$$ Tourist
Mitropóleos 21, Thessaloníki
Tel: (031) 27 63 35
Fax: (031) 22 68 65
High-ceiling, Belle Epoque pile
that's deservedly popular; officially
D-class, because very limited
communal areas, but C-class room
standard.

$$ Vergina
19 Monastiríou Street,
Thessaloníki 54627
Tel: (031) 51 60 21
In the centre of Thessaloníki.
Recently renovated rooms with air-
conditioning; business class rooms
also available.

Panórama

$$$ Nepheli
1 Komninón Street,
Panórama 55236
Tel/fax: (031) 34 20 02
Small roof garden, nightclub,
convention facilities, parking.

$$$ Panórama
26 Analípseos Street,
Panórama 55236
Tel: (031) 34 12 66
Fax: 34 12 29
Built in the late 1960s this hotel
has all the usual facilities for its
class.

Peloponnese

Arhá Kórinthos

$ Shadow
Approach road, Arhá Kórinthos
Tel: (0741) 31 48 1
Rear rooms at this simple but en
suite inn, with their views over the
lush plain, are the best; some noise

Price Guide

Price categories are based on the cost of a double room for one night in the high season:
$$$ Expensive 35–60,000dr
$$ Moderate 12–35,000dr
$ Inexpensive under 5,000dr – 12,000 dr

For details of the Greek Tourist Authority's hotel classification system see Hotel Categories on page 337.

from live music at weekends in ground-floor restaurant.

Mykínes
$$ Belle Helene
Through road, Mykínes
Tel: (0751) 76 22 5
Alias "House of Schliemann", as the building housed the archeologist during his work here. Quite reasonable, with the feel of an English country B&B, since preservation considerations mean no en suite baths. Attached restaurant has guestbook with signatures of the great and infamous.

Olymbía
$$ Pelops
Varelá 2
Tel: (0624) 22 54 3
Fax: (0624) 22 21 3
Quiet location opposite a church, with a loyal repeat clientele (unusual in a "ruins" village) who appreciate the friendly Australian-Greek management.

Paralía Ástrous
$ Chryssi Akti
Seafront
Tel: (0755) 51294
Maybe not the most comfortable hotel in town – and with hospital decor – but the rooms are large, en suite, reasonably priced and have the further advantage of looking right out onto the beach.

Stemnítsa
$$ Trikoloneio
Tel: (0795) 81 297
Two 19th-century mansions mated

to a modern annexe have bred this underrated C-class hotel with an excellent attached restaurant; the best standard of accommodation for some distance around.

Koróni
$$ Auberge de la Plage
Zánga beach
Tel: (0725) 22 40 1
Fax: (0725) 22 50 8
No prizes for its 1970s modernist architecture, but an incomparable setting overlooking the sand and sea.

Areópoli
$ Pyrgos Kapetanakou
Máni
Tel: (0753) 51 23 3
One of the better executed EOT restoration projects, this three-storey tower, set in mature gardens, comprises various sized rooms, with communal balconies and a ground-floor refectory.

Ghythio
$$ Aktaion
Vassiléos Pávlou 39
Tel: (0733)22 29 4
Refurbished neo-classical pile at the north end of the quay; some traffic noise, but all balconied rooms have sea view and air conditioning.

Néos Mystrás
$ Vyzantion
Tel: (0731) 83 30 9
Fax: (0731) 20 01 9
This 1960s-vintage B-class hotel is perhaps showing its age, but bathrooms have full sized tubs, and most rooms enjoy an unbeatable view of the Byzantine ruins.

Monemvasía
$$$ Malvasia
Tel: (0732) 61 32 3
Fax: (0732) 61 7 22
The scattered units of this restoration complex are the best of several in the town; each room, furnished to a high standard in wood, marble and bright textiles, is unique, with features such as fireplaces and private balconies. Unit sizes vary from simple doubles to a family-sized apartment.

Náfplion
$$ Byron
Plátonos 2
Tel: (0752) 22 35 2
Fax: (0752) 26 33 8
Occupies an old stucco mansion at the top end of town; top-floor rooms have better views and the odd balcony, though bathrooms could be better. Ground floor bar/breakfast salon, plus small terrace.
$ Epidavros
Kokkínou 2
Tel: (0752) 27 54 1
Another renovation job, all pine floors and coffered ceilings, and more affordable than the Byron – but no views as it's in the flatlands.

NE Aegean Islands

Samothráki
$$ Xenia
Sanctuary of the Great Gods, Paleópoli
Tel: (0551) 41166
Not state-of-the-art accommodation by any means, but this old stone-clad, one-storey outfit, originally built to accommodate archeologists, is much in demand – no wonder, poised as it is on a knoll between sea and ruins. Price of room includes breakfast.

$$ Kaviros
Thermá
Tel: (0551) 98 27 7
Fax: (0551) 98 27 8
Pricey 1980s-built hotel under the plane trees at this spa resort; well-landscaped and traffic-free.

Thássos
$ Alkyon
Seafront, Liménas
Tel: (0593) 22 14 8
Fax: (0593) 23 66 2
Spacious rooms, with harbour or garden view, plus gregarious Anglo-Greek management and afternoon tea, make this a firm favourite with English-speaking independent travellers. Open much of the year.
$ Myroni
Back of town. Liménas
Tel: (0593) 23 25 6
Fax: (0593) 22 13 2
Very well priced and comfortable

spot with a large breakfast salon; orientated towards independent travellers, also with a cheaper annexe.

$ Thassos Inn
Top of Panayía village
Tel: (0593) 61 61 2
Fax: (0593) 61 02 7
Quiet except for the sound of water in runnels all around, this modern building in traditional style has most rooms facing the sea. Open much of the year.

Límnos

$$$ Akti Myrina
Just north of Mýrina
Tel: (0254) 22 31 0
Fax: (0254) 22 35 2
Elegant, very expensive bungalows with private beach and all activities to hand; try not to get booked into the ugly new annexe.

$$ Ifestos
Andhróni district, Mýrina
Tel: (0254) 24 960
Fax: (0254) 23 62 3
Attractive, quietly located C-class a block or two behind Romeïkós Yialós town beach.

$$ Villa Aphrodite
Platý beach
Tel: (0254) 23 14 1
Fax: (0254) 25 03 1
Run by returned South African Greeks, this comfortable small hotel sits amidst well-landscaped grounds, with a poolside restaurant (supper only) and sumptuous buffet breakfasts.

Lésvos

$$ Villa 1900
P. Vostáni 24, Mytilíni town
Tel: (0251) 23 44 8
Fax: (0251) 28 03 4
Rooms in a restored neo-classical mansion with period furnishings and ceiling murals.

$$ Vatera Beach
Vaterá
Tel: (0252) 61 21 2
Fax: (0252) 61 16 4
This rambling, well-run hotel with Greek and American management, is situated just opposite the best beach on the island; good attached restaurant out front, loyal repeat clientele.

$$ Olive Press
Shore road, Mólyvos
Tel: (0253) 71205
Fax: (0252) 71647
Converted from an old olive mill – look for the smokestack – this stone-clad hotel offers a mix of simple rooms and self-catering studios arranged around a courtyard.

$$ Clara
Avláki district, Pétra
Tel: (0253) 41 53 2
Fax: (0253) 41 53 5
A bit isolated, but designer-furnished rooms of this pastel-shaded bungalow complex look north to Pétra and Mólyvos. Tennis courts, pool and short walk to a beach.

Híos

$ Kyma
Evghenías Handhrí, Híos Town
Tel: (0271) 44 50 0
A converted neo-classical mansion with a modern extension; family management, willing service and good breakfasts in a painted-ceiling salon.

$$ Perivoli
Kámbos
Tel: (0271) 31 51 3
Fax: (0271) 32 04 2
A tasteful renovation project utilizing an old mansion in the aristocratic Kámbos district.

$$$ Volissos Houses
Volissós village
Tel: (0274) 21 12 8
Fax: (0274) 21 01 3
Quite stunning old-house restoration project, British-built and managed; currently 5 self-contained, self-catering units, but set to grow to 7 in the year 2000.

Sámos

$$ Olympia Beach
Kokkári
Tel: (0273) 92 42 0
Fax: (0273) 92 45 7
Small hotel facing the west beach, not usually blocked out by tours.

$ Vathi
Neapóli district, Áno Vathý
Tel: (0273) 28124
Fax: (0273) 24045
Slight remoteness is offset by large view rooms, a small plunge-pool

and welcoming management; a favourite of independent travellers.

$$ Galaxy
Angéou 1, Katsoúni district, Vathý
Tel: (0273) 22 66 5
Garden surroundings, a fair-sized pool, ordinary rooms; takes packages but there are often vacancies.

$ Galini Hotel
Pythagorio
Tel: (0273) 61 16 7
Modern, small, quiet hotel near the top end of town, welcomes (unusually here) walk-in clientele.

Ikaría

$$ Messakti Village
Messakhtí beach, Armenistís
Tel: (0275) 71 33 1
Fax: (0275) 71 33 0
Imposing communal areas and large private terraces compensate for rather plain rooms at this self-catering complex; the large pool is a necessity, as the sea here can be dangerously rough.

Sporades Islands/Évvia

Skiáthos

$$ Boúrtzi Hotel
Skíathos Town,
Skiathos 37002
Tel: (0427) 21304
Fax: (0427) 23243

$ Póthos Hotel
Evangelistrias,
Skíathos Town,
Skíathos 37002
Tel: (0427) 22694
Both clean, simple and moderately priced.

$$ Troúlos Bay
Koukounariés, Troúlos
Tel: (0427) 49390
Fax: (0427) 49218
Attractive and comfortable, on the beach. No single rooms.

$$ Atrium Hotel
Platanias, Skíathos 37002.
Tel: (0427) 49345
Fax (0427) 49444
Casual elegance, with traditional architecture, resembles monastery. Chic, beautiful.

Skópelos
$$ Kyr Sótos Hotel
Skópelos town, Skopelos 37003
Tel: (0424) 22 54 9
Remodelled family house set on the
waterfront, inexpensive and casual
with tiny rooms. No single rooms.
$$$ Skópelos Village
Skópelos 37003
Tel: (0424) 22 51 7
Spacious maisonettes on the far
side of the harbour with pool and
playground.
$$ Adrina Beach
Pánormos
Tel: (0424) 23373
Casual elegance, with private
beach. No single rooms.

Alónissos
$$ Paradise Hotel
Patitíri, Alónissos 3700
Tel: (0424) 65160
Fax: (0424) 65161
Has pool and close to the rocks for
sea bathing.
$ Liadromia
Patitíri
Tel: (0242) 65521
Fax: (0424) 65096
Private traditional house on
peninsula overlooking the sea.
Carefully refurbished in 1998.
Garden. No single rooms.
$$ Nereídes
Tel: (0424) 65 64 3
Fax: (0424) 65 09 6
Studio apartments with pool. No
single rooms.

Skýros
$$ King Likomides
Linariá 34007, Skýros
Tel: (0222) 96 24 9
Fax: (0222) 93 41 2
Small hotel by the pier where the
ferries dock. Small fridges in
rooms.
$$ Linariá Bay
Linariá
Tel: (0222) 96 27 4–5
Small white hotel on the
promontory above the pier. Small
fridges in rooms. Moderately priced,
slightly more expensive than King
Likomides.
$$ Skýros Palace
Magaziá
Tel: (0222) 91 99 4

Fax: (0222) 92 07 0
About 1km (about half a mile) from
the Molos below the Magaziá and
about 45 metres (50 yards) from
the beach. Bar, restaurant,
swimming pool. This is the island's
class hotel.
$$$ Xenia
Magaziá
Tel: (0222) 91 20 9
Fax: (0222) 92 06 2
One of the cement boxes that
usually disfigure, but this "modern"
hotel on the low bluff directly
behind the beach is now part of the
scenery. The location is wonderful,
the rooms comfortable. Bar, good
restaurant. Expensive.

Évvia
$$ Akti Aetos
Kárystos, 34001, Évvia.
Tel: (0224) 23 44 7
Fax: (0224) 22 46 1
Small two-storey white hotel and
bungalows. Restaurant, bar with
view down the beach about 65
metres (70 yards) away.
$$ Karystion
Kárystos
Tel: (0224) 22 19 1/391
Fax: (0224) 22 72 7
Small family-run hotel 360 metres
(400 yards) from port, built right on
the water and surrounded by a
park. All rooms overlook the sea
and have minibar, TV and air-
conditioning. Bar and bar snacks.
Moderately priced. Bookings made
on the Internet get 10 percent
discount: http://agn.hol.gr./hotels/
karystio/karystio.htm
$$ Límni
Límni
Tel: (0227) 31 31 6
Medium-sized hotel towards the far
end of the village, 10 metres/yards
from the sea.
$$ Plaza
Límni 34005, Évvia.
Tel: (0227) 31 23 5
Very small 19th-century hotel with
arches right on the water.
$$$ Aígli
18 25th Martiou, Edhipsós 34300,
Évvia.
Tel: (0226) 22 21 5
Fax: (0226) 22 99 1
Hotel dating from *circa* 1930 in the

centre of town, now faded but a
historical building well maintained,
across the road from the sea.
Restaurant, bar, garden. The hot
baths for which many people visit
the place are also inside the hotel.
$$ Agápi
7 Filellínon, Edhipsós 34300, Évvia
Tel: (0226) 23 88 3–4
Fax: (0226) 23 57 32
Medium-sized hotel 90 metres (100
yards) from the sea and separated
by park from the NTGO-run thermal
baths. All rooms have TV, small
fridge and air-conditioning.

Dodecanese Islands

Rhodes
$$ Andreas Hotel
Omirou 28d, Rhodes old town
Tel: (0241) 34 15 6
Fax: (0241) 74 28 5
Imaginative old-house restoration,
perennially popular, reasonably
priced; wood-trimmed rooms have
sinks only.
$$ Casa de la Sera
Thisséos 38, Old town
Tel: (0241) 75 15 4
Airy, tiled-floor en suite rooms and a
small breakfast bar make this a
good choice.
$$$ S. Nikolis Hotel
Ippodhámou 61, old town
Tel: (0241) 34 56 1
Fax: (0241) 32 03 4
Rambling restoration project
encompassing the hotel plus self-
catering studios; rooftop breakfast
terrace, fair-sized suites at the
hotel.
$$ Nymph Inn
Sálakos
Tel: (0246) 22 20 6
A converted Italian-era mansion
next to the mineral-water-bottling
plant makes a fine woodland base
near the centre of the island.

Kárpathos
$ Blue Bay Hotel
Vróndi beach, Pigádhia
Tel: (0245) 22 47 9
Fax: (0245) 22 39 1
Comfortable and just a few steps
back from the sand.
$$ Aphrodite
Ólymbos village

Price Guide

Price categories are based on the cost of a double room for one night in the high season:

$$$ Expensive 35–60,000dr
$$ Moderate 12–35,000dr
$ Inexpensive under 5,000dr – 12,000 dr

For details of the Greek Tourist Authority's hotel classification system see Hotel Categories on page 337.

Tel: (02435) 51 45 4
The only en suite rooms here, plus views south to the ocean.

Kassos
$ Anessis
Tel: (0245) 41 23 4
and **$ Anagenessis**
Tel: (0245) 41 49 5
Exceedingly modest though they are, these represent nearly half the beds available in Frý, the capital and port town.

Kastellorizo
$$ Megisti Hotel
Tel: (0241) 49 27 2
This is overpriced but the only really luxurious place, at the north end of the waterfront, with its own swimming lido.
$$ Mavrothalassitis Pension
Tel: (0241) 49 20 2
In the centre of town, this is one of the very few here with en suite plumbing; lovely Australian-Greek family also runs a restaurant.

Tílos
$ Eirini Hotel
Livadia
Tel: (0241) 44 29 3
Fax: (0241) 44 23 8
Long the top hotel on the island, now being challenged by others, but still wins on points for its beautiful grounds.
$ Livadia
Tel: (0241) 44 26 6
Upgraded in 1994, and is good value, especially the upper floor "suites"; also offers self-catering studios nearby.

$ Miliou Apartments
Megálo Horió
Tel: (0241) 44 20 4
Self-catering units near the centre of this attractive village; an excellent base for nearby Éristos beach, which curiously doesn't yet have a completed hotel.

Symi
$ Horio
Tel: (0241) 71 80 0
Mock-traditional architecture, and great views, at the top of the stair-street up from the port (minibus transfer available).
$$ Alyki
Tel: (0241) 71 66 5
Fax: (0241) 71 65 5
Genuinely olde worlde – this used to be the opera house – next to the clocktower on the quay.
$$ Opera House Hotel/Apartments
Tel: (0241) 72 03 4
Fax: (0241) 72 03 5
New units but in traditional style, run by Austrian-Symian family. Very quiet despite proximity to port. Choice of rooms or self-catering suites.

Hálki
$$ The Captain's House
Tel: (0241) 57 20 1
English-and-Greek-run – a delightful outfit in an old mansion, recently converted to en suite.
$$ Hotel Halki
Tel/fax: (0241) 45 29 5
Installed in a converted sponge factory, with 28 rooms and a restaurant bar.

Nissyros
$$ Porfyris Hotel
Mandhráki, inland
Tel: (0242) 31 37 6
Comfortable, with a good pool and views over orchards.
$ Pension Nissyros
At the foot of the castle, Mandhráki
Tel: (0242) 31 05 2
More modest, close to the sea.

Kos
$ Pension Alexis
Irodhótou 9, Kós Town
Tel: (0242) 28 79 8
Backpacker's home-from-home;

self-catering kitchen, bicycle hire, good communal area.
$ Hotel Afendoulis
Evripílou 1
Tel: (0242) 25 32 1
Fax: (0242) 25 79 7
More upscale hotel run by the same friendly family, with large en suite rooms, good communal areas, and full breakfasts. Alexis is a wonderful host, and loves to lead gustatory safaris with willing guests.

Astypálea
$$ Vangelis
Skála port
Tel: (0243) 61 28 1
Newish (1994) studio units above a respected restaurant, on the less congested side of the bay.
$$ Studios Electra
Livádhia
Tel: (0243) 61 27 0
Castle-view studios just inland at the island's main beach resort.

Kálymnos
$$ Villa Themelina
Tel: (0243) 22 68 2
Installed in a 19th-century mansion with a pool and gardens, this is the town's top choice; unfortunately package companies seem aware of this.
$$ Greek House Pension
Amoudhára
Tel: (0243) 23 75 2
En suite, eccentrically furnished rooms and almost maniacally friendly proprietress.

Télendhos
Most establishments here – surprisingly numerous for such a small islet – are taverna/accommodation combos.
$$ Hotel Port Potha
Tel: (0243) 47 32 1
Fax: (0243) 48 10 8
An exception to the above rule, this is the 1997 debut of relative luxury here.
$ Uncle George's
Tel: (0243) 47 50 2
With an excellent taverna downstairs from simple but clean rooms, this is more typical for Télendhos.

Price Guide

Price categories are based on the cost of a double room for one night in the high season:
$$$ Expensive 35–60,000dr
$$ Moderate 12–35,000dr
$ Inexpensive under 5,000dr
– 12,000 dr

For details of the Greek Tourist Authority's hotel classification system see Hotel Categories on page 337.

Léros
$$ Pension Fanari
in Pandéli
Tel: (0247) 23 15 2
Secluded setting, with views across to the castle, make this a winner.
$ Hotel Gianna
Álinda
Tel: (0247) 23 15 3
Modern hotel overlooking the Allied World War II cemetery and Álinda's narrow but clean beach.

Lipsí
$ Apartments Galini
Tel: (0247) 41 21 2
The first building you see overhead at the ferry jetty, but a good choice nonetheless; very friendly family, well-appointed rooms with balconies.
$$ Aprhodite Hotel
Tel: (0247) 41 00 0
A 1997-built, attractive studio bungalow complex, just inland from the town beach of Liendoú; geared to packages but not averse to speculative trade at slow times.

Pátmos
$$ Hotel Australis
Mérihas district, Skála
Tel: (0247) 31 57 6
Plain, en suite rooms in a 1970s building, but big breakfasts and the very kind Australian-Greek managing family ensures a loyal following.
$$ Blue Bay Hotel
Just out of Skála on the way to Gríkou
Tel: (0247) 31 16 5
Fax: (0247 32 30 3

Hotels at the fishing port can be noisy; the extra 400 metres (437 yards) remoteness here makes all the difference. Comfortable, with knock-out sea views.

Ionian Islands

Corfu
There are more than 200 hotels on Corfu, ranging from the luxurious Corfu Palace on down. Choose according to where you want to be and what is available. In Corfu town, avoid the hotels in Kanoni, as they are in the airport flight path. Visit the Greek National Tourist Office (EOT) at the corner of Rizospastón Vouleftón and Iakóvou Políla for information about hotels and less formal accommodation.
Tel: (0661) 37 52 0/37 63 9–40.
$$$ Cavalieri Hotel
4 Kapodistriou, Corfu Town, 49100
Tel: (0661) 39 33 6
Fax: (0661) 39 28 3
Pleasant, well-run hotel, with attractive roof garden. Rooms have TV, air-conditioning and most have small fridges.
$$ Astron
15 Donzelot, Corfu Town, 49100
Tel: (0661) 39 50 5
Fax: (0661) 33 70 8
Medium-sized hotel in the old harbour near the law courts over-looking the sea. TV in each room.
$$ Bella Venezia
Corfu Town 49100
Tel: (0661) 46 50 0
Fax: (0661) 20 70 8
Near Plateía Dimarchíou behind the Cavalieri Hotel. Rooms have TV and air-conditioning and small fridge.
$$ Arkadion
44 Kapodistriou, Corfu Town. 49100
Tel: (0661) 37 67 0
Fax: (0661) 74 50 8
Centrally located right by the Liston facing the esplanade. No frills.
$$ Ermónes Beach Hotel
Ermones, Corfu, 49100
Tel: (0661) 94 24 1
Fax: (0661) 94 24 8
This well-landscaped, large hotel/bungalows set on a wooded hillside provides a cable car to take guests down to the beach.

$$ Glyfada Beach Hotel
Glyfada
Tel: (0661) 94 25 8
Medium-sized hotel on the beach, no frills.
$$ Louis Grand Hotel
Glyfada, Corfu, 49100
Tel: (0661) 94 14 0
Fax: (0661) 94 14 6
Large hotel on the beach with all the trimmings. Rooms have air-conditioning and minibar. Restaurant, three bars and swimming pool.

Paxí
$$ Paxos Beach
Gaios, Paxi, 49082
Tel: (0622) 32 21 1
Attractive bungalows above beach 2km (about a mile) from town.

Lefkáda
$$ Lefkas
2 F. Panagou, Lefkáda Town, Lefkáda, 31100
Tel: (0645) 23 91 6
Fax: (0645) 24 57 9
The larger and more pretentious of two hotels facing the sea as you enter town, with large arches on the facade. Rooms have TV and air-conditioning. Restaurant and bar.
$$ Nirikos
Lefkáda Town, Lefkáda 31100
Tel: (0645) 24 13 2
Fax: (0645) 23 75 6
Next to the Lefkas, smaller and a better deal. Rooms have TV and ceiling fans. Restaurant and bar.
$$ Apollon
Vasilikí, Lefkáda, 31082
Tel: (0645) 31 12 2
Fax: (0645) 31 14 2
Small family-run hotel in the village, 275 metres (300 yards) from the harbour. Rooms have small fridges.
$$ Vasiliki Bay Hotel
Vasilikí, Lefkáda, 31082
Tel: (0645) 31 07 77
Pretty similar to the Apollon in the village 55 metres (60 yards) from the harbour.
$$ Ammoudia
Nydrí, Lefkáda, 31100
Tel: (0645) 92 77 1
Pleasant small hotel on the edge of Nydrí, 45 metres (50 yards) from the sea. Bar, snack bar, pool.

Itháki

The two tourist agencies, Della (tel: 0674 32 11 04) and Polyctor (tel: 0674 32 11 04) can arrange rooms in private houses in much of the island.

$$ Mentor
Paralia, Vathy,
Itháki, 28300
Tel: (0674) 32 43 3
Fax: (0674) 32 29 4
Basic, clean, sometimes noisy.

$$ Odysseas
Vathy, Itháki, 28300
Tel: (0674) 32 38 1
Smaller and somewhat less expensive than the Mentor.

$$ Nostos
Frikes, Itháki, 28301
Tel: (0674) 31 64 4
Fax: (0674) 31 71 6
Attractive, family-run small hotel, 180 metres (200 yards) from the sea with restaurant and bar.

$$ Captain Apartments
Kióni
Tel: (0674) 31 48 1
Fax: (0674) 31 36 2
Family-run rented apartments, each with kitchen and TV, in a very attractive small village. On top of the hill overlooking the sea, 135 metres (150 yards) from the water.

Kefalloniá

The Greek National Tourist Office (EOT) in the harbour across from the police station can help you find the full range of accommodation available on the island.

$$ Mouikis
3 Vyronos, Argostóli.
Kefallonia, 28100
Tel: (0671) 23 45 6
Fax: (0671) 24 52 8
In town some 45 metres (50 yards) from the harbour with wonderful views over the water. Well-kept rooms have TV and air-conditioning.

$$ Mouikis Village
Argostóli, Kefallonia, 28100
Tel: (0671) 41 56 2
Fax: (0671) 24 52 8
Wonderful small apartments 6km (4 miles) from Argostóli, with pool, tennis and children's playground. Moderately expensive, but becoming a good bargain for larger apartments.

$$ Olga
Argostóli, Kefallonia 28100
Tel: (0671) 24 98 1
Fax: (0671) 24 98 5
In center of town on the waterfront. Rooms have air conditioning, TV, balcony, bar

$$ WhiteRocks
Platý Yialó, Kefallonia, 28100
Tel: (0671) 23 16 7
Fax: (0671) 28 75 5
The best of the resort area, set in among the trees and about 45 metres (50 yards) from the water. Hotel and bungalows. All rooms have air-conditioning. Two bars, two restaurants and a snack bar on the beach. Half-board.

$$ Lara
Lourdáta
Tel: (0671) 31 15 7
Fax: (0671) 31 15 6
Wonderful, quiet, family-run hotel shaded by very tall olive trees, 250 metres (280 yards) from the beach. Rooms have small fridges and those that are not well shaded have ceiling fans you probably won't need.

Fisárdo

$$ Filoxenia
Fiskárdo, Kefallonia, 28084
Tel: (0674) 41 31 9
19th-century house beautifully refurbished as a small hotel, with six large apartments in the village not far from the water.

$$ Panormos
Fiskárdo, Kefallonia, 28084
Tel: (0674) 41 20 3
Six rooms above restaurant right on the water.

Zákynthos

$$ Bitzaro
46 D. Roma, Zákynthos Town, Zakynthos 29100
Tel: (0695) 23 64 4
Fax: (0695) 23 49 3
Near the town beach, ivy covered, quiet. Rooms have TV, ceiling fans.

$$ Diana
Kapodistriou & 2 Mitropoleos, Zákynthos Town, Zákynthos 29100
Tel: (0695) 28 54 7
Fax: (0695) 45 04 7
In town on a quiet pedestrian street. Rooms have air conditioning, TV, balcony, with view on the sea.

$$ Zante Beach
Laganás,
Zakynthos 29092
Tel: (0695) 51 13 0
Fax (0695) 51 13 5
Large cement hotel, with large pool and children's pool, restaurant, bar, on the beach. Pleasant management actively supports the measures protecting Loggerhead turtles.

$$$ Caravel Zante
Plános, Zakynthos 29100
Tel: (0695) 45 26 1
Fax (0695) 45 54 8
6 km (3 and a half miles) northwest of Zákynthos town. Beautifully set on a small cove right by the water.

$$ Plághos Beach
Tragáki,
Zakynthos 29100
Tel: (0695) 62 42 9
Fax (0695) 45 99 7
Arguably the most beautiful hotel on the island, surrounded by gardens and on the water. Large swimming pool.

$$ La Grotta
Volímes, Zakythos 29091
Tel: (0695) 31 22 4
Small hotel in Aghios Nikolaos.

Crete

Aghia Galini

This beautifully sited resort seems to consist of nothing but hotels and pensions.

$ Candia
Tel: (0832) 91 20 3
This is a friendly hotel with a view over the harbour and sea (open all year).

$$ Andromeda pension,
tel: (0832) 91 28 4, and
$$ Rea, tel: (0832) 91 39 0 are slightly better appointed.

Aghia Roumeli

$$ Agia Roumeli pension
Tel: (0821) 25 65 7
Only has a few rooms, but they are panelled with wood. Sea view,

Agios Georgios

$ Kourites
Tel: (0844) 22 19 4
A basic but good pension in Tzermiado.

$ Rea in Agios Georgios
Tel: (0844) 31 20 9
This is a more modest
establishment but nicely furnished.

Agios Nikolaos
$$ Alfa
Tel: (0841) 23 70 1
There are smaller pensions around
the bus station, but Alfa, on the
peninsula is better.
$$ Ormos
On the edge of the town on the
Elounda side
Tel: (0841) 28 14 4
Fax: (0841) 25 39 4
The Ormos has comfortable
bungalows and swimming pool.
$$$ Minos Palace
Tel: (0841) 23 80 1
fax: (0841) 23 81 6
If money is no obstacle, then try the
luxury Minos Palace, built to
resemble the architectural style of
the Minoan palaces.

Almirida
$$ Almirida Bay
Tel: (0821) 31 75 1
50-bed hotel with restaurant and
swimming pool.
$$ Farma Almirida
Tel: (0821) 31 73 2
Fax: (0821) 31 58 9
Farma Almirida is a popular hotel
situated only a few hundred yards
from the beach and offers its
guests a "holiday on the farm".

Bali
$$ Bali Beach
Tel: (0834) 94 21 0
A single-storey hotel occupying a
pleasant site on the bay.

Hania
A number of the Venetian town
houses have been opulently
converted into luxurious pensions.
$$ Casa Delfino
Theofanous 9,
near Zambeliou
Tel: (0821) 93 09 8
Fax: (0821) 96 50 0
A moderately expensive pension
with comfortable rooms.
$$ Contessa
Theofanous 15
Tel: (0821) 98565

With expensive furniture, wooden
floors and ceilings.
$$ Porto Veneziano
Tel: (0821) 27100
Fax: (0821) 44 05 3
Situated some distance from the
bustle of the main harbour near the
yacht marina and fishing harbour.
$ Elena Beach
Tel: (0821) 97 63 3
Fax: (0821) 92 97 2
One of the smaller, quieter beach
hotels that can be found in Nea
Chora, a 15-minute walk from the
town centre.

Hersonisos
$$$ Creta Maris
Tel: (0897) 22 11 5
Fax: (0897) 22 13 0
This is one of the two top-grade
luxury hotels in Hersonisos.
Situated by the beach Creta Maris
has 1,000 beds, single-storey
accommodation and a design in
sympathy with Cretan architectural
style.
$$$ Knossos Royal Village
Tel: (0897) 23 37 5
Fax: (0897) 23 15 0
Opened in 1991 and, as the name
suggests, attempts to recreate a
Minoan settlement.

Hora Sfakion
$$ Vritomartis
Tel: (0825) 91 11 2
Fax: (0825) 91 22 2
A 100-room hotel just a short
distance from the town. Open all
year, it is popular with long-stay
winter guests. Swimming pool and
tennis courts available.

Elounda
$$$ Elounda Beach
Tel: (0841) 41 81 2
Fax: (0841) 41 37 3
A member of the 'Leading Hotels of
the World' group, this hotel stands
out as one of island's best.
$$$ Elounda Mare
Relais et Châteaux
Tel: (0841) 41 10 2
Fax: (0841) 41 30 7
Another fine hotel offering luxury
facilities.
$$ Aristea
Tel: (0841) 41 30 1

A moderately-priced hotel with good
facilities situated adjacent to the
sea.
$ Olous
Tel: (0841) 41 27 0
Situated on the main street, the
Olous very reasonable both in price
and quality.

Georgioupolis
Mainly private rooms and pensions.
In the east, however, the sandy
beach is lined by big hotels.
$ Zorbas
Tel: (0825) 61 38 1
The Zorbas has 17 rooms. It has a
good reputation, and is also near
the platia.
$$$ Mare Monte
Next to the beach
Tel: (0825) 61 39 0
Fax: (0825) 61 27 4
This is a pleasant beach hotel with
swimming pool and organised
activities.

Iraklion
It is not easy to find a quiet hotel in
this noisy town and the beach
hotels in the west of the town
should be avoided. Light sleepers
could ask for a room at the back.
$ Cretan Sun
In the Old Town, by the market
Tel: (081) 24 37 94
$$ Daedalus
Tel: (081) 22 43 91
In the pedestrianised zone at the
heart of the old town. Relatively
quiet.

Ierapetra
$$$ Lyktos Beach
Tel: (0842) 61 28 0
Fax: (0842) 61 31 8
A beach hotel of superior quality,
with tennis courts, 7km (4 miles)
out of town.

Kastelli Kissamou
$ Galini Beach
Tel: (0822) 23 28 8
Pension by the beach.

Matala
$$ Matala Bay
Tel: (0892) 45 10 6
A good hotel, but is some distance
from the sea.

Open all the year round are:
$$ Eva Marina,
tel: (0892) 45 12 5, and
$$ Frangiskos,
tel: (0892) 42 38 0.
All three are modern holiday hotels.

Mirtos
$ Myrtos
Tel: (0842) 51 21 5
In the middle of the village and open all year.
$$ Esperides
Tel: (0842) 51 20 7
This hotel is the best in town. Facilities include a swimming pool

Palaeochora
$$ Polydoros
Tel: (0823) 41 15 0
In a cul-de-sac near the beach. Small but well-appointed hotel. **$ Hotel Rea**
Tel: (0823) 41 30 7
In the town. Twelve clean rooms with bath.

Plakias
$ Phoenix
Tel: (0832) 31 33 1
To the west of Plakias in a quiet location.
$$$ Damnoni Resort
Tel: (0832) 31 99 1
Fax: (0832) 31 89 3
A beach hotel with good watersport facilities.

Rethymnon
$$ Kyma Beach
On the Platia Iroon
Tel: (0831) 55 50 3
Fax: (0831) 22 35 3
A 35-room hotel with a good à la carte menu. It has central heating and stays open all year.
$$$ Grecotel Rethimna Beach
Tel: (0831) 71 00 2
Fax: (0831) 20 08 5
One of the series of A-Category hotels found beside the long sandy beach. Grecotel Rethimna Beach offers watersports and children's activities. Mountain bike tours can also be arranged from here.

Sitia
$$$ Helios Club
Tel: (0841) 28 82 1

Fax: (0841) 28 82 6
160-room beach hotel out on the road to Vai.
$$ Crystal
Tel: (0843) 22 28 4
The best of the bunch of C-category hotels in the Kapetan Sifi near the harbour.
$$ Idi
Tel: (0894) 31 30 2
Mountain hotel with an old water mill which still functions. The hotel farms its own trout in a nearby pond. Good restaurant.

Saronic Gulf Islands

Salamína
$$ Gabriel
Tel: 01 466 2275
Not plush, but the best hotel on the island in the pleasant village of Eándio right by the water.

Aegina
$$ Areti
9 Kazantsaki and Paralia,
Aegina Town, Aegina 18010
Tel: (0297) 23 59 3
Across from the ferryboat landing, no frills. Also has other rooms.
$$ Danae
43 Kazantzaki, Aegina Town,
Aegina 18010
Tel: (0297) 22 42 4
Fax (0297) 26 50 9
Family run, friendly hotel 650 metres (700 yards) from harbour on bluff overlooking the sea. Restaurant, bar, swimming pool with bar. A good choice

Less expensive rooms to rent can be found from Antonis Marmarinos (0297 22954).

$$ Apollo
Aghia Marina, Aegina 18010
Tel: (0297) 32 27 1
Fax (0297) 32 68 8
Large cement block accommodation with all the trimmings, restaurant, bar, swimming pool, tennis, right on the sea.
$$ Argo
Aghia Marina, Aegina 18010
Tel: (0297) 32 26 6
Near the Apollo and similar to it, but smaller and less expensive.

Price Guide

Price categories are based on the cost of a double room for one night in the high season:
$$$ Expensive 35–60,000dr
$$ Moderate 12–35,000dr
$ Inexpensive under 5,000dr
– 12,000 dr

For details of the Greek Tourist Authority's hotel classification system see Hotel Categories on page 337.

Anghístri
$$ Mylos
Anghístri 18010
Tel: (0297) 91 24 1
Fax (0297) 91 44 9
Rooms have small refrigerator and fans are available. About 90 metres (100 yards) from the sea.

Porós
$$ Epta Adelfia
1 Tombazi and Plateia Iroon,
Póros 18020
Tel: (0298) 23 41 2
Small family run hotel in town near harbour. Some rooms have air conditioning.
$$ Latsi
74 I. Papadopoulou,
Póros 18020
Tel: (0298) 22 39 2
150 yards from the harbor, just before the naval school. Restaurant, bar.
$$ Pavlou
Neórion, Póros 18020
Tel: (0298) 22 73 4
Fax (0298) 24 91 1
2 km from town, 15 yards from the water. Refurbished 1998. Restaurant, bar, two tennis courts, swimming pool.

The package tour companies are on Póros in force, controlling many hotel rooms. You may find less expensive accommodation through the Tourist Police (0298 22 46 2) or try across the narrow straits in Galatás:

$$ Galátia
Galatás, 18020

Tel: (0298) 22 22 7
Provides comfortable but
unadorned accommodation at a
reasonable price.

Hydra
$$ Miranda
Hydra 18040
Tel: (0298) 52 23 0
Fax (0298) 53 51 0
Renovated traditional island
mansion. Rooms have air
conditioning and small verandah.
Breakfast served in garden.
$$ Orlof
9 Rafalia,
Hydra 18040
Tel: (0298) 52 56 4
Fax (0298) 53 53 2
Renovated old island mansion now
offering the most attractive
accommodation on the island.
Rooms have air conditioning, TV,
small refrigerator. Generous buffet
breakfast served in pleasant
garden.
$$ Angelika,
42 Andrea Miaouli,
Hydra 18040.
Tel: (0298) 53 20 2
Fax (0298) 53 69 8
Renovated old island mansion, 250
yards from harbour, not as posh as
the Orlof but very pleasant. The
rooms have air conditioning and TV.
Breakfast is served in the
courtyard.
$$ Leto
Hydra 18040
Tel: (0298) 53 38 5
Fax (0298) 53 80 6
180 metres (200 yards) from the
harbour up the road by the clock
tower. Air conditioning.

Many small pensions/private
homes provide perfectly
comfortable rooms at more
reasonable rates; to find them
check with the island's Tourist
Police (tel: 0298 52 20 5).

Spétses
$$ Léka Palace
Spétses 18050
Tel: (0298) 72 31 1
Fax (0298) 72 16 1
The old Xenia, then the Kasteli, now
with new name and new

management, just renovated and
upgraded. Beyond Kounoupítsa
northwest from the Dapia. Large
rooms with TV, mini fridge, air
conditioning. Bar and restaurant
overlooking the sea, 5 minute walk
down to beach. Large swimming
pool, tennis courts, extensive
garden.
$$$ Spétses
Spétses 18050
Tel: (0298) 72 60 2
Fax (0298) 72 49 4
In Kounoupítsa, 500 metres (450
yards) from the Dapia. Rooms have
air conditioning, and TV. Restaurant,
bar, and a second bar on the
hotel's pleasant private beach.
$$ Soleil
Spétses 18050
Tel: (0298) 72 48 8
Small hotel on the water near the
Dapia between the fish market and
the town beach. The rooms have TV
and small refrigerator. Scrupulously
clean.
$$ Villa Christina
Spétses 18050
Tel: (0298) 72 21 8
Small hotel 3 minutes from the
Dapia, about 130 metres (150
yards) below Lazarosís taverna.
Most rooms have small
refigerators, all have fans.
Cafeteria/bar. Three gardens.
$$ Villa Martha
Spétses 18050
Tel: (0298) 72 14 7
Out of town, southeast of the Old
Harbour, 230 metres (250 yards)
before the sea at Aghia Marina, set
among trees and flowers.
Cafeteria/bar. Rooms overlook
either the sea or the wooded
mountain. Ceiling fans.

Cyclades Islands
Ándhros
$$$ Paradissos
Ándhros town
Tel: (0282) 22 18 7
Fax: (0282) 22 34 0
An elegant mansion near the centre
of town, 700 metres (760 yards)
from the beach. Airy rooms with
superb views from the balconies.
$$ Andros Holiday Hotel
Gávrio

Tel: (0282) 71 38 4
Right on the beach just outside
town. Attractive rooms, swimming
pool, tennis courts, sauna, gym.
$$ Hryssí Aktí
Batsí
Tel: (0282) 41 23 6
Deservedly popular for its location,
in the centre of town, across from
the beach.

Kéa
$$ Ioulis
Kéa town
Tel: (0288) 22 17 7
Delightfully quiet spot in the *kástro*,
with lovely views from the terrace.
$$ Kéa Beach
Koúndouros Bay
Tel: (0288) 31 23 0
Luxury bungalow complex built in
traditional Cycladic style, with all
facilities from a nightclub to
watersports. 5 km (3 miles) south
of Písses.

Tínos
$$ Tinion
Hóra
Tel: (0283) 22 26 1
fax: (0283) 24 75 4
Charming old-world hotel with tiled
floors, lace curtains and a large
balcony.
$$ Aeolos Bay Hotel
Ághios Fókas
Tel: (0283) 23 33 9
Fax: (0283) 23 08 6
Smart, comfortable hotel a short
walk out of town, overlooking the
beach. Swimming pool, pleasant
gardens, breakfast on the terrace.

Kýthnos
$$ Kythnos
Mérihas Bay
Tel: (0281) 32 24 7
Basic but friendly hotel situated right
on the waterfront. Rooms at the front
have balconies overlooking the sea.

Sýros
$$$ Omiros
Ermoúpoli
Tel: (0281) 24 91 0
150-year-old Neo-Classical mansion
restored to a high standard. Rooms
furnished in traditional style, with
views of the lively harbour.

$$$ Dolphin Bay Hotel
Galissás
Tel: (0281) 42 92 4
The largest and most modern hotel on the island, with all facilities, large swimming pool and beautiful views over the bay.
$$ Europe Hotel
Ermoúpoli
Tel: (0281) 28 77 1
An early 19th-century hospital converted into a pleasant hotel with large rooms round a cloister-like pebbled courtyard.

Mýkonos
$$$ Princess of Mýkonos
Ághios Stéfanos beach
Tel: (0289) 23 80 6
Fax: (0289) 23 03 1
A five-star hotel popular with stars such as Jane Fonda. 2 km (1 mile) from Hóra and just 30 metres (33 yards) above the beach, with all the luxury facilities. Air conditioned rooms (some with kitchenettes), satellite TV, Italian restaurant, swimming pool and gym.
$$$ Cavo Tagoo
Hóra
Tel: (0289) 23 69 2
Fax: (0289) 24 92 3
Jet-set luxurious, set on a hillside 500 metres (547 yards) north of Hóra. Prize-winning Cycladic architecture, beautiful furnishings, impeccable service, friendly atmosphere and wonderful views over the Aegean.
$$$ Despotiko Hotel
Hóra
Tel: (0289) 22 00 9
Fax: (0289) 23 46 2
A converted 18th-century mansion named after a 19th-century bishop, an ancestor of the family that runs the hotel today. Bar, swimming pool.
$$ Hotel Elena
Hóra
Tel: (0289) 23 45 7
Fax: (0289) 23 45 8
Located in the heart of town, yet quiet and impeccably clean, with great views of the harbour. Rooms have air conditioning and TV. Good buffet breakfast. Watch the sunset from the veranda bar.
$$ Apollonia Bay Hotel
Ághios Ioánnis

Tel: (0289) 27 89 0
Traditional, Cycladic cluster of small villa-studios located on its own bay about 3½ km (2¼ miles) from Hóra. Gracious, friendly service, incomparable views. Rooms have air conditioning, TV, hairdryers. Large swimming pool, bar.

Sérifos
$$ Areti
Livádi
Tel: (0281) 51 47 9
Fax: (0281) 51 54 7
Family-run hotel (and cake-shop) near the ferry landing, built on a hill with superb views. Peaceful terraced garden overlooking the sea.

Sífnos
$$$ Platýs Yialós Hotel
Platýs Yialós
Tel: (0284) 71 32 4
Large, Cycladic-style hotel at far end of beach. Well furnished and tastefully decorated with wood-carvings and wall paintings. Rooms have air conditioning and fridge.
$$ Artemónas Hotel
Artemón
Tel: (0284) 31 30 3
Simple, beautiful, family hotel with rooms that overlook fields rolling towards the sea.
$ Apollonia
Apollonía
Tel: (0284) 31 49 0
Charming small hotel (only 9 rooms) with traditional island architecture and friendly service.
$ Moní Hrysopighí
Apókofto
Tel: (0284) 31 25 5
This 17th-century monastery, situated on an islet reached by footbridge, rents out simple cells in summer. Book well in advance.

Andíparos
$$ Hryssí Aktí
near Kástro
Tel: (0284) 61 22 0
Elegant hotel with good rooms right on the beach on the island's east coast.
$ Mandalena
Kástro
Tel: (0284) 61 20 6
Clean but simple rooms on the

Price Guide

Price categories are based on the cost of a double room for one night in the high season:
$$$ Expensive 35–60,000dr
$$ Moderate 12–35,000dr
$ Inexpensive under 5,000dr – 12,000 dr

For details of the Greek Tourist Authority's hotel classification system see Hotel Categories on page 337.

waterfront, with good views of the harbour and across to Páros.

Páros
$$$ Astir of Paros
Náousa
Tel: (0284) 51 97 6
One of Greece's finest deluxe hotels, right on the beach. Spacious rooms with all the facilities, balconies and bathrooms lined with Parian marble. Large pool, three-hole (sic) golf course, horseback riding, art gallery.
$$ Golden Beach
Hrysí Aktí
Tel: (0284) 41 36 6
Fax: (0284) 41 19 5
Modern low-rise hotel on the beautiful east coast. Good rooms with balconies overlooking the Golden Beach. Excellent service. Very popular with windsurfers.
$ Dina
Parikía
Tel: (0284) 21 32 5
Friendly hotel in the heart of the old town. Spotlessly clean rooms set around a lovely flowered courtyard. Only 8 rooms, so book early.

Náxos
$$$ Pyrgos Zevgoli
Hóra
Tel: (0285) 22 99 3
Quiet, plush and exclusive, high up in the old town. A mansion with only 10 rooms (book early). One has a four-poster bed, most have great views.
$$ Grotta
Hóra
Tel: (0285) 22 21 5

Price Guide

Price categories are based on the cost of a double room for one night in the high season:
$$$ Expensive 35–60,000dr
$$ Moderate 12–35,000dr
$ Inexpensive under 5,000dr – 12,000 dr

For details of the Greek Tourist Authority's hotel classification system see Hotel Categories on page 337.

Modern Cycladic-style hotel beautifully situated on a headland with good views over the sea and the *kástro*.
$ Anixi
Hóra
Tel: (0285) 22 11 2
Modest, very Greek, family-run pension overlooking the sea and the Grotta quarter. Communal bathroom, garden.

Mílos
$$$ Popi's Windmill
Trypití
Tel: (0287) 22 28 6
A luxuriously converted windmill with all the amenities of an elegant hotel, plus beautiful views towards Adamás port.
$$ Kapetan Tassos
Apollónia
Tel: (0287) 41 28 7
Modern apartments in traditional blue-and-white island architecture, with good sea views.
$ Panorama
Klíma
Tel: (0287) 21 62 3
Fax: (0287) 22 11 2
Small seafront hotel, family-run with friendly service. The owner sometimes takes guests fishing.

Folégandhros
$$$ Anemomylos
Hóra
Tel: (0286) 41 30 9
A fully-equipped apartment complex built in traditional Cycladic style around a courtyard. Stunning views from the balconies overhanging the cliff edge.

$$$ Fani-Vevis
Hóra
Tel: (0286) 41 23 7
Comfortable hotel in a Neo-Classical mansion with rooms overlooking the sea.
$ Kástro
Hóra
Tel: (0286) 41 23 0
A 500-year-old traditional house that is actually part of the ancient Kástro walls. Quaint rooms have pebble mosaic floors, barrel ceilings and spectacular views down sheer cliffs to the sea.

Síkinos
$$$ Porto Síkinos
Aloprónia
Tel: (0286) 51 22 0
The best accommodation on the island: a complex of 18 Cycladic-style buildings right on the beach. Bar and restaurant.
$$ Kamares
Aloprónia
Tel: (0286) 51 23 4
Traditional-style, affordable hotel with average but comfortable rooms.
$ Flora
Aloprónia
Tel: (0286) 51 21 4
Another Cycladic-style development, this time simple chalet rooms built around courtyards on the hillside above the port. Great sea views.

Íos
$$$ Íos Palace
Mylopótas
Tel: (0286) 91 26 9
Modern hotel designed and decorated in the traditional style. Near the beach, with very comfortable rooms, marble-lined bathrooms and balconies overlooking the sea.
$$ Philippou
Hóra
Tel: (0286) 91 29 0
Small, comfotable hotel in the centre of Íos's hectic nightlife. Great location if you plan to party all night. Otherwise, bring earplugs or choose somewhere out of town.
$ Acropolis
Mylopótas
Tel: (0286) 91 30 3

Clean, simple rooms with balconies overlooking the beach below.

Amórgos
$$$ Aegiali
Órmos Aigiális
Tel: (0285) 73 39 3
Smart modern hotel complex with good facilities, including a taverna and large swimming pool. Lovely views over the bay from the veranda.
$ Minoa
Katápola
Tel: (0285) 71 48 0
Fax: (0285) 71 00 3
Traditional-style hotel on the harbour square. Can be noisy.

Santoríni
$$$ Atlantis
Firá
Tel: (0286) 22 23 2
Fax: (0286) 22 82 1
This is an elegant hotel that was built in the 1950s. Spacious rooms, the majority of them with balconies offering magnificent views of the town and the volcano.
$$$ Fanari
Ía
Tel: (0286) 71 00 8
Traditional *skaftá* cave houses converted into luxury holiday accommodation. Swimming pool, breakfast terrace, bar, and 240 steps down to Ammoudiá Bay below.
$$ Ermis
Kamári
Tel: (0286) 31 66 4
Friendly, family-run hotel set in beautiful gardens not far from the town centre and the black beach.
$ Esperides
Kamári
Tel: (0286) 31 18 5
Small, friendly new hotel which includes the ruins of a Byzantine town in its pistachio grove.

Camping

Large numbers of visitors to Greece rough it in one form or another. Those who want to camp at organised campsites will find them all over Greece, a few owned by the Greek Touring Club, but most of them owned privately, including a few dozen ex-EOT sites that were privatized in 1998.

The most beautiful campsites in Greece, however, are usually the ones you find on your own. While in most places it is officially illegal just to lay out your sleeping bag or pitch a tent, if you're discreet you will rarely be bothered. That means asking permission if you seem to be on private property, avoiding unofficial campsites set up in popular tourist areas, and always leaving the place looking better than it did when you came.

Youth Hostels

Greece has a number of youth hostels for which you need a youth hostel card. However, you can often buy one on the spot or just pay an additional charge. There are youth hostels in Athens, Mykínes, Náfplion, Olymbía, Pátras, Dhélfi, Litóhoro, Thessaloníki, Corfu, Santoríni and on Crete at Iráklion, Mália, Sitía, Réthymnon, Plakiás and Mýrthios. There are also private, unaffiliated "student houses" of varying quality and repute in Athens, and on youth-orientated islands like Santoríni and Náxos.

Monasteries

Monasteries and convents can often provide lodging as well for travellers. Mount Áthos, of course, has a long tradition of this hospitality (for men). Certain other monasteries in Greece also welcome overnight visitors on a more informal basis. If you have found a monastery that does accept overnight guests, you will have to dress (no shorts) and behave accordingly. The doors may close as early as sunset and some kind of donation may be expected.

Mountain Refuges

Mountain refuges are run by the various Greek mountaineering clubs and can range from a small 12-bed ski hut where you need to bring your own food and supplies to 100-bed

lodges where all meals are provided. There are over 40 of them, but only a few are permanently staffed, and getting the key for the others from the controlling club is generally more trouble than it's worth.

Traditional Settlements

The traditional settlements (*paradhosiakós ikismós*) are villages recognised by the Greek government as forming an important part of the national heritage. Buildings in these villages have been restored and originally set up by the NTOG for tourist use. Such houses and villages are, in their different ways, strikingly beautiful, and highly recommended for a week or month's retreat in rural Greece.

Restored accommodation in traditional settlements, some of it now under private management, includes:
Kapetanakos Tower
Areópolis, Máni
Tel: (0733) 51233
Fax: (0753) 51401
Paradhosiakós Ikismós Ías
Ía, Santoríni
Tel: (0286) 71234
Paradhosiakós Ikismós
Mestá, Híos
Tel: (0271) 76319
Psará Island
Tel: (0274) 61293
Mansions at Makrinítsa
Mt. Pílion
Tel: (0428) 99228/99250
Mansions at Vizítsa
Mt Pílion
Tel: (0423) 86765/86717
Megálo Pápingo
Epirus
Tel: (0653) 41615
Reservations should be made by contacting the phone or fax numbers listed above rather than going through EOT/NTOG.

Where to Eat

What To Eat

Eating out in Greece is above all a social affair. Whether it be with your family or *paréa*, that sacred circle of friends, a meal out is an occasion to celebrate.

This may have something to do with the fact that eating out in Greece continues to be affordable and popular, not something restricted to those who have American Express cards. And the predominance of the *tavérna*, that bastion of Greek cuisine, reflects this popularity. These casual eating establishments have more or less the same style and set-up throughout Greece, and the menu is similar: no frills, no packaging that tries to convince the consumer that this *tavérna* is different from the others, special or distinct. The place, and your being there, is somehow taken for granted: you eat the good food at Yannis's or Yorgos's, you enjoy yourself, and you don't end up paying an arm and a leg for it.

This is the general background for eating out in Greece against which we find, of course, considerable variation. The *tavérna* is by no means the only kind of establishment. You will also encounter the *estiatório*, the restaurant as we usually think of it, which ranges from the tradesman's lunch-hour hangout, with ready-cooked (*maghireftó*) food and bulk wine, to pricey linen-tablecloth places with bow-tied staff.

The *psistariá* is a barbecue-style restaurant specialising in lamb, pork or chicken on a spit; the *psarotavérna* specialises in fish; while the *ovelistírio* (*yíros* stall) and *souvlatzídhiko* purvey *yíros* and *souvláki* respectively, sometimes to a sit-down trade, garnished with salads. More popular of late among students and urban intelligentsia are the so-called *kultoúra* restaurants, nouvelle Greek cuisine based on updated traditional recipes, and *ouzerí* (called *tsipourádhika* in the north), where the local tipple serves as accompaniment to *mezédhes* or small plates of speciality dishes.

Seafood is now one of the most expensive dishes (except squid and octopus, which are widely available). Fish are usually in a drawer full of ice for you to choose from, and your dish is priced by the weight of the fish of your choice. Although the best *souvláki* are made from lamb, most are pork nowadays. Vegetarians are not well catered for in Greece – your best bet is mixing and matching from a selection of *mezédhes*.

There is considerable regional variety in Greek cuisine and you should keep an eye out for specialities of the house you haven't seen before. Another thing you'll quickly learn is how strikingly different the same dish can be when it is prepared well or badly. It is therefore worthwhile shopping around for your *tavérna* (especially in heavily visited areas), asking the locals what they suggest, walking into the kitchen to look at the food (a customary practice), instead of getting stuck with a tourist trap that spoils your taste for *moussakás* for the rest of the trip.

Some *tavérnes* may not have menus, some have menus without prices. Prices are usually in two

Greek Salad

"Greek" salad is a staple of Greek cuisine. *Horiátiki*, the full monty with tomatoes, cucumber, feta cheese and olives, is a lunch in itself with bread – and this is what you'll get if you ask for salad. If all you want is a small side salad, say so: this will usually be tomatoes and cucumbers.

columns: the first without and the second with tax. It is a good idea to enquire how much things cost before you eat. The listings below mention some of the more popular foods you will find.

Athens

Coffee Shops
Metropol
1 Pándhróssou and Mitropóleos Square
On the traffic-free square by the Cathedral, this is a pleasant oasis, summer and winter.

Zonars
9 Panepistimíou Street
Tel: 323 0336
A grand boulevard café. Breakfast, lunch and dinner are also available here, but Zonars is best for coffee and sweets like Black Venus. Expensive.

Chic Little Bars & (not very Greek) Restaurants
Mets
14 Márkou Mousoúrou Street, in Mets
Tel: 922 9454
Another haunt of the young, trendy and thirsty, this lively little place is conveniently located in the same area as the excellent *tavérnes* Manesis and Myrtia.

Montparnasse or **Ratka**
30–32 Háritos Street
Kolonáki
Tel: 729 0746
This split-level bar is one of the most fashionable district's most fashionable spots. (It is also the reason Montparnasse is named as it is: it is across the street from Ratkas.) Reserve for a late dinner. The food is definitely not Greek. A hot spot, packed after 10pm. Closed in summer. Expensive.

Ouzeri (Mezodhopolía in formal Greek)
To Kafeneio
26 Loukianoú Street
Kolonáki
Tel: 722 9056
One of four places to book for dinner if you have only a day or so in the city. This 19th-century

lookalike features 40 starters on the superb menu. Order four or five plates, and get a true feeling for the country's cuisine. The restaurant is refined, intimate, downright sexy, and the service a pleasant surprise. Expensive. (The other three musts are **Gherofinikas**, **Vasilenas** and **Rodiá**: *see below*)

Kafeneio
1 Epiharmoú
Pláka
Tel: 324 6916
A less pricey version of the above, with a more limited menu, but warm-hearted Pláka atmosphere. A cosy place till the wee hours, especially in winter. Try the *saganáki* and *keftethákia* meatballs. Expensive.

O Kouklis
14 Trípodhon, Pláka
Tel: 324 7605
Another bargain-basement of *mezédhes*, including herring or Greek sausage flambé, this starters-only spot is best in summer, when the tables spill out onto the raised verandah. A bit of a tourist trap, though. Inexpensive.

Perix
14 Glýkonos Street, across from Dexamini Square
Tel: 723 6917
A pleasant, reasonable place for starters and Perix *oúzo*, as well as dinner, if you like. Perix spills out into the square in summer. Inexpensive.

Kolonaki
Rodiá
44 Aristípou Street
Tel: 722 9883
One of the author's favourites, this is the haunt of foreign archeologists. In summer or winter, the barrel wines are good. Order veal in lemon or oregano sauce, *bourekákia* (cheese croquettes), *dolmáthes* (stuffed vine leaves), and a *horiatiki* (Greek salad).

To Kioúpi
Kolonáki Square
Basement restaurant with no frills, good food, low prices.

To Kotópoulo
3 Kolonáki Square
Between Citibank and Skoufa Street

is a little hole in the wall with a few tables wobbling out front where, at lunch or dinner time, you can eat heavenly grilled chicken, *souvlakia* in *pítta* rolls, French fries, salad and beer. Too good to miss. Inexpensive.

In & Near Mets
Karavítis
Arktinoú 4
Tel: 721 5155, 721 1610
An old friend of Athenians for nearly six decades, Mr Linardos's garden is open May–October. Order grilled meats and *retsína*, all accompanied by guitar music. Moderate.
Pergouliá
16 Márkou Mourourou
Tel: 923 4062
Run by an English-Greek couple. Family-style eating, fixed price for seven *hors d'oeuvres*, two main courses, *baklava*, fruit and all the wine you can drink. Inexpensive.

Plaka
Kalokerinos Tavern
10 Kékropos Street
Tel: 323 2054, 322 1679
This is an after-nine *tavérna* featuring traditional Greek fare, a *bouzouki* band (and Romanian violinist) plus a floor show of Greek dancing. Reservations are required. Moderate.
Platanos
4 Dioghénous Street, near the Tower of the Winds
Tel: 322 0666
Stifado and other oven-ready dishes are the specialities here at this venerable spot with pavement seating; competent cooking. Moderate.
Socrates' Prison
20 Mitséon Street
Tel: 922 3434
In Koukaki, just across the street from the Acropolis, this pleasant Greek taverna with tables on the pavement is the real thing. After enjoying Athens Festival performances, indulge in grilled chicken or lamb with your Pikermi bulk wine. Moderate.
Xynos
4 Angélou Gerónda Street
Tel: 322 1065

Founded in 1936, this restaurant has a genuine old-Athens ambience, serves lamb fricassé and barrel wine, and has three strolling guitarists. Closed in July. Moderate.
Bakalarakia (also known as *O Damingos*, after the owner)
41 Kydathinéon Street
Tel: 322 5084, 322 0395
The author's favourite winter *tavérna*, this basement is supported by a truly ancient marble column and has a reputation for phenomenal *retsína*, fried cod with garlic sauce, radishes, herring and *loukanika* (spicy Greek sausages). Closed late May through September. Inexpensive.

Great Restaurants
Gherofinikas
10 Pindhárou Street
Tel: 363 6710, 362 2719
Another favourite of the author's, this is the place to use your plastic. Reservations are a must. Order *Imam Baïldí* (aubergine starter), squab (baby chicken) with currant and pine nut pilaf, and finish with chocolate soufflé. Expensive.
Kuyu-Kaplanis
23 Navárhou Vótsi Street, at Mikrolimano in Piraeus
Tel: 411 1623
Choose from 25 *mezédhes* at your table by the harbour, and go on to shrimp and lobster. Expensive.
Ta Nissia
at The Athens Hilton
Tel: 722 0201
Try the dinner buffet here, a vast array of Greek and Turkish *mezédhes*. The wine list is impressive: try a hearty Nemean, red or white. Expensive.
Vasilenas
72 Etolikoú Street, Piraeus
Tel: 461 2457
Reserve a table, starve for at least a day, and then arrange for a taxi to pick you up afterwards: the *table d'hôte* consists of some 16 courses. Since Winston Churchill and Tyrone Power signed the guestbook, this unpretentious, underpriced beauty of a restaurant has been drawing gastronomes from

the world over. Allow several hours to savour your meal. Moderate.

Not Greek At All
L'Abreuvoir
51 Xenokrátous Street
Tel: 722 9106
This elegant French restaurant serves fine French food at tables set under mulberry trees. Expensive.
Boschetto Ristorante-Bar
Evangelismós Park
Tel: 721 0893/722 7324
Alone in the green park behind the Evangelismó Hospital, this Italian restaurant is a pricey gem. Reserve ahead.
Kona Kai
Ledra Marriott Hotel
115 Syngroú Avenue
Tel: 934 7711
Reserve ahead for authentic Polynesian cuisine. Expensive.
Michiko
27 Kydathinéon St
Pláka
Tel: 322 0980
Sushi and saki in old Athens. Moderate.
Eden
Lyssíou 12, Pláka
Tel: 324 8858
Athens's first, and still most durable, vegetarian restaurant, though quality can be erratic. A good antidote to too many grills. Moderate.

Bakeries & Street Food
As you make your way around Athens on foot, you will pass a neighbourhood bakery about every 10 minutes. Stop in. This is where Athenians buy and eat breakfast, generally standing up.

Busy shoppers on Ermou Street should stop in at the Ariston, at 10 Voulís St, where morning queues trailing out the door advertise this shop's fine cheese pies.

Street vendors have other goodies: nuts and coconut sticks; *kouloúria*, the chewy, sesame-seed crusted bracelets commuters wear to work to eat with their coffee; roasted chestnuts, which scent the air downtown in autumn and winter; and roasted corn.

Gustatory Note

Many Greek specialities are cooked in the morning and left to stand, so food can be lukewarm (if not cold!), but the Greeks believe this is better for the digestion.

Zacharoplasteia or Patisseries

Athens is heaven for the visitor with an advanced case of sweet tooth. The place to indulge is the *zacharoplasteíon*, or confectioner's shop. In the city centre, the old-fashioned **Zonars**, at 9 Panepistimíou Avenue, is hard to beat. The elegant tables facing the street are a fine vantage point from which to watch the passing parade while consuming enormous numbers of calories.

Flocas at 118 Kifissiás Avenue in Ambelokipi is another oasis for sugar addicts.

For Greek pastries with a Middle Eastern flavour, **Farouk Hanbali**, at 4 Messinías Street, also in Ambelokipi, has *baklavás* and other filo-and-nut delicacies, for sale by the kilo.

The **Lalaggis** shop, at Spefsíppou 23 in Kolonáki, features chocolate *baklavás* among other things. Take a box home to make friends' mouths water.

Breakfast

Kolonaki Square is a great place to have breakfast and people-watch.

The **Ellinikon** café, at the corner of the square and Koumbári Street, has elegant tables, outdoors in season, great coffee and western breakfasts.

Another nice place to start your day, especially if you are heading into the Flea Market, is the **Hermion Restaurant**, at 15 Pándhrossou Street in Pláka.

Roúmeli and Thessaly

Delphi

The restaurants in Delphi are along the lower road in the village. They are not particularly good but have wonderful views down over the olive plains towards Itéa and Ámfissa.

Galaxídi

Several good fish *tavérnes* are wonderfully placed along the harbour.

Vólos

Good, moderately expensive fish tavernas are on the waterfront on N. Plastiras Street, near the archaeological museum.

Kastráki

There are several pleasant *tavérnes* around the central square.

Thessaloníki

Restaurants

Tsarouhas
Olýmbou 78
Most noted, and one of the best, of the city's *patsatzídhika* or tripe-soup-kitchens; lots of other dishes, and Anatolian desserts. Open long hours. Inexpensive.

Ta Adhelfia tis Pixarias
Platía Navarínou 7
One of the better among several *tavérnes* on this pedestrianized square. Macedonian delicacies.

Archipelagos
Kanári 1, Néa Kríni
Fancy seafood out in the southwestern coastal suburbs. Expensive.

Loutros
Komninón 15
Operates out of a former *hamam* (Turkish bath). Good fried seafood and retsina on pavement seating. Shut summer. Moderate.

Ouzeri and Tsipourádhika

Ta Pringiponissia
Krítis 60, east of 25-Martíou
Constantinople-Greek food served in a 1997-revamped designer interior; you choose from the proffered *dhískos* or tray. Shut Sunday. Moderate.

O Myrovolos tis Smyrnis
Modhiáno market
Tel: 27 41 70
Doyenne of several competing *tsipouradhika* at the market hall's west entrance, strong on seafood, bags of atmosphere. Air-conditioned interior, or seating in the arcade – either way reservations recommended.

Aristotelous

Aristotélous 8
Upmarket *ouzerí* with courtyard seating and all the standards; shut Sunday and August.

To Yedi
Paparéska 13
Kástra district. Just opposite the entrance of the old Yedikule prison, this *ouzerí* has the fullest menu of several in the neighbourhood, and an unbeatable location.

Breakfast & Snacks

Family
Mitropóleos 67
Carbohydrate-rich breakfasts and lunches: crêpes, pizzas, pastries and so on.

Corner
Ethnikís Amýnis 5
The original flagship of the small wood-fired pizzeria chain with branches in many Greek cities; full beer bar, loud music, youth-orientated. There's a quieter branch on Aghías Sofías.

Epirus & Northwest

Messolóngi

Famous for its eels, which can be found along with a variety of other traditional foods in several places along Athanasíou Razikotsíka Street, near the central square.

Vónitsa

Some pleasant but not special fish *tavérnes* are along the waterfront.

Ioánnina

Mezedhadhiko Syn 2
Pamvotídhas Ave, Lakefront
The best by some way of the various waterfront eateries, this *ouzerí* has an ample menu, reasonable prices and a loyal local following.

Métsovo

Athens/Athenai
By central plaza
The ground-floor restaurant of this hotel purveys excellent local *maghireftá* recipes, plus wine from vineyards down in the river valley; this was one of the first inns in Epirus.

Monodhéndhri
To Petrino Dhassos
Bus-stop plaza, Zagoriá
Good home-style dishes, including local specialities like *alevrópitta*, served in the well-appointed former *kafenío*.

Kónitsa
To Dhendro
Bend in the approach road
Tel: (0655) 23 98 2
Trout, grills and interesting things done with peppers distinguish this taverna-inn from the run-of-the-mill eating place, with seating under the vast plane tree of the name.

Sývota
O Faros
Waterfront
Much the best *maghireftá* available here, crisply executed without grease, at this up-and-coming resort.

Párga
To Kyma
Waterfront
Despite its outwards appearance, not a tourist-trap, but a reliable source of *maghireftá* and one of the oldest *tavérnes* in town.

Préveza
Amvrosios
Opposite Venetian clock tower, Préveza bazaar
Wonderful grilled sardines and nothing but; no relation whatsoever to the canned variety.

Árta
Skaraveos
Priovólou 13
This cool and trendily appointed but very reasonable lunch-only spot has ample choice for vegetarians; well worth planning a stop for.

Kastoriá
Omonia
Platía Omonías
Enduringly popular eatery, especially at lunch, with all the standard *maghireftá* plus a few grills. Outdoor seating on the square.

Véria
Kostalar
Afodhítis 2d, Papákia district
Tasty clay-pot oven dishes and grills on offer since 1939 at this locally popular spot on a plane-shaded square. Shut Monday; supper only.

Kavála
Imaret
Poulídhou, Panayía district
Somewhat pricey, and brief menu, but who cares when you've the chance to eat inside the Imaret; claimed to be the largest Islamic civic building in Europe, an 18th-century almshouse and hostel for theological students.

Xánthi
Nisaki
Pindhárou
Incomparable setting on the Podhonýfi riverbank, with all the usual *mezédhes* – some spicy in the Thracian manner – and grills on offer.

Marónia
O Yerasimos
Platanítis beach
Friendly, reasonable seafood taverna with a little terrace within sight of much the best Thracian beach for some way in either direction.

Komótini
Apolavsis
Old bazaar
One of a handful of *ouzerí* that line the vine-shaded lanes of the old Ottoman bazaar; only really gets going by night.

Kórinthos
Arhondiko
4km (about 2 miles) west of modern Kórinthos on shore road
Tel: (0741) 27 96 8
Mezédhes tend to be more interesting than main courses; open all year, with indoor and outdoor seating.

Pátra
Beau Rivage
Platía 25-Martíou
Fancy but surprisingly reasonable restaurant with the emphasis on grills, but also mussels and squid.
En Patrais
Corner Aghíou Nikoláou and Iféstou
Classic old taverna with a steady clientele, proffering all the Greek standards.

Olympía
O Kladhios
Behind the train station on the riverside
A find in tourist-clogged Olympia: real *mezédhes*. Go early as outdoor seating is limited.

Koróni
Ouzeri Kangelarios
Waterfront
Tel: (0725) 22 64 8
The most imaginative of several eateries here, with mussels, sea urchins, prawns and small local fish, all reasonably priced.

Andhrítsena
O Gheorghis
Central square
Tel: (0626) 22 00 4
Sit amid the remains of the morning market, beside the tree that has grown around a water spout, and enjoy standard oven fare and grills.

Methóni
Iy Klimataria
A block from castle
Tel: (0723) 31 54 4
Somewhat pricey gourmet preparation of the Greek standards, with emphasis on own-grown produce transformed into vegetarian dishes.

Gustatory Note

The Greeks are more generous with oil in food than most northern Europeans palates are used to. Although you can ask for no oil on a salad, for instance (*hóris ládi*), most waiters will think this an odd request as Greeks generally regard oil as good for the digestion.

Pýlos
O Grigoris
Gheorghíou Krassánou
Tel: (0723) 22 62 1
Oven-baked *maghireftá* and
occasional grilled fish, served in a
pleasant garden in summer.

Kardhamýli
Lela's
Waterfront
Tel: (0721) 73 54 1
This is the oldest and most
traditional taverna here, with only
German draft beer as a concession
to the predominant clientele;
terrace seating and occasional live
music.

Neos Mystras
O Mystras
100 metres (109 yards) from
central fountain
Tel: (0731) 93 43 2
This is what Greeks eat for Sunday
lunch: vegetable stew, fat olives,
chops or sausages, accompanied
by plenty of rough-and-ready wine –
heaven. Indoor and outdoor
seating.

Monemvasía
Matoulla's
Lower Monemvasía
Tel: (0732) 61 66 0
For years the only taverna here,
this has recently become gentrified,
with seating out back on the fine
terrace, but the cooking still
passes muster.

Náfplio
Omorfi Poli
Kotsonopoúlou 1
Tel: (0752) 25 94 4
Greek casseroles and grills with a
nouvelle twist, but biggish, un-
nouvelle portions. Book in advance
as seating is limited, and come
hungry.
Ta Fanaria
Staïkopoúlou 13
Best at lunch when up to 20
dishes emerge from the oven;
good Megara *retsína* and moderate
prices, especially on a street
known for tourist rip-offs.

Stemnítsa
Iy Klinitsa
Central square
Basic but sympathetic taverna
dishing out home-style vegetables
or marinated salads alongside
grilled meat, plus barrel wine; an
oasis in an area otherwise bereft
of good food.

NE Aegean Islands

Samothráki
Orizontas
Kamariótissa
Quick-served *maghireftá* and good
bulk wine make this by far the best
of several *tavérnes* situated in the
port.
To Kastro
Kentrikí Platía,
Hóra
Excellent, unpretentious *ouzerí*

whose outdoor seating glimpses the
ruins of the Genoese castle.

Thássos
O Glaros
South end of the beach,
Alykí hamlet
Longest-lived, least expensive and
most authentic of several *tavérnes*
here; usually has a modest breed of
local fresh fish.
O Platanos
Under the tree,
Sotíros village
This is a summer-only taverna run
by a sympathetic young couple from
nearby Rahóni village; elaborate
dishes when trade justifies it,
simple grills otherwise, and
powerful homemade *tsípouro* if
you ask.
Iy Pighi
Kentriki Platía,
Liménas
Old warhorse dishing out
dependable *maghireftá* next to the
spring of the name; best at supper.

Límnos
Platanos
Mýrina town
Traditional purveyor of *maghireftá* in
the bazaar, beneath two plane trees.
Iliovasilemata
Ághios Ioánnis beach
Concrete-block building and tacky
verandah that's not much to look
at, but the seafood is excellent.
Zimbabwe
Platý village

Coffee and Tea

Greeks generally drink their coffee
and tea with lots of sugar. An
essential phrase for those who
like their hot drinks without sugar
is *horís záhari*, "without sugar".
Tag this phrase at the end of
whatever drink you are ordering:
for example, *Nescafé horís záhari*.
You can also ask for your drink
skéto which means the same
thing in a less emphatic way. If
you like some sugar ask for
métrio. If you love sugar say
nothing and they'll probably dump
a few teaspoons into whatever

you're drinking. *Me gála* means
"with milk".
Whole beans suitable for
cafetiere or percolator coffee only
arrived in Greece in the early
1990s; they are making steady
inroads among locals and tourists
fed up with the ubiquitous
"Nescafé", which has become the
generic term for any instant coffee.
In our view the only palatable use
for it is in *frapé*, cold instant
coffee whipped up in a shaker.
Gallikós "French", in other words
percolated coffee, usually quite

acceptable.
Ellenikós cafés Greek coffee,
boiled and served with the grounds
in the cup. If you want a large cup
of it ask for a *dhiplós. Ellenikó
cafés* is also known as *turkikós
cafés* but this sometimes provokes
patriotic objections.
Tsaï Tea either with milk or with
lemon, *me lemóni*
Hamomíli Camomile tea
Tsaï tou vounóu Mountain tea. Tea
made with mountain sage leaves.
Easy to find in shops, and at more
traditional *kafenía*.

Secluded but popular grill-*ouzerí*, strong on meats, run by a returned family from southern Africa; outdoor seating.

Lésvos
The Captain's Table
Old port, Mólyvos
Greek and Australian-run fish restaurant with grills and good vegetarian *mezédhes* too; excellent all-round, where you can take anyone regardless of food habits.
Ya Mas
Skála Eressoú, Waterfront
Canadian-Greek run breakfast and after-hours bar with pancakes, whole-grain bread and decadent chocolate desserts.
Dhouladhelli
South entrance to Aghiássos village
Inexpensive taverna with local specialities, including (in autumn) stuffed squash blossoms.
Iy Eftalou
Just before the thermal baths, Eftaloú
Reliable favourite, much resorted to by locals. Seating outdoors under the trees in summer; open indoors during winter.
Women's Agricultural Tourism Co-op
Kentrikí Platía, Pétra
Upstairs restaurant with lots of simple grills - plenty of seafood - *mezédhes*, and rather fewer *maghireftá*. Outdoor seating with sea views (and breezes).
Ilias
Vafiós village entrance
Both taverna-*ouzerí* here are decent, as long as you stay away from fried things; this one has a slight edge for the sake of whole-grain bread and good bulk wine.

Híos
O Dholomas
Karfás
Frankly tacky decor, but this is an excellent *ouzerí*; open May – September, and winter weekends.
Ouzeri Theodhosiou
Neoríon quay, Híos Town
Longest-lived and still one of the best *ouzerí* in town, despite dissenting grumbles about the occasional tinned item.

O Tsambos
Katarráktis
Fish *tavérnes* are often a rip-off; this homey place near the anchorage isn't.
O Pyrgos
Avgónyma village
Returned Greek-American family has set up shop in the old arcaded *kafenío*; food, if occasionally over-fried, is abundant and fresh.
Stelios's (Tou Koupelou)
Waterfront, Langádha
Last remaining – and happily one of the best – of the seafood *tavérnes* which once graced the quay here, swept away by the new craze for *barákia* and patisseries.
Kafenio E
Pýrgos district, Volissós
Vegetarian snack bar catering largely to the patrons of the two restored-house complexes here; reservations, tel: (0274) 21 48 0, are advised as space is limited.

Sámos
Nissi
Aghía Paraskeví bay
Grilled seafood, an abundant *dhiskos* (tray) of *mezédhes* and a seafront terrace make this a good choice.
Iy Haravghi
Kerveli beach
Better-than-average beach taverna with a full bar, good *mezedhes* and *maghireftá*.
Remataki
Town beach, Pythagorio
Most *tavérnes* in Pythagorio are clip joints; this is one of the few places locals will be seen at, for the sake of dishes like *anginares a La Polita* (artichokes with carrots, potatoes, vinegar and oil).
Blue Chairs
Vourliótes
Four *tavérnes* compete hotly in the photogenic central square here; this one, has an edge for crisply executed standards like *revithokeftédhes* (chickpea croquettes).
To Kyma
Ághios Konstandínos
This full-service taverna at the east

Eating Greek-style

For Greeks the main meal of the day is eaten between 2pm and 3.30pm, and, even in the cities, is usually followed by a siesta break lasting until 5.30 or 6pm.

The evening meal can either be another full meal, or an assortment of *mezédhes*. This is usually eaten between 9pm and 11pm.

Breakfast in Greece is traditionally small, usually bread and coffee. There are, however, wonderful options available from bakeries.

end of the quay has good bulk wine (not common on Sámos) and occasionally tasty local delicacies such as rabbit stew.
Iy Psaradhes
Aghios Nikolaos anchorage, Kondakéïka
Seafood and little else, at its best in spring.
To Kyma
Shore road, Limáni Karlóvassi
Long-running (since 1984) *ouzerí* specialising in reasonable seafood *pikilíes*.

Ikaría
Paskhalia
Armenistís
Ground-floor diner of a small pension has both wonderful breakfasts (for all comers) and reasonable fish washed down by good bulk wine at supper.
Delfini
Armenistís
Across the way from Paskhalia. More traditional, less polished, even more popular than its neighbour for the sake of the waves lapping the terrace – and the sustaining cooking.

Foúrni
Rementzo (Nikos')
Best of the three full-service waterfront *tavérnes*; here you'll almost definitely find *astakós*, Aegean lobster, and the succulent *skathári* or black bream, as Foúrni has an active fishing fleet.

Sporades Islands/Évvia

Skópelos
Spyros
Skópelos town
Popular taverna on the waterfront.
Perivóli
Skópelos town
Refined Greek cooking. You'll need to reserve a table.
Térpsis
Skópelos town
Head here for grilled chicken near Stafylos beach.

Alónissos
Several moderately priced restaurants are along the waterfront in Patitíri. Try **Astroftengiá** in the old town, which has better food, or **Paraport** in the castle, which has the view.

Skýros
Kristina's
Skýros town
Down the street branching away from the post office. Upmarket, very good non-Greek food.
Margétis
Main street, Skýros town
Good Greek food.

Évvia
Anemone
Kaárystos
Reasonably priced taverna near the Karystion Hotel.
In Límni Platanos, under the plane tree, is the popular favourite, and the **Kamares** and **Avra** opened in 1998.

Dodecanese Islands

Rhodes
Le Bistrot
Omírou 22–24, Old town
A genuine French-run bistro; pricey and a bit nouvelle, but very good, and always packed.
O Meraklis
Aristotélous 32
The last surviving patsatzídhiko (patsás kitchen) in town attracts a rather lurid clientele from 3–7am only; just the thing if you've stumbled off the overnight ferry.

Alatopipero
Miḥaïl Petrídhi 76, New town near Rodhíni park
Nouvelle-Greek ouzerí with recherché dishes like stuffed cyclamen leaves and hortópitta (wild greens pie), plus bottlings from Greece's better microwineries. Supper only; closed Monday.
O Yiannis
In Koskinoú village, 5 km (3 miles) south of Rhodes town Very reasonable mezédhes.
Tommy's
Haráki
Best of the waterfront fish tavérnes, run by a professional fisherman.
Epta Pighes
Eptá Pighés
This streamside exohikó kéndro has been going since 1948, and because of its Rhodian clientele is far better than its location would have you believe.
Platanos
Lahaniá village
Atmospheric seating by the double-spouted fountain here in the square; food's basic but normally priced.

Kárpathos
Olympia
Pigádhia waterfront away from the quay
Does reasonable grills.
Kali Kardhia
Pigádhia shore road
The spot for fish, though they do other things too.
To Limanaki
south end of Vróndi beach
There's only one independent tavérna the length of the beach; fortunately it's good, with nice touches like homemade rice pudding. Lunch only.
Parthenonas
Centre, Ólympos village
The place to go for local titbits like makaroúnes (homemade pasta with onions and cheese) or myrgouátana (a type of fried seaweed).

Halki
Mavri Thalassa
Emborio waterfront
None of the half-dozen tavérnes

here are bad, but this currently has the edge for its carefully prepared mezédhes and crab salad.

Kastellorizo
Ouzeri Megisteas
Behind the arcaded market building Best value for money, with a good line in goat chops (generally better than lamb in Greece).
Little Paris
Waterfront
Longest-running and most reliable of several fish tavérnes, most of which cater to not-very-discriminating yachties.

Tilos
Blue Sky
Above the ferry dock, Livádhia
The more reasonable of two spots for grilled fish.
Stelios
East end of Livádhia bay
Newish (1997) entrant on the scene, currently about the best for Greek maghireftá.
Kali Kardhia
Megálo Horió
This has much the best food in the western half of the island and fine views over the kámbos to Éristos beach.

Symi
Gheorghios's
Horio
This is an island institution, decades old and still very good; nouvelle Greek cuisine in non-nouvelle big portions served on the pebbled courtyard.
O Meraklis
Rear of Yialos bazaar
Well-executed dishes, if a bit pricey (especially the baby native shrimp).
Tholos
Past the Haráni shipyards
A ouzerí with tasty food and an excellent view of town.

Nissyros
Taverna Nissyros
Inland lane of Mandhráki
The oldest and one of the most popular outfits here.
Taverna Irini
Platía Ilikioméni, Mandhráki

Big portions of fish and meat, unlike many other *mezédhes*-orientated spots in town.

Aphroditi
Páli fishing port
Good for *maghireftá*, homemade desserts and bulk Cretan wine.

Kos

Ambavris
Ambávris hamlet, 800 metres (875 yards) south of Kós town
Outdoor courtyard seating means only summer operation; go for the *pikilía* or house medley.

Gin's Palace
Platáni village
Ethnic Turkish management dishes out tasty Anatolian-style *mezédhes* and grills all year round.

Psistaria Apostolis
Marmári access road
Fresh fish and own-produced meat, an amazing wine list and reasonable prices, what more could you want? Open all summer and winter weekends for locals.

Olympiada
Ziá village
Perhaps the only one of a dozen *tavérnes* here without a sunset view, so the food – lots of stews with *pligoúri* (bulgur wheat) on the side – has to be good. Open most of the year.

Iy Pighi
Pylí village
Inexpensive, basic (*loukánika* etc) but nourishing taverna hidden away beside a giant cistern fountain with lion-headed spouts, best for a lunch while touring.

Limionas
Limiónas fishing anchorage, near Kéfalos
Where you go for fresh fish on Kós; limited menu otherwise.

Kálymnos

Barba Petros/Adherfi Martha
East quay, Póthia
Excellent and reasonable seafood, if rather plainly served.

Xefteris
Inland
Good and traditional *maghireftá* dishes, though not as cheap as they might be – probably due to their fame.

Iliovasilema
Myrtiés
Run by the local butcher, so good grills; never mind the tacky decor.

Astralea

Iy Monaxia/Viki's
Inland from ferry jetty, Skála
Most reliable purveyor of *maghireftá* on the island; open much of the year.

Leros

Ouzeri Kapetan Mihalis
Little alley in Aghía Marína
Basic but authentic and cheap (no sea view) place where you can sample local salt-marinated (*pastós*) seafood. Open for lunch.

Mezedhopolio Kapaniri
Aghía Marína seafront
Plenty of fried vegetable first courses, then meat or seafood. Best for supper.

To Stéki
Next to Allied war cemetery, Álinda
Good grills and *mezédhes*, open all year for a local clientele.

Iy Thea Artemi
Blefoútis beach
Better-than-average beach taverna in the middle of nowhere; the usual *marídhes* or *kalamária* with chips.

Lípsí

Barbarosa
Good for vegetable-based *maghireftá*; great view terrace.

Delfini
By the police station
Eclectic menu including fish and vegetables, popular with British groups.

Fish Restaurant
On the quay
Only opens when the owner has freshly caught something – a good sign.

Pátmos

O Grigoris
Skála waterfront
Seating is noisy – at the corner with the road up to Hóra – but the food, all the Greek standards, is carefully prepared and abundant.

Vangelis
Main square, Hóra

Eating out with Kids

Children regularly dine out with their parents until late at night. There's no formality about this – kids are as likely to be racing round the taverna playing tag or under the table teasing the stray cats as sitting up at the table. The Greeks are extremely indulgent to their children, so don't be embarrassed to make any special food request for your own.

Eat out on the pavement or inside on the raised pavillion at this long-running classic *maghireftá* spot. Check out the amazing juke-box, if it's still there.

Melloi/Stefanos's
Melóï beach
A superb taverna, especially at a beach; from cavernous 1970s premises issue a stream of well-executed *maghireftá*, with plenty for vegetarians.

Lambi
Lámbi beach
Besides Stefanos, the most reliable of Pátmos' various beach eateries; food's much simpler, emphasizing grilled meat.

Ionian Islands

Corfu

Trípa
Kinopiástes, just south of Corfu town
Fixed, moderately high-priced, but an endless flow of very good food.

Lefkáda

Reganto
Lefkáda town
Down the first road leading off the main square to the right as you come down from the harbour. Colourful atmosphere, good food.

Nikiána
Lefkáda town
Breath of Zorba with tables right by the water.

Nydri
Lefkáda town
Nick the Greek's standard good *tavérna* on the harbour.

Ithaki
Gregory's
Vathy
Just outside town, Gregory's has a romantic setting under the trees and good food, both meat and fish.

Kefalloniá
In Lourdáta there are several good *tavérnes* near the Lara hotel, the closest of which is the traditional **Thalasino Trifylli**, just across from the hotel.

Zákynthos
Arekia Taverna and the **Village Inn** in Zakynthos Town are both good places to enjoy an evening meal.

Crete

Haniá
Karnaghio
In old harbour
Tholos
Typical Cretan fare.
Dino's
Seafood restaurant.

Réthymnon
Agrimia
Typical Cretan fare.
Famagusta
Cypriot and Cretan food.

Irákleion
Kyriakos

Ordering Drinks

bíra	beer
kokkinélli	resinated rosé wine *krasí* wine
mávro	red
me to kiló, or *hima*	wine by the kilo local, from the barrel
neró	water
retsína	resin-flavoured wine
oúzo	aniseed-flavoured grape distillate
rakí	distilled spirit from vintage crushings
tsípouro	north-mainland version of rakí, up to 48 percent alcohol

Reliable *tavérna*.
Ippokambas
Best mezé in town.

Saronic Gulf Islands

Aegína
Vostitsano
Aegina town

Or try any of the numerous fish *tavérnes* in Perdika.

Cylades

Santorini
Taverna Katina Coletta
Ammoudi, Oia
In many people's eyes, the fresh fish, prawns, lobster and Santorini specialities make this the island's best taverna. Easter until October; from lunch until the wee hours.
Taverna Ambrosia
Kamari
Fotis and his Australian wife, Nicki, have been written up in *Vogue* for the exquisite things they do with seafood. Moderate.
Taverna Pyrgos
Pyrgos Village
This is an elegant restaurant with an unusual view. Order a table-full of their excellent *mezédhes*, or starters, especially the smoky aubergine salad. Expensive.
Restaurant Nikolaos
On Stavros Street, parallel to the caldera road, near the Kira Thira Jazzbar in Phira.
Only traditional Greek food and very fresh fish is served here, simply prepared for reasonable prices; red and white barrel wines. Serving Santorinians for 35 years. Order the *koliós* fish. Open year round for lunch and dinner. Moderate.
Every Day Cafe
A few doors south of the Kira Thira Jazzbar in Phira
Gild the lily and order their chocolate-covered *baklava* with your Lavazza coffee. Open all day long, from (contrary to its name) 20 March until the end of October. Inexpensive.
Neptune
Near the blue-domed Church of the Virgin, Oia
The Karvounis family has been

serving seafood, meat-stuffed lettuce leaves and superb *tiropitas* etc, for 35 years. Lunch here is superb – matched by the view. Moderate.
Mama's Café (at the Blue Note Bar)
Surely Mama Irini serves the best US-style breakfasts in Greece: pancakes, french toast and Maxwell House coffee. Inexpensive.
O Kritikos ("Psistaria")
At Yothonas on the airport road. Barbara and Michaelis have brought this taste of Crete to Santorini. Grilled pork, lamb and veal plus speciality meats are featured. Try *saganaki* (fried cheese) and Cretan house wines.

For after-hours tippling, you can't beat the **Kira Thira Jazzbar**, a barrel-vaulted jazz and blues haunt in central Phira, next to Every Day Cafe. Dimitris Tsavdarides brews a mean sangria. Alternatively, **Franco's Bar**, on the caldera in Phira, has been rated one of the world's best by no less than *Newsweek International*. The tall drinks it serves are works of art; so is the wonderful view. **The Blue Note Pub**, also in Phira, is one of the current hot spots in town for the (good) beer and rock bunch.

Mykonos
Efthimios Efthimiou's Patisserie
Fl. Zouganeli Street, Hora
For over 40 years, Efthimiou has served up Mykonos's famed 'little baskets' (*kalathakia*) and macaroons in his immaculate sweet shop – for 15 years at this location. (Takeaway only.) Expensive.
L'Angolo Bar
Lakka district, Hora
The place for espresso, cappuccino and a quick breakfast, as well as packed lunches for Delos or the beach. Moderate.
Nikola's Taverna
Aghia Anna Beach (after Plati Yialos)
A locals' favourite: an authentic Greek *tavérna* on a pretty, tiny beach. Moderate.
Taverna Niko's
Just off the harbour, up from

St. Nicholas church
For a quarter of a century, Niko's have made fresh fish and lobster their speciality. Try homemade moussaka, salads with capers and roka. Great service. Moderate.

Sesame Kitchen
Three Wells district, Hora
Hazel Fouski is English, and the charming bistro she has established in Hora is a vegetarian's haven, though meat dishes appear on the menu as well. A great place to sample Greek bottled wines. High season 7pm–1am.

Katrin's
Aghios Yerasimos district, Hora
For 20-odd years, 'Bobbys' has featured pricey French cuisine with a Mykonian twist. Order his seafood starters and finish with chocolate mousse. Mr Giziotis also owns Super Paradise Beach's Coco Bar. High season 7pm–4am. Expensive.

Matthew Taverna
Tourlos (on San Stefanos road)
This is a polished *tavérna*, and the service on the cool terrace is personalised and genuine. Try *Bekri Meze*, a kind of Greek boeuf bourgignon, or lamb wrapped in vine leaves. High season noon–1am. Inexpensive to moderate.

La Bussola
Laka district, Hora
Chef Giovanni Marale serves up excellent Genovese dishes, but the pizza is also delicious. Whatever you choose as a main course, be sure to try the *pannacotta* afterwards. Moderate.

Sea Satin Market
Alefkhandra quarter, directly below the windmills
Absolutely unique waveside restaurant, Sea Satin is open from breakfast until tea-time. Creative, home-made cuisine, Easter until mid-September. Inexpensive.

Naxos

The Meltemi Restaurant
Extreme southern end of Hora's waterfront, on the sea.
The Meltemi's been here some 50 years, serving Greek cuisine, including fresh fish. It's authentic, reserved and very Greek. Easter till

end October, all day till midnight. Inexpensive to moderate.

Oniro Restaurant/Roof Garden/Bar
In Hora downhill from Pradounas Square, just outside Kastro quarter
It's the roof garden's view that's an *oniro*, or dream. The food is simply reliable Hellenic/international. Order the *kaloyeros*, eggplant with veal, or *baxes*, which is a vegetarian's delight. Open Easter till end October. Moderate to expensive.

To Kastro Taverna
On Pradounas Square
This is a good place for Greek rabbit stew, or *stifado*, and *exohiko*, a layered pastry with lamb, cheese and vegetables. Easter till end October. Moderate to expensive.

After dark, head for the little square of Nikiforos Mandilaras, also called Villandoni Square, next to Takis Probonas's liquor store. Late of an evening here, you may have the good fortune to hear guitarists accompanying Naxian men of a certain age singing either distinctive Naxian songs or mainland ballads of the early 20th century.

For rowdier entertainment, head north out of town 3km (2 miles) for Platanos/Bouzouki Greek dancing. Harbourfront bars in Hora, such as the second-storey **Greek Bar**, midway down the waterfront, and **Veggera**, a Mýkonos clone at the southern end of the port, are good.

Paros

Tamarisko Garden Restaurant
Neos Dromos Street, Paroikia
Located in the Old Agora marketplace. Order Pork Stew Tamarisko, mushrooms in sauce, and the dreamy chocolate mousse. March till end-October 7pm onwards. Closed Monday. Moderate.

Cafe Nostros Crêperie
Near the National Bank, Paroikia
Mrs Panagaki, the owner, is a delight. Try her homemade apple pielets and crêpes. Come for breakfast, snacks, decent coffee and freshly squeezed fruit juices. Open all year, all day. Inexpensive.

The wine Greece is most known for, retsina, is flavoured with pine resin, It's an acquired taste but in hot weather is an ideal "solvent" for greasy, heavy food.

Ouzerie/Psarotaverna Boudaraki
Harbour road, Paroikia
Situated just before the Pandrossos Hotel, this is a typical Greek *ouzerí* with drinks and Greek starters such as grilled octopus and fresh sea urchins. Open Easter till early October. Inexpensive.

The Levanti
Old Agora, Paroikia
Next to the Vietnamese restaurant called May-Tey, order mixed Lebanese starters, falafel and tabouli, as well as one of several diverse salads. Open year round; garden in summer and autumn. Expensive.

O Christos
Opposite the Church of the Panagia Pantanassa, Naoussa
Very elegant; very nice. Stick to seafood, their speciality, and expect to pay somewhat more than usual. Expensive.

Perivolaria Restaurant
Near Naoussa's police station, and opposite Artio Travel
Snails, schnitzel and shrimp – take your pick. It's all good. A fancy, international restaurant with a short summer season and pricey (for Greece) rates. Expensive.

Greek wines have yet to obtain the status of their French counterparts, though young oenologists trained abroad are definitely having a go at it, and there are an increasing number of quality micro-wineries on the mainland.

Additionally, many islands produce excellent vintages that they can't or won't export, so they remain unknown. Miles Lambert-Gócs' The Wines of Greece (Faber & Faber) is recommended as a guide to the better bottles, though coverage ceases in 1993.

All this wonderful wine however, costs as much as anywhere else; cheaper but palatable mainland labels include Carras (Macedonia), Boutari (Macedonia), Cambas (Attica), and Tsantali (Macedonia). Examples include:

Boutari Nemea: the best mid-range red. Full bodied, not too tanniny. Other, premium versions of Nemea – merely a region in the north-central Peloponnese – exist; the pricier, the smoother, as a rule.

Boutari Lacs des Roches: their upper mid-range white, is considered superior to Rotonda.

Katoghi: a wonderfully smooth red from Métsovo.

Hatzimihali, red and white: the first, and still one of the best of central Greek microwineries; what fancy *tavérnes* tend to have as a premium wine, it can also be found in rather provincial bottle-shops.

Athanasiadhi, red and white: similar to Hatzimihali, and as readily available.

Gheorghiadi: the best bottled *retsína*, from Thessaloníki, far superior to the usually preferred Kourtaki or Malamatina.

Island Wines

Many islands bottle (or barrel) wines that are sold only locally. Although barreled (*me to kiló, híma*) wines tend to be rough and ready, they're very cheap and certainly authentic. You may have to ask around for the following:

Ionian Islands

Kefalloniá Robola, a delicate expensive white.

Corfu Theotoki is the local wine (red or white); the speciality of the island is a very sweet orange liqueur called Kumquat.

Antípaxi The local grapes are much appreciated; ask for wine from the barrel.

Zákynthos Try the wines made from grapes grown in Zákynthos's lush green vineyards: Comouto rosé or the white Verdea.

Dodecanese Islands

Rhodes A visit to one of the numerous off-licences in Rhodes town will find a whole range of locally produced drinks; wines from Rhodes are consumed all over the Dodecanese. CAIR, the cooperative originally founded by the Italians, has the ubiquitous white Ilios (named after the sun god) and red Chevalier du Rhodes, but the private, Émbonas-based winery Emery is more esteemed for its Mythiko and Villaré red and white labels. CAIR Brut "champagne" is exported to many islands and can also be found in Athens.

Níssyros Produces a non-alcoholic drink called soumádha, similar to Italian orgeat, made from almonds; you dilute the syrup 3:1 with water for a refreshing drink.

Northeast Aegean

Sámos is one of the few islands to export wine, not only to the mainland but also abroad; the French in particular like the sweet dessert wines. A number of premium white bottles in particular are produced, but surprisingly the **ouzo** is reckoned better: try Ghiokarinis brand.

Híos Particularly around Mestá a heavy, sherry-like but very palatable wine is made from raisins. Ouzo is made here too – try Tetteris brand.

Lésvos Quite a few local ouzos emanate from the distilling centre of Plomári; Varvaghiannis is the most celebrated, and expensive, but many consider it too sweet. EPOM is the principal cooperative, marketing among others the "Mini" brand, with its rampantly sexist label, a staple of ouzerí across the country.

Limnos Like most volcanic islands, Límnos produces excellent whites, fewer reds; almost anything is worth trying, and easily available from Myrina bottle shops.

Thássos Not wine, not *oúzo*, but tsípouro – often flavoured with exotic spices or pear extract rather than the anise of *oúzo* – is the tipple here. Homemade firewater gets lethally strong; anything over 50 percent alcohol must be barrelled, not bottled, lest it explode

Beer & Wine

Greeks never simply "go out drinking". Even if an evening involves heavy drinking of *retsína* or *oúzo*, these will always be accompanied by food, an inveterate habit which minimises the effects (and after-effects) of the alcohol.

When it comes to ordering your wine, check to see if they serve wine from the barrel (ask for *híma*). This is the inexpensive local stuff which varies from town to town. Otherwise you can choose among the various bottled wines, some of the better Greek labels being Cambas, Boutari, Carras and Calliga. *Áspro* is white, *mávro* is red, rosé is rosé, retsína is resinated white wine, and *kokinélli* is resinated rosé.

Easter Celebrations

Easter is Greece's big festive occasion, like Christmas in northern Europe. Stay in one of the larger villages and you'll be sucked into the celebrations, including Good Friday funereal processions, a candlelit mass at midnight on Easter Saturday and festivities, dancing and spit roast throughout Sunday in village centres.

Celebrations in the mountain island of Ídhra, Corfu, Olymbos and Patmos are reputed to be the best. But book your accommodation well in advance.

Culture

Dance & Music

A considerable part of the good music and dance performances take place during the various festivals (*see Cultural Events, below*). Besides these performances, however, there are numerous other events worth attending in both Athens and Thessaloníki.

In Athens, outstanding Greek and foreign musicians often perform at the Lykavittós Theatre on Mount Lykavittós, not to mention the larger concerts that take place in the soccer stadiums. Opera can be seen at the Olympia Theatre, performed by the Lyriki Skini (the National Opera Company), while classical music is typically performed at the Megaron Musikis near the American Embassy.

In Thessaloníki, summertime venues include the Theatro Dhassos, on the slopes beyond Kastra, and Theatro Kipou, near the archeological museum; in winter performances of music, opera, dance and theatre move indoors to the nearly adjacent State Theatre and Royal Theatre, near the White Tower. More cutting-edge are events at the multi-functional cultural centre, Mylos, a converted flour mill 2km (about a mile) southeast of the centre, comprising cinemas, concert halls, exhibition space, musical *boites* and a theatre.

In both Athens and Thessaloníki, the cultural institutes (Goethe, British Council, French) sometimes sponsor interesting events.

Athens has an active dance scene with ballet, folk, modern, jazz and experimental dance troupes.

Greek Music

Greece has an incredible range of musics, ranging from folk to light popular, *rembétika* to Byzantine chanting, Theodorakis to Haris Alexiou. Endless muzak soundtracks on boats and in *tavérnes* notwithstanding, there *is* musical life after Zorba.

Owing to Greece's geographical position and the vast number of cultures that have called it home, there is astonishing regional variety in folk music. Crete has one of the more vital traditions, characterised by the *lyra* (three-string spike fiddle) and *laouto* (mandolin-like lute). In the Dodecanese, these are often joined by either *tsamboúna*, a goatskin bagpipe, or *sandoúri*, the hammer dulcimer popularised in the islands by refugees from Asia Minor.

Nisiótika is the general name for island music; that of the Ionians is the most Italian-influenced and western in scale. Mainland music is also unmistakable, characterised by the extensive use of the *klaríno* (clarinet) and, in Epirus, an extraordinary, disappearing tradition of polyphonic singing.

Rembétika, despite its 1970s revival in clubs in Athens and Patras, is now a rather static artform, but one enduringly popular and well-documented on CD. When combing the stacks at record stores, keep an eye out for such stalwart artists as Vassilis Tsitsanis, Roza Eskenazi, Rita Ambatzi, Ioannis Papaioannou, Markos Vamvakaris, Marika Papaghika and Andonis Dalgas.

Contemporary sounds include original syntheses or derivations of the folk and rembetic traditions by such artists as Thessalonian Dionysis Savvopoulos, who first challenged the supremacy of bouzouki in the mid-1960s with his guitar and orchestral-based

Cultural Events

April–October Sound and Light performances in Athens at the Pnyx; on Corfu at Venetian Castle; Rhodes at Grand Master's.
May–September Folk dancing by the Dora Stratou Group in Athens, and Nelly Dimoglou Group in Rhodes Old Town.
May–October Rhodes. Theatre, concerts, dance and so on.
June Jazz & Blues Festival, Lykavittós Theatre, Athens
Mid-June-September Pátras International Festival: ancient drama, classical music and contemporary theatre up in the medieval castle grounds and the Odeon.

June–September Athens Festival at the Herod Atticus Odeon, among other venues.
Late June–late Sept Symi Festival. Concerts and musical events; newish but apparently set for success.
July–August Epídhavros Festival. Performances of ancient drama in the open-air Epidaurus amphitheatre.
Late July Music Festival on the island of Itháki (Ithaca).
Early August Iráklion concerts, theatre, opera and so on.
August Lefkádha Festival of Music, Folklore and Theatre, with overseas groups.

August Kavala Festival: includes ancient drama performed at Philippi.
Late August Wine Festival in Rodhíni Park, south of Rhodes town.
July–August "Epirot Summer" at Ioánnina; includes ancient drama performances at nearby Dodona amphitheatre.
Aug–Sept Santorini Music Festival
Aug–Oct Rhodes Festival
Aug–Sept Réthymnon Renaissance Fair: cultural activities at the Venetian Fort.
October Thessaloniki Dhimitria Festival. Theatre, music, ballet, followed by a self-contained film-festival.

compositions, and spawned a whole generation of disciples and protegés such as rock-influenced Nikos Papazoglou, Nikos Xydhakis and Heimerinoi Kolymvites. Revival artists who have updated folk traditions with varying degrees of success include Haïnidhes, Loudovikos ton Anogheion, and the Irishman Ross Daly.

Theatre

Athens has an active theatre life but, as most productions are in Greek, options for English-speakers are limited. Most productions in English take place during festivals (*see Cultural Events*). You will do best to check the *Athens News* for up-to-date information.

One recent cultural initiative has provided some excellent productions of both modern and ancient drama in English at one of Greece's most striking open-air theatres – the Stone (Pétra) Theatre in Petropolis in the suburbs of Athens. In summer, plays are produced under the auspices of the Stones and Rocks Festival.

Movies

Going to the cinema in Greece during the summer is a special pleasure not to be missed. Nearly all the movie theatres that run in the summer (the others shut down unless air-conditioned) are open-air, sometimes tucked among apartment buildings (whose tenants

Traditional Greek Dancing

Each region and island of Greece has its own version of the folk dance. This ranges from the basic *sta tria* – three steps to one side, followed by a kick (growing gradually faster and faster) – to a frenzied combination of complicated footwork, jumps, slaps and kicks. Troupes, dressed in traditional Greek costume, are

watch the film from their balconies), in other areas, perched on a seaside promontory under rustling palm trees, stars and the moon. Tickets are slightly cheaper than indoor movie houses and soundtracks are in the original language. It's also a great way to beat the dog-day heat of high-summer in Greece.

Cultural Hubs

In Athens there are two main cultural centres for those who speak English: the British Council and the Hellenic American Union.

The British Council in Kolonáki Square (tel: 36 33 211) sponsors occasional lectures, exhibitions and performances (although its library is no longer open to the public).

The Hellenic American Union, Massalías 22, 4th Floor (tel: 36 37 740) sponsors various cultural events and also runs several courses in Greek dance, film, language, literature and so on for

most likely to be performing on public holidays.

Probably the best-known professional group is Dora Stratou Greek Folk Dances, which holds regular shows from May to September.
Dora Stratou Theatre, Philoppapou Hill, Athens. Tel: 32 43 95.

foreign visitors. Open Monday–Friday 9.30am–2pm; Monday–Thursday 5.30pm–8.30pm.

The Athens Centre, 48 Arhimídhous, Pangráti, runs the best language courses in town.

In Thessaloníki there are also two main cultural centres for those who speak English: the British Council, 9 Ethnikís Amýnis, corner Egnatias (tel: 23 52 36) and the American Centre, 34 Mitropóleos Street, 1st floor, just off Aristotelous Square (tel: 27 63 47). Though somewhat more limited in scope, their activities are similar to those of the Athens centres.

It's all Greek to You

You may not know a word of Greek, but it's still worth going to one of the Greek plays that are on over the summer.

All the ancient amphitheatres – such as Epídhavros, Pátras, Dodona, Philippi and Athens' Herod Atticus Odeon – put on evening productions of plays written by the famous ancient playwrights (such as Aristophanes, Sophocles and Euripides). They're in the original

ancient Greek, but they're fairly easy to follow if you read the play beforehand or a brief synopsis of the plot – worth watching for the spectacle alone.

Nothing beats the atmosphere in these imposing ancient amphitheatres as the sun sets and the audience lights up tiny candles and settles back for the performance. Bring along a cushion and blanket as you're sitting on the old stone seats.

Festivals

Annual Festivals

January 1 Feast of Ághios Vasílios (St Basil): celebrated all over Greece. Greek for Happy New Year is *kali kroniá*.
January 6 Epiphany – Blessing of the waters: all over Greece.
January 8 "Gynaecocracy"– men and women switch roles on the feast of St Domenica (Dhomniki), patron of midwives: villages in the areas around Komotiní, Xánthi, Kilkís and Sérres (village of Monoklissia).
February–March Carnival season for three weeks before Lent: all over Greece. Some villages with celebrations of special interest are: Náoussa, Véria, Kozáni, Zánte, Skýros, Xánthi, Híos (Mestá, Olýmbi), Lésvos (Aghiássos), Galaxídi, Thebes, Polýgyros,

Athens Festival

The Athens Festival runs from June to September and hosts numerous cultural events, including ballet, opera, jazz and modern music, and modern and classical plays from worldwide artists.

Top performances are popular, so book tickets as soon as you arrive in Greece. Information and tickets can be obtained from the GNTO (EOT) Festival Office, 2 Spýrou Milíou Arcade (entrance from 4 Stadou Street). Tel: 32 21 459 or 32 23 222, ext 240.

Otherwise, you can often get seats on the day of the performance by calling in at the box office of the Herod Atticus Odeon 6pm–9pm.

Thimianá, Lamía, Kefalloniá, Messíni, Sohós, Sérres, Kárpathos, Iráklion, Ámfissa, Efxinoupolis (Vólos), Aghía Anna (Euboea), Réthymnon and (best of all) Pátra.
"Clean" Monday Beginning of fast for Lent. Picnics in the countryside and kite flying, all over Greece.
March 25 Feast of Annunciation/ Independence Day. Anniversary of Bishop Ghermanos of Pátra raising the standard of revolt against the Turks near Kalávryta in 1821: military parades in all main towns, pilgrimage to Tínos.
Easter Cycle Good Friday, Holy Saturday and Easter Sunday are celebrated throughout the whole of Greece.
April 23 Feast of St George: celebrated especially in Kaliópi (Límnos), Aráhova, Así Gonía (near Haniá) and Pylí (Kos).
May 1 Labour Day: picnics in the countryside all over Greece.
May 21 *Anastenáridhes*: fire-walking ritual at Aghía Eléni (near Sérres) and at Langádha (near Thessaloníki).
August 15 Assumption of the Virgin: festivals all over Greece. Major pilgrimage to the island of Tínos.
September Cricket on Corfu.
October 28 "Ohi (No) Day" – anniversary of Greek defeat of Italian army in 1940 and Metaxas' supposed one-word response to Italy's ultimatum. Military parades in major cities.
Christmas season All over Greece. Children sing *kálanda* (carols) from door to door for a small gratuity.
December 31 New Year's Eve. More carols. Many Greeks play cards for money on this occasion, and cut the *vassilópitta* with a lucky coin hidden in it. Special celebration in the town of Híos.

Nightlife

Nightlife

Metropolitan nightlife in Greece (essentially Athens, Thessaloníki, Iráklion and Pátra) can be roughly divided into four categories: bars; live music clubs with jazz, Greek music (most likely *laïki*, or a watered-down version of *rembétika*) and rock; discos; and musical *tavérnes* where food prices reflect the live entertainment.

It should be noted first, however, that for most Greeks, the simple *tavérna* remains the most popular site for a night out spent eating, drinking and, sometimes, singing with your friends. In general, younger Greeks frequent the bars, music clubs and discos, while the locales for popular Greek music are more patronised by the older generations.

In Athens, the weekly *Athinórama* (in Greek) has an extensive listing of all the various venues and events. If you really want to find out what's going on in the city, ask a Greek friend to help you sort through the listings. However, do take note that during the late summer (July–August) many clubs and music halls close down, with musicians of all stripes touring the countryside for the summer festival season, or setting up shop at a beachfront "annexe" of a trendy island or resort.

The true Greekophile will gain the truest flavour of Athens nightlife only during the winter months, when small (sometimes slightly seedy) clubs called *boites* open their doors to singers crooning love songs into the early hours of the morning. Eat and drink first, though, as the price for indifferent wine is exorbitant at these clubs.

Gay Life

Overt gay behaviour is not a feature of Greek society. Homosexuality is legal at the age of 17, and bisexuality fairly common among men, but few couples (male or female) are openly gay. Mýkonos is famous as a gay Mecca, and Lésvos (where the Greek poetess Sappho was born) for lesbians. But elsewhere in Greece single-sex couples are liable to be regarded as odd, although usually welcomed as any other tourists.

Let the *kefi* take you

Like the Spanish, the Greeks are famous for their impromptu dancing. If you stay on an island you'll be unlucky not to witness a local, empowered by a few retsinas and egged on by friends, suddenly get up from his table in the taverna to girate to the music. When the *kefi*, or spirit of the dance, really takes hold, you may even see glasses on heads and jigging on tables through to the early hours.

Join in and you'll work off a few moussakas and have friends for life (and as likely as not an extra glass of wine or two on the house). Don't worry if you've got two left legs or no sense of rhythm – no one will even notice.

Though plate breaking was a regular feature in the 1960s and 1970s, and still goes on in a few "Greek" restaurants in London, this is now outlawed in Greece. Some establishments turn a blind eye to the law, but any tourist who gets carried away in the spirit of the moment is more than likely to be paying for breakages at the end of the night.

Sport

Participant Sports

Greece offers a wide variety of possibilities for sports and recreation. The following is a partial listing of these:

Cave Exploration

Greece is honey-combed with caves. Usually the local Tourist Police have information on where local caves are and how you go about visiting them. The following have set hours and facilities for public visits: Koutoúki, Peaneía, Attica; Pérama, near Ioánnina; Drogharáti and Melissáni, Kefalloniá; Andíparos, the Cyclades; Glyfádha and Alepótripa at Dhirós, Máni, Peloponnese; Petrálona, at Kókkines Pétres, Halkidhikí.

Diving

Scuba-diving in Greece is tightly controlled, with the aim of preserving the nation's heritage of submerged antiquities. However, there is a growing number of authorized sites for diving — consult your nearest EOT/GNTO branch for an updated list. Those of long standing include Órmos Kallithás on Rhodes, Vlihádhia Bay on Kálymnos, and much of southern Mýkonos.

Do not, however, expect undersea fauna and flora of Caribbean splendour; free-diving with mask, fins and snorkel is likely to be just as rewarding in Greek waters.

Fishing

There are plenty of places where you can fish in Greece. In the villages of most islands you will find boats and fishing tackle for hire. If you'd like some suggestions

contact the **Amateur Anglers and Maritime Sports Club**, Aktí Moutsopoúlou, in Piraeus, tel: (451) 5731.

Golf

Greece is by no means carpeted with golf courses, but, if you get the yen to tee up, try:
The Glyfada Golf Course and Club, tel: (894) 6820 (18 holes)
The Afandou Golf Club, Rhodes, tel: (0214) 51225–6 (18 holes)
The Corfu Golf Club, Ropa Valley, tel: (0661) 94220/1 (18 holes)
The Pórto Carrás Golf Course, near Néos Marmarás, Halkidhikí, tel: (0375) 71381/71221 (18 holes).

Health Spas

You'll find health spas with hydrotherapy in the following locations: Loutrá Edipsós, Évvia (Euboea); Loutrá Eléftheron, Kavála; Loutrá Kaïáfas, Illia; Kaména Voúrla; Loutrá Kyllini, Illia; Kýthnos, the Cyclades; Langádha, Thessaloniki (also mud baths); Loutráki, Corinth; Méthana, Saronic Gulf; Platistomo, Smókovo, Kardítsa; Thermá, Ikaría; Thermopylae; Vouliagméni, Attica; Ípati, Roúmeli.

Most of these are decidedly institutional, locally pitched and old-fashioned, though refurbishment with EU grants is promised in many spots.

Hiking & Mountaineering

Greece is a paradise for hikers and mountain climbers, with many surviving footpaths in the mainland mountains and on certain islands, threading through forested areas untouched by the tourist masses. For information on trails, maps, refuges and excursions, consult one of the specialist guides in the booklist, or if you'd prefer an organized excursion, see the list of trekking operators on page 326. The GNTO also produces several walking leaflets with details of recommended tracks and wildlife to look out for en route.

Sailing

Numerous companies offer sailing packages and cruises round the coast of Greece that can be booked from home. Much of the sailing is in flotillas helmed by the hire companies, but experienced sailors can charter their own yacht. Alternatively, once you're in Greece you can hire boats by the day or week at many marinas.

The best times to sail are spring and autumn, as winds can be high through the summer months and prices are hiked up to many times that of the cooler seasons.

There are sailing schools, housed in the naval clubs of the following cities: Athens (Paleó Fáliro); Thessaloníki; Corfu; Vólos; Rhodes; Syros; Kalamáta; Alexandhroúpolis. Further information can be obtained from: **Hellenic Yachting Federation**, 7 Akti Navárhou Koundourióti, Piraeus. Tel: 4137531, fax: 4131119.

Horse Riding

Many small riding schools offer horse riding. Contact the Riding Club of Greece, Paradissos, tel: 6826128, or in the capital the Riding Club of Athens, tel: 6611088.

Skiing

Most Greek mountains above 2,000m (6, 562 ft) high have good snow cover for skiing from December to March, with some of the higher mountains (Olympos, Parnassus and the Píndhos) skiable until May.

The following mountains have ski-lifts and are almost exclusively devoted to down-hill skiing, though there are also cross-country ski rentals: Mount Vérmio, Náoussa (chair-lift); Mount Pílion (chair-lift); Mount Parnassós (chair-lift); Mount Tymvristós, Karpeníssi (chair-lift); Métsovo, Epirus (chair-lift); Khelmós, near Kalávryta (chair-lift); Mount Vítsi, Vígla Pissodheríou, near Flórina; Mount Vróndou, near Sérres; Mount Dhírfys, Évvia; Mount Ménalon, near Trípoli; Mount Olympus, Vryssopoúles; Mount Pangéo, Kiládha Orfeá, near Kavála; Mount Falakró, near Drama.

For further information contact the Greek Skiing and Alpine Federation, 7 Karagheórghi Servías Street, Athens, tel: 3234555. Or the GNTO has a brochure listing mountain refuges and ski centres, with details of pistes, lifts and accommodation at each resort.

Tennis

Although there are tennis clubs in most larger cities, most are not open to non-members/non-residents. But most island hotels and inclusive complexes of A or Luxury class have more user-friendly tennis facilities.

Waterskiing

Waterskiing (and in some places parasailing as well) is far cheaper in Greece than in most Mediterranean resorts. You will find facilities for water skiing at: Vouliagméni (on the coast southeast of Athens); Agrínio (Lake Trihonídha); Vólos; Édhessa (Lake Vegoritídha); Ioánnina; Thessaloníki; numerous locations on Corfu; Haniá, Crete; Eloúnda, Crete; Kýhera; Mytilíni; Pórto Héli; Páros; Rhodes; Skiáthos; Gherakina; Halkidhikí; Kallithéa ; Halkídha; Híos.

For general information contact: **Water Skiing Association**, 32 Stournára Street, Athens. Tel: 5231875.

Windsurfing

Greece is ideal for learner windsurfers, with gentle breezes blowing round its many small coves. Windsurf boards are rented, and lessons available (at very reasonable rates), at many popular Greek beaches, and at all the beaches run by the GNTO. For information contact the Hellenic Windsurfing Association, 7 Filellinon Street, Athens. Tel: 3230068, 3230330.

Spectator Sports

Greece has a limited range of spectator sports. **Football** is the main one, with matches played nearly every Wednesday and Sunday afternoon during the season. The top teams are AEK of Athens, Olympiakós of Piraeus, PAOK of Thessaloníki and Panathanaíkos. Check the local papers for information or contact the Soccer Federation, 137 Syngroú, Athens, tel: 9336410.

Basketball is becoming the second most popular sport in Greece after soccer. The national team has a reasonable track record, and the national league competition is followed keenly. Check the local papers or call the Basketball Federation, 11 N Saripolou Street, Athens, tel: 8245125, 8224131.

Horse racing takes place at the Fáliron Racecourse at the seaward end of Syngroú Avenue in Athens. There are races every Monday, Wednesday and Saturday at 6.30pm. For information call: 9417761.

Language

About the Greek language

The language of Greece is modern Greek. It is the outcome of developments that have taken place in the Greek language since the Classical period (4th–3rd centuries BC). Modern Greek is still very close to Ancient Greek: it uses the same alphabet and much of the same vocabulary, and it retains much of the same grammar. This guide to Greek phrases cannot deal with the complexities of the grammar, but aims to provide the simplest (if not necessarily the most elegant) way of saying some basic things. It's well worth investing in a good phrase-book, and possibly a pocket dictionary.

All Greeks learn English at school, and many speak it very well. There are also plenty of Greeks who have lived abroad (in America, Australia, Germany or elsewhere) and have picked up an excellent command of English there. More importantly, Greeks aren't used to foreigners knowing any Greek at all, and even a couple of words from you in their native language are likely to provoke admiration and encouragement.

Pronunciation tips

The words and phrases in this language section are transcribed into the Latin alphabet; the only items given in Greek characters are a few words and phrases commonly used in notices. Most of the sounds of Greek aren't difficult to pronounce for English speakers.

There are only five vowel sounds: a is pronounced as in English 'pat';

e is as in 'red'; i as in 'bid'; o is like the vowel sound in standard English 'more'; and u is as in 'pull'. The letter y here is always pronounced as in 'yes', not as in 'why' or in 'silly'. The letter 's' in this guide is always pronounced 's', never 'z'. The sound represented here as th is always pronounced as in 'thin', not 'that'; the first sound in 'that' is represented by dh.

The only difficult sounds are h, which is pronounced like the 'ch' in Scottish 'loch', and gh, which has no equivalent in English, but you can try producing it by pronouncing the 'ch' in 'loch' and humming at the same time! If that doesn't work, just pronounce it "g" as in "get".

Even some of the most common Greek words tend to be quite long: four or five syllables are quite usual. The position of the stress in Greek words is of the utmost importance, and Greeks will often fail to understand you if you don't stress the right syllable; in this guide, stress is marked by an accent (á): compare póli 'town' (pronounced something like 'Polly') and polí 'much', 'many' or 'very' (pronounced "poll-ee")

Greek word order is flexible, so you may often hear phrases in a different order from the one in which they are given here.

Like the French, the Greeks use the plural of the second person when addressing someone politely. We have used the polite (formal) form throughout this language section, except where an expression is specified as 'informal'.

Communication

Yes *ne*
No *óhi*
Thank you *efharistó*
You're welcome *parakaló*
Please *parakaló*
Okay/All right *endáxi*
Excuse me (to get attention, or I'm sorry) *me syghoríte*
Excuse me (to ask someone to get out of the way) *syghnómi*
Can I ask you something? (normal

way of beginning a request for information) *na sas rotíso káti?*
Could you help me? *boríte na me voithísete?*
Certainly *vevéos* or *efharístos*
Can I help you? *boró na sas voithíso?*
Can you show me... *boríte na mou dhíxete...*
I want... *thélo...*
I need... *hriázome*
Wait a minute! *periménete!*
I'm lost *éhasa to dhrómo*
I don't know *dhen xéro*
I don't understand *dhen katálava*
Do you speak *xérete*
English/French/Greek? *angliká/ghaliká/eliniká?*
Can you please speak more slowly? *parakalo miláte sighá-sigha*
Could you say that again, please? *parakaló xanapéste to*
Slowly/quietly *sighá-sigha*
Here *edhó*
There *ekí*
Up/above *páno*
Down/below *káto*
Now *tóra*
Early *norís*
Late *arghá*
What? *ti?*
When? *póte?*
Why? *yatí?*
Where? *pou?*
Where is the toilet? *pou íne i toualéta?*

Telephone Calls

The telephone *to tiléfono*
phone-card *tilekárta*
May I use the phone please? *boró na tilefoníso parakaló?*
Hello (on the phone) *embrós*
My name is... *léghomai...*
Could I speak to... *boró na milíso me...*
Wait a moment *periménete mía stighmí*
He/she isn't here *dhen íne edhó*
When will he/she be back? *póte tha íne ekí?*
Should he/she call you back? *na sas pári?*
I'll try again later *tha xanapáro arghótera*
I didn't hear what you said *dhen ákousa*

In the Hotel

The hotel *to xenodhohío*
Do you have any vacant rooms? *éhete dhomátia?*
I've booked a room *ého kratísi éna dhomátio*
I'd like... *tha íthela...*
a single/double room (with double bed) *éna monó/dhipló dhomátio*
a twin-bed/three-bed room *éna dhíklino/tríklino*
a room with a bath/shower *éna dhomátio me bányo/dous*
How long will you stay? *póso tha mínete?*
One night *éna vrádhi*
Two nights *dhýo vrádhia*
How much is it? *póso káni?*
Is breakfast included? *mazí me to proinó?*
It's expensive *íne akrivó*
Is it quiet? *íne ísiho?*
Is there a balcony? *éhi balkóni?*
Do you have a room with a sea-view? *éhete dhomátio me théa pros ti thálasa?*
Is the room heated/air-conditioned? *to dhomátio éhi thérmansi/klimatismós?*
Can I see the room please? *boró na dho to dhomátio parakaló?*
What floor is it on? *se pio órofo íne?*
On the first floor *ston bróto órofo*
Is there a lift? *éhi asansér?*
The room is *to dhomátio íne*
too hot *polí zestó*
cold/small *krío/mikró*
It's noisy *éhi polí fasaría*
Could you show me another room please? *boríte na mou dhíxete álo dhomátio parakaló?*
I'll take it *tha to páro*
Sign here, please *mía ipoghrafí parakaló*
What time is breakfast? *ti óra servírete to proinó?*
Please give me a call at... *parakaló xipníste me stis...*
Come in! *embrós!*
Can I have the bill, please? *mou kánete to loghariazmó parakaló?*
Can you call me a taxi, please? *tha kalésete éna taxí parakaló?*
dining room *trapezaría*
key *klidhí*
towel *petséta*
sheet *sendóni*

pillow *maxilári*
soap *sapoúni*
hot water *zestó neró*
toilet paper *hartí toualétas*

At a Bar, Café or Patisserie

bar/café/patisserie *bar/kefenío* (or *kafetéria*)/*zaharoplastío*
I'd like... *tha íthela...*
a coffee *éna kafé*
Greek coffee *elinikó kafé*
filter coffee *ghalikó kafé/kafé fíltro*
instant coffee *neskafé*
cappuccino *kapoutsíno*
white (with milk) *me ghála*
black (without milk) *horís ghála*
with sugar *me záhari*
without sugar *horís záhari* (or *skéto*)
a cup of tea *éna tsái*
a lemon tea *éna tsái me lemóni*
(bottled/canned) orange/lemon juice *mía portokaládha/lemonádha*
fresh orange juice *éna himó portokáli*
a glass/bottle of water *éna potíri/boukáli neró*
with ice *me págho*
a whisky/ouzo/brandy *éna ouíski/ouzo/koniak*
a beer (draught) *mia bíra* (*apó varéli*)
an ice-cream *éna paghotó*
a pastry *mia pásta*
Anything else? *típot' álo?*
sweet pastries *baklavá/kataífi*

In a Restaurant

restaurant *estiatório/tavérna*
Have you got a table for... *éhete trapézi yia...*
How many are you? *pósa átoma íste?*
There are (four) of us *ímaste (téseris)*
Could we change tables? *boroúme n' aláxoume trapézi?*
vegetarian *hortofághos*
Can we see the menu? *boroúme na dhoúme ton katálogho?*
What have you got to eat? *ti éhete na fáme?*
Come and see what we've got *eláte na dhíte ti éhume*
We would like to order *théloume*

na parangíloume
What will you have? *ti tha párete?*
What would you like to drink? *ti tha píte?*
Have you got wine by the carafe? *éhete krasí híma?*
a litre/half-litre *éna kiló/misókilo*
of white/red *áspro/kókino*
wine *krasí*
Would you like anything else? *thélete típot' álo?*
No, thank you *óhi efharistó*
glass *potíri*
knife/fork/spoon *mahéri/piroúni/koutáli*
plate/napkin *piáto/petséta*
The bill please *to loghariazmó parakaló*

Food

Mezédhes
Although Greek cuisine doesn't have a strict division into courses, *mezédhes* are small dishes of starters, which are usually shared out among the party eating together; the dishes are put in the middle, and everyone helps themselves with their forks. Note that hummus, commonly found in Greek restaurants in Britain, is not served in Greece.

taramosaláta smoked fish-roe dip
dzadzíki yoghurt with garlic dip
melidzánes tighanités/ kolokithákia tighanitá sliced aubergines/courgettes fried in batter
loukánika sausages
tiropitákia cheese pies
andsoúghes anchovies
elyés olives
dolmádhes vine-leaves stuffed with rice
saghanáki fried cheese
fáva pease pudding

Meat Dishes

kréas meat
arní lamb
hirinó pork
kotópoulo chicken
moshári veal, beef
kounéli rabbit
psitó roast or grilled
sto foúrno roast
sta kárvouna grilled

sti soúvla on the spit
souvláki spit-roast
kokinistó stewed in tomato sauce
krasáto stewed in wine sauce
tighanitó fried
kapnistó smoked
brizóla (pork or veal) chop
paidhákia lamb chops
sikóti liver
biftéki hamburger (without bun)
keftédhes meat-balls (fried or grilled)
soutzoukákia/ meatballs
gouvarlákia kimá (stewed) minced meat
makarónia me kimá spaghetti with minced meat
piláfi me kimá rice with minced meat
makarónia me sáltsa spaghetti with tomato sauce (may contain meat gravy)
piláfi me sáltsa rice with tomato sauce (may contain meat gravy)
mousaká moussaka (minced meat and aubergine topped with béchamel sauce)
pastítsio minced meat and macaroni topped with béchamel sauce
yíros me píta doner kebab (slices of grilled meat served in pitta bread)
domátes/piperiés yemistés stuffed tomatoes/peppers
yemistés (me rízi/kimá) stuffed (with rice/minced meat)

Seafood

frésko/katepsighméno fresh/frozen
psári fish
glósa sole
xifías swordfish
kolyós mackerel
barboúnia red mullet
sardhéles sardines
marídhes whitebait
mídhia mussels
bakaliáros dried salted cod
strídhia oysters
kidhónia clams
kalamarákia squid
soupiés cuttlefish
htapódhi octopus
garídhes prawns
kávouras crab
astakós lobster

Vegetables and Vegetarian food

anghináres artichokes
arakás peas
domátes tomatoes
fakés brown lentils
fasólia/fasoláda stewed white beans
fasolákia green beans
(fréska) stewed in tomato sauce
hórta various kinds of boiled greens
karóta carrots
kolokithákia courgettes
kounoupídhi cauliflower
koukiá broad beans
láhano cabbage
maroúli lettuce
melidzánes aubergine/eggplant
pandzária beetroot
patátes (tighanités/sto foúrno) potatoes (chips/roast)
piperiés peppers
radhíkia boiled dandelion leaves
revíthya chickpeas
spanáki spinach
spanakópita spinach pie
tyrópita cheese pie
vlíta kind of boiled greens
yíghandes stewed butter beans
saláta salad
domatosaláta tomato salad
angourodomáta tomato and cucumber salad
horiátiki "Greek salad" (tomato, cucumber, onions, olives and feta cheese)

Basic Foods

psomí bread
aláti salt
pipéri pepper
ládhi (olive) oil
xídhi vinegar
mustárdha mustard
kremídhia onions
skórdho garlic
voútiro butter
tyrí cheese
féta feta (sheeps-milk cheese)
avghá (tighanitá) (fried) eggs
omeléta omelette
marmeládha jam, marmelade
rízi rice
yiaoúrti yoghurt
méli honey
záhari sugar

Fruit (ta frúta)

mílo apple
veríkoka apricots
banánes bananas
kerásia cherries
síka figs
stafília grapes
lemóni lemon
pepóni melon
portokáli orange
rodhákino peach
ahládhi pear
fráules strawberries
karpoúzi watermelon

Visiting a site

Is it possible to see the church/archaeological site? *boroúme na dhoúme tin eklisía/ta arhéa?*
Where can I find the custodian/key? *pou boró na vro to fílaka/klidhí?*
We've come a long way to see it. It's a pity it's closed (this can be tried if entry seems a problem!) *írthame apo polí makriá na to dhoúme. Kríma pou ína klistó*

Sightseeing

art gallery *pinakothíki*
beach *plaz*
bridge *yéfira*
castle *kástro/froúrio*
cathedral *mitrópoli*
church *eklisía*
excavations *anaskafés*
forest *dhásos*
fresco *ayoghrafía*
garden *kípos*
icon *ikóna*
lake *límni*
library *vivliothíki*
market *aghorá*
minaret *minaré*
monastery *monastíri*
monument *mnimío*
mosque *dzamí*
mountain *vounó*
museum *mousío*
old town *paliá póli*
park *párko*
river *potamós*
ruins *erípia/arhéa*
sea *thálasa*
temple *naós*

information *plirofories*
open/closed *anihtó/klistó*

At the shops

shop *maghazí/katástima*
What time do you open/close? *ti óra anígete/klínete?*
Are you being served? *exiperitíste?*
Whose turn is it? *pios éhi sirá?*
What would you like? *oríste/ti thélete?*
I'm just looking *aplós kitázo*
How much does it cost? *póso éhi?*
Do you take credit cards? *pérnete pistotikés kártes?*
I'd like... *tha íthela...*
this one *aftó*
that one *ekíno*
one of these/those *éna tétyo*
Have you got... *éhete...*
Yes, of course *málista/ne vévea/vevéos*
(Unfortunately) we haven't got (any) *(dhistihós) dhen éhoume*
size (for clothes & shoes) *noúmero*
Can I try it on? *boró na to dhokimáso?*
What size do you take? *ti noúmero pérnete?*
It's too expensive *íne polí akrivó*
cheap *ftinó*
Don't you have anything cheaper? *dhen éhete típota pio ftinó?*
Please write it down for me *to ghráfete parakaló?*
It's too small/big *íne polí mikró/meghálo*
colour *hróma*
black *mávro*
blue *ble*
brown *kafé*
gold *hrisó*
green *prásino*
grey *grízo*
pink *roz*
red *kókino*
silver *aryiró*
white *áspro*
yellow *kítrino*
It's lovely *íne polí oréo*
No thank you, *óhi efharistó,*
I don't like it *dhen m'arési*
I'll take it *tha to páro*
I don't want it *dhen to thélo*
This is faulty *aftó éhi éna*
Can I have a replacement?

elátoma. boró na to aláxo?
Can I have a refund? *boró na páro píso ta leftá?*
Anything else? *típot'álo?*
Pay at the cash desk *plirónete sto tamío*
a kilo *éna kiló*
half a kilo *misókilo*
a quarter (of a kilo) *éna tétarto*
two kilos *dhýo kilá*
100 grams *ekató gramária*
200 grams *dhyakósa gramária*
300 grams *trakósa gramária*
more *perisótero*
less *lighótero*
a little *lígho*
very little *polí lígho*
with/without *me/horís*
That's enough *ftáni*
That's all *tipot'álo*

Types of Shop

bakery *foúrnos*
bank *trápeza*
barber's *kourío*
bookshop *vivliopolío*
butcher's *hasápiko/kreopolío*
chemist's *farmakío*
department store *megálo katástima*
dry cleaner's *steghnotírio*
fishmonger's *ihthiopolío/psarádhiko*
florist *anthopolío*
greengrocer's *manáviko*
grocer's *bakáliko*
hairdresser's (women's) *komotírio*
kiosk (for newspapers and a variety of other goods) *períptero*
laundry *plindírio*
liquor store *káva*
market *aghorá*
photographer's (e.g. for film processing) *fotoghrafío*
post office *tahydhromío*
stationer's *hartopolío*
supermarket *soupermárket*
tobacconist *kapnopolío*
travel agency *taxidhiotikó ghrafío/praktorío*

Times and Dates

(in the) **morning/afternoon/evening** *to proí/to apóyevma/to vrádhi*
the middle of the day *to mesiméri*
(at) **night** *(ti) níhta*
yesterday *htes*

today *símera*
tomorrow *ávrio*
the day before yesterday *proxtés*
the day after tomorrow *methávrio*
now *tóra*
early *norís*
late *arghá*
a minute *éna leptó*
five/ten *pénde/dhéka*
minutes *leptá*
an hour *mía óra*
half an hour *misí óra*
a quarter of an hour *éna tétarto*
at one/ *sti mía/*
two (o'clock) *stis dhýo (i óra)*
a day *mía méra*

Greetings

Good morning *kaliméra*
Good evening *kalispéra*
Good night *kaliníhta*
Hello/Goodbye *yásas* (informal *yásou*)
Mr/Mrs/ *kýrios/kyría*
Miss *dhespinís*
Pleased to meet you (formal) *héro polí*
What is your name? *pos léyeste?/pos íne t' onomá sas?* (informal *pos se léne?*)
I am English/American *íme anglídha/amerikanídha* (masculine *ánglos/amerikanós*)
Irish/Scottish *irlandhéza/skotséza* (masculine *irlandhós/skotsézos*)
Canadian/Australian *kanadhéza/afstraléza* (masculine *kanadhós/afstralós*)
I'm here on holiday *káno dhiakopés edhó*
Is this your first trip to Greece/Athens? *próti forá érheste stin Elládha/Athína?*
Do you like it here? *sas arési edhó?*
How are you? *ti kánete?* (informal *ti kánis?*)
Fine, thanks. And you? *kalá, esís?* (informal *esí*)
Cheers/Your health! (when drinking) *yámas!*
Do you like...? *sas arési...?*
Very much *pára polí*
It's lovely/beautiful *íne polí oréa*
Never mind/It doesn't matter *dhembirázi*

a week *mia evdhomádha*
(on) Monday *(ti) dheftéra*
(on) Tuesday *(tin) tríti*
(on) Wednesday *(tin) tetárti*
(on) Thursday *(tin) pémti*
(on) Friday *(tin) paraskeví*
(on) Saturday *(to) sávato*
(on) Sunday *(tin) kyriakí*
on the first (of the month) *tin próti (tou minós)*
on the second/third *stis dhýo/tris*

Travelling

Transport
airport *aerodhrómio*
aeroplane *aeropláno*
boarding card *kárta epivívasis*
boat *plío/karávi*
bus *leoforío*
bus station *stathmós leoforíon*
bus stop *stási*
coach *poúlman*
ferry *feribót*
first/second *próti/défteri*
class *thési*
flight *ptísi*
hydrofoil *iptámeno*
motorway *ethnikí odhós*
No smoking *apaghorévete to kápnisma*
port *limáni*
return ticket *isitírio me epistrofí*
single ticket *aplo isitírio*
station *stathmós*
taxi *taxí*
train *tréno*
WC *toualéta*

Travelling by Public Transport

Can you help me, please? *boríte na me voithísete parakaló*
Where can I buy tickets? *pou na kópso isitírio?*
At the counter *sto tamío*
Does it stop at... *káni stási sto...*
You need to change at... *tha prépi n' aláxete sto...*
When is the next train/bus/ferry to... *póte févyi to tréno/leoforío/feribót yia...*
How long does the journey take? *pósi óra káni to taxídhi?*
What time will we arrive? *ti óra tha ftásoume?*
How much is the fare? *póso íne to isitírio*

Next stop, please *stási parakaló*
Can you tell me where to get off? *tha mou píte pou na katévo?*
Should I get off here? *edhó na katévo?*
Excuse me, I want to get off now *signómi thélo na katévo tóra*

At the airport

Where are the offices of BA/Olympic? *pu íne ta ghrafía tis British Airways/olimbiakís?*
I'd like to book a seat to Thessaloniki *tha íthela na kratíso mía thési ya thesaloníki*
When is the next flight to... *póte tha íne i epómeni ptísi ya...*
Are there any seats available? *párhoun thésis?*
How many suitcases have you got? *póses valítses éhete?*
Can I take this with me? *boró na to páro aftó mazí mou?*
My suitcase has got lost *háthike i valítsa mou*
My suitcase has been damaged *i valítsa mou épathe zimyá*
The flight has been delayed *i ptísi éhi kathistérisi*
The flight has been cancelled *i ptísi mateóthike*
I can put you on the waiting list *boró na sa válo sti lísta anamonís*

Directions

right/left *dhexiá/aristerá*
Take the first/second right *párte ton próto/déftero dhrómo dhexiá*
Turn right/left *strípste dhexiá/aristerá*
Go straight on after the traffic lights *tha páte ísya/efthía metá ta fanárya*
Is it near/far away? *ína kondá/makriá?*
How far is it? *póso makriá íne?*
It's five minutes walk *íne pénde leptá me ta pódhya*
It's ten minutes by car *íne dhéka leptá me to aftokínito*
100 metres *ekató métra*
opposite/next to *apénandi/dhípla*
up/down *páno/káto*
junction *dhiastávrosi*
house/building/apartment block *spíti/ktírio/polikatikía*
Where is/are... *pou íne...*

Emergencies

Help! *voíthia!*
Stop! *stamatíste!*
I've had an accident *íha éna atíhima*
Watch out! *proséxte!*
Call a doctor *fonáxte énayatró*
Call an ambulance *fonáxte éna asthenofóro*
Call the police *fonáxte tin astinomía*
Call the fire brigade *fonáxte tus pirozvéstes*
Where's the telephone? *pou íne to tiléfono?*
Where's the nearest hospital? *pou íne to pio kondhinó nosokomío?*
I would like to report a theft *éghine mía klopí*
Thank you very much for your help *efxaristó polí pou me voithísate*

Where can I find a bank/petrol station/bus stop/hotel? *pu boró na vro mía trápeza/éna venzinádhiko/mía stási/éna xenodohío?*
How do I get there? *pos na páo ekí?*
Can you show me where I am on the map? *boríte na mu díxete sto hárti pou íme?*
Am I on the right road for... *ya... kalá páo?*
No, you're on the wrong road *óhi, pírate láthos dhrómo*

On the Road

Where can I rent a car? *pu boró na nikyáso aftokínito?*
What is it insured for? *ti asfália éhi?*
Can another driver drive it? *borí na to odhiyísi álos odhighós?*
By what time must I return it? *méhri ti óra prépi na to epistrépso?*
driving licence *dhíploma*
licence plate *pinakídha*
petrol *venzíni*
petrol station *venzinádhiko*
oil *ládhi*
How much should I put in? *pósi na válo?*
Fill it up, please *óso pérni*

lead-free *amólivdhi*
My car won't start *to aftokínito
dhen pérni bros*
My car has broken down *hálase to
aftokinitó mou*
I've had an accident *íha éna
atíhima*
How long will it take to repair?
pósi óra thélete na to ftyáxete?
Can you check... *boríte na
elénxete...*
There's something wrong with...
káti éhi... (plural *káti éhoun...*)
accelerator *to gázi*
the brakes *ta fréna*
the clutch *to ambrayáz*
the engine *i mihaní*
the exhaust *i exátmisi*
the fanbelt *i zóni*
the gearbox *i tahítites*
the headlights *ta fanárya*
the radiator *to psiyío*
the spark plugs *ta bouzí*
the tyre(s) *to lástiho (ta lástiha)*
the windscreen *to parbríz*

Health

Is there a *ipárhi éna*
chemist's nearby? *farmakío edhó
kondá?*
Which chemist is open all night? *pio
farmakío dianikterévi?*
I don't feel well *dhen esthánome
kalá*
I'm ill *íme árostos* (feminine *árosti*)
He/she's ill *íne árostos/árosti*
Where does it hurt? *pou ponái?*
It hurts here *ponái edhó*
I suffer from... *pás-ho apo...*
**I have a headache/sore
throat/stomach ache** *éxo
ponokéfalo/ponólemo/
stomahóponos*
**Have you got something for travel
sickness?** *éhete típota yia ti naftía?*
Do I need a *hriázete*
prescription? *syndhaghí?*
It bit me *me dhángose* (of an
animal)
It bit me *me tsímbise* (of an insect)
It stung me *me kéntrise*
bee *mélisa*
wasp *sfíka*
mosquito *kounoúpi*
sticking plaster *lefkoplástis*
tissues *hartomándhila*
toothpaste *odhondhókrema*
diarrhoea pills *hápia yia ti dhiária*

Numbers

1	*éna/mía*
2	*dhýo*
3	*tris/tría*
4	*tésera*
5	*pénde*
6	*éxi*
7	*eptá*
8	*ohtó*
9	*enéa*
10	*dhéka*
11	*éndeka*
12	*dhódheka*
13	*dhekatrís/dhekatría*
14	*dhekatéseris*
15	*dhekapénde*
16	*dhekaéxi*
17	*dhekaeptá*
18	*dhekaohtó*
19	*dhekaenéa*
20	*íkosi*
30	*triánda*
40	*saránda*
50	*penínda*
60	*exínda*
70	*evdhomínda*
80	*ogdhónda*
90	*enenínda*
100	*ekató*
200	*dhyakósa*
300	*trakósa*
400	*tetrakósa*
500	*pendakósa*
1,000	*hílies/hília*
2,000	*dhýo hiliádhes*
a million	*éna ekatomírio*

Further Reading

Ancient History & Culture

Burkert, Walter. **Greek Religion** (Basil Blackwell). Translation of the German-language classic study of belief in ancient Greece.

Burn, A.R. **The Penguin History of Greece** (Penguin, various reprints). A good, single-volume introduction to ancient Greece, though of course more detailed period studies are available.

Dodds, E.R. **The Greeks and the Irrational**. (University of California Press, various reprints). Modern Greeks like you to think that their seers put reason on a pedestal; this explores the prevalence of the Other and the unconscious in ancient Greece.

Finley, M.I. **The World of Odysseus**. (Penguin, various reprints). Mycenean myths as borne out by archeological facts.

Fox, Robin Lane **Alexander the Great** (Penguin). All about the man on the 100-dr coin; psychobiography wedded to a conventional history.

Grimal, Pierre, ed **Dictionary of Classical Mythology** (Penguin). Though translated from the French, this is still considered to be tops among a handful of available alphabetical gazetteers.

Hornblower, Simon **The Greek World, 479-323 BC** (Routledge). Covers the eventful period from the end of the Persian Wars to Alexander's demise; the standard university text.

Byzantine History & Culture

Trans. By E.R.A. Sewter. **The Alexiad of Anna Comnena** (Penguin, various reprints) Chronicle of the great Emperor Alexios Komnenos by his daughter, an important literary and political figure in her own right.

Norwich, John Julius, **Byzantium** (3 vols): **The Early Centuries, The Apogee & The Decline** (Viking-Penguin, 1988-1995). The most readable and masterful popular history, by the noted Byzantinologst.

Psellus, Michael. **Fourteen Byzantine Rulers.** (Penguin, various reprints). That many centuries of rule in a single century (10th-11th), as told by a near-contemporary historian.

Runciman, Steven. **Byzantine Style and Civilization.** (Penguin, UK only). Art, culture and monuments. (Same author) **The Fall of Constantinople, 1453** (Cambridge-Canto). Definitive study of an event which continues to exercise modern Greek minds. **The Orthodox Church** (Penguin, various reprints). Good introduction to what's essentially the established religion of modern Greece.

Anthropology & Culture of Modern Greece

Campbell, John. **Honor, family and patronage: A study of institutions and moral values in a Greek mountain community** (Oxford University Press). Classic study of Sarakatsáni in the Píndhos, with much wider application to Greece in general, which however got the author banned from the area by touchy officialdom.

Dalven, Rae. **The Jews of Ioannina** (Lycabettus Press, Athens). History and culture of the pre-World War II community; Dalven herself was an Epirot Jew.

Danforth, Loring H. and Tsiaras, Alexander. **The Death Rituals of Rural Greece** (Princeton University Press).

Du Boulay, Juliet. **Portrait of a Greek Mountain Village** (Oxford/Clarendon Press). Ambeli, a mountain village in Évvia, as it was in the mid-1960s.

Holst, Gail. **Road to Rembetika : Songs of Love, Sorrow and Hashish** (Denise Harvey, Athens). The most user-friendly introduction to the enduringly popular musical form; complete with translated lyrics of

standards, and updated discographies (get the most current edition possible).

Karakasidou, Anastasia (University of Chicago Press). **Fields of Wheat, Hills of Blood: Passages to Nationhood in Greek Macedonia 1870-1990**. A fascinating study about the process of Hellenisatikon, this book provoked death threats upon the author from extreme Greek nationalists who had neither understood the text nor read it (see p. 101).

Mackridge, Peter. **The Modern Greek Language**. (Oxford University Press). Analysis by one of the foremost scholars of the tongue's evolution.

Useful Websites

The official Greek Tourist Office (GNTO/EOT) has a site which can be found at two locations:
www.areianet.gr/infoxenios/GNTO
www.gmor.com/infoxenios/GNTO
Much of this information can also be found at:
www.vacation.net.gr
This site claims to list all the hotels in Greece, along with their telephone numbers:
www.all-hotels.gr
Shipping schedules are available at:
www.gtpnet.gr
For general tourist information and links have a look at:
www.greektravel.com
www.travel-greece.com
A new site said by the government to show "contemporary Greece" is at:
www.greece.gr
The Ministry of Culture site has impressive coverage of many of the country's museums:
www.culture.gr

Cuisine

Dalby, Andrew **Siren Feasts** (Routledge). Analysis of Classical and Byzantine texts shows just how little Greek food has changed in three millennia; good too on the arrival and etymology of exotic vegetables and herbs.

Davidson, Alan **Mediterranean Seafood** (Penguin). Recently re-

issued 1972 classic that's still the standard reference, and guaranteed to end every argument as to just what that fish is on your *tavérna* plate. Complete with recipes.

Harris, Andy. **A Taste of the Aegean**. Photographs by Terry Harris. (Pavilion Books). Two Greek-resident brothers and renowned food experts take you on a gastronomic tour, with recipes.

Stavroulakis, Nicholas. **Cookbook of the Jews of Greece:** (Athens: Lycabettus Press). Recipes you can follow interspersed with their relation to the Jewish liturgical year, and a potted history of the Greek Jewish community.

Modern History & Politics

Clogg, Richard. **A Concise History of Greece** (Cambridge University Press). Clear and lively account of Greece from Byzantine times to 1991, with helpful maps and well-captioned artwork. The best single-volume summary.

Fourtouni, Eleni. **Greek Women in Resistance**. (New Haven: Thelphini Press). Accounts and journals of women interned post-civil war on Tríkeri and Makrónissos – as much, one suspects, for being uppity in a patriarchal society as for being communists or fellow travellers.

Mazower, Marc. **Inside Hitler's Greece: The Experience of Occupation 1941–1944** (Yale University Press). Shows, among other things, how the complete demoralization of the country and imcompetence of establishment politicians fuelled the rise of ELAS – and guaranteed civil war. Some harrowing photos as well.

Murtagh, Peter. **The Rape of Greece** (Simon and Schuster). Partisan account of the imposition of the junta, and how Greece has generally been taken advantage of by her ostensible allies.

Ward, Michael **Greek Assignments, SOE 1943-UNSCOB 1948** (Lycabettus Press, Athens). Another parachuted-in guerrilla who walked from Píndhos to Pílion and survived to marry a Greek and serve as British consul in Thessaloníki. Makes vividly clear how the Germans sat in the main towns and pretty much gave free run of the countryside to the resistance.

Woodhouse, C.M. **Modern Greece: A Short History** (Faber and Faber). Spans the period from early Byzantium to the early 1980s; dryer and more right-wing than Clogg, but still useful.

Ancient Greek Literature & History

Aeschylus. **The Oresteia**. (Viking-Penguin).

Aesop. **Fables of Aesop** (Penguin). Moral tales, complete with talking animals, by the native of Lésvos and resident of ancient Sámos.

Aristophanes. **Lysistrata/The Acharnians/The Clouds**. (Penguin). A trilogy from the greatest ancient comedian.

Herodotus. **The Histories** (Penguin). Fifth-century BC chronicle of the Persian Wars, and the diverse peoples of Anatolia caught up in the conflict.

Homer, translation by Richard Lattimore. His verse translations of **The Iliad** (University of Chicago) and **The Odyssey** (Harper Collins) remain unsurpassed. The first relates the semi-mythical Bronze Age campaign against Troy; the latter follows the hero Odyssues on his convoluted way home to Ithaca from the war.

Plato. **The Republic** and **The Symposium** (Penguin). The standard

Bookshops

Athens has various bookshops that carry books in English:
Compendium, Níkis 28, located just behind Sýndagma Square (tel: 322-6931).

Eleftheroudakis, Panepistimíou 17 (tel: 331 4180 5).

Kakoulides – The Book Nest, Panepistimíou 25-29, Stoa Megárou Athinón (tel: 322-5209).

Pantelides, Amerikís 11 (tel: 362-3673).

undergraduate philosophy texts, perhaps even more meaningful if read on the spot.

Thucydides **History of The Peloponnesian Wars** (Penguin). Bleak, month-by-month account of the conflict by a relegated Athenian general; a pioneer of the genre.

Xenophon **The History of My Times** (Penguin). Thucydides ceases coverage in 411 BC; this continues events up to 362 BC.

Modern Literature by Greeks

Beaton, Roderick **An Introduction to Modern Greek Literature** (Oxford University Press). Readable survey of Greek literature since independence, but tendentious and with some surprising gaps (best-selling quality novels like *Loxandra* and *Cassandra and the Wolf* get one sentence each).

Cavafy, C.P. **Collected Poems**, trans. by Edmund Keeley and Philip Sherrard (Princeton University Press) or **The Complete Poems of Cavafy**, translated by Rae Dalven (Harcourt Brace Jovanovich). Each have their partisans and are considered the two best versions available in English.

Elytis, Odysseus. **The Axion Esti**. (Anvil/University of Pittsburgh) , **Selected Poems** (Anvil/Penguin) and **The Sovereign Sun** (Bloodaxe/Temple University Press). Pretty much the complete works of the Nobel laureate, in translation.

Kazantzakis, Nikos. **Zorba the Greek** is a surprisingly dark and nihilistic work, worlds away from the crude, two-dimensional character of the film; **The Last Temptation of Christ**, which provoked riots by Orthodox fanatics in Athens in 1989; **Report to Greco** explores his Cretanness/Greekness; while **Christ Recrucified (The Greek Passion)** encompasses the Easter drama within Christian-Muslim dynamics on Crete. All are published by Faber & Faber/Touchstone, plus in cheap offcut editions in Greece. Nobel laureate, wooly Marxist and

self-imposed exile Kazantzakis embodies the old maxims of a prophet being without honour in his own country, and that classics are books praised but generally unread. Whether in intricate, untranslatable Greek or wooden English, Kazantzakis can be hard going.

Leontis, Artemis, ed **Greece: a Traveler's Literary Companion** (Whereabouts Press, San Francisco). Various regions of the country as portrayed in very brief fiction or essays by modern Greek writers; an excellent corrective to the often condescending Grand Tourist accounts.

Myrivilis, Stratis. **Life in the Tomb**, translated by Peter Bien (Quarter/New England University Press). Harrowing account of the Macedonian front during World War I; first part of a loose trilogy comprising **The Mermaid Madonna** and **The Schoolmistress with the Golden Eyes**, the latter two set on the author's home island of Lésvos, eventually filmed for television, but badly translated and shabbily produced by Greek touristic presses.

Papandreou, Nick **Father Dancing** (Penguin). Thinly disguised, page-turning *roman-à-clef* by the late prime minister's younger son; Papandreou père comes across as an egotistical monster (*quelle surprise*).

Ritsos, Yannis, Papadiamantis, Alexandros. **The Murderess**. Translation by Peter Levi (London: Writers and Readers). Landmark demotically written novel, set on Skiáthos at the turn of the century. An old woman concludes that little girls are better off dead than grown up into drudgery; mayhem ensues.

Seferis, George. **Collected Poems 1924-1955/Complete Poems**. Trans. by Edmund Keeley. (Princeton University Press). The former, out of print, has Greek-English texts on facing pages and is preferable to the so-called *Complete Poems* of Greece's other Nobel literary laureate.

Sotiriou, Dido **Farewell Anatolia** (Kedros, Athens). A best-selling classic since its appearance in 1962, this traces the end of the millennial presence of Greeks in Asia Minor from 1914 to 1922, using a character based on the author's father.

Tsirkas, Stratis. **Drifting Cities.** Trans. by Kay Cicellis. (Athens: Kedros). Welcome paperback re-issue of this epic novel on wartime leftist intrigue in Alexandria, Cairo and Jerusalem.

Vassilikos, Vassilis. **Z.** (Four Walls Eight Windows). Based closely enough on the assassination of leftist MP Grigoris Lambrakis in 1963 to get the book – and author – banned by the colonels' junta; brilliantly filmed by Costa-Gavras.

Foreign Writers on Greece

De Bernières, Louis **Captain Corelli's Mandolin** (Secker & Warburg/Minerva). Heart-rending tragicomedy set on occupied Kefaloniá during World War II which has acquired cult status and seemingly permanent best-seller-list tenancy since its appearance in 1994.

Durrell, Lawrence. **Prospero's Cell** and **Reflections on a Marine Venus** (Faber and Faber/Penguin). Corfu in the 1930s, and Rhodes in 1945–47, now looking rather old-fashioned, alcohol-fogged and patronizing of the "natives", but still entertaining enough.

Fowles, John. **The Magus.** (Vintage/Dell). Blockbuster, inspired by author's spell teaching on Spétses during the 1950s, of post-adolescent manipulation, conspiracy and cock-teasing (ie, the usual Fowles obsessions).

Gage, Nicholas. **Eleni** (Collins Harvill/Ballantine). Epirus-born American correspondent returns to Greece to avenge the death of his mother at the hands of an ELAS firing squad in 1948. Good on pre-1940s village life, not so good on intepretation of events.

Leigh Fermor, Patrick. **Roumeli: Travels in Northern Greece** and **Mani** (Penguin). Written during the late 1950s and early 1960s, before the advent of mass tourism, these remain some of the best compendia

of the then already-vanishing customs and relict communities of the mainland.

Miller, Henry. **The Colossus of Maroussi.** (Minerva/New Directions). Miller takes to Corfu, the Argolid, Athens and Crete of 1939 with the enthusiasm of a first-timer in Greece who's found his element; deserted archeological sites and larger-than-life personalities.

Pausanias, translation by Peter Levi. **The Guide to Greece** (2 vols, Penguin, various reprints). In effect the first-ever guidebook, aimed at pilgrims and travellers in imperial Roman Greece; alas, most sites described have deteriorated beyond recognition or even disappeared altogether.

Pettifer, James **The Greeks: the Land and People since the War** (Penguin). Useful, if hastily written and edited, general introduction to politics, family life, food, tourism and other contemporary topics.

Salmon, Tim. **The Unwritten Places** (Lycabettus Press). Veteran Hellenophile describes his love affair with the Greek mountains, and the Vlach pastoral communities of Epirus in particular; includes a fine account of one of the last strictly-on-foot transhumant sheep transfers from summer to winter pastures.

Spencer, Terence. **Fair Greece, Sad Relic** (Denise Harvey, Athens). Literary and Grand Tour philhellenism, from the fall of Constantinople to the War of Independence.

Storace, Patricia. **Dinner with Persephone** (Granta/Panthon). New York poet resident a year in Athens successfully takes the pulse of modern Greece, with all its shibboleths, foundation myths, carefully nurtured self-image and rampant misogyny. Very funny, and spot-on.

Regional & Archeological Guides

Burn, A. R. and Mary **The Living Past of Greece** (The Herbert Press). Worth toting its oversized format into the field for the sake of lively

text and clear plans; unusually, covers most major sites from Minoan to medieval.

Dubin, Marc. **Hiking in Epirus** (Road Editions, Athens). Detailed guide to the best treks of the Píndhos

Hetherington, Paul **Byzantine and Medieval Greece** (John Murray). Erudite and authoritative dissection of the castles and churches of the mainland; frustratingly omits the islands.

Various Titles (Lycabettus Press Guides, Athens). Assorted booklets to various Greek destinations; though most have not been updated in years, those for Kos, Patmos, Nafplion, Paros, Idhra and the travels of St Paul are especially worthwhile.

Stavroulakis, Nicholas, and Timothy J. DeVinney **Jewish Sites and Synagogues in Greece** (Talos Press, Athens). Alphabetical gazetteer to the communities and suriviving Jewish monuments across Greece; some of the latter have disappeared since publication, however.

Botany

Baumann, Helmut **Greek wildflowers and Plant Lore in Ancient Greece** (Herbert Press). As the title says; lots of interesting ethnobotanical trivia.

Polunin, Oleg **Flowers of Greece and the Balkans** (Oxford University Press). This book is also showing its age, but has lots of colour photos.

Polunin, Oleg and Anthony Huxley **Flowers of the Mediterranean** (Hogarth Press). Lots of colour plates to aid in identification, and includes flowering shrubs.

Other Insight Guides

Companion titles that highlight destinations in this region include **Insight Guides** to **Greek Islands, Athens, Crete, Cyprus** and **Turkish Coast.**

The **Insight Pocket Guide** series, designed to guide short-stay visitors around their destinations by means of carefully timed itineraries, includes books on *Athens*, *Crete*, the *Aegean Islands*, and *Rhodes*. Each book contains a full-size fold-out map.

The **Insight Compact Guide** series, whose fact-packed portable format makes them ideal for on-the-spot use, includes **Greece**, **Rhodes** and **Crete**.

Insight Flexi Maps have clear cartography with a weather-resistant laminated finish which can also be written on with a non-permanent marker. Maps to this part of the world include **Crete**, **Athens** and **Cyprus**.

ART & PHOTO CREDITS

INSIGHT GUIDE
GREECE

Cartographic Editor **Zoë Goodwin**
Production **Stuart A. Everitt**
Design Consultants
Klaus Geisler, Graham Mitchener
Picture Research **Hilary Genin**

Index

Numbers in italics refer to photographs

INSIGHT GUIDES

The world's largest collection of visual travel guides

A range of guides and maps to meet every travel need

Insight Guides

This classic series gives you the complete picture of a destination through expert, well written and informative text and stunning photography. Each book is an ideal background information and travel planner, serves as an on-the-spot companion – and is a superb visual souvenir of a trip. Nearly 200 titles.

Insight Pocket Guides

focus on the best choices for places to see and things to do, picked by our local correspondents. They are ideal for visitors new to a destination. To help readers follow the routes easily, the books contain full-size pull-out maps. 120 titles.

Insight Maps

are designed to complement the guides. They provide full mapping of major cities, regions and countries, and their laminated finish makes them easy to fold and gives them durability. 60 titles.

Insight Compact Guides

are convenient, comprehensive reference books, modestly priced. The text, photographs and maps are all carefully cross-referenced, making the books ideal for on-the-spot use when in a destination. 120 titles.

Different travellers have different needs. Since 1970, Insight Guides has been meeting these needs with a range of practical and stimulating guidebooks and maps

" I was first drawn to the Insight Guides by the excellent "Nepal" volume. I can think of no book which so effectively captures the essence of a country. Out of these pages leaped the Nepal I know – the captivating charm of a people and their culture. I've since discovered and enjoyed the entire Insight Guide series. Each volume deals with a country in the same sensitive depth, which is nowhere more evident than in the superb photography. "

Sir Edmund Hillary

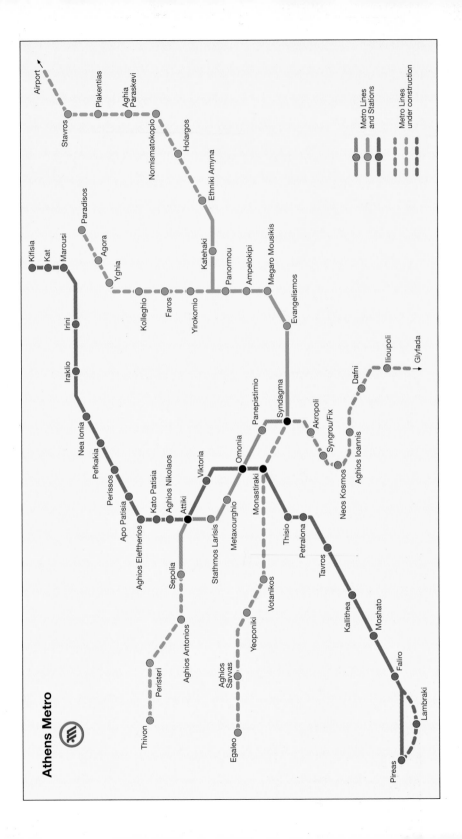